CompTIA® A+®
Complete Practice Tests
Exam Core 1 (220-1001) and Exam Core 2 (220-1002)
Second Edition

D1530964

Jeff T. Parker

Quentin Docter

SYBEX®
A Wiley Brand

Senior Acquisitions Editor: Kenyon Brown
Development Editor: John Sleeva
Technical Editor: Audrey O'Shea
Senior Production Editor: Christine O'Connor
Copy Editor: Judy Flynn
Editorial Manager: Pete Gaughan
Production Manager: Kathleen Wisor
Associate Publisher: Jim Minatel
Book Designers: Judy Fung and Bill Gibson
Proofreader: Nancy Carrasco
Indexer: Jack Lewis
Project Coordinator, Cover: Brent Savage
Cover Designer: Wiley
Cover Image: Getty Images, Inc. / Jeremy Woodhouse

To my faithful canine companion, Abby. For me, Abby starts with A+.
—Jeff

To my girls
—Quentin

Acknowledgments

Genuine thanks to the Sybex/Wiley team, particularly to Kenyon Brown for the opportunity to author this edition. Thank you to John Sleeva for his patience and support. Without Development Editors like John, authors are ships without a captain. Finally, to Audrey O'Shea as technical editor, I thank you for the untiring second pair of eyes. Readers have these people to thank for the excellence found in the book.

About the Authors

Jeff Parker resides on the Canadian east coast while consulting for a firm in Virginia specializing in IT risk management and compliance. Jeff started in information security while working for HP in Boston, Massachusetts. Jeff then took the role of Global IT Risk Manager for Deutsche Post to enjoy Prague, Czech Republic, with his family for several years. There he developed and oversaw implementation of a new IT risk management strategy. Today, Jeff most enjoys watching his two children grow up in Nova Scotia, Canada.

Jeff holds several certifications, including the CISSP, the CompTIA CASP, CySA+, and ITT+. He also co-authored the Wiley book *Wireshark for Security Professionals: Using Wireshark and the Metasploit Framework* Other Author is Jessey Bullock (Wiley, 2017) as well as authored preparation books for other CompTIA certifications, including CASP and the CySA+.

Quentin Docter is an IT consultant who started in the industry in 1994. Since then, he's worked as a tech and network support specialist, trainer, consultant, and webmaster. Throughout his career he's obtained CompTIA A+, Network+, IT Fundamentals certifications and numerous Microsoft, Cisco, Sun, and Novell certifications. He has written several books for Sybex, including books on A+, Server+, IT Fundamentals, Windows, and Solaris 9 certifications as well as PC hardware and maintenance. Quentin can be reached at qdocter@yahoo.com.

About the Technical Editor

Audrey O'Shea (A+, Network+, IT Fundamentals, Project +, Security+, Storage +, CSIS, CIOS, and several CIW certifications) is an IT instructor, consultant, and author who has worked in the industry since 1989. In those 30 years, she has held the positions of network administrator, tech support specialist, trainer, and consultant and has been a public speaker advocating for women to enter the tech field. Audrey can be reached at aoshea@live.com.

Contents

Introduction

If you're picking up this book, there's a good chance that you want to pass the CompTIA A+ exam. It means that you're likely either an IT professional looking for certifications or someone who has a bit of computer knowledge and wants to start an IT career. The A+ exam is entry level and is often the first certification test IT technicians will take.

While still considered an entry-level credential, the exam has become more challenging compared to what it was a few years ago. You'll see why when comparing exam objectives, prior versus new. First, the breadth of material has expanded, including an entirely new domain "Virtualization and Cloud Computing." Second, the exam coverage for the domain "Operational Procedures" has nearly doubled. To achieve this, CompTIA balances the remaining domains more evenly. Overall, our opinion is the industry will understand this exam to be more practical and vigorous, and the credential will be even more valued. The time to gain this credential is now.

While we're confident that if you can answer all the questions in this book, you can pass the exam, we encourage you to go beyond memorizing questions and answers. One reason is that the questions on the actual exams will be different than the ones written for this book. Another (better) reason is that life isn't a multiple-choice exam. When you're in the field and trying to fix a computer, you won't have possible solutions given to you—you need to have a solid base of knowledge to work from.

CompTIA A+ Complete Practice Tests, Second Edition, combined with the Sybex *CompTIA A+ Complete Study Guide, Fourth Edition* (both the Standard and Deluxe Editions), will help give you the foundation you need to pass the exams. Study them well and they will also give you the tools you need to navigate a myriad of technical topics and make you more valuable to prospective employers.

What Is A+ Certification?

The A+ certification program was developed by the Computing Technology Industry Association (CompTIA) to provide an industry-wide means of certifying the competency of computer service technicians. The A+ certification is granted to those who have attained the level of knowledge and troubleshooting skills that are needed to provide capable support in the field of personal computers and mobile devices. It is similar to other certifications in the computer industry, such as the Cisco Certified Network Associate (CCNA) program and the Microsoft certification programs. The theory behind these certifications is that if you need to have service performed on a certain vendor's products, you would prefer to use a technician who has been certified in one of the appropriate certification programs rather than just the first "expert" that pops up in a Google search. The difference with A+ is that it's an industry-wide certification and vendor agnostic. That means by passing it, you're capable of handling different issues regardless of the software or hardware vendor.

Everyone must take and pass two exams: Core 1 (220-1001) and Core 2 (220-1002). You don't have to take the 220-1001 exam and the 220-1002 exam at the same time, but the A+ certification isn't awarded until you've passed both tests.

Tests are administered by CompTIA's global testing partner, Pearson VUE. For more information on taking the exam, visit the CompTIA website at www.comptia.org. You can also visit Pearson VUE at www.pearsonvue.com.

Who Should Buy This Book?

If you want to pass the A+ exam, this book is definitely for you. This book is an exam prep book. If you're an experienced computer professional, a book like this may be all you need to pass the exam.

However, a book of exam questions isn't designed to give you all the background you need to truly understand the basics of personal computers, mobile devices, and virtualization. If you're newer to the industry, we encourage you to buy a study guide as well, such as the Sybex *CompTIA A+ Complete Study Guide*. The study guide will provide more depth and context to help you acquire the skills and knowledge you need to be successful. This book then becomes a great companion as you prepare to take the exam.

How to Use This Book and the Interactive Online Learning Environment and Test Bank

This book includes 1,200 practice test questions, which will help you get ready to pass the A+ exam. The interactive online learning environment that accompanies *CompTIA A+ Complete Practice Tests* provides a robust test bank to help you prepare for the certification exams and increase your chances of passing them the first time! By using this test bank, you can identify weak areas up front and then develop a solid studying strategy using each of these testing features.

The test bank also offers two practice exams. Take these practice exams just as if you were taking the actual exam (without any reference material). When you've finished the first exam, move on to the next one to solidify your test-taking skills. If you get more than 90 percent of the answers correct, you're ready to take the certification exams.

You can access the Sybex interactive online test bank at http://www.wiley.com/go/Sybextestprep.

Tips for Taking the A+ Exams

Here are some general tips for taking your exams successfully:

- Bring two forms of ID with you. One must be a photo ID, such as a driver's license. The other can be a major credit card or a passport. Both forms must include a signature.

- Arrive early at the exam center so you can relax and review your study materials, particularly tables and lists of exam-related information.

- Read the questions carefully. Don't be tempted to jump to an early conclusion. Make sure you know exactly what the question is asking.

- Don't leave any unanswered questions. Unanswered questions are scored against you.

- There will be questions with multiple correct responses. When there is more than one correct answer, a message at the bottom of the screen will prompt you to either "Choose two" or "Choose all that apply." Be sure to read the messages displayed to know how many correct answers you must choose.

- When answering multiple-choice questions you're not sure about, use a process of elimination to get rid of the obviously incorrect answers first. Doing so will improve your odds if you need to make an educated guess.

- On form-based tests (nonadaptive), because the hard questions will eat up the most time, save them for last. You can move forward and backward through the exam.

- For the latest pricing on the exams and updates to the registration procedures, visit CompTIA's website at www.comptia.org.

Exam Objectives

CompTIA goes to great lengths to ensure that its certification programs accurately reflect the IT industry's best practices. The company does this by establishing Cornerstone Committees for each of its exam programs. Each committee comprises a small group of IT professionals, training providers, and publishers who are responsible for establishing the exam's baseline competency level and who determine the appropriate target audience level.

Once these factors are determined, CompTIA shares this information with a group of hand-selected subject-matter experts (SMEs). These folks are the true brainpower behind the certification program. They review the committee's findings, refine them, and shape them into the objectives you see before you. CompTIA calls this process a Job Task Analysis (JTA).

Finally, CompTIA conducts a survey to ensure that the objectives and weightings truly reflect the job requirements. Only then can the SMEs go to work writing the hundreds of questions needed for the exam. And, in many cases, they have to go back to the drawing board for further refinements before the exam is ready to go live in its final state. So, rest assured, the content you're about to learn will serve you long after you take the exam.

A+ Certification Exam Objectives: Core 1 (220-1001)

The following table lists the domains measured by this examination and the extent to which they are represented on the exam:

Domain	Percentage of Exam
1.0 Mobile Devices	14%
2.0 Networking	20%
3.0 Hardware	27%
4.0 Virtualization and Cloud Computing	12%
5.0 Hardware and Network Troubleshooting	27%
Total	100%

Objective	Chapter
1.0 Mobile Devices	
1.1 Given a scenario, install and configure laptop hardware and components.	1, 10
Hardware/device replacement	1, 10

- Keyboard
- Hard drive
  - SSD vs. hybrid vs. magnetic disk
  - 1.8in vs. 2.5in
- Memory
- Smart card reader
- Optical drive
- Wireless card/Bluetooth module
- Cellular card
- Video card
- Mini PCIe
- Screen
- DC jack
- Battery
- Touchpad
- Plastics/frames
- Speaker
- System board
- CPU

Objective	Chapter
Repeater	2, 10
Hub	2, 10
Cable/DSL modem	2, 10
Bridge	2, 10
Patch panel	2, 10
Power over Ethernet (PoE) - Injectors - Switch	2, 10
Ethernet over Power	2, 10
2.3 Given a scenario, install and configure a basic wired/wireless SOHO network.	2, 10
Router/switch functionality	2, 10
Access point settings	2, 10
IP addressing	2, 10
NIC configuration - Wired - Wireless	2, 10
End-user device configuration	2, 10
IoT device configuration - Thermostat - Light switches - Security cameras - Door locks - Voice-enabled, smart speaker/digital assistant	2, 10
Cable/DSL modem configuration	2, 10
Firewall settings - DMZ - Port forwarding - NAT - UPnP - Whitelist/blacklist - MAC filtering	2, 10

Objective	Chapter

Network cables
- Ethernet
  - Cat 5
  - Cat 5e
  - Cat 6
  - Plenum
  - Shielded twisted pair
  - Unshielded twisted pair
  - 568A/B
- Fiber
- Coaxial
- Speed and transmission limitations
	3, 10

Video cables - VGA - HDMI - Mini-HDMI - DisplayPort - DVI - DVI-DDVI-I	3, 10
Multipurpose cables - Lightning - Thunderbolt - USB - USB-C - USB 2.0 - USB 3.0	3, 10
Peripheral cables - Serial	3, 10
Hard drive cables - SATA - IDE - SCSI	3, 10
Adapters - DVI to HDMI - USB to Ethernet - DVI to VGA	3, 10

xxiv Introduction

Objective	Chapter
Error correcting	3, 10
Parity vs. non-parity	3, 10
3.4 Given a scenario, select, install and configure storage devices.	3, 10
Optical drives - CD-ROM/CD-RW - DVD-ROM/DVD-RW/DVD-RW DL - Blu-ray - BD-R - BD-RE	3, 10
Solid-state drives - M2 drives - NVME - SATA 2.5	3, 10

Magnetic hard drives
- 5,400rpm
- 7,200rpm
- 10,000rpm
- 15,000rpm
- Sizes:
  -2.5
  -3.5
	3, 10

Hybrid drives	3, 10
Flash - SD card - CompactFlash - MicroSD card - MiniSD card - xD	3, 10
Configurations - RAID 0, 1, 5, 10 - Hot swappable	3, 10

Objective	Chapter
3.5 Given a scenario, install and configure motherboards, CPUs, and add-on cards.	3, 10

Objective	Chapter
Motherboard form factor - ATX - mATX - ITX - mITX	3, 10
Motherboard connector types - PCI - PCIe - Riser card - Socket types - SATA - IDE - Front panel connector - Internal USB connector	3, 10

BIOS/UEFI settings
- Boot options
- Firmware updates
- Security settings
- Interface configurations
- Security
  - Passwords
  - Drive encryption
    - TPM
    - LoJack
    - Secure boot
	3, 10

CMOS battery	3, 10
CPU features - Single-core - Multicore - Virtual technology - Hyperthreading - Speeds - Overclocking - Integrated GPU	3, 10

Objective	Chapter
3.10 Given a scenario, configure SOHO multifunction devices/printers and settings.	3, 10

Use appropriate drivers for a given operating system.
- Configuration settings
  - Duplex
  - Collate
  - Orientation
  - Quality
	3, 10

Device sharing
- Wired
  - USB
  - Serial
  - Ethernet
- Wireless
  - Bluetooth
  - 802.11(a, b, g, n, ac)
  - Infrastructure vs. ad hoc
- Integrated print server (hardware)
- Cloud printing/remote printing
	3, 10

Public/shared devices
- Sharing local/networked device via operating system settings
  - TCP/Bonjour/AirPrint
- Data privacy
  - User authentication on the device
  - Hard drive caching
	3, 10

3.11 Given a scenario, install and maintain various print technologies.	3, 10
Laser - Imaging drum, fuser assembly, transfer belt, transfer roller, pickup rollers, separate pads, duplexing assembly - Imaging process: processing, charging, exposing, developing, transferring, fusing, and cleaning - Maintenance: Replace toner, apply maintenance kit, calibrate, and clean.	3, 10
Inkjet - Ink cartridge, print head, roller, feeder, duplexing assembly, carriage, and belt - Calibrate. - Maintenance: Clean heads, replace cartridges, calibrate, and clear jams.	3, 10

Objective	Chapter
Thermal - Feed assembly, heating element - Special thermal paper - Maintenance: Replace paper, clean heating element, and remove debris.	3, 10
Impact - Print head, ribbon, tractor feed - Impact paper - Maintenance: Replace ribbon, replace print head, and replace paper.	3, 10
Virtual - Print to file. - Print to PDF. - Print to XPS. - Print to image.	3, 10
3D printers - Plastic filament	3, 10
4.0 Virtualization and Cloud Computing	4, 10
4.1 Compare and contrast cloud computing concepts.	4, 10
Common cloud models - IaaS - SaaS - PaaS - Public vs. private vs. hybrid vs. community	4, 10
Shared resources - Internal vs. external	4, 10
Rapid elasticity	4, 10
On-demand	4, 10
Resource pooling	4, 10
Measured service	4, 10
Metered	4, 10
Off-site email applications	4, 10

Objective	Chapter
Cloud file storage services - Synchronization apps	4, 10
Virtual application streaming/cloud-based applications - Applications for cell phones/tablets - Applications for laptops/desktops	4, 10
Virtual desktop - Virtual NIC	4, 10
4.2 Given a scenario, set up and configure client-side virtualization.	4, 10
Purpose of virtual machines	4, 10
Resource requirements	4, 10
Emulator requirements	4, 10
Security requirements	4, 10
Network requirements	4, 10
Hypervisor	4, 10
5.0 Hardware and Network Troubleshooting	5, 10
5.1 Given a scenario, use the best practice methodology to resolve problems.	5, 10
Always consider corporate policies, procedures, and impacts before implementing changes.	5, 10
1. Identify the problem. - Question the user and identify user changes to the computer and perform backups before making changes. - Inquire regarding environmental or infrastructure changes. - Review system and application logs.	5, 10
2. Establish a theory of probable cause (question the obvious). - If necessary, conduct external or internal research based on symptoms.	5, 10
3. Test the theory to determine cause. - Once the theory is confirmed, determine the next steps to resolve the problem. - If the theory is not confirmed reestablish a new theory or escalate the problem.	5, 10

Objective	Chapter
4. Establish a plan of action to resolve the problem and implement the solution.	5, 10
5. Verify full system functionality and, if applicable, implement preventive measures.	5, 10
6. Document findings, actions, and outcomes.	5, 10
5.2 Given a scenario, troubleshoot problems related to motherboards, RAM, CPUs, and power.	5, 10
Common symptoms - Unexpected shutdowns - System lockups - POST code beeps - Blank screen on bootup - BIOS time and setting resets - Attempts to boot to incorrect device - Continuous reboots - No power - Overheating - Loud noise - Intermittent device failure - Fans spin – no power to other devices - Indicator lights - Smoke - Burning smell - Proprietary crash screens (BSOD/pin wheel) - Distended capacitors - Log entries and error messages	5, 10
5.3 Given a scenario, troubleshoot hard drives and RAID arrays.	5, 10
Common symptoms - Read/write failure - Slow performance - Loud clicking noise - Failure to boot - Drive not recognized - OS not found - RAID not found - RAID stops working. - Proprietary crash screens (BSOD/pin wheel) - S.M.A.R.T. errors	5, 10

Objective	Chapter
5.4 Given a scenario, troubleshoot video, projector, and display issues.	5, 10
Common symptoms - VGA mode - No image on screen - Overheat shutdown - Dead pixels - Artifacts - Incorrect color patterns - Dim image - Flickering image - Distorted image - Distorted geometry - Burn-in - Oversized images and icons - Multiple failed jobs in logs	5, 10
5.5 Given a scenario, troubleshoot common mobile device issues while adhering to the appropriate procedures.	5, 10
Common symptoms - No display - Dim display - Flickering display - Sticking keys - Intermittent wireless - Battery not charging - Ghost cursor/pointer drift - No power - Num lock indicator lights - No wireless connectivity - No Bluetooth connectivity - Cannot display to external monitor - Touchscreen non-responsive - Apps not loading - Slow performance - Unable to decrypt email - Extremely short battery life - Overheating - Frozen system - No sound from speakers - GPS not functioning - Swollen battery	5, 10

Objective	Chapter
Disassembling processes for proper reassembly	5, 10
- Document and label cable and screw locations.	
- Organize parts.	
- Refer to manufacturer resources.	
- Use appropriate hand tools.	
5.6 Given a scenario, troubleshoot printers.	5, 10
Common symptoms	5, 10
- Streaks	
- Faded prints	
- Ghost images	
- Toner not fused to the paper	
- Creased paper	
- Paper not feeding	
- Paper jam	
- No connectivity	
- Garbled characters on paper	
- Vertical lines on page	
- Backed-up print queue	
- Low memory errors	
- Access denied	
- Printer will not print.	
- Color prints in wrong print color	
- Unable to install printer	
- Error codes	
- Printing blank pages	
- No image on printer display	
5.7 Given a scenario, troubleshoot common wired and wireless network problems.	5, 10
Common symptoms	5, 10
- Limited connectivity	
- Unavailable resources	
- Internet	
- Local resources	
- Shares	
- Printers	
- Email	

Objective	Chapter
- No connectivity	
- APIPA/link local address	
- Intermittent connectivity	
- IP conflict	
- Slow transfer speeds	
- Low RF signal	
- SSID not found	

A+ Certification Exam Objectives: Core 2 (220-1002)

The following table lists the domains measured by this examination and the extent to which they are represented on the exam.

Domain	Percentage of Exam
1.0 Operating Systems	27%
2.0 Security	24%
3.0 Software Troubleshooting	26%
4.0 Operational Procedures	23%
Total	100%

Objective	Chapter
1.0 Operating Systems	
1.1 Compare and contrast common operating system types and their purposes.	6, 11
32-bit vs. 64-bit - RAM limitations - Software compatibility	6, 11
Workstation operating systems - Microsoft Windows - Apple Macintosh OS - Linux	6, 11

Objective	Chapter
Cell phone/tablet operating systems - Microsoft Windows - Android - iOS - Chrome OS	6, 11
Vendor-specific limitations - End-of-life - Update limitations	6, 11
Compatibility concerns between operating systems	6, 11
1.2 Compare and contrast features of Microsoft Windows versions.	6, 11
Windows 7	6, 11
Windows 8	6, 11
Windows 8.1	6, 11
Windows 10	6, 11
Corporate vs. personal needs - Domain access - Bitlocker - Media center - Branchcache - EFS	6, 11
Desktop styles/user interface	6, 11
1.3 Summarize general OS installation considerations and upgrade methods.	6, 11
Boot methods - USB - CD-ROM - DVD - PXE - Solid state/flash drives - Netboot - External/hot-swappable drive - Internal hard drive (partition)	6, 11

Objective	Chapter
Type of installations	6, 11
- Unattended installation	
- In-place upgrade	
- Clean install	
- Repair installation	
- Multiboot	
- Remote network installation	
- Image deployment	
- Recovery partition	
- Refresh/restore	
Partitioning	6, 11
- Dynamic	
- Basic	
- Primary	
- Extended	
- Logical	
- GPT	
File system types/formatting	6, 11
- ExFAT	
- FAT32	
- NTFS	
- CDFS	
- NFS	
- ext3, ext4	
- HFS	
- Swap partition	
- Quick format vs. full format	
Load alternate third-party drivers when necessary.	6, 11
Workgroup vs. Domain setup	6, 11
Time/date/region/language settings	6, 11
Driver installation, software, and Windows updates	6, 11

Objective	Chapter
Task Manager	6, 11
- Applications	
- Processes	
- Performance	
- Networking	
- Users	
Disk Management	6, 11
- Drive status	
- Mounting	
- Initializing	
- Extending partitions	
- Splitting partitions	
- Shrink partitions	
- Assigning/changing drive letters	
- Adding drives	
- Adding arrays	
- Storage spaces	
System utilities	6, 11
- Regedit	
- Command	
- Services.msc	
- MMC	
- MSTSC	
- Notepad	
- Explorer	
- Msinfo32	
- DxDiag	
- Disk Defragmenter	
- System Restore	
- Windows Update	
1.6 Given a scenario, use Microsoft Windows Control Panel utilities.	6, 11
Internet Options	6, 11
- Connections	
- Security	
- General	
- Privacy	
- Programs	
- Advanced	

Objective	Chapter
Display/Display Settings - Resolution - Color depth - Refresh rate	6, 11
User Accounts	6, 11
Folder Options - View hidden files. - Hide extensions. - General options - View options	6, 11
System - Performance (virtual memory) - Remote settings - System protection	6, 11
Windows Firewall	6, 11
Power Options - Hibernate - Power plans - Sleep/suspend - Standby	6, 11
Credential Manager	6, 11
Programs and features	6, 11
HomeGroup	6, 11
Devices and Printers	6, 11
Sound	6, 11
Troubleshooting	6, 11
Network and Sharing Center	6, 11
Device Manager	6, 11
Bitlocker	6, 11
Sync Center	6, 11

Objective	Chapter
1.7 Summarize application installation and configuration concepts.	6, 11
System requirements - Drive space - RAM	6, 11
OS requirements - Compatibility	6, 11
Methods of installation and deployment - Local (CD/USB) - Network-based	6, 11
Local user permissions - Folder/file access for installation	6, 11
Security considerations - Impact to device - Impact to network	6, 11
1.8 Given a scenario, configure Microsoft Windows networking on a client/desktop.	6, 11
HomeGroup vs. Workgroup	6, 11
Domain setup	6, 11
Network shares/administrative shares/mapping drives	6, 11
Printer sharing vs. network printer mapping	6, 11
Establish networking connections. - VPN - Dial-ups - Wireless - Wired - WWAN (Cellular)	6, 11
Proxy settings	6, 11
Remote Desktop Connection	6, 11
Remote Assistance	6, 11
Home vs. Work vs. Public network settings	6, 11

Objective	Chapter
Features	6, 11
- Multiple desktops/Mission Control	
- Key Chain	
- Spot Light	
- iCloud	
- Gestures	
- Finder	
- Remote Disc	
- Dock	
- Boot Camp	
Basic Linux commands	6, 11
- ls	
- grep	
- cd	
- shutdown	
- pwd vs. passwd	
- mv	
- cp	
- rm	
- chmod	
- chown	
- iwconfig/ifconfig	
- ps	
- su/sudo	
- apt-get	
- vi	
- dd	
- kill	
2.0 Security	7, 11
2.1 Summarize the importance of physical security measures.	7, 11
Mantrap	7, 11
Badge reader	7, 11
Smart card	7, 11
Security guard	7, 11
Door lock	7, 11

Objective	Chapter
Shared files and folders - Administrative shares vs. local shares - Permission propagation - Inheritance	7, 11
System files and folders	7, 11
User authentication - Single sign-on	7, 11
Run as administrator vs. standard user	7, 11
BitLocker	7, 11
BitLocker To Go	7, 11
EFS	7, 11
2.7 Given a scenario, implement security best practices to secure a workstation.	7, 11
Password best practices - Setting strong passwords - Password expiration - Screensaver required password - BIOS/UEFI passwords - Requiring passwords	7, 11

Account management
- Restricting user permissions
- Logon time restrictions
- Disabling guest account
- Failed attempts lockout
- Timeout/screen lock
- Change default admin user account/password.
- Basic Active Directory functions
  - Account creation
  - Account deletion
  - Password reset/unlock account
  - Disable account.
	7, 11

Objective	Chapter
Disable autorun.	7, 11
Data encryption	7, 11
Patch/update management	7, 11
2.8 Given a scenario, implement methods for securing mobile devices.	7, 11
Screen locks - Fingerprint lock - Face lock - Swipe lock - Passcode lock	7, 11
Remote wipes	7, 11
Locator applications	7, 11
Remote backup applications	7, 11
Failed login attempts restrictions	7, 11
Antivirus/Anti-malware	7, 11
Patching/OS updates	7, 11
Biometric authentication	7, 11
Full device encryption	7, 11
Multifactor authentication	7, 11
Authenticator applications	7, 11
Trusted sources vs. untrusted sources	7, 11
Firewalls	7, 11
Policies and procedures - BYOD vs. corporate-owned - Profile security requirements	7, 11

Objective	Chapter
3.0 Software Troubleshooting	8, 11
3.1 Given a scenario, troubleshoot Microsoft Windows OS problems.	8, 11
Common symptoms - Slow performance - Limited connectivity - Failure to boot - No OS found - Application crashes - Blue screens - Black screens - Printing issues - Services fail to start - Slow bootup - Slow profile load	8, 11
Common solutions - Defragment the hard drive. - Reboot. - Kill tasks. - Restart services. - Update network settings. - Reimage/reload OS. - Roll back updates. - Roll back device drivers. - Apply updates. - Repair application. - Update boot order. - Disable Windows services/applications. - Disable application startup. - Safe boot - Rebuild Windows profiles.	8, 11

Objective	Chapter
Avoid distractions.	9, 11
- Personal calls	
- Texting/social media sites	
- Talking to coworkers while interacting with customers	
- Personal interruptions	
Dealing with difficult customers or situations	9, 11
- Do not argue with customers and/or be defensive.	
- Avoid dismissing customer problems.	
- Avoid being judgmental.	
- Clarify customer statements (ask open-ended questions to narrow the scope of the problem, restate the issue, or question to verify understanding).	
- Do not disclose experiences via social media outlets.	
Set and meet expectations/timeline and communicate status with the customer.	9, 11
- Offer different repair/replacement options, if applicable.	
- Provide proper documentation on the services provided.	
- Follow up with customer/user at a later date to verify satisfaction.	
Deal appropriately with customers' confidential and private materials.	9, 11
- Located on a computer, desktop, printer, etc.	
4.8 Identify the basics of scripting.	9, 11
Script file types	9, 11
- .bat	
- .ps1	
- .vbs	
- .sh	
- .py	
- .js	
Environment variables	9, 11
Comment syntax	9, 11
Basic script constructs	9, 11
- Basic loops	
- Variables	

NOTE Exam objectives are subject to change at any time without prior notice and at CompTIA's sole discretion. Please visit the certification page of CompTIA's website at www.comptia.org for the most current listing of exam objectives.

Exam 220-1001

Chapter

1

Mobile Devices

THE FOLLOWING COMPTIA A+ EXAM 220-1001 TOPICS ARE COVERED IN THIS CHAPTER:

✓ **1.1   Install and configure laptop hardware and components.**

- Hardware/device replacement
- Keyboard
- Hard drive
- SSD vs. hybrid vs. magnetic disk
- 1.8in vs. 2.5in
- Memory
- Smart card reader
- Optical drive
- Wireless card/Bluetooth module
- Cellular card
- Video card
- Mini PCIe
- Screen
- DC jack
- Battery
- Touchpad
- Plastics/frames
- Speaker
- System board
- CPU

✓ **1.2   Given a scenario, install components within the display of a laptop.**

- Types
- LCD

- OLED
- WiFi antenna connector/placement
- Webcam
- Microphone
- Inverter
- Digitizer/touchscreen

✓ **1.3   Given a scenario, use appropriate laptop features.**

- Special function keys
- Dual displays
- Wireless (on/off)
- Cellular (on/off)
- Volume settings
- Screen brightness
- Bluetooth (on/off)
- Keyboard backlight
- Touch pad (on/off)
- Screen orientation
- Media options (fast forward/rewind)
- GPS (on/off)
- Airplane mode
- Docking station
- Port replicator
- Physical laptop lock and cable lock
- Rotating/removable screens

✓ **1.4   Compare and contrast characteristics of various types of other mobile devices.**

- Tablets
- Smartphones
- Wearable technology devices
- Smart watches
- Fitness monitors

- VR/AR headsets
- E-readers
- GPS

✓ **1.5   Given a scenario, connect and configure accessories and ports of other mobile devices.**

- Connection types
- Wired
- Micro-USB/Mini-USB/USB-C
- Lightning
- Tethering
- Proprietary vendor-specific ports (communication/power)
- Wireless
- NFC
- Bluetooth
- IR
- Hotspot
- Accessories
- Headsets
- Speakers
- Game pads
- Extra battery packs/battery chargers
- Protective covers/water proofing
- Credit card readers
- Memory/MicroSD

✓ **1.6   Given a scenario, configure basic mobile device network connectivity and application support.**

- Wireless/cellular data network (enable/disable)
- Hotspot
- Tethering
- Airplane mode
- Bluetooth

- Enable Bluetooth
- Enable pairing
- Find a device for pairing
- Enter the appropriate pin code
- Test connectivity
- Corporate and ISP email configuration
- POP3
- IMAP
- Port and SSL settings
- S/MIME
- Integrated commercial provider email configuration
- iCloud
- Google/Inbox
- Exchange Online
- Yahoo
- PRI updates/PRL updates/baseband updates
- Radio firmware
- IMEI vs. IMSI
- VPN

✓ **1.7   Given a scenario, use methods to perform mobile device synchronization.**

- Synchronization methods
- Synchronize to the cloud
- Synchronize to the desktop
- Synchronize to the automobile
- Types of data to synchronize
- Contacts
- Applications
- Email
- Pictures

- Music
- Videos
- Calendar
- Bookmarks
- Documents
- Location data
- Social media data
- E-books
- Passwords
- Mutual authentication for multiple services (SSO)
- Software requirements to install the application on the PC
- Connection types to enable synchronization

1. Which type of laptop backlight is typically used in smaller mobile devices and consumes the least amount of power?

    A. IPS

    B. TN

    C. LED

    D. CCFL

2. In which scenario would you use the Fn key and the F10 key?

    A. To turn the screen brightness down

    B. To turn the screen brightness up

    C. To turn the speaker volume down

    D. To turn the speaker volume up

3. You are purchasing a mobile device that allows you to use your finger to input information. What type of touch screen technology does this device use?

    A. Capacitive

    B. Human based

    C. Warmth

    D. Resistive

4. You are using a public Wi-Fi hotspot and believe that someone is trying to hack into your laptop. Which laptop feature should you use to immediately turn off all wireless connections?

    A. Silent mode

    B. Quiet mode

    C. Airplane mode

    D. Connectionless mode

5. You have been asked to purchase a new camera for the company photographer. Some of the cameras are marketed as "smart" cameras. What key feature does this likely mean the camera includes?

    A. Wi-Fi

    B. RJ-45

    C. Separate video processor

    D. Internal hard drive

6. A user approaches you and asks for a CPU upgrade so his Lenovo laptop will run faster. What is most likely the easiest way to meet this user's needs?

    A. Remove the CPU and replace it with a faster one that fits the same socket.

    B. Replace the laptop with one with a faster CPU.

    C. Replace the motherboard with a standard laptop motherboard with a faster processor.

    D. Replace the motherboard with a Lenovo laptop motherboard with a faster processor.

7. In which scenario would you use the Fn key and the F4 key shown here?

    A. To turn the touch pad on or off

    B. To change the video output to an external monitor

    C. To change the screen orientation from landscape to portrait

    D. To turn the keyboard backlight on or off

8. You are using a laptop computer and the wireless network card fails. There are no wired ports nearby. You need to send a file to your boss, who is in another country, in the next 10 minutes. What should you do to fix the situation?

    A. Remove the defective network card and install a new one.

    B. Install a USB to RJ-45 dongle.

    C. Install a USB to Wi-Fi dongle.

    D. Install a USB to Bluetooth dongle.

9. Which type of mobile device is known for using electrophoretic ink?

   A. E-reader

   B. Smart watch

   C. Smart glasses

   D. Tablet

10. What type of connection are you using if you use a USB cable to connect your laptop to your cellular phone in order to use the cellular wireless connection from the laptop?

    A. Hotspot

    B. Tethering

    C. USB networking

    D. Phoning

11. For which characteristic was the BlackBerry smartphone most famous?

    A. Wi-Fi

    B. Hardware keyboard

    C. Anti-glare

    D. Trackball

12. Which laptop accessory should you purchase if you want to protect the device against theft?

    A. Docking station

    B. Change Protective cover

    C. Cable lock

    D. LoJack

13. The hard drive in your manager's desktop has failed, and you need to replace it. Your manager asks about the benefits of replacing it with an SSD instead of an HDD. What should you tell her? (Choose two.)

    A. They are cheaper.

    B. They take up less space.

    C. They consume less power and generate less heat.

    D. They operate silently.

14. Which laptop expansion port was designed as an industry standard to replace VGA and DVI ports and is backward compatible with both standards?

    A. DisplayPort

    B. VideoPort

    C. Thunderbolt

    D. HDMI

15. In a laptop, which display type illuminates each pixel individually rather than by LED backlight?

    A. CCFL

    B. E Ink

    C. LCD

    D. OLED

16. You have recently purchased a laptop computer with a touch screen. It allows you to draw images on the screen and save them on the computer. Which device is responsible for converting the input into the image that you are able to save?

    A. Inverter

    B. Touch pad

    C. Digitizer

    D. Touch screen

17. A technician has a failed Lenovo laptop, and he suspects the motherboard is bad. He has several other laptops available from which he can harvest parts. Which of the following statements is most likely true regarding the replacement motherboard he selects?

    A. The motherboard is not replaceable.

    B. He can choose a motherboard from any other laptop.

    C. He can choose a motherboard from any other Lenovo laptop.

    D. He must choose a motherboard from that same model of Lenovo laptop.

18. A technician needs to replace a failed laptop hard drive. The user stores a large amount of video on her computer and needs the largest-capacity drive possible. What type of hard drive should you install?

    A. SSD

    B. Magnetic

    C. Hybrid

    D. Flash

19. Which of the following wireless communication types has a maximum distance of about 4″?

    A. NFC

    B. Wi-Fi

    C. IR

    D. Bluetooth

20. Which two components of a laptop are the most useful when making a video conference call? (Choose two.)

    A. Digitizer

    B. Webcam

    C. Microphone

    D. Inverter

21. Which mobile accessory is shown here?

    A. Credit card reader

    B. Memory card reader

    C. External battery pack

    D. Wi-Fi range extender

22. Which mobile connection type allows you to share your cellular Internet connection with a Wi-Fi enabled device?

    A. Hotspot

    B. NFC

    C. Bluetooth

    D. IR

23. You are responsible for replacement parts within your company's IT department. Because of the critical nature of your business, you need to have replacement parts on hand in the event of a hardware failure. Your company uses four different types of laptops, two HP and two Dell. How many different types of motherboards do you most likely need to stock?

    A. One

    B. Two

    C. Three

    D. Four

24. In a laptop computer, which component is responsible for providing light to the display?

 A. Backlight

 B. Inverter

 C. LCD

 D. Screen

25. You need to purchase a memory card reader and removable memory for your mobile device. You need to transfer approximately 1 TB of data at a time. Which technology should you invest in?

 A. SDHC

 B. miniSD

 C. microSDHC

 D. SDXC

26. What type of mobile device would use the connector shown here?

 A. Apple iPhone 4

 B. Apple iPhone 6

 C. Samsung Galaxy S5

 D. Fitbit Surge

27. You are replacing a motherboard in a laptop computer. When you open the case, you notice that there is a small circuit board attached to the motherboard that appears to have video and network circuitry built into it. What is the name of this small circuit board?

 A. Daughterboard

 B. Secondary motherboard

 C. Junior board

 D. Expansion board

28. You are visiting a remote office and need to print some documents. Your host tells you that the printer you need is configured on a piconet. What type of expansion option should you use to connect to this printer?

    A. USB to RJ-45 dongle

    B. USB to Wi-Fi dongle

    C. USB to Bluetooth

    D. USB to Thunderbolt

29. You will be traveling to another country for work and will have a 10-hour airplane flight. You need to work on your laptop while on the flight, but your battery won't last that long. What should you buy to allow you to use the auxiliary power outlets on the airplane?

    A. AC adapter

    B. DC adapter

    C. Power inverter

    D. Docking station

30. Your laptop has an internal Mini PCIe expansion slot. The documentation for an expansion card says that it supports Mini PCIe 2.0 x1 functionality. At what speed does the expansion card run?

    A. 500 Mbps

    B. 2.5 Gbps

    C. 5.0 Gbps

    D. 6.0 Gbps

31. Of the laptop components listed, which one is least likely to be built into the display?

    A. Wi-Fi antenna

    B. Speakers

    C. Webcam

    D. Digitizer

32. A defining characteristic of a phablet is a screen of approximately what size?

    A. Between 3″ and 5″

    B. Between 5″ and 7″

    C. Between 7″ and 12″

    D. Between 12″ and 24″

33. You are interested in buying a smart watch that has an OS compatible with your Android-based smartphone. Which brand of smart watch uses the Android Wear OS?

    A. Apple Watch

    B. Samsung Gear S

    C. Sony SmartWatch 3

    D. Pebble Time

34. You want to enable hands-free cellular conversations for when you are driving, so you purchase a wireless headset. Which wireless technology does the headset most likely use?

    A. Wi-Fi

    B. IR

    C. Bluetooth

    D. NFC

35. The AC adapter for your Dell laptop is not working properly, and you are searching for a replacement. Which two factors should be most important when selecting a new AC adapter? (Choose two.)

    A. Polarity

    B. Same wattage as or higher wattage than the original

    C. Brand of the adapter

    D. Size of the adapter

36. A laptop user wants to have a full-sized monitor and keyboard, as well as an external hard drive, available to him when he is at his desk. Which accessory can he purchase so that he doesn't need to plug in each of these devices separately to his laptop every time he returns to his desk?

    A. KVM switch

    B. Port bay station

    C. Desktop station

    D. Docking station

37. Identify the laptop connector, typically located on the bottom of the laptop, shown here.

    A. Mini PCIe

    B. Smart card reader

    C. Docking port

    D. Battery port

38. You need to replace a failed hard drive in a user's laptop, and it's a model you are unfamiliar with. You look at the bottom of the laptop and see no obvious entrance points. Which component will you most likely need to remove to access the hard drive bay?

    A. Plastics/frames

    B. Battery

    C. System board

    D. Keyboard

39. A new laptop user asks you to explain airplane mode to her. Which of the following statements best describes what airplane mode does?

    A. It turns off all your wireless connections.

    B. It turns off your Wi-Fi connection.

    C. It turns off your Wi-Fi and cellular connections.

    D. It turns off your Wi-Fi and Bluetooth connections.

40. Which memory cards have a capacity of up to 32 GB? (Choose two.)

    A. miniSDHC

    B. microSDHC

    C. SD

    D. microSDXC

41. The iPhone 8 and iPhone X use what type of connector for charging?

    A. Thunderbolt

    B. Lightning

    C. ApplePower

    D. USB-C

42. You have a laptop with an ExpressCard/34 slot. Which type of device or devices are you unlikely to be able to use as an expansion option in that slot?

    A. Hard drive

    B. Sound card

    C. Network card

    D. eSATA adapter

43. You have enabled the GPS service in your tablet. What is the minimum number of GPS satellites your tablet needs to be in contact with to determine its location?

    A. One

    B. Two

    C. Three

    D. Four

44. You are investigating new laptops for your company. You want the laptop displays to have a wide viewing angle. Which technology is best suited for your needs?

- **A.** LED
- **B.** CCFL
- **C.** IPS
- **D.** TN

45. You are using a USB flash drive to transfer files from a laptop. You plug the USB drive in and then copy the files to it. What is the recommended way to remove the drive?

- **A.** Unplug the drive.
- **B.** Use the Safely Remove Hardware icon in the system tray, stop the drive, and then unplug it.
- **C.** Close the drive's window in Windows Explorer and unplug it.
- **D.** Use the Shut Down Hardware icon in the system tray, stop the drive, and then unplug it.

46. What is the name of the OS used by the Apple Watch, which was designed specifically for the watch?

- **A.** iOS
- **B.** OS X mobile
- **C.** WatchOS
- **D.** Tizen

47. The new model of laptop just purchased by your company has a Universal ExpressCard slot. Which of the following types of cards can you install into that slot?

- **A.** ExpressCard/54 only
- **B.** ExpressCard/34 and ExpressCard/54
- **C.** ExpressCard/24, ExpressCard/34, and ExpressCard/54
- **D.** ExpressCard/34, ExpressCard/54, and CardBus

48. You have a MacBook Pro computer with a Thunderbolt 3 port. What is the maximum throughput of a device plugged into this port?

- **A.** 5 Gbps
- **B.** 10 Gbps
- **C.** 20 Gbps
- **D.** 40 Gbps

49. A technician needs to replace a failed laptop hard drive. What are the possible form factors of this hard drive? (Choose two.)

- **A.** 1.3"
- **B.** 1.8"
- **C.** 2.5"
- **D.** 3.5"

50. Your laptop has an internal Mini PCIe expansion slot. The documentation for an expansion card says that it supports Mini PCIe USB 2.0 functionality. At what speed does the expansion card run?

   A. 480 Mbps

   B. 2.5 Gbps

   C. 5.0 Gbps

   D. 6.0 Gbps

51. Which laptop component can take input from a stylus and convert it into an image on the computer?

   A. Digitizer

   B. Touch pad

   C. Point stick

   D. Inverter

52. What type of wearable technology device is specifically designed to track a user's movements and heart rate and may include features such as GPS?

   A. Smart watch

   B. Fitness monitor

   C. Smart glasses

   D. Smart headset

53. Your company is producing posters for an upcoming public relations campaign. The project leader wants to embed information into an NFC tag in the poster. How much information can this tag hold?

   A. 8 KB

   B. 144 KB

   C. 1.4 MB

   D. 4.4 MB

54. You want to play video games on your tablet computer. Which accessory would you purchase if you wanted to play the game much like you would on a gaming console?

   A. Docking station

   B. Touch pad

   C. Point stick

   D. Game pad

55. Which laptop expansion port technology was developed by Apple and supports a wide variety of peripheral devices?

   A. USB

   B. DisplayPort

   C. eSATA

   D. Thunderbolt

56. You have a laptop with an ExpressCard/34 slot. Which of the following statements is true regarding installing expansion cards?

   A. You can only plug in an ExpressCard/34 card.

   B. You can plug in an ExpressCard/34 card or an ExpressCard/22 card.

   C. You can plug in an ExpressCard/34 card or an ExpressCard/54 card.

   D. You can plug in an ExpressCard/34 card or an ExpressCard Universal card.

57. You are wearing your smart watch, which allows you to make payments like a credit card. What type of connection technology does this service use?

   A. Bluetooth

   B. NFC

   C. Wi-Fi

   D. IR

58. Which laptop display component is capable of discharging energy and causing severe injuries to technicians?

   A. Screen

   B. Backlight

   C. Inverter

   D. LCD

59. Your new laptop has 4 GB system RAM and an integrated video card. The default setting specifies 512 MB of video memory. How much RAM is available for the processor to use?

   A. 4 GB

   B. 3.5 GB

   C. 3 GB

   D. It's variable.

60. Oculus, Samsung, and HTC are manufacturers of what type of wearable technology devices?

   A. Smart glasses

   B. Smart headsets

   C. Smart watches

   D. VR/AR headsets

61. You need to install a memory upgrade in a laptop computer. The computer's documentation says that the laptop uses DDR3 SODIMMs. How many pins will be on the SODIMM?

   A. 144

   B. 200

   C. 204

   D. 240

62. What type of mobile device would use the connector shown here?

    A. Apple iPhone 4

    B. Apple iPhone X

    C. Samsung Galaxy S9

    D. Fitbit Surge

63. You need to replace a failed laptop hard drive. The user has asked that the new hard drive be as fast as possible, regardless of disk space or cost. What type of drive should you install?

    A. SSD

    B. Magnetic

    C. Hybrid

    D. External

64. Which type of mobile connection uses a process called pairing to logically connect two devices?

    A. Bluetooth

    B. Wi-Fi

    C. NFC

    D. IR

65. Tablet computers feature touch screens that are approximately what size?

    A. Between 5″ and 7″

    B. Between 3″ and 5″

    C. Between 7″ and 12″

    D. Between 12″ and 24″

66. What type of connectors are the two shown in the center here?

- **A.** Lightning
- **B.** Thunderbolt
- **C.** IEEE 1394
- **D.** Power

67. Which mobile technology device makes use of an augmented reality display?
- **A.** Smartphone
- **B.** Smart watch
- **C.** Smart camera
- **D.** Smart glasses

68. Which type of laptop backlight generally does not require the use of an inverter?
- **A.** TN
- **B.** IPS
- **C.** CCFL
- **D.** LED

69. You have traveled to the office of one of your suppliers. It does not have wireless networking, and your laptop does not have a wired network connection. If you need to get on the supplier's network, what is the best solution?
- **A.** Install a Mini PCIe network card with an RJ-45 port.
- **B.** Install a USB to RJ-45 dongle.
- **C.** Install a USB to Bluetooth dongle.
- **D.** Install a USB to Wi-Fi dongle.

70. You are on the phone talking to a technician who is trying to upgrade a laptop. He is having trouble identifying the Mini PCIe card. How wide should you tell the technician that the card is?
- **A.** 27 mm
- **B.** 30 mm
- **C.** 51 mm
- **D.** 60 mm

71. You have been asked to burn a DVD with several videos on it, but your laptop does not have an internal optical drive. You are certain that this request will be made several times. Which option is the best for you to install or replace a DVD burner?

   A. Remove the secondary hard drive bay and install an internal DVD burner.

   B. Remove the battery pack and install a DVD burner in its place.

   C. Install an external DVD burner using a USB port.

   D. Install an external DVD burner using the DB-15 port.

72. Which type of network connection is least likely to be found on a tablet computer?

   A. Wi-Fi

   B. Bluetooth

   C. RJ-45

   D. Cellular

73. A Lightning connector would be used with what type of device?

   A. Samsung Galaxy S9

   B. Fitbit Surge

   C. Apple iPhone 4

   D. Apple iPhone X

74. You have decided to start playing video-intensive games on your laptop computer. The video appears jumpy and slow to respond. What should you do first to try to increase the performance during gameplay?

   A. Upgrade the video card.

   B. Install additional video memory.

   C. Use Windows Control Panel to increase the amount of video memory available.

   D. Use the system BIOS to increase the amount of video memory available.

75. A guest presenter plugs an external projector into his laptop using the VGA port on the back of the laptop. He then uses the Fn key and his video toggle switch; the projector displays his presentation, but his laptop screen goes dark. What should he do if he wants to see the presentation on both the projector and his laptop?

   A. Install a second video driver and then use the video toggle key to switch the video output to both screens.

   B. Unplug the projector and plug it back in to synchronize it with the laptop.

   C. Unplug the projector, use the video toggle key to switch the video output, and then plug the projector back in.

   D. Press the video toggle key again until the presentation is shown on both screens.

76. You need to replace a failed motherboard in a laptop computer. Which of the following components are most likely integrated into the motherboard? (Choose two.)

   A. Video card

   B. Network card

   C. Hard drive

   D. RAM

77. A user has a laptop that is intermittently locking up. Initial diagnostics indicate that the processor is overheating. What can you do to try to remediate the issue? (Choose two.)

   A. Leave the case open while the system is running to allow for better airflow and cooling.

   B. Lower the CPU voltage in the system BIOS.

   C. Lower the CPU clock speed in the system BIOS.

   D. Run the laptop on AC power instead of battery power.

78. A client has an older Windows 7 laptop with an integrated video card. The system seems to boot but produces no video, even with an external monitor hooked up. What can you do to fix this?

   A. Add an external USB video card and connect the monitor to it.

   B. Remove the old video card, and replace it with a new internal video card.

   C. Replace the motherboard.

   D. Leave the old card in the system, and add an internal Mini PCIe video card.

79. You are upgrading a laptop with a Mini PCIe card. What type of connector does Mini PCIe use?

   A. 52-pin

   B. 78-pin

   C. 144-pin

   D. 200-pin

80. Which of the following are ways to input information or commands into Google Glass? (Choose two.)

   A. Touch screen

   B. Touch pad

   C. Voice command

   D. Virtual keyboard

81. Which of the following wireless communication methods are the least susceptible to hacking? (Choose two.)

   A. Wi-Fi

   B. IR

   C. Bluetooth

   D. NFC

82. Of the laptop LCD technologies, which consumes the least amount of power?

   A. LED

   B. IPS

   C. TN

   D. CCFL

83. What types of networking will smart cameras often have built into them? (Choose two.)

   A. Bluetooth

   B. IR

   C. RJ-45

   D. 802.11b/g/n

84. What type of connector is shown here on the right?

By Techtonic, edited from USB types.jpg (public domain), via Wikimedia Commons

   A. USB micro

   B. USB mini

   C. USB type A

   D. Lightning

85. A user has brought his laptop to you because the screen is intermittently flickering. Which display component is most likely causing this?

   A. Backlight

   B. LCD

   C. Screen

   D. Inverter

86. Which of the following wireless communication types has a maximum distance of 1 meter and requires line of sight?

A. NFC

B. Bluetooth

C. Wi-Fi

D. IR

87. What is the likely type of Wi-Fi antenna connector you will find on a laptop?

A. SMA-female-RP

B. N-male

C. SMA-male-RP

D. N-female

88. A user needs ports for external devices in addition to what his laptop is capable of connecting. The user would like to have these devices available even without the laptop. What device provides that additional connectivity without the laptop?

A. Docking station

B. Port replicator

C. KVM switch

D. Docking port

89. A warehouse manager at a factory is required to supervise productivity while walking and taking notes. She finds the laptop awkward to type on while walking but does not want to have to use two devices. What would you recommend she do?

A. Get a small tablet to synchronize with the laptop.

B. Place accessible workstations throughout the factory.

C. Get a laptop with a rotating or removable screen.

D. Get a smaller laptop.

90. After enabling your device for communication using the IEEE 802.15.1 standard, what is the next step?

A. Entering the PIN code

B. Finding a device for pairing

C. Enter the IMAP server and port.

D. Opening the firewall for 802.15.1 traffic

91. When attempting to pair with a Bluetooth device, what is the typical next step?

A. Enabling Bluetooth on both devices simultaneously

B. Entering the Bluetooth password

C. Entering the Bluetooth PIN code

D. Exiting out of any running Bluetooth applications

92. Your client is frustrated that her Bluetooth earpiece that was working yesterday is no longer working? As she asks you for help, what is the likely source of the problem?

    A. Earpiece has paired to a different device.

    B. Broken earpiece

    C. Weak Wi-Fi signal

    D. Bluetooth connectivity was lost.

93. Which mail protocol keeps all emails stored on a single device and can only be accessed from one device?

    A. IMAP

    B. SMTP

    C. POP3

    D. S/MIME

94. Which mail protocol keeps all emails stored on the server, allowing messages to be synchronized between multiple devices?

    A. IMAP

    B. SMTP

    C. POP3

    D. S/MIME

95. Which protocol is used for sending and receiving encrypted email?

    A. S/MIME

    B. SMTP

    C. SNMP

    D. SignE

96. What service is built into Apple-developed devices and permits users and subscribers to store documents, media, and contact information off their devices?

    A. iStore

    B. BackCloud

    C. iCloud

    D. CloudOnline

97. What is the hosted messaging version of Microsoft's Exchange mail server that saves customers off-site?

    A. Google Inbox

    B. Exchange Online

    C. iExchange

    D. On-Prem Exchange

98. What email configuration settings are commonly used when setting up email on a device?

   A. Active Directory domain name

   B. Port and SSL settings

   C. DNS server

   D. Administrative contact

99. What type of update is done to mobile devices over the air?

   A. PRI and PRL

   B. IMEI

   C. Screen resolution

   D. IMSI

100. Which number is hard-coded into the phone and identifies your physical phone hardware to the cellular tower?

   A. PRI

   B. IMSI

   C. IMEI

   D. MAC

101. Which unique mobile number identifies you as a user and is coded into the SIM card, allowing you to transition it from one phone to another?

   A. PRI

   B. IMSI

   C. IMEI

   D. MAC

102. A user is traveling to a country that employs content blocking technology on the cellular network. What would you suggest he uses to bypass the content blocking as well as keep his mobile browsing more private?

   A. S/MIME

   B. PRL

   C. Baseband

   D. VPN

103. What best practice can save someone from losing her data on her mobile device if the device is lost?

   A. Synchronization

   B. VPN

   C. Encryption

   D. Updating

104. A user wants a list of favorite websites to be readily available between multiple devices, including his mobile device. What is his best option?

    A. Email weblinks to self.

    B. Send links to a URL shortening service.

    C. Synchronize bookmarks.

    D. Print web URLs to carry.

105. When two parents wish to share appointment dates and times between devices, what is their best option?

    A. Synchronizing calendars

    B. Sharing calendar passwords

    C. Texting calendar data to each other

    D. Emailing calendar invites to each other

106. What technology lets you minimize how often a user must log in for multiple services?

    A. SSO

    B. SMTP

    C. Synchronization

    D. Repudiation

107. A user comments he needs to use his phone to find a person's cell number because the desktop mail application's address book has some phone numbers but is missing the person's phone number. What would you suggest that user do to make life easier?

    A. Copy phone numbers on one central piece of paper.

    B. Verify all contact information as still current.

    C. Synchronize contact information between devices.

    D. Erase duplicate numbers, then manually copy missing information.

108. Before starting to install a new application on an older system, what should be done?

    A. Verify that the operating system is compatible.

    B. Confirm software requirements to install the application.

    C. Upgrade the memory on the system to the maximum amount.

    D. Expand the storage capacity on the system to the maximum.

Chapter

2

Networking

THE FOLLOWING COMPTIA A+ EXAM 220-1001 TOPICS ARE COVERED IN THIS CHAPTER:

✓ **2.1 Explain common TCP and UDP ports, protocols, and their purposes.**

- Ports and protocols
  - 21 – FTP
  - 22 – SSH
  - 23 – TELNET
  - 25 – SMTP
  - 53 – DNS
  - 80 – HTTP
  - 110 – POP3
  - 143 – IMAP
  - 443 – HTTPS
  - 3389 – RDP
  - 137-139 – NetBIOS/NetBT
  - 445 – SMB/CIFS
  - 427 – SLP
  - 548 – AFP
  - 67/68 – DHCP
  - 389 – LDAP
  - 161/162 – SNMP
- TCP vs. UDP

✓ **2.2 Compare and contrast common networking hardware devices.**

- Routers
- Switches

- Managed
- Unmanaged
- Access points
- Cloud-based network controller
- Firewall
- Network interface card
- Repeater
- Hub
- Cable/DSL modem
- Bridge
- Patch panel
- Power over Ethernet (PoE)
  - Injectors
  - Switch
- Ethernet over Power

✓ **2.3   Given a scenario, install and configure a basic wired/ wireless SOHO network.**

- Router/switch functionality
- Access point settings
- IP addressing
- NIC configuration
  - Wired
  - Wireless
- End-user device configuration
- IoT device configuration
  - Thermostat
  - Light switches
  - Security cameras
  - Door locks
  - Voice-enabled, smart speaker/digital assistant
- Cable/DSL modem configuration

- Firewall settings
  - DMZ
  - Port forwarding
  - NAT
  - UPnP
  - Whitelist/blacklist
  - MAC filtering
- QoS
- Wireless settings
  - Encryption
  - Channels
  - QoS

✓ 2.4 Compare and contrast wireless networking protocols.

- 802.11a
- 802.11b
- 802.11g
- 802.11n
- 802.11ac
- Frequencies
  - 2.4Ghz
  - 5Ghz
- Channels
  - 1–11
- Bluetooth
- NFC
- RFID
- Zigbee
- Z-Wave
- 3G
- 4G
- 5G
- LTE

✓ **2.5 Summarize the properties and purposes of services provided by networked hosts.**

- Server roles
  - Web server
  - File server
  - Print server
  - DHCP server
  - DNS server
  - Proxy server
  - Mail server
  - Authentication server
  - syslog
- Internet appliance
  - UTM
  - IDS
  - IPS
  - End-point management server
- Legacy/embedded systems

✓ **2.6 Explain common network configuration concepts.**

- IP addressing
  - Static
  - Dynamic
  - APIPA
  - Link local
- DNS
- DHCP
  - Reservations
- IPv4 vs. IPv6
- Subnet mask
- Gateway
- VPN
- VLAN
- NAT

✓ **2.7 Compare and contrast Internet connection types, network types, and their features.**

- Internet connection types
  - Cable
  - DSL
  - Dial-up
  - Fiber
  - Satellite
  - ISDN
  - Cellular
    - Tethering
    - Mobile hotspot
  - Line-of-sight wireless Internet service
- Network types
  - LAN
  - WAN
  - PAN
  - MAN
  - WMN

✓ **2.8 Given a scenario, use appropriate networking tools.**

- Crimper
- Cable stripper
- Multimeter
- Tone generator and probe
- Cable tester
- Loopback plug
- Punchdown tool
- Wi-Fi analyzer

1. Which of the following network devices receives network traffic and makes a decision on whether to send it on based on the destination hardware address?

    A. Hub

    B. Bridge

    C. Access point

    D. Repeater

2. A technician installed a UTP splitter on one of your network segments that has CAT6e cable. What is the maximum speed supported by this connection?

    A. 10 Mbps

    B. 100 Mbps

    C. 1 Gbps

    D. 10 Gbps

3. You are installing a fiber-optic cable between two buildings. To install the cable, you must run it through a conduit between the buildings, and access to the conduit is not easy. Before you run the cable, you want to ensure that it's working properly. Which tool should you use?

    A. Cable tester

    B. Multimeter

    C. Loopback plug

    D. Tone generator and probe

4. Which TCP/IP protocol, designed to download email, allows for multiple clients to be simultaneously connected to the same mailbox?

    A. SMTP

    B. POP3

    C. IMAP

    D. SMB

5. You are using your laptop on the company network. In your web browser, you type in www.google.com and press Enter. The computer will not find Google. You open the browser on your phone, and using your cellular connection, you can open Google without a problem. Your laptop finds internal servers and can print without any issues. What is the most likely reason you can't open Google?

    A. DNS server problem

    B. DHCP server problem

    C. Missing subnet mask

    D. Duplicate IP address

6. A technician needs to run a network cable to a remote building, which is approximately 15 kilometers from his base station. He's not sure if any cable will span that distance. What is the maximum distance of SMF cable?

   A. 300 meters

   B. 550 meters

   C. 40 kilometers

   D. 100 kilometers

7. You have been asked to install a run of RG-59 cable from one end of a building to the other. What is the maximum distance for this type of cable run?

   A. 100 meters (328 feet)

   B. 228 meters (750 feet)

   C. 304 meters (1,000 feet)

   D. 500 meters (1,645 feet)

8. Which one of the following TCP/IP protocols was designed as a replacement for Telnet?

   A. SMB

   B. SSH

   C. SFTP

   D. FTPS

9. Which of the following network connectivity devices operate at Layer 2 of the OSI model? (Choose two.)

   A. Hub

   B. Switch

   C. Bridge

   D. Router

10. In IPv4, what is the function of the subnet mask?

   A. It tells hosts where to route packets.

   B. It differentiates between the network ID and host ID.

   C. It determines which subnet the host is on.

   D. It masks external networks from the host.

11. Which of the following TCP/IP protocols is connection-oriented and attempts to guarantee packet delivery?

   A. IP

   B. TCP

   C. UDP

   D. ICMP

12. Which TCP/IP protocol allows a user to log into a remote computer and manage files as if they were logged in locally?

    A. FTP

    B. SFTP

    C. SMB

    D. Telnet

13. You are given a network configuration of 155.100.63.0/26 from your ISP. When you configure your network hosts, what subnet mask should you assign them?

    A. 255.255.0.0

    B. 255.255.255.0

    C. 255.255.255.192

    D. 255.255.255.240

14. Which Wi-Fi standard specifies a maximum of 54 Mbps transmissions in the 2.4 GHz frequency range?

    A. 802.11a

    B. 802.11b

    C. 802.11g

    D. 802.11n

15. Which TCP/IP protocol is used to provide shared access to files and printers on the network?

    A. FTP

    B. SSH

    C. SMB

    D. SNMP

16. What port does the Telnet protocol use?

    A. 21

    B. 22

    C. 23

    D. 25

17. You have just installed a wireless 802.11ac network for a client. The IT manager is concerned about competitors intercepting the wireless signal from outside the building. Which tool is designed to test how far your wireless signal travels?

    A. Tone generator and probe

    B. Protocol analyzer

    C. Packet sniffer

    D. Wi-Fi analyzer

18. Some of your network users are concerned about submitting confidential information to an online website. What should you tell them?

    A. It's fine, because all Internet traffic is encrypted.

    B. If the website address starts with TLS://, it should be OK to submit confidential information to a trusted site.

    C. If the website address starts with HTTPS://, it should be OK to submit confidential information to a trusted site.

    D. Don't ever submit confidential information to any online website.

19. Which TCP/IP Internet layer protocol is responsible for delivering error messages if communication between two computers fails?

    A. ICMP

    B. IP

    C. TCP

    D. UDP

20. Which type of IPv6 address identifies a single node on the network?

    A. Multicast

    B. Anycast

    C. Unicast

    D. Localcast

21. You are configuring a wireless 802.11n router for a small network. When setting it up, which security option should you choose?

    A. WPA2

    B. WPA

    C. WEP

    D. SSID

22. What type of network covers large geographical areas and often supports thousands of users?

    A. LAN

    B. WAN

    C. PAN

    D. MAN

23. Which TCP/IP protocol, developed by Microsoft, allows users to connect to remote computers and run programs on them?

    A. RDP

    B. SMB

    C. CIFS

    D. Telnet

24. What port does the SSH protocol use?

    A. 21

    B. 22

    C. 23

    D. 25

25. Which of the following IP addresses is not routable on the Internet?

    A. 10.1.1.1

    B. 11.1.1.1

    C. 12.1.1.1

    D. 13.1.1.1

26. Which network connectivity device does not forward broadcast messages, thereby creating multiple broadcast domains?

    A. Hub

    B. Switch

    C. Bridge

    D. Router

27. You have a desktop computer that is behaving erratically on the network. The wired connection will often disconnect without warning. Which tool should you use to troubleshoot the network adapter?

    A. Multimeter

    B. Tone generator and probe

    C. Loopback plug

    D. Cable tester

28. Your company just expanded and is leasing additional space in an adjacent office building. You need to extend the network to the new building. Fortunately, there is a conduit between the two. You estimate that the cable you need to run will be about 300 meters long. What type of cable should you use?

    A. CAT5

    B. CAT5e

    C. CAT7

    D. MMF

29. You want to ensure that client computers can download email from external email servers regardless of the protocol their email client uses. Which ports do you open on the firewall to enable this? (Choose two.)

    A. 23

    B. 25

    C. 110

    D. 143

30. You are installing network cabling in a highly secure facility. The cables need to be immune to electronic eavesdropping. What type of cable should you use?

   A. Fiber-optic

   B. UTP

   C. STP

   D. Coaxial

31. Which networking device is capable of reading IP addresses and forwarding packets based on the destination IP address?

   A. Hub

   B. Switch

   C. Bridge

   D. Router

32. Which network device is designed to be a security guard, blocking malicious data from entering your network?

   A. PoE injector

   B. Bridge

   C. Firewall

   D. Router

33. You are manually configuring TCP/IP hosts on the network. What configuration parameter specifies the address of the router that enables Internet access?

   A. Subnet mask

   B. DHCP server

   C. DNS server

   D. Default gateway

34. A senior administrator calls you and tells you that she is working from home and trying to use RDP, but it won't connect. What port do you need to ensure is open on the firewall to grant her access?

   A. 143

   B. 443

   C. 548

   D. 3389

35. Identify the cable connector in the picture.

- **A.** F-connector
- **B.** BNC
- **C.** SC
- **D.** ST

36. What type of network is most commonly associated with Bluetooth devices and covers a small area?

- **A.** LAN
- **B.** WAN
- **C.** PAN
- **D.** MAN

37. Which TCP/IP Internet layer protocol is responsible for resolving physical MAC addresses to logical IP addresses?

- **A.** IP
- **B.** ICMP
- **C.** ARP
- **D.** RARP

38. Which of the following IPv6 addresses is equivalent to an address in the 169.254.0.0/16 range in IPv4?

- **A.** 2000::/3
- **B.** FC00::/7
- **C.** FE80::/10
- **D.** FF00::/8

39. You need to configure a wireless router for an office network. The office manager wants new devices to be able to automatically join the network and announce their presence to other networked devices. Which service should you enable to allow this?

- **A.** DHCP
- **B.** NAT
- **C.** QoS
- **D.** UPnP

40. You are troubleshooting a computer with an IPv6 address that is in the FE80::/10 range. Which of the following statements are true? (Choose two.)

  A. The computer will not be able to get on the Internet.

  B. The computer will be able to get on the Internet.

  C. The computer is configured with a link local unicast address.

  D. The computer is configured with a global unicast address.

41. You have set up your web server to function as an FTP server as well. Users on the Internet complain that they are not able to access the server using FTP clients. What port are they trying to access the server on?

  A. 21

  B. 22

  C. 23

  D. 25

  E. 80

42. Which TCP/IP port and protocol allows you to access data such as employee phone numbers and email addresses that are stored within an information directory?

  A. 427 - SLP

  B. 25 - SMTP

  C. 445 - CIFS

  D. 389 - LDAP

43. You are configuring network hosts with static IP addresses. You have chosen to use a class B network address. What is the default subnet mask that you should configure on the hosts?

  A. 255.0.0.0

  B. 255.255.0.0

  C. 255.255.255.0

  D. 255.255.255.255

44. You are installing a new network and working in a wiring closet. You need to attach several network cables to a 110 block. Which tool should you use to perform this task?

  A. Crimper

  B. Cable stripper

  C. Cable tester

  D. Punchdown tool

45. Which of the following Internet connection types offers the fastest download speeds?

  A. Cable

  B. DSL

  C. Fiber-optic

  D. ISDN

46. Which TCP/IP protocol uses TCP ports 137–139 and 445 by default?

    A. FTP

    B. SSH

    C. SMB

    D. SNMP

47. For IPv6, which of the following statements are not true? (Choose two.)

    A. Each IPv6 interface can have only one address.

    B. Each IPv6 interface is required to have a link local address.

    C. IPv6 addresses are incompatible with IPv4 networks.

    D. IPv6 no longer uses broadcasts.

48. Which of the following network architecture devices operate at Layer 1 of the OSI model? (Choose two.)

    A. Switch

    B. Hub

    C. Extender

    D. Router

49. Which TCP/IP protocol was developed by Apple and used to transfer files between computers?

    A. FTP

    B. AFP

    C. ATP

    D. SMB

50. Which of the following IPv6 addresses is equivalent to 127.0.0.1 in IPv4?

    A. ::0

    B. ::1

    C. ::127

    D. 2000::/3

51. A technician is configuring a wireless 802.11ac router for a home network. For security purposes, he enables the firewall. He wants to configure it so that if a computer makes an outbound request on a specific port, subsequent inbound traffic on that port would be allowed through the firewall. Which option does he need to configure to manage these settings?

    A. Port forwarding

    B. Port triggering

    C. NAT

    D. QoS

52. You are asked to perform consulting work for a medium-sized company that is having network connectivity issues. When you examine the patch panel, you notice that none of the dozens of UTP cables are labeled. Which tool can you use to identify which cable goes to which workstation?

    A. Cable tester

    B. Loopback plug

    C. Punchdown tool

    D. Tone generator and probe

53. Which TCP/IP protocol is responsible for dynamically assigning IP addresses to client computers?

    A. DNS

    B. DHCP

    C. RDP

    D. LDAP

54. Which networking device works at Layer 2 of the OSI model, has multiple ports in which each is its own collision domain, and examines the header of the incoming packet to determine which port it gets sent to?

    A. Hub

    B. Switch

    C. Bridge

    D. Router

55. Which TCP/IP port will an email client use to push email to its email server?

    A. 23

    B. 25

    C. 110

    D. 143

56. A technician is going to set up a Wi-Fi network using standard omnidirectional antennae. Because of the building configuration, transmitting signals for the greatest distance is his primary criterion. Which standard should he choose?

    A. 802.11a

    B. 802.11g

    C. 802.11n

    D. 802.11ac

57. You are troubleshooting an intermittently failing CAT7 network connection. You suspect that there is a short in the connection. Which tool can you use to determine this?

   A. Tone generator and probe

   B. Loopback plug

   C. Multimeter

   D. Crimper

58. Which TCP/IP protocol gathers and manages network performance information using devices called agents?

   A. SNMP

   B. SMTP

   C. LDAP

   D. SMB

59. In which type of office environment would you perform a cable/DSL modem configuration?

   A. Multiple buildings in a single country

   B. Multiple buildings in many countries

   C. Single tenant building with 300-500 employees

   D. Small office or home office with 3-5 employees

60. Which Wi-Fi encryption standard was the first to include the use of a 128-bit dynamic per-packet encryption key?

   A. WEP

   B. WPA

   C. WPA2

   D. AES

61. You are installing an 802.11n Wi-Fi network with five wireless access points. The access points are set up so their ranges overlap each other. To avoid communications issues, what principle should you follow when configuring them?

   A. Configure all access points to use the same channel.

   B. Configure all access points to use adjacent channels.

   C. Configure all access points to use nonoverlapping channels.

   D. Channel configuration will not cause communications issues.

62. Which TCP/IP protocol is designed to send email from clients to mail servers?

   A. SMTP

   B. POP3

   C. IMAP

   D. SMB

63. You are setting up a small network in your neighbor's house. She is concerned about wireless security, so she doesn't want to use wireless networking at all. She needs to connect two computers to each other, but it will be impossible to run a network cable between them. Which technology can help her network these computers?

   A. Ethernet over power

   B. Power over Ethernet

   C. Firewall

   D. Access point

64. You have been asked to install a Wi-Fi network in a building that is approximately 100 meters long and 25 meters wide. Because of cost considerations, you will need to use 802.11g. At a minimum, how many wireless access points will you need?

   A. Two

   B. Three

   C. Four

   D. Six

65. You are installing network cabling in a drop ceiling of an office space. The ceiling area is used to circulate breathable air. What type of cable do you need to install?

   A. Coaxial

   B. UTP

   C. Fiber-optic

   D. Plenum

66. You need to install a wireless hub in a drop ceiling where there is no access to a power source. Which technology will allow you to get power to that device?

   A. Ethernet over power

   B. Power over Ethernet

   C. Wireless access point

   D. Repeater/extender

67. Which of the following IP addresses is not a private address and therefore is routable on the Internet?

   A. 10.1.2.3

   B. 172.18.31.54

   C. 172.168.38.155

   D. 192.168.38.155

68. You are configuring a wireless 802.11n router. The office manager insists that you configure the router such that traffic from her computer receives higher priority on the network than other users' traffic. Which setting do you need to configure to enable this?

    A. QoS

    B. UPnP

    C. DMZ

    D. Port forwarding

69. If you are connecting to a website that encrypts its connection using TLS, what port does that traffic travel on?

    A. 21

    B. 80

    C. 143

    D. 443

70. Your network is currently running a mix of 802.11b and 802.11g devices. At the end of the year, you have extra budget to upgrade some, but not all, of the wireless infrastructure. You want to upgrade to the newest technology but still maintain backward compatibility. Which standard should you choose?

    A. 802.11g

    B. 802.11ac

    C. 802.11r

    D. 802.11n

71. You are consulting with a small field office that needs a dedicated, digital point-to-point network connection to its parent office. Which Internet connection type will meet this requirement?

    A. Dial-up

    B. Cable

    C. DSL

    D. ISDN

72. What type of network spans multiple buildings or offices but is confined to a relatively small geographical area?

    A. LAN

    B. WAN

    C. PAN

    D. MAN

73. Which of the following shorthand notations corresponds to the CIDR subnet mask 255.255.224.0?

    A. /19

    B. /20

    C. /21

    D. /22

74. You are configuring hosts on a network running IPv4. Which elements are required for the computer to connect to the network?

    A. IP address

    B. IP address and subnet mask

    C. IP address, subnet mask, and default gateway

    D. IP address, subnet mask, default gateway, and DNS server address

75. Which TCP/IP protocol was developed by Microsoft and has been the default file and print sharing protocol on Windows-based computers since Windows 2000?

    A. CIFS

    B. SMB

    C. FTP

    D. LDAP

76. Which of the following statements regarding IPv4 configuration is true?

    A. All hosts on a network must have a unique subnet mask.

    B. All hosts on a network must have their network ID set to all 1s.

    C. All hosts on a network must have a default gateway.

    D. All hosts on a network must have a unique host address.

77. Which Wi-Fi encryption standard uses a static key, which is commonly 10, 26, or 58 characters long?

    A. WPA

    B. WPA2

    C. TKIP

    D. WEP

78. Which TCP/IP port number does SNMP use?

    A. TCP 143

    B. UDP 143

    C. TCP 161

    D. UDP 161

79. Because of a recent security breach, your IT team shut down several ports on the external firewall. Now, users can't get to websites by using their URLs, but they can get there by using IP addresses. What port does the IT team need to open back up to enable Internet access via URLs?

    A. 21

    B. 53

    C. 67

    D. 80

80. All your network hosts are configured to use DHCP. Which IP address would indicate that a host has been unable to locate a DHCP server?

  A. 192.168.1.1

  B. 10.1.1.1

  C. 172.16.1.1

  D. 169.254.1.1

81. A technician is trying to establish a dial-up network connection using a legacy modem. What is the fastest data throughput for a modem?

  A. 28.8 Kbps

  B. 56 Kbps

  C. 1 Mbps

  D. 4 Mbps

82. You have reason to believe that several network users are actively browsing prohibited content on unsecured sites on the Internet. Which port can you disable on the firewall to immediately stop access to these websites?

  A. 53

  B. 67

  C. 80

  D. 443

83. Which TCP/IP protocol is designed to help resolve hostnames to IP addresses?

  A. ARP

  B. RARP

  C. DHCP

  D. DNS

84. You need to install an Internet connection for a forest ranger outlook tower, located far away from electrical lines. Which option would be best for broadband Internet access?

  A. Cable

  B. DSL

  C. ISDN

  D. Satellite

85. Which TCP/IP host-to-host protocol makes its best effort to deliver data but does not guarantee it?

  A. IP

  B. TCP

  C. UDP

  D. ICMP

86. What type of network is typically defined as being contained within a single office or building?

   A. LAN

   B. WAN

   C. PAN

   D. MAN

87. Which port is AFP capable of using?

   A. 427

   B. 443

   C. 445

   D. 548

88. You are installing a wireless network for a small company. It wants to have 100 Mbps or better wireless transmission rates. Which of the following standards will allow you to provide this? (Choose two.)

   A. 802.11g

   B. 802.11i

   C. 802.11n

   D. 802.11ac

89. What legacy network protocol allows NetBIOS-dependent computer applications to communicate over TCP/IP?

   A. IPX

   B. SPX

   C. NetBT

   D. BGP

90. What networking protocol allows systems to discover local systems and other devices?

   A. DHCP

   B. DNS

   C. HTTP

   D. SLP

91. Which of the following features does not require a managed network switch?

   A. Priority of traffic

   B. VLAN configuration

   C. Directing Layer 2 traffic

   D. Port mirroring

92. The senior network administrator struggles to configure company network devices spanning several cities. The challenge is because he is required to be on premises for the network infrastructure of each building. What would be a cost-effective solution?

    A. Employ network administrators at each building.

    B. Go to a flat network.

    C. Train a local sales associate.

    D. Employ a cloud-based network controller.

93. What is the maximum distance allowed between a power over Ethernet injector and the Ethernet device?

    A. 50 meters

    B. 100 meters

    C. 250 meters

    D. 450 meters

94. When setting up a small office, home office (SOHO) network, what end-user device configuration must be performed?

    A. Network switch broadcasts configuration settings.

    B. Devices utilize service location protocol.

    C. NIC set with static address or be DHCP-served

    D. End users configure as needed.

95. What is the typical method for IoT device configuration to connect to the wireless network?

    A. DNS

    B. AD

    C. SLP

    D. DHCP

96. What method is effective in defining how a firewall allows outbound access when the group of approved devices rarely changes?

    A. MAC filtering

    B. Dynamic DNS

    C. Whitelist

    D. Blacklist

97. What firewall rule technique allows only a known list of applications or traffic as legitimate?

    A. MAC filtering

    B. Dynamic DNS

    C. Whitelist

    D. Blacklist

98. What communication technology establishes connectivity between enabled devices only when the devices are placed within 4 cm of each other?

   A. RFID

   B. NFC

   C. Wi-Fi

   D. UHF

99. What communication technology allows for low power, close-proximity passive reading of a small tag or patch on an object?

   A. RFID

   B. NFC

   C. Wi-Fi

   D. UHF

100. What is the role of the server responsible for publishing information about the company's values, purpose, and available products or services to the public?

   A. FTP server

   B. Proxy server

   C. File server

   D. Web server

101. What server would function as a central repository of documents and provide network shared file storage for internal users?

   A. FTP server

   B. Proxy server

   C. File server

   D. Web server

102. What server sits between the protected, controlled network and the public Internet, functioning as a gatekeeper of traffic?

   A. FTP server

   B. Proxy server

   C. File server

   D. Web server

103. What type of server can host files for easy access and fetching, similar to how a web server serves web pages?

   A. FTP server

   B. Proxy server

   C. File server

   D. Web server

104. What server is added to a company infrastructure to avoid the need to attach printers to each individual desktop?

  A. Syslog server

  B. DNS server

  C. Print server

  D. Authentication server

105. What server is used to resolve domain names to IP addresses to facilitate web browsing or locating a directory resource on the network?

  A. Syslog server

  B. DNS server

  C. Print server

  D. Authentication server

106. What server is accessed each time it's necessary to challenge and validate a user's credentials in order for the user to access a network resource?

  A. Syslog server

  B. DNS server

  C. Print server

  D. Authentication server

107. What service can collect and journal all the system-generated messages produced by servers and network devices?

  A. Syslog server

  B. DNS server

  C. Print server

  D. Authentication server

108. A company wanting to monitor network traffic or host system behavior to identify suspect activity will install what type of service?

  A. Proxy server

  B. IDS

  C. UTM

  D. Email

109. What is the primary difference between an IDS and IPS?

  A. IDS works both on a host and a network.

  B. IDS will not actively alert on suspect activity.

  C. IPS works in pairs.

  D. IPS will actively react to suspect activity.

110. Your client is interested in a security device that will take action when suspicious activity is identified, as well as filter traffic and perhaps also provide some antivirus functionality. What type of device is the client looking for?

    A. Proxy server

    B. Firewall

    C. UTM

    D. IPS

111. Your client is now looking at improving control over all the user devices. Particularly, the client wants resource access controlled based on policy and the users meeting a few criteria. What device would you suggest?

    A. End-point management server

    B. Perimeter authentication server

    C. RADIUS server

    D. SFTP server

112. Last weekend you installed and booted several more computers to be ready for Monday morning. Later Monday morning you hear from employees as they come in that they cannot log in. Their desktops don't seem to want to connect. You investigate and find that each faulty workstation has a 169.254.x.x IP address. What might you look at next?

    A. DHCP reservation

    B. LAN connector broken

    C. Windows patch unable to install

    D. Corrupted Registry

113. What network segmentation technique reduces broadcast domains?

    A. VPN

    B. VLAN

    C. BGP

    D. EIGRP

114. What connectivity technique can ensure that your network traffic is encrypted from endpoint to endpoint?

    A. VPN

    B. VLAN

    C. BGP

    D. EIGRP

115. Which of the follow components is not typically found in a wireless mesh network (WMN)?

    A. WMN router

    B. WMN gateway

    C. WMN server

    D. WMN client

116. Of the following fiber connectors, which is used for duplex (two strands instead of one)?

   A. ST

   B. SC

   C. FC

   D. RJ-11

117. What twisted pair connectors are commonly found for telephone wire?

   A. RJ-45

   B. Coaxial

   C. RJ-11

   D. FC

118. Using the T568B wiring standard on both ends of a cable would produce what type of network cable?

   A. T568B on both ends is not a working network cable.

   B. T568B is a telephone wiring standard.

   C. T568B on both ends is a crossover network cable.

   D. T568B on both ends is a straight-through network cable.

119. What IoT device configuration most likely includes continuous remote monitoring?

   A. Thermostat

   B. Light switches

   C. Security cameras

   D. Door locks

120. What IoT device configuration requires a microphone? (Choose two)

   A. Voice-enabled smart speaker

   B. Light switches

   C. Door locks

   D. Voice-activated Digital assistant

121. Which wireless networking protocol is most limited by the number of potential connected devices?

   A. LTE

   B. 3G

   C. Zigbee

   D. Z-wave

122. Which wireless networking protocol is expected to reach speeds of 1 Gbps?

   A. 3G

   B. 4G

   C. 5G

   D. Z-wave

Chapter

3

Hardware

THE FOLLOWING COMPTIA A+ EXAM 220–1001 TOPICS ARE COVERED IN THIS CHAPTER:

✓ **3.1 Explain basic cable types, features, and their purposes.**

- Network cables
  - Ethernet
    - Cat 5
    - Cat 5e
    - Cat 6
    - Plenum
    - Shielded twisted pair
    - Unshielded twisted pair
    - 568A/B
  - Fiber
  - Coaxial
  - Speed and transmission limitations
- Video cables
  - VGA
  - HDMI
  - Mini-HDMI
  - DisplayPort
  - DVI
  - DVI-DDVI-I
- Multipurpose cables
  - Lightning
  - Thunderbolt
  - USB
  - USB-C

- USB 2.0
- USB 3.0
- Peripheral cables
  - Serial
- Hard drive cables
  - SATA
  - IDE
  - SCSI
- Adapters
  - DVI to HDMI
  - USB to Ethernet
  - DVI to VGA

✓ **3.2   Identify common connector types.**

- RJ-11
- RJ-45
- RS-232
- BNC
- RG-59
- RG-6
- USB
- Micro-USB
- Mini-USB
- USB-C
- DB-9
- Lightning
- SCSI
- eSATA
- Molex

✓ **3.3   Given a scenario, install RAM types.**

- RAM types
  - SODIMM
  - DDR2

- DDR3
- DDR4
- Single channel
- Dual channel
- Triple channel
- Error correcting
- Parity vs. non-parity

✓ **3.4 Given a scenario, select, install, and configure storage devices.**

- Optical drives
  - CD-ROM/CD-RW
  - DVD-ROM/DVD-RW/DVD-RW DL
  - Blu-ray
  - BD-R
  - BD-RE
- Solid-state drives
  - M2 drives
  - NVME
  - SATA 2.5
- Magnetic hard drives
  - 5,400rpm
  - 7,200rpm
  - 10,000rpm
  - 15,000rpm
  - Sizes:
    - 2.5
    - 3.5
- Hybrid drives
- Flash
  - SD card
  - CompactFlash

- MicroSD card

- MiniSD card

- xD

- Configurations

  - RAID 0, 1, 5, 10

  - Hot swappable

✓ **3.5 Given a scenario, install and configure mother-boards, CPUs, and add-on cards.**

- Motherboard form factor

  - ATX

  - mATX

  - ITX

  - mITX

- Motherboard connectors types

  - PCI

  - PCIe

  - Riser card

  - Socket types

  - SATA

  - IDE

  - Front panel connector

  - Internal USB connector

- BIOS/UEFI settings

  - Boot options

  - Firmware updates

  - Security settings

  - Interface configurations

  - Security

  - Passwords

  - Drive encryption

  - TPM

- LoJack
- Secure boot
- CMOS battery
- CPU features
  - Single-core
  - Multicore
  - Virtual technology
  - Hyperthreading
  - Speeds
  - Overclocking
  - Integrated GPU
- Compatibility
  - AMD
  - Intel
- Cooling mechanism
  - Fans
  - Heat sink
  - Liquid
  - Thermal paste
- Expansion cards
  - Video cards
    - Onboard
    - Add-on card
  - Sound cards
  - Network interface card
  - USB expansion card
  - eSATA card

✓ **3.6 Explain the purposes and uses of various peripheral types.**

- Printer
- ADF/flatbed scanner
- Barcode scanner/QR scanner

- Monitors
- VR headset
- Optical
- DVD drive
- Mouse
- Keyboard
- Touchpad
- Signature pad
- Game controllers
- Camera/webcam
- Microphone
- Speakers
- Headset
- Projector
  - Lumens/brightness
- External storage drives
- KVM
- Magnetic reader/chip reader
- NFC/tap pay device
- Smart card reader

✓ **3.7 Summarize power supply types and features.**

- Input 115V vs. 220V
- Output 5.5V vs. 12V
- 24-pin motherboard adapter
- Wattage rating
- Number of devices/types of devices to be powered

✓ **3.8 Given a scenario, select and configure appropriate components for a custom PC configuration to meet customer specifications or needs.**

- Graphic/CAD/CAM design workstation
  - Multicore processor

- High-end video
- Maximum RAM
- Audio/video editing workstation
  - Specialized audio and video card
  - Large, fast hard drive
  - Dual monitors
- Virtualization workstation
  - Maximum RAM and CPU cores
- Gaming PC
  - Multicore processor
  - High-end video/specialized GPU
  - High-definition sound card
  - High-end cooling
- Standard thick client
  - Desktop applications
  - Meets recommended requirements for selected OS
- Thin client
  - Basic applications
  - Meets minimum requirements for selected OS
  - Network connectivity
- Network attached storage device
  - Media streaming
  - File sharing
  - Gigabit NIC
  - RAID array

✓ **3.9 Given a scenario, install and configure common devices.**

- Desktop
  - Thin client
  - Thick client
  - Account setup/settings

- Laptop/common mobile devices
  - Touchpad configuration
  - Touchscreen configuration
  - Application installations/configurations
  - Synchronization settings
  - Account setup/settings
  - Wireless settings

✓ **3.10 Given a scenario, configure SOHO multifunction devices/printers and settings.**

- Use appropriate drivers for a given operating system.
  - Configuration settings
    - Duplex
    - Collate
    - Orientation
    - Quality
- Device sharing
  - Wired
    - USB
    - Serial
    - Ethernet
  - Wireless
    - Bluetooth
    - 802.11(a, b, g, n, ac)
    - Infrastructure vs. ad hoc
  - Integrated print server (hardware)
  - Cloud printing/remote printing
- Public/shared devices
  - Sharing local/networked device via operating system settings
    - TCP/Bonjour/AirPrint
  - Data privacy
    - User authentication on the device
    - Hard drive caching

✓ **3.11 Given a scenario, install and maintain various print technologies.**

- Laser
  - Imaging drum, fuser assembly, transfer belt, transfer roller, pickup rollers, separate pads, duplexing assembly
  - Imaging process: processing, charging, exposing, developing, transferring, fusing, and cleaning
  - Maintenance: Replace toner, apply maintenance kit, calibrate, clean
- Inkjet
  - Ink cartridge, print head, roller, feeder, duplexing assembly, carriage, and belt
  - Calibrate
  - Maintenance: Clean heads, replace cartridges, calibrate, clear jams
- Thermal
  - Feed assembly, heating element
  - Special thermal paper
  - Maintenance: Replace paper, clean heating element, remove debris
- Impact
  - Print head, ribbon, tractor feed
  - Impact paper
  - Maintenance: Replace ribbon, replace print head, replace paper
- Virtual
  - Print to file
  - Print to PDF
  - Print to XPS
  - Print to image
- 3D printers
  - Plastic filament

1. What is the distance limitation of the FireWire 800 standard when implemented over fiber-optic cable?

   A. 4.5 meters

   B. 100 meters

   C. 400 meters

   D. 800 meters

2. Which motherboard form factor measures 6.7″ × 6.7″?

   A. Mini-ITX

   B. Nano-ITX

   C. Pico-ITX

   D. Mobile-ITX

3. Which of the following statements are not true regarding CPUs and operating systems? (Choose two.)

   A. A 32-bit OS can run only on a 32-bit CPU.

   B. A 64-bit OS can run only on a 64-bit CPU.

   C. A 64-bit OS can run on a 32-bit CPU or a 64-bit CPU.

   D. A 32-bit OS can run on a 32-bit CPU or a 64-bit CPU.

4. The DCPS within a laser printer converts AC power into what three voltages? (Choose three.)

   A. +5 VDC

   B. −5 VDC

   C. +24 VDC

   D. −24 VDC

5. Identify the cable type shown here.

   A. Component

   B. Composite

   C. Coaxial

   D. RCA

6. A technician is looking to buy a new LCD monitor. Which type of LCD monitor has faster response times and is less expensive than others?

   A. TN

   B. IPS

   C. LED

   D. Plasma

7. Which computer peripheral is most likely to use a mini-DIN 6 connector?

   A. Keyboard

   B. Monitor

   C. Hard drive

   D. Sound card

8. Which type of storage device is composed of a conventional hard drive and a substantial amount of solid-state storage?

   A. SSD

   B. HDD

   C. Mesh

   D. Hybrid

9. An administrator ordered replacement printer paper that is a thicker caliper than recommended by the printer manufacturer. What is the biggest risk in using this paper?

   A. Smeared images

   B. Paper will not feed.

   C. Paper will jam.

   D. Images will not print.

10. You need to share printers on your network with multiple client operating systems, such as Windows, MacOS, and Linux. Which of the following services will best meet your needs?

    A. Bonjour

    B. AirPrint

    C. TCP printing

    D. Virtual printing

11. Which one of the following connector types are you most likely to find on the end of a CAT6a cable?

    A. RJ-11

    B. RJ-45

    C. BNC

    D. SATA

12. Identify the video connector shown here.

    A. DVI

    B. VGA

    C. HDMI

    D. Composite

13. What type of printer technology will often use a roll of paper as opposed to individual sheets?

    A. Ink-jet

    B. Thermal

    C. Laser

    D. Fax machine

14. Which RAM feature will detect errors within memory but is not able to fix them?

    A. Parity

    B. Non-parity

    C. ECC

    D. Non-ECC

15. Which of the following types of printers require the replacement of some sort of ink or toner? (Choose all that apply.)

    A. Laser

    B. Thermal

    C. Impact

    D. Ink-jet

16. You are working on repairing a defective laser printer. Which of the following is a true statement regarding the imaging drum in a laser printer?

    A. It can hold a charge only when it's not exposed to light.

    B. It can hold a charge only when it's exposed to light.

    C. It can hold a charge regardless of light exposure.

    D. It is not required to hold a charge.

17. What are the dimensions of a MicroATX motherboard?

    A. 12″ × 9.6″

    B. 9.6″ × 9.6″

    C. 6.7″ × 6.7″

    D. 3.9″ × 2.8″

18. When discussing video monitors, what is the term used to describe the number of pixels used to draw the screen?

    A. Refresh rate

    B. Frame rate

    C. Aspect ratio

    D. Resolution

19. You have three hard disks, each 1 TB in size. After installing them as a RAID-5 array in a computer, how much usable storage space will you have?

    A. 1.5 TB

    B. 2 TB

    C. 2.5 TB

    D. 3 TB

20. Which of the following statements most accurately describes the functionality of the execute disable bit?

    A. It prevents the CPU from working if the computer is stolen.

    B. It prevents the CPU from working if the CPU has been set to run at too high a speed (overclocking).

    C. It prevents the computer from being booted remotely in a PXE boot environment.

    D. It protects the computer from certain types of viruses or malicious code.

21. You need to enable clients to print to your networked printers, regardless of the printers' location worldwide. Which service will best suit your needs?

    A. Bonjour

    B. AirPrint

    C. Virtual printing

    D. Cloud printing

22. Identify the computer component shown here.

   A. CPU heat sink and fan
   B. Passive CPU heat sink
   C. Power supply fan
   D. Secondary cooling fan

23. Which of the following connectors transmit analog signals? (Choose two.)

   A. VGA
   B. RJ-45
   C. RJ-11
   D. HDMI

24. A business partner who is visiting your corporate office wants to print to a printer using a Bluetooth connection. What type of connection is this?

   A. Permanent
   B. Ad hoc
   C. On demand
   D. Infrastructure

25. You have a motherboard that supports up-plugging. Which of the following statements regarding PCIe are true? (Choose two.)

   A. You can put an x1 card into an x8 slot.
   B. You can put an x8 card into an x16 slot.
   C. You can put an x8 card into an x1 slot.
   D. You can put an x16 card into an x8 slot.

26. A technician needs to increase the fault tolerance of his computer's storage system, and he has two hard drives available. Which of the following options is his best choice?

   A. Install both drives and configure them as separate volumes.

   B. Install both drives and implement RAID-0.

   C. Install both drives and implement RAID-1.

   D. Install both drives and implement RAID-5.

27. During which step of the laser printer imaging process does a fluorescent lamp discharge the photosensitive drum?

   A. Cleaning

   B. Charging

   C. Exposing

   D. Developing

28. Which type of laptop monitor technology uses a current of electricity to stimulate a sealed panel of inert gas?

   A. OLED

   B. LED

   C. Plasma

   D. LCD

29. What type of front- or top-panel connector uses a standard 3.5 mm jack to make connections?

   A. USB

   B. Audio

   C. FireWire

   D. Thunderbolt

30. The motherboard in your desktop computer supports dual-channel memory. Which of the following statements regarding RAM is true?

   A. The RAM will work only if it's installed in pairs.

   B. The RAM will work only if it's installed in pairs or if one double-sided RAM module is used.

   C. The RAM will work if only one module is installed, but only at half of its rated speed.

   D. The RAM will work if only one module is installed.

31. A single lane of PCIe 4.0 operates at what data rate?

   A. 250 MBps

   B. 500 MBps

   C. 1 GBps

   D. 2 GBps

32. A technician needs to replace a failed power supply in a desktop computer. When choosing a replacement power supply, which two specifications are most important to consider? (Choose two.)

   A. Wattage

   B. Dual rail

   C. Dual voltage options

   D. Number of connectors

33. What is an advantage of using double-sided memory over single-sided memory?

   A. It allows the memory to operate twice as fast.

   B. It allows the CPU to access twice as much RAM at one time.

   C. It's required for use in dual-channel motherboards.

   D. It allows for twice as much memory to be used in the same amount of space.

34. You need to replace the magnetic hard drive in your manager's laptop. She wants a high-speed, high-capacity drive. What are the most common issues associated with her request? (Choose two.)

   A. Increased battery usage

   B. Increased heat production

   C. Decreased component life span

   D. Decreased space for other peripherals

35. What are the two speeds at which PCI expansion buses can operate in desktop computers? (Choose two.)

   A. 33 MHz

   B. 66 MHz

   C. 133 MHz

   D. 266 MHz

36. A designer from the corporate office is visiting your field office. He tries to print from his MacBook Pro to a networked printer, but it does not work. Local users in the office are able to print to the device using their Windows 8 computers. What would most likely solve the problem?

   A. Select the Enable Mac Printing option in the print server configuration settings.

   B. Select the Enable Bonjour option in the print server configuration settings.

   C. Install a Mac printer driver on the print server.

   D. Stop and restart the print spooler service.

37. The users on your network in the Human Resources department often have sensitive materials shown on their computer screens. What is their best option to dramatically limit the viewing angle of their monitors?

    A. Lower the brightness setting.

    B. Lower the contrast setting.

    C. Install an antiglare filter.

    D. Install a privacy filter.

38. Identify the peripheral connector shown here.

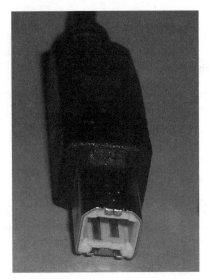

    A. USB Type A

    B. USB Type B

    C. USB Standard mini-B

    D. Thunderbolt

39. You have an OLED monitor that you just plugged into a desktop computer. One of your co-workers changes the resolution from 1920×1080 to 1920×1200, but then the image looks highly distorted. What is the most likely cause of this?

    A. The video driver does not support 1920×1200 resolution.

    B. The monitor has a native resolution of 1920×1080.

    C. The video adapter has a native resolution of 1920×1080.

    D. The monitor is plugged into the wrong monitor interface to support the new resolution.

40. Which of the following are advantages of using a CPU liquid cooling system over an air-based system? (Choose two.)

    A. Easier to install and maintain

    B. More efficient

    C. Quieter

    D. Safer for internal components

41. You need to perform preventive maintenance on an impact printer. What are two areas you should examine that you would not need to on most ink-jet printers? (Choose two.)

    A. Ink cartridges

    B. Output tray

    C. Print head

    D. Tractor feed mechanism

42. Which expansion bus technology uses lanes, which are switched point-to-point signal paths between two components?

    A. PCI

    B. PCI-X

    C. PCIe

    D. Mini-PCI

43. You are installing new computers in a machine shop. The computers on the shop floor don't need to run local applications or have their own hard drives, but they do need to connect to the shop's server. What type of custom configuration should you recommend?

    A. Thin client

    B. Thick client

    C. Virtualization workstation

    D. CAD/CAM workstation

44. Which PC component reboots the computer from a cold startup point without removing power from the components?

    A. Power button

    B. Suspend button

    C. Reset button

    D. Reboot button

45. Which type of LCD panel is considered to have the best color representation at wider angles of viewing?

    A. TN

    B. IPS

    C. LED

    D. Plasma

46. You have a user who needs recommendations for installing a home server PC. She wants her family to be able to share files and videos on their home network. She also wants her data to be protected in the event of a hard drive failure. Which two components do you recommend she include?

   A. Dedicated print server

   B. RAID array

   C. Gigabit NIC

   D. Dual processors

47. Your motherboard does not support up-plugging for PCIe adapter cards. Which of the following statements is true?

   A. You can't put an x8 card into an x16 slot.

   B. You can put an x8 card into an x16 slot, but it will run at x1 speed.

   C. You can put an x8 card into an x16 slot, and it will run at x8 speed.

   D. You can put an x8 card into an x16 slot, and it will run at x16 speed.

48. Which system component enables the use of Secure Boot technology?

   A. BIOS

   B. UEFI

   C. AMI

   D. SATA

49. Which type of DIMM has 184 pins?

   A. DDR

   B. DDR2

   C. DDR3

   D. SODIMM

50. Which CPU technology allows for the assignment of two logical cores for every physical core present?

   A. Multicore

   B. 32-bit vs. 64-bit

   C. Integrated GPU

   D. Hyperthreading

51. On what type of printer are you most likely to use tractor feed paper?

   A. Dot-matrix

   B. Thermal

   C. Laser

   D. Ink-jet

52. Which type of flash memory is capable of being embedded on the circuit board of mobile devices?

  A. xD

  B. MiniSD

  C. MicroSD

  D. eMMC

53. Which motherboard form factor is common in desktop computers and measures 12″ × 9.6″?

  A. ATX

  B. MicroATX

  C. Mini-ITX

  D. ITX

54. What two components within an ink-jet printer are responsible for moving the print head into proper position?

  A. Carriage and belt

  B. Roller and belt

  C. Carriage motor and roller

  D. Carriage motor and belt

  E. Belt motor and roller

55. Your company just hired a video producer to create exciting videos for the sales team. For her custom computer, which two upgrades are the most useful? (Choose two.)

  A. Video card

  B. CPU

  C. NIC

  D. Hard drive

56. You need to enable virtualization support for one of your Windows 8–based desktop computers using an Intel Core i5 CPU. Which two of the following must be true? (Choose two.)

  A. The CPU must have Intel VT.

  B. The CPU must have Intel VR.

  C. You need to enable virtualization in Windows 8.

  D. You need to enable virtualization in the BIOS.

57. Your business employs four graphic designers who need new computers. These designers create graphical content such as advertisements, posters, and full-color brochures. Which of the following components is the least important to enhance in their custom-configured machines?

    A. Hard drive

    B. Processor

    C. Video card

    D. RAM

58. An analog LCD monitor is most likely to have what type of connector?

    A. DisplayPort

    B. RCA

    C. VGA

    D. BNC

59. What is the name of the measure that specifies how many times an image can be redrawn on a computer screen in one second?

    A. Refresh rate

    B. Frame rate

    C. Native resolution

    D. Aspect ratio

60. Which PC peripheral connection type operates at 20 Gbps bandwidth, with a port that provides 18 V and 9.9 W of power?

    A. FireWire 800

    B. USB 3.0

    C. eSATA

    D. Thunderbolt

61. Inside a laser printer, approximately what temperature does the fuser get heated to?

    A. 250° F

    B. 350° F

    C. 450° F

    D. 550° F

62. You have a user who needs a custom PC configuration to run common desktop applications and simply meet the recommended requirements for a selected operating system. What should you recommend?

    A. Thin client

    B. Thick client

    C. Home server PC

    D. Virtualization workstation

63. In the laser printer printing process, which step immediately follows the exposing step?

   A. Charging

   B. Fusing

   C. Developing

   D. Transferring

64. What are the two power requirements that a PCI expansion bus may have in a desktop computer? (Choose two.)

   A. 1.7 V

   B. 3.3 V

   C. 5 V

   D. 6.6 V

65. Which of the following is a standard for a secure cryptoprocessor that can secure hardware (and the system boot process) using cryptographic keys?

   A. TPM

   B. LoJack

   C. Secure Boot

   D. BitLocker

66. In a laser printer, what is the function of the transfer corona assembly?

   A. It transfers a positive charge to the paper.

   B. It transfers a positive charge to the imaging drum.

   C. It transfers the toner from the imaging drum to the paper.

   D. It transfers the image from the laser to the imaging drum.

67. What type of connector is shown here?

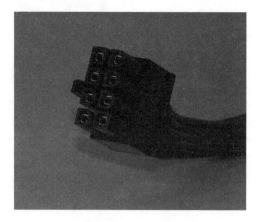

A. Molex

B. SATA

C. PCIe

D. ATX

68. A technician has installed a printer driver on a Windows 8 client computer. What is the best next step the technician can take to ensure that the printer is installed properly?

A. Ping the printer's IP address.

B. Check the printer status and ensure that it says "Ready."

C. Stop and restart the spooler service.

D. Print a test page.

69. Which component within a laser printer converts AC current into usable energy for the charging corona and transfer corona?

A. LVPS

B. HVPS

C. ACPS

D. Transfer corona assembly

70. You are connecting a laptop to a printer on the network using Wi-Fi. The user will need to use the printer frequently when they are in the office. What type of wireless connection will you establish with the printer?

A. Permanent

B. Ad hoc

C. On demand

D. Infrastructure

71. What is the maximum throughput of PCI-X adapters?

A. 533 MBps

B. 1066 MBps

C. 4266 MBps

D. 8533 MBps

72. What is the name of the boot routine that verifies the size and integrity of the system memory?

A. RAMCheck

B. BIOS

C. UEFI

D. POST

73. You have been asked to install and configure a RAID-10 storage array for a computer. What is the minimum number of hard disks required for this configuration?

   A. Two

   B. Three

   C. Four

   D. Five

74. Identify the peripheral connector shown here.

   A. HDMI

   B. PATA

   C. SATA

   D. eSATA

75. A technician is recommending that his company use removable memory cards. Which of the following should he tell his manager?

   A. MiniSD and microSD cards work in a standard SD card slot.

   B. MiniSD cards work in a standard SD slot, but microSD cards do not.

   C. MicroSD cards work in a standard SD slot, but miniSD cards do not.

   D. Neither miniSD nor microSD cards will work in a standard SD slot.

76. You are purchasing new laptops for your company. When thinking about the monitor quality, which type of backlight will produce better-quality pictures?

   A. LED

   B. OLED

   C. Plasma

   D. Fluorescent

77. Which component of the motherboard chipset is responsible for managing high-speed peripheral communications?

   A. Northbridge

   B. Southbridge

   C. Eastbridge

   D. Westbridge

78. A graphical designer in your office needs two monitors to do her work. Which of the following should you install to set up her desktop computer for this configuration?

   A. A video splitter

   B. A second video driver

   C. A second video adapter

   D. A video replicator

79. Which of the following statements are true regarding buffered memory modules? (Choose two.)

   A. They increase the electrical load placed on the controller.

   B. They decrease the electrical load placed on the controller.

   C. When used, the memory controller communicates in series with the register.

   D. When used, the memory controller communicates in parallel with the memory chips.

80. You have a desktop computer that is about five years old, with a single-channel memory architecture. You want to upgrade the memory. After checking the documentation, you purchase a higher-capacity RAM module that runs at the required bus speed. After you install it, the new RAM is not recognized, but the old RAM is. The computer store tests the RAM and it's fine. What should you try next?

   A. Flash the BIOS.

   B. Purchase a second memory module of the same type, and install them as a pair.

   C. Return the memory module and purchase a lower-capacity one.

   D. Replace the motherboard.

81. A client needs to connect to the Internet using telephone lines. What type of expansion card should you configure in his computer?

   A. USB

   B. Cellular

   C. Modem

   D. NIC

82. Which of the following types of computer peripherals are considered input and output devices? (Choose two.)

    A. Digitizer

    B. Touch screen

    C. KVM

    D. Printer

83. You have a motherboard designed to hold DDR3 1600 memory. What will happen if you attempt to install DDR2 667 memory into the motherboard?

    A. It won't fit.

    B. It will operate at 667 MHz.

    C. It will operate at 1133 MHz.

    D. It will operate at 1600 MHz.

84. What happens during the transferring step of the laser printer printing process?

    A. The image is transferred to the imaging drum.

    B. The toner is transferred to the imaging drum.

    C. The toner is transferred to the paper.

    D. A strong, uniform negative charge is transferred to the imaging drum.

85. The set of signal pathways on a motherboard between the CPU and RAM is called what?

    A. Northbridge

    B. Southbridge

    C. Frontside bus

    D. Backside bus

86. One of your users needs to print several copies of a 20-page document. She wants to ensure that all the pages print in order so she doesn't have to reorganize the documents later. Which option does she need to set properly in her printer configuration settings?

    A. Duplex

    B. Collate

    C. Page order

    D. Orientation

87. Which of the following video resolutions is compatible with the 4:3 aspect ratio?

    A. UXGA 1600×1200

    B. ATSC 1920×1080

    C. WUXGA 1920×1200

    D. WQXGA 2560×1600

88. You upgraded the RAM on your system and are now having boot issues. The manufacturer's website recommends updating the BIOS. What is the easiest way to do this?

   A. Replace the BIOS chip.

   B. Replace the CMOS battery.

   C. Install a new motherboard.

   D. Flash the BIOS.

89. A technician needs to install an optical storage device as cheaply as possible. His client needs to store approximately 500 MB of data at a time. Which technology is the best solution for this situation?

   A. CD-RW

   B. DVD-RW

   C. DVD-RW DL

   D. BD-RE

90. A technician needs to install an optical disc system with capacity to burn discs storing about 12 GB of data at one time. What is the minimum technology required to get him over this threshold?

   A. DVD-R SS, DL

   B. DVD-R DS, SL

   C. DVD-R DS, DL

   D. BD-R SS, DL

91. Identify the connector type on the cable shown here.

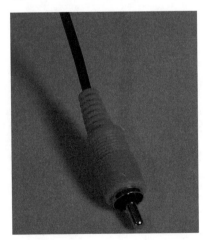

   A. BNC

   B. RCA

   C. Mini-DIN

   D. HD15

92. You are buying a new video projector for the executive conference room. The administrative assistant tells you that the room often has bright sunlight, so the projector needs to be bright. What is the key specification you should pay attention to when selecting this projector?

    A. Frame rate

    B. Native resolution

    C. Aspect ratio

    D. Lumens

93. Which home and office printing technology typically employs a reservoir of ink, contained in a cartridge, as its medium to form images on paper?

    A. Laser

    B. Thermal

    C. Ink-jet

    D. Impact

94. You have been asked to purchase new RAM for three workstations. The workstations call for DDR3 1600 chips. What throughput will these modules support?

    A. 1600 Mbps

    B. 3200 Mbps

    C. 6400 Mbps

    D. 12,800 Mbps

95. Historically, which display type has been preferred to watch fast-motion programs such as sporting events?

    A. Plasma

    B. Fluorescent

    C. LED

    D. LCD

96. A technician needs to purchase new RAM for a motherboard. The motherboard specifications call for 400 MHz DDR2 RAM. Which RAM modules should the technician use?

    A. PC3200

    B. PC6400

    C. PC2–3200

    D. PC2–6400

97. Identify the connector type shown here in the center.

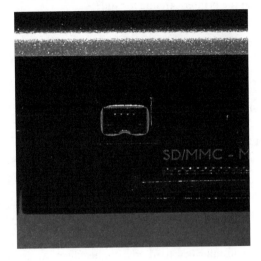

    A. eSATA

    B. Thunderbolt

    C. PCIe

    D. FireWire

98. On your network, users want to print easily from their iPads and iPhones. Which service supports this?

    A. Bonjour

    B. AirPrint

    C. TCP printing

    D. Virtual printing

99. You have a new computer that needs to communicate with other computers on a wireless network. What type of expansion card do you need to install?

    A. WAP

    B. NIC

    C. KVM

    D. WPA

100. The WUXGA video standard, running at a resolution of 1920×1200, operates at what aspect ratio?

    A. 4:3

    B. 5:4

    C. 16:9

    D. 16:10

101. When printing, which component is responsible for converting the data being printed into the format that the printer can understand?

A. PDL

B. Printer driver

C. Print feeder

D. Print spooler

102. Which of the following statements best describes the function of a typical power supply fan?

A. It cools the power supply by blowing in air from outside the case.

B. It cools the power supply by blowing hot air out the back of the power supply.

C. It cools the computer by blowing in air from outside the case, through the power supply, and into the computer.

D. It cools the computer by pulling hot air from inside the case, through the power supply, and blowing it out the back of the power supply.

103. A technician needs to install a new hard drive for her client. Access speed is far more important to this client than disk space. What type of hard drive is best suited for this client?

A. SSD

B. HDD

C. SD

D. BD-R

104. Serial and Parallel ATA port communication to other components on a motherboard is managed by what?

A. Northbridge

B. Southbridge

C. Frontside bus

D. Backside bus

105. What is the maximum data rate for a USB 2.0 connection?

A. 12 Mbps

B. 480 Mbps

C. 1 Gbps

D. 5 Gbps

106. A technician has been asked to install and configure a RAID-5 array in a working computer that contains one hard drive. How many additional hard drives, at a minimum, does he need to bring with him to the job?

A. One

B. Two

C. Three

D. Four

107. You need to increase network security. A consultant suggests that you install a peripheral device to scan user fingerprints as a requirement to log in. What type of device will you install?

A. Scanner

B. Digitizer

C. Biometric device

D. Touch pad

108. Which CPU architecture term describes a CPU with multiple physical processor dies in the same package?

A. Multicore

B. 64-bit

C. Integrated GPU

D. Hyperthreading

109. Which of the following optical disc standards provides the highest capacity?

A. DVD-R SS, SL

B. DVD-R DS, SL

C. DVD-R SS, DL

D. DVD-R SS, TL

110. Your company recently shipped five desktop computers from Germany to the United States. After switching the power cord to an American-style plug, you try to power one on and it doesn't work. You try the others and none of them power on either. What is the most likely cause?

A. All of the computers were damaged during shipping.

B. German power supplies work only with German power cords.

C. The power supplies won't work because they expect 50 Hz frequency from the wall outlet and the United States standard is 60 Hz.

D. The power supply voltage switch needs to be moved.

111. What are the dimensions of a mobile-ITX motherboard?

A. 9.6″ × 9.6″

B. 6.7″ × 6.7″

C. 3.9″ × 2.8″

D. 2.4″ × 2.4″

112. Which of the following printer types are considered impact printers? (Choose two.)

A. Laser

B. Daisy-wheel

C. Dot-matrix

D. Thermal

113.   Which type of video display technology does not require a separate display unit and light source?

   A.   Plasma

   B.   OLED

   C.   LED

   D.   LCD

114.   Which type of bus architecture provides faster speeds?

   A.   Serial (1 bit at a time)

   B.   Parallel (8 bits at a time)

   C.   They are the same speed.

   D.   More information is needed to answer this question.

115.   Which hardware component is responsible for storing prefetched data or code that the CPU will need to use and storing most recently used data or code?

   A.   RAM

   B.   SSD

   C.   Buffer

   D.   Cache

116.   Which two CPU sockets are capable of supporting Intel Core i7 processors? (Choose two.)

   A.   LGA1156 (Socket H)

   B.   LGA2011 (Socket R)

   C.   Socket AM3+

   D.   Socket FM2

117.   You are discussing data storage needs with a client who is a videographer and media producer. She needs to store dozens of large files and needs immediate access to them for editing. What is the most appropriate storage technology for her to use?

   A.   NAS

   B.   HDD

   C.   SD

   D.   BD-R

118.   You have a client who wants to build a high-end custom home theater PC. Which two components will you suggest he install in the computer? (Choose two.)

   A.   Sound card with surround sound

   B.   High-end cooling

   C.   Video card with HDMI outputs

   D.   Multicore processor

119. You are searching for a new monitor on the Internet and find a used digital LCD monitor for sale. What are the two most likely types of connector you will find on this monitor? (Choose two.)

    A. Composite

    B. DVI-D

    C. HDMI

    D. VGA

120. A technician needs to purchase a new laptop for a manager. The manager has had several laptops fail and wants her new one to have as few components as possible to reduce the risk of failure. Which type of light source technology does not require an inverter and therefore is a better choice?

    A. OLED

    B. Plasma

    C. Fluorescent

    D. LED

121. Which of the following are typical formats supported by virtual printing? (Choose three.)

    A. Print to PDF.

    B. Print to XPS.

    C. Print to DOC.

    D. Print to image.

122. A bidirectional PCIe 1.1 x1 link provides how much data throughput?

    A. 250 MBps

    B. 500 MBps

    C. 1 GBps

    D. 2 GBps

123. Which component in a laser printer is responsible for heating up and melting the toner into the paper to create a permanent image?

    A. Transfer corona assembly

    B. Pickup rollers

    C. Exit assembly

    D. Fuser assembly

124. During which step in the laser printer printing process does a wire or roller apply a strong, uniform negative charge to the surface of the imaging drum?

    A. Charging

    B. Conditioning

    C. Exposing

    D. Transferring

125.   You are installing two new RAM modules into a single channel of a dual-channel motherboard. Which of the following is true?

   A.   Both RAM modules need to have the same parameters.

   B.   The RAM modules can be different sizes but must be the same speed.

   C.   The RAM modules can be different speeds but must be the same size.

   D.   The RAM modules can have different speeds and sizes, as long as they are the same type.

126.   Which of the following printer components is not found in a laser printer?

   A.   Fuser assembly

   B.   Imaging drum

   C.   Transfer roller

   D.   Carriage motor

127.   What type of common printer can potentially release harmful ozone into the atmosphere and therefore may contain an ozone filter?

   A.   Laser

   B.   Ink-jet

   C.   Thermal

   D.   Impact

128.   There are four servers in your server closet. You need to access each of them, but not at the same time. Which device will allow you to share one set of input and output devices for all four servers?

   A.   Touch screen

   B.   Docking station

   C.   Set-top controller

   D.   KVM switch

129.   A user on your network has an older laser printer with no Ethernet connection. It's connected to his computer with a parallel cable. He has shared it on the network for others to use. Now, he wants no part of the printer, but others still need to use it on the network. What would be the best upgrade to install in this printer to allow others to send print jobs to it directly over the network?

   A.   A network card

   B.   An integrated print server

   C.   TCP/IP printing

   D.   AirPrint

130.   A technician needs to perform maintenance on an ink-jet's dirty paper pickup rollers. What should she use to clean them?

   A.   Rubbing alcohol

   B.   Mild soap and water

   C.   A dry lint-free cloth

   D.   Compressed air

131. During which step in the laser printer imaging process is toner attracted to the imaging drum?

    A. Exposing

    B. Transferring

    C. Fusing

    D. Developing

132. You are installing and configuring a magnetic hard drive and have several models to choose from. Which hard drive is most likely to have the highest data throughput rates?

    A. 500 GB, 7200 rpm

    B. 750 GB, 5400 rpm

    C. 750 GB, 10,000 rpm

    D. 1 TB, 7200 rpm

133. What is the name of the software package, typically enabled in the BIOS, that allows you to track the location of a stolen laptop or remotely lock it so it's inaccessible?

    A. TPM

    B. LoJack

    C. Secure Boot

    D. Drive Encryption

134. Identify the white connector on the section of motherboard shown here.

    A. RAM

    B. PATA

    C. Mini-PCI

    D. ATX

135. You need to purchase RAM for a computer. Which factor determines the speed of memory you should purchase?

- **A.** CPU speed
- **B.** FSB speed
- **C.** BSB speed
- **D.** ECC speed

136. Your manager tells you to buy a high-capacity magnetic hard drive with the highest data transfer rate possible. Which hard drive parameter do manufacturers modify to increase hard drive data transfer rates?

- **A.** Read/write head size
- **B.** Connector size
- **C.** Spin rate
- **D.** Platter size

137. Three of these four motherboard form factors can be mounted in the same style of case. Which ones are they? (Choose three.)

- **A.** ATX
- **B.** MicroATX
- **C.** Mini-ITX
- **D.** Nano-ITX

138. Which RAM feature can detect and possibly fix errors within memory?

- **A.** Parity
- **B.** Non-parity
- **C.** ECC
- **D.** Non-ECC

139. You have a client who needs a hot-swappable, nonvolatile, long-term storage technology that lets him conveniently carry data with him from one location to another in his pocket. Which technologies can you recommend? (Choose two.)

- **A.** USB flash drive
- **B.** Hybrid SSD
- **C.** PATA
- **D.** SD

140. What type of expansion slots are the first, third, and fifth slots (from the top down) on the motherboard shown here?

A. PCIe x1

B. PCIe x8

C. PCIe x16

D. PCI

141. You have been asked to assemble 20 new desktop PCs for a client. When you look at the first motherboard, you see four memory slots. The one closest to the CPU is colored blue. Then in order they are white, blue, and white. Which of the following statements are true? (Choose two.)

A. This is a quad-channel motherboard.

B. This is a dual-channel motherboard.

C. For optimal performance, you should install RAM modules into the two slots closest to the CPU.

D. For optimal performance, you should install RAM modules into the two blue slots.

142. One of your Windows 8 users has a file she wants to print as a PDF file, but the application she is using does not support printing to PDF. What would be her best option?

   A. There is no way to print to PDF if the application does not support it.

   B. Use the Windows 8 native feature to print to PDF.

   C. Install a third-party app that installs support for printing to PDF.

   D. Use the Windows 8 native feature to print to XPS and then convert the XPS file into PDF.

143. You have a computer running Windows 8. Every time you boot, the computer insists on trying to boot from the DVD-ROM drive. Where can you change the setting to have the system boot to the hard drive first?

   A. BIOS

   B. Windows Configuration

   C. System Manager

   D. Device Manager

144. Which of the following types of connectors are generally found on the front or top panel of the computer? (Choose two.)

   A. Hard drive

   B. Optical disk

   C. Power button

   D. USB

145. Your manager is excited because he just purchased a fast USB 3.0 external hard drive for his work team. He wants to set it in the middle of the cubicles and let everyone have access to it. Some of the cubicles are about 15 feet away from each other. What is the recommended maximum cable length for this type of device?

   A. 3 meters

   B. 5 meters

   C. 10 meters

   D. 15 meters

146. A technician has just installed a duplexer on a laser printer. The duplexer was sold by the manufacturer and is compatible with the printer. However, the printer properties will not let anyone choose to print on both sides of the paper. What might resolve the issue?

   A. Removing and reinstalling the duplexer

   B. Turning the printer off and back on

   C. Upgrading the printer's firmware

   D. Stopping and restarting the spooler service

147. You have a desktop computer with three PCI expansion slots. What will happen when you mix cards of different speeds on the same motherboard?

    A. The cards will operate at their original speeds.

    B. None of the cards will function.

    C. The cards will all operate at the faster speed.

    D. The cards will all operate at the slower speed.

148. Which of the following statements accurately explains what happens during the exposing step in the laser printer printing process?

    A. A laser reduces areas of the drum from a strong negative charge to a slight positive charge.

    B. A laser reduces areas of the drum from a strong negative charge to a slight negative charge.

    C. A laser increases areas of the drum from a slight negative charge to a strong negative charge.

    D. A laser increases areas of the drum from a slight positive charge to a strong positive charge.

149. Which of the following is the defining characteristic of a passive cooling system for a CPU?

    A. It uses water.

    B. It uses heat pipes.

    C. It uses liquid nitrogen or helium.

    D. It does not require a fan or power.

150. You have an older laptop with a CD burner in it. What is the approximate capacity of the CDs you will be able to create with this device?

    A. 350 MB

    B. 700 MB

    C. 1.4 GB

    D. 4.7 GB

151. Which of the following system settings are configurable in the BIOS? (Choose two.)

    A. Date and time

    B. Enabling and disabling services

    C. Enabling and disabling devices

    D. System cooling fan speeds

152. 64-bit SODIMM modules come in which pin configurations? (Choose two.)

    A. 184-pin

    B. 200-pin

    C. 204-pin

    D. 240-pin

153. Which level of cache is typically the smallest and closest to the processor die in a computer?

    A. L1

    B. L2

    C. L3

    D. L4

154. Which computer component gets power from the connector shown here?

    A. Motherboard

    B. Hard drive

    C. Expansion card

    D. Secondary case fan

155. Which of the following are types of CPU sockets? (Choose two.)

    A. LGA

    B. CGA

    C. IGA

    D. PGA

156. You just purchased several used computers from another company. They came with no documentation. When looking at the RAM, you see a sticker that says PC3–10600. What is the FSB speed of this computer?

    A. 667 MHz

    B. 1066 MHz

    C. 1333 MHz

    D. 1600 MHz

157. Your engineering team is creating a product prototype that requires a video display. They need the display to be flexible to wrap somewhat around the prototype. What type of technology should they use?

A. LED

B. LCD

C. OLED

D. Plasma

158. Your office has an ink-jet printer, and the manager asks if it can be upgraded to print on both sides of the paper. What type of device can add this functionality?

A. Flipping assembly

B. Dual paper feed assembly

C. Duplexing assembly

D. Rear paper feed assembly

159. Which component in a laser printer is responsible for converting AC current into usable energy for the logic circuitry and motors?

A. LVPS

B. HVPS

C. DCPS

D. ACPS

160. What types of RAM modules are shown here, from top to bottom?

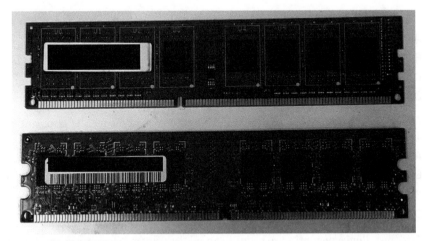

A. DDR and DDR2

B. DDR2 and DDR

C. DDR2 and DDR3

D. DDR3 and DDR2

161. The Acme company has a laser printer in its Chicago office that has been used for three months. A technician needs to ship the printer to the Detroit office for use there. What, if any, preparations should be made for the toner cartridge?

   A. No preparations are needed for the toner cartridge before shipping.

   B. Insert a toner blocker into the toner cartridge before shipping.

   C. Seal the toner cartridge with tape before shipping.

   D. Remove the toner cartridge from the printer before shipping.

162. You have been asked to implement an external backup solution for a small company. When considering tape backup solutions, which standard provides the best storage capacity?

   A. QIC

   B. DLT

   C. DAT

   D. LTO

163. A client wants you to upgrade his desktop computer to have two video cards. You want to be sure that his computer can support the extra adapter. What type of open internal expansion slot should you look for?

   A. PCIe

   B. ISA

   C. VGA

   D. DVI

164. Which step immediately follows the fusing step in the laser printer imaging process?

   A. Processing

   B. Transferring

   C. Exposing

   D. Cleaning

165. Which of the following are services created by Apple to allow for the automatic discovery of printers on local networks? (Choose two.)

   A. Bonjour

   B. AirPrint

   C. TCP printing

   D. Virtual printing

166. After installing a new print cartridge in an ink-jet printer, what process must be run before printing to the device?

   A. Degaussing

   B. Driver installation

   C. Rasterizing

   D. Calibration

167. The most common RAM slots used in desktop and laptop computers, respectively, are what?

    A. SODIMM and DIMM

    B. Mini-DIMM and DIMM

    C. DIMM and Mini-DIMM

    D. DIMM and SODIMM

    E. SODIMM and Mini-DIMM

    F. Mini-DIMM and SODIMM

168. Which type of printing technology uses a heating element to make images on waxy paper?

    A. Laser

    B. Ink-jet

    C. Thermal

    D. Dye sublimation

    E. Solid ink

169. You have a laser printer that is displaying the message "Perform user maintenance." What should you do to resolve this situation?

    A. Apply a maintenance kit and clear the message.

    B. Use compressed air to blow out the inside of the printer and clear the message.

    C. Turn the printer off and back on again to clear the message.

    D. Replace the toner cartridge and clear the message.

170. PCI-X expansion slots are compatible with what other adapters?

    A. 33 MHz PCI

    B. 66 MHz PCI

    C. 133 MHz PCI

    D. 533 MHz PCI

171. A user wants to create the ultimate gaming PC. Which of the following peripherals would be most appropriate for this type of system?

    A. Chip reader

    B. Magnetic reader

    C. Joystick

    D. Smart TV

172.   Identify the type of cable connectors shown here.

- **A.**   F-connector
- **B.**   BNC
- **C.**   SC
- **D.**   ST

173.   Identify the connectors shown here, from left to right.

- **A.**   ST and SC
- **B.**   SC and ST
- **C.**   RJ-45 and RJ-11
- **D.**   RJ-11 and RJ-45

174. Identify the connector shown here.

  ✗ **A.** ST

    B. SC

    C. LC

    D. MFF

175. You need to create several UTP cables from a roll of bulk cable. Your company uses the T568B standard. What is the correct order for wires in the connectors?

    A. White/orange, orange, white/green, blue, white/blue, green, white/brown, brown

    B. White/orange, orange, white/green, green, white/blue, blue, white/brown, brown

    C. White/orange, green, white/green, blue, white/blue, orange, white/brown, brown

    D. Orange, white/orange, white/green, blue, white/blue, green, white/brown, brown

176. You are installing network cable that will support digital cable television signals. What type of cable should you install?

    A. RG-6

    B. RG-8

    C. RG-58 A/U

    D. RG-59

177. You need to replace a faulty 250-foot section of RG-6 cable, but all you have available is RG-59. Which of the following statements is true?

    A. The replacement cable will not work because the distance exceeds RG-59 specifications.

    B. The replacement cable will not work because RG-6 and RG-59 use different connectors.

    C. The replacement cable will not work because RG-6 and RG-59 have different impedance.

    D. The replacement cable should work.

178. You have been asked to design a new network that requires 10 Gbps transmission speeds. Which cable types will meet the minimum specifications? (Choose two.)

    A. MMF

    B. CAT5

    C. CAT5e

    D. CAT7

179. What characteristic differentiates STP from UTP?

    A. It uses RJ-45s connectors instead of RJ-45.

    B. It follows the T568A wiring standard.

    C. It does not produce poisonous gas when burned.

    D. It has a layer of foil shielding.

180. You are investigating remnants of an old network setup in an unused building. At the end of a conduit, all you see are the connectors shown here. What type of cable do you expect these connectors to be attached to?

    A. Coaxial

    B. STP

    C. UTP

    D. Fiber-optic

181. Identify the connector shown here.

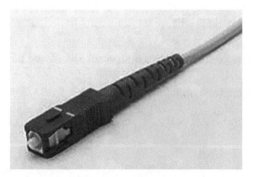

    A. ST

    B. SC

    C. LC

    D. MFF

182. While cleaning out a storage room, a technician finds several rolls of CAT5e network cable. He thinks that he might be able to use it to create replacement cables for his network. What is the maximum speed that this cable will support?

    A. 100 Mbps

    B. 1 Gbps

    C. 10 Gbps

    D. 20 Gbps

183. Which type of coaxial cable connector locks by twisting the connector one-quarter turn?

    A. F-connector

    B. BNC

    C. SC

    D. ST

184. Your network uses UTP cabling. Which of the following types of network connections require the use of a crossover cable? (Choose two.)

    A. Computer to hub

    B. Computer to switch

    C. Computer to router

    D. Switch to switch

185. You are replacing a connector at the end of coaxial cable. What type of connector is threaded and screws into place?

    A. F-connector

    B. BNC

    C. SC

    D. ST

186. You are installing UTP network cabling. The network has a mixture of network cards, but the minimum required speed is 100 Mbps. What is the minimum grade of cable you can install to meet this requirement?

    A. CAT3

    B. CAT5

    C. CAT5e

    D. CAT6a

187. You are installing UTP network cable for a client. The client's policies require that network cables do not produce poisonous gas when burned. What type of cable do you need to install?

    A. Plenum

    B. PVC

    C. STP

    D. CAT5e or higher

188. You have been asked to create a UTP crossover cable. Which pins need to be crossed over to make the cable work properly?

    A. 1 and 2, 3 and 6

    B. 1 and 3, 2 and 6

    C. 1 and 6, 2 and 3

    D. None of the above

189. You are trying to replace a hard drive in an older system. The connector has 68 pins, along two rows. You believe from printing on the motherboard it is a 16-bit connection. What type of drive do you have to replace?

    A. SATA

    B. ATA

    C. SCSI

    D. NVMe

190. A technician has a tablet that he is told is capable to connect to an HDMI monitor. However, the tablet has a port far smaller than HDMI. What type of video connection would be typical for this small form factor device?

    A. USB-C

    B. RS-232

    C. DB-9

    D. MiniHDMI

191. What was the connectivity cable end Apple used between 2012 and 2019, between the 30-pini dock connector and the USB-C?

    A. RS-232

    B. MiniHDMI

    C. Micro-USB

    D. Lightning

192. With what connection standard is the Apple Thunderbolt 3 cable fully compatible?

    A. USB-C

    B. MiniHDMI

    C. Micro-USB

    D. DB-9

193. Which of the following connection types can be inserted or first flipped over and inserted?

    A. DB-9

    B. RS-232

    C. Micro-USB

    D. USB-C

194. What serial connection standard was first developed in 1960 and had been the standard for microsystems for a few decades?

    A. DB-9

    B. RS-232

    C. Micro-USB

    D. ~~USB-C~~

195. What 9-pin connector type was commonly used for keyboards, mice, or game controllers before USB became popular?

    A. SCSI

    B. PS/2

    C. DB9

    D. Lightning

196. Which of the following does not apply with triple channel memory?

    A. Triple the 64-bit communication path to the CPU

    B. Triple the speed with which memory is accessed

    C. Requires installation of three matched memory modules

    D. Triple the power distributed to the memory

197. What form factor for solid-state hard drives measures 22 mm wide and lengths varying between 30 mm, 42 mm, 60 mm, and longer?

    A. NVM.e

    B. SATA

    C. PCIe

    D. M.2

198. What form factor for solid-state hard drives has dimensions that mirror the older, platter-type drives?

    A. M.2

    B. PCIe

    C. RPM

    D. 2.5"

199. Your friend has just finished building a computer. After installing the operating system, all seems fine except that he found that flash drives placed in the USB ports on the top of the case do not get noticed by the OS. Where do you suspect the problem is?

  A. Device drivers outdated

  B. USB settings misconfigured

  C. Motherboard's internal USB connector disconnected

  D. System clock

200. You wish to protect your system from someone not authorized to start the OS. What is your best option?

  A. Password protect the locked screen.

  B. Password protect in the BIOS/UEFI settings.

  C. Encrypt the hard drive.

  D. Use a 12-character login password.

201. What is used to ensure an efficient and effective heat exchange away from the CPU?

  A. Thermal paste

  B. High-tension clamps to heatsink

  C. Dihydrogen monoxide coolant

  D. Lower CPU speeds

202. If you require more USB ports than your system can provide, what is your most cost-effective option?

  A. Install a USB expansion board.

  B. Swap peripherals for those requiring different connectors.

  C. Replace the motherboard for one with additional USB ports.

  D. Swap out peripherals as you use them.

203. You have been asked to make the touch pad less sensitive. Where would you do this in Windows 10?

  A. Windows Settings | Apps

  B. Windows Settings | Devices

  C. Windows Settings | Personalization

  D. Windows Settings | Ease of Access

204. Someone who uses multiple laptops has asked you if it's possible to synchronize the settings for Internet Explorer across all his devices. Is it possible, and where would you do this in Windows 10?

  A. Not possible

  B. Possible. Under Devices | Sync Your Settings

  C. Possible. Under Personalization | Sync Your Settings

  D. Possible. Within Microsoft Account | Sync Your Settings

205. What technology allows you to generate a tangible product from a computer-aided drafting application?

   A. Smart card reader

   B. 3D printer

   C. Touch pad

   D. VR headset

206. An employee whose job duties include having to "sign" digital documents is frustrated with how sloppily the mouse re-creates her signature. What would you recommend to the employee?

   A. Scan her true signature, and then copy/paste the image.

   B. Procure a signature pad for signing more naturally.

   C. Lessen the mouse sensitivity.

   D. Use only PKI digital signatures.

207. What is the wiring difference between 568a and 568b networking cable?

   A. Both have 8 wires, but two are switched

   B. 568a uses positive voltage; 568b uses negative voltage

   C. 568b has only 6 wires

   D. Both have 8 wires, but four are switched

208. What is the difference between a DVI-D and a DVI-I cable?

   A. DVI-I cable sends both audio and video

   B. DVI-D cable sends both audio and video

   C. DVI-I cable sends both analog and digital

   D. DVI-D cable sends both analog and digital

209. What is the common purpose of an IDE cable?

   A. Connecting an expansion card to the motherboard

   B. Connecting an optical drive to the motherboard

   C. Terminating a hard drive

   D. Connecting a hard drive to a SCSI adapter

210. What is the difference between drive form factors such as M2 and SATA 2.5 inch when installing and configuring solid-state drives?

   A. SATA 2.5 connect with two cables while M2 uses one cable

   B. M2 supports magnetic hard drives running at 15,000rpm

   C. SATA 2.5 drives and M2 drives use the same slot

   D. M2 drives can use either the SATA or the PCIe bus

211.   Which of the following is not a difference when selecting 2.5 inch and 3.5 inch hard drives?

   A.   While clearly different lengths, both are the same thickness

   B.   Generally, 2.5 are in laptops, while 3.5 is found in desktops

   C.   If SATA drives, both have two connections: data and power

   D.   Both can be found in SATA or IDE standard

212.   You want to replace a hard drive and see the 40 pin connector on the motherboard. What type of drive is needed?

   A.   NVMe

   B.   Serial ATA

   C.   M2

   D.   IDE

213.   What is described by video card companies when they offer AIBs?

   A.   AIBs are video graphic add-in boards

   B.   AIBs is a specialized ASIC bios for video processing

   C.   AIBs are video all-included boards

   D.   AIBs are not offered by video card companies

214.   What peripheral type is commonly used by a store for tracking inventory or checking out at the register?

   A.   Mouse/trackball

   B.   Barcode scanner/QR scanner

   C.   External ZIP drive or flash drive

   D.   Screen projector

215.   When purchasing a new power supply from abroad, what must be considered before connecting the power supply to your machine?

   A.   Input 115V vs 220V

   B.   Output 5.5V vs. 12V

   C.   Input 5.5V vs. 12V

   D.   Output 115V vs 220V

216.   What commonly draws the output 5.5V vs. 12V voltages? (Choose two)

   A.   Motors such as fans and hard drive spindles use 12V

   B.   Integrated circuits and phones use 12V

   C.   Integrated circuits and phones use 5V

   D.   Motors such as fans and hard drive spindles use 5V

217. The corporate sales engineers are required to carry with them their laptop/common mobile devices. What is a likely requirement for these employees when configuring their laptop and mobile device?

   A. Log in account with elevated privileges

   B. Accompanying laser printer and scanner peripherals

   C. Remote access and VPN

   D. Portable file cabinet

218. During what issue may require troubleshooting a device's touchscreen configuration?

   A. A user complains their alarm goes off periodically

   B. The display no longer responds correctly

   C. The phone's battery discharges very quickly

   D. A user mentions their phone stays unlocked all the time

219. One employee's system has a direct wired connection to a USB printer. Occasionally, other coworkers need to use the printer, prompting disconnecting the wired USB printer from one system and reconnecting to another. What is the cost-efficient solution to this inconvenience?

   A. Device sharing

   B. Buy an inexpensive printer for the other coworkers' systems

   C. Purchase a serial device server

   D. Create accounts for other employees on the connected laptop

220. A small company discovers a legacy wired serial printer in storage. The boss would like to utilize the printer through device sharing on the network. What is a possible configuration to accomplish the boss's goal?

   A. Purchasing a powered USB hub

   B. Connecting the printer to the network directly

   C. Purchasing a RS232 to RJ45 converter

   D. Configuring a reverse proxy at the perimeter

221. Which of the following directly helps ensure data privacy on the system?

   A. Employing user authentication on the device

   B. Keeping backups of critical data

   C. Purchasing a strong device case

   D. Using a surge protector

222. The security analyst recommends turning off hard drive write caching, despite the risk of data loss from a sudden power loss. What might be likely rationale for disabling hard drive caching?

   A. Less power used

   B. Data privacy

   C. Longer hard drive lifespan

   D. Quieter drive noise

223. Users complain print jobs are appearing very dim. What would be the likely action to try on an inkjet printer? (Choose two)

    A. Clear jams

    B. Replace cartridges

    C. Clean heads (printer heads)

    D. Replace paper

224. Users complain the text on print jobs appears skewed or tilted. What would be the likely action to try on an inkjet printer?

    A. Calibrate

    B. Remove debris

    C. Clean heating element

    D. Clean heads

225. What is used in an 3d printer which allows it to print or create three dimensional objects?

    A. compressed air

    B. plastic filament

    C. dihydrogen monoxide

    D. plastic ink

Chapter

4

Virtualization and Cloud Computing

THE FOLLOWING COMPTIA A+ EXAM 220-1001 TOPICS ARE COVERED IN THIS CHAPTER:

✓ **4.1 Compare and contrast cloud computing concepts.**

- Common cloud models

    - IaaS

    - SaaS

    - PaaS

    - Public vs. private vs. hybrid vs. community

- Shared resources

    - Internal vs. external

- Rapid elasticity

- On-demand

- Resource pooling

- Measured service

- Metered

- Off-site email applications

- Cloud file storage services

    - Synchronization apps

- Virtual application streaming/cloud-based applications

    - Applications for cell phones/tablets

    - Applications for laptops/desktops

- Virtual desktop

    - Virtual NIC

✓ **4.2 Given a scenario, set up and configure client-side virtualization.**

- Purpose of virtual machines
- Resource requirements
- Emulator requirements
- Security requirements
- Network requirements
- Hypervisor

1. Microsoft offers users free access to a cloud-based storage account. What is the name of that service?

   A. OneDrive

   B. WinCloud

   C. Shadow Copy

   D. Microsoft Cloud

2. What type of cloud service offers the best security?

   A. Community

   B. Private

   C. Public

   D. Hybrid

3. Your manager tells you to purchase cloud-based services. Your network needs extra processing power and file storage. What type of service should you purchase?

   A. PaaS

   B. IaaS

   C. SaaS

   D. FWaaS

4. Your company has decided to purchase cloud services from Google. What type of cloud does Google provide?

   A. Public

   B. Private

   C. Hybrid

   D. Community

5. You have recently connected your Windows 7 workstation to a cloud storage service. You want to ensure that the cloud-based service synchronizes with your desktop every morning at 2:30 a.m. Which Windows management utility should you use to enable this?

   A. Task Scheduler

   B. Event Viewer

   C. Component Services

   D. Data Sources

6. Your company produces software and employs about 20 developers. They need to program apps for different operating systems. You decide to purchase cloud-based services to support the development team. What type of service should you purchase so they can develop their programs and then test them in environments other than where they were developed?

   A. IaaS

   B. SaaS

   C. PaaS

   D. NaaS

7. Which type of cloud service provides your company with the network hardware, infrastructure, and software needed to run your business?

A. PaaS

B. FWaaS

C. IaaS

D. SaaS

8. Which feature of cloud service allows you to instantly obtain additional storage space or processing power as your company needs it?

A. Ubiquitous access

B. Rapid elasticity

C. Resource pooling

D. Measured service

9. You are configuring the Mail app on an iPhone to use an Outlook.com email address. What configuration information do you need to enter to establish connectivity?

A. Email address and password

B. Email address, password, and server name

C. Email address, password, server name, and mail protocol

D. Email address, password, server name or IP address, and mail protocol

10. What feature of Windows 8 allows users to log into the OS, download apps from the Windows Store, and sync files to the cloud with only one sign-on?

A. Microsoft SSO

B. Login sync

C. OneDrive

D. Live sign-in

11. You are installing virtualization on a workstation that needs to support multiple operating systems. Which type of hypervisor is best suited for this environment?

A. Type 1

B. Type 2

C. Either Type 1 or Type 2 will function in the same way.

D. Virtual machine manager

12. You are configuring client-side virtualization on an existing Windows 8.1 64-bit workstation. You will be running OS X Yosemite in the virtual environment. Each OS requires 2 GB of RAM. Windows needs 20 GB of disk space and Yosemite needs 8 GB. What are the minimum hardware requirements for this workstation?

A. 4 GB RAM, 28 GB disk space

B. 2 GB RAM, 20 GB disk space

C. 2 GB RAM, 28 GB disk space

D. 4 GB RAM, 20 GB disk space

13. You are setting up virtualization on a server that will be running four instances of Windows Server 2012 R2. Four different departments will be using one instance each, and all departments have been promised 16 GB RAM. Using resource pooling and using a bare-metal hypervisor, what is the minimum amount of physical RAM needed on the server?

    A. 16 GB

    B. 32 GB

    C. 64 GB

    D. 8 GB

14. Your company has an application developer who creates programs for Windows, Linux, and MacOS. What is the most cost-effective solution for her to be able to test her programs in multiple operating systems as quickly as possible?

    A. Buy workstations for each of the OSs she codes in.

    B. Set up her workstation to dual boot.

    C. Set up her workstation with virtual machines.

    D. Create one version of each application that will run in all three OSs.

15. For which operating system can you get a preconfigured virtual machine (that runs in the Windows Virtual PC emulator) that allows users to run Windows XP–based applications?

    A. Windows Vista

    B. Windows 7

    C. Windows 8

    D. Windows 8.1

16. For which operating systems can you run or install Microsoft's native hypervisor, allowing you to run virtual machines? (Choose two.)

    A. Windows Server 2003

    B. Windows 8 Education

    C. Windows 7 Professional

    D. Windows 10 Professional

17. Your company wants to begin transferring particular services to the cloud, but the team cannot yet decide on the migration schedule. Management wants to pay for cloud computing based on usage, not a fixed flat fee. What payment model would you recommend?

    A. On-demand

    B. Resource pool

    C. Metered

    D. Waterfall

18. You are an avid fan of Twitch, the streaming application where you entertain yourself as you watch other people play games. Twitch works well at your house and at your friend's house. However, when you visit the website at work, the website looks fine but you can't watch anyone play games. You tried this on both your phone and your laptop. Which of the following should you suspect as the reason?

   A. Your immediate supervisor
   B. Your company's Wi-Fi connection bandwidth
   C. Your company data retention policy
   D. Your company firewall

19. What is a primary benefit to the virtual desktop feature in Windows 10?

   A. Control the desktop of a remote Windows machine.
   B. Share the desktop of a local Windows machine.
   C. Copy a Windows desktop to install on multiple machines.
   D. Host multiple desktops on a local Windows machine.

20. A client complains about the occupied space, abundant power usage, and hardware costs of the multiple machines used in its small data center. Still, the client does not wish to lose control over any of the machines. What might you recommend to the client to resolve all of those issues?

   A. Establish clusters for high availability.
   B. Create virtual machines.
   C. Outsource to an IaaS provider.
   D. Shut down the nonessential machines.

21. Which term describes printers, copiers, and other assets on the local network that are available to employees?

   A. Measured resources
   B. Shared resources
   C. Private cloud
   D. Community cloud

22. Network control and security management of cloud assets is the difference between what two types of shared resources?

   A. Internal vs. external
   B. Private vs. public
   C. Hybrid vs. community
   D. Synchronized vs. unsynchronized

23. A company using cloud services wishes to better prepare for surges for what it needs. What sort of capacity provisioning by its cloud provider should the company ask for?

    A. Rapid metering

    B. Infrastructure as a service

    C. On-demand

    D. Resource pooling

24. Which term best describes when a cloud provider monitors and controls resource availability depending on usage?

    A. Elasticity

    B. Pooling

    C. Measured service

    D. On-demand

25. The company's sales manager wants to ensure that the laptop files of its traveling sales engineers stay consistent with the files on the company cloud. What sort of applications could assist with that business need?

    A. Security monitoring apps

    B. Virtualization apps

    C. Emulator apps

    D. Synchronization apps

26. What technique describes when an organization moves applications normally restricted to a local desktop to the cloud?

    A. On-demand desktop

    B. Binary application desktop

    C. Virtual application streaming

    D. Desktop streaming

27. How can an organization permit employees who need to run an application on one mobile device to instead run it from multiple devices?

    A. Virtual application streaming

    B. Wrapping

    C. Binary application desktop

    D. On-demand desktop

28. An employee travels between multiple offices, using a desktop system in each office. What technology would ensure that the employee's desktop icons, files, and applications stay uniform across systems in all the offices?

    A. On-demand desktop

    B. Virtual desktop

    C. Desktop emulation

    D. Synchronized folders

29. What enables a guest machine to connect to a network?

  A. CAT5 network cable

  B. Guest applications

  C. Virtual NIC

  D. Host operating system

30. In setting up and configuring client-side virtualization, what is necessary to consider before purchasing computing and storage hardware?

  A. Resource requirements

  B. Management response

  C. Resale value

  D. Physical size

31. In setting up and configuring client-side virtualization, what is necessary to consider before configuring a VLAN?

  A. Network requirements

  B. Emulation demands

  C. Cloud service providers

  D. Storage capacity

32. What must be defined when wanting to maintain confidentiality, integrity, and availability of the system resources?

  A. Scalability

  B. Emulation

  C. Elasticity

  D. Security requirements

33. When considering how efficiently a hypervisor runs, which of the following is best when it is minimized?

  A. Storage

  B. Emulator requirements

  C. Memory

  D. Scalability

Chapter

5

Hardware and Network Troubleshooting

✓ **5.1 Given a scenario, use the best practice methodology to resolve problems.**

- Always consider corporate policies, procedures, and impacts before implementing changes.

- 1. Identify the problem.

  - Question the user and identify user changes to the computer and perform backups before making changes.

  - Inquire regarding environmental or infrastructure changes.

  - Review system and application logs.

- 2. Establish a theory of probable cause (question the obvious).

  - If necessary, conduct external or internal research based on symptoms.

- 3. Test the theory to determine cause.

  - Once the theory is confirmed, determine the next steps to resolve the problem.

  - If the theory is not confirmed reestablish a new theory or escalate the problem.

- 4. Establish a plan of action to resolve the problem and implement the solution.

- 5. Verify full system functionality and, if applicable, implement preventive measures.

- 6. Document findings, actions, and outcomes.

✓ **5.2 Given a scenario, troubleshoot problems related to motherboards, RAM, CPUs, and power.**

- Common symptoms
  - Unexpected shutdowns
  - System lockups
  - POST code beeps
  - Blank screen on bootup
  - BIOS time and setting resets
  - Attempts to boot to incorrect device
  - Continuous reboots
  - No power
  - Overheating
  - Loud noise
  - Intermittent device failure
  - Fans spin – no power to other devices
  - Indicator lights
  - Smoke
  - Burning smell
  - Proprietary crash screens (BSOD/pin wheel)
  - Distended capacitors
  - Log entries and error messages

✓ **5.3 Given a scenario, troubleshoot hard drives and RAID arrays.**

- Common symptoms
  - Read/write failure
  - Slow performance
  - Loud clicking noise
  - Failure to boot
  - Drive not recognized
  - OS not found

- RAID not found

- RAID stops working.

- Proprietary crash screens (BSOD/pin wheel)

- S.M.A.R.T. errors

✓ **5.4 Given a scenario, troubleshoot video, projector, and display issues.**

- Common symptoms

  - VGA mode

  - No image on screen

  - Overheat shutdown

  - Dead pixels

  - Artifacts

  - Incorrect color patterns

  - Dim image

  - Flickering image

  - Distorted image

  - Distorted geometry

  - Burn-in

  - Oversized images and icons

  - Multiple failed jobs in logs

✓ **5.5 Given a scenario, troubleshoot common mobile device issues while adhering to the appropriate procedures.**

- Common symptoms

  - No display

  - Dim display

  - Flickering display

  - Sticking keys

  - Intermittent wireless

  - Battery not charging

  - Ghost cursor/pointer drift

  - No power

- Num lock indicator lights
- No wireless connectivity
- No Bluetooth connectivity
- Cannot display to external monitor
- Touchscreen non-responsive
- Apps not loading
- Slow performance
- Unable to decrypt email
- Extremely short battery life
- Overheating
- Frozen system
- No sound from speakers
- GPS not functioning
- Swollen battery
- Disassembling processes for proper reassembly
  - Document and label cable and screw locations.
  - Organize parts.
  - Refer to manufacturer resources.
  - Use appropriate hand tools.

✓ **5.6 Given a scenario, troubleshoot printers.**

- Common symptoms
  - Streaks
  - Faded prints
  - Ghost images
  - Toner not fused to the paper
  - Creased paper
  - Paper not feeding
  - Paper jam
  - No connectivity
  - Garbled characters on paper
  - Vertical lines on page

- Backed-up print queue
- Low memory errors
- Access denied
- Printer will not print.
- Color prints in wrong print color
- Unable to install printer
- Error codes
- Printing blank pages
- No image on printer display

✓ **5.7 Given a scenario, troubleshoot common wired and wireless network problems.**

- Common symptoms
  - Limited connectivity
  - Unavailable resources
    - Internet
    - Local resources
      - Shares
      - Printers
      - Email
  - No connectivity
  - APIPA/link local address
  - Intermittent connectivity
  - IP conflict
  - Slow transfer speeds
  - Low RF signal
  - SSID not found

1. You are troubleshooting a computer that will not boot. It tells you that there is no bootable device. You check the BIOS, and it does not show any installed hard drives. What should you do next?

   A. Run `bootrec /fixmbr`.

   B. Replace the hard drive with one in an external enclosure.

   C. Flash the BIOS.

   D. Check the hard drive connections.

2. A technician just replaced a failed internal hard drive in a desktop computer with an empty hard drive. She needs to boot to the network to connect to an imaging server to restore the computer. How should she do this?

   A. During boot, press the F2 key to boot to the network.

   B. During boot, enter the BIOS and change the boot sequence to boot to the network.

   C. Let the boot complete normally. When the BIOS does not find a bootable partition on the hard drive, it will boot from the network.

   D. During boot, press the F7 key to edit the boot sequence menu.

3. A user's laptop computer does not display anything on the screen, although the power light and other indicator lights are on. You plug in an external monitor and it does not display either. Which component is most likely causing the problem?

   A. Inverter

   B. Backlight

   C. Screen

   D. Video card

4. You are troubleshooting a computer making a loud whining noise. Looking at the exhaust fan, you see a thick coating of dust. What should you do next?

   A. Use compressed air to clean the fan.

   B. Use a computer vacuum to clean the fan.

   C. Use a damp cloth to clean the fan.

   D. Replace the power supply.

5. A user reports that his laptop battery does not charge when his laptop is plugged into an AC outlet. What is the best resolution to try first?

   A. Replace the battery.

   B. Replace the AC adapter.

   C. Remove and reinsert the battery.

   D. Drain the battery completely and then recharge it.

6. A technician has determined that she needs to replace a motherboard in a laptop. Which of the following procedures should you follow? (Choose two.)

    A. Never use a power screwdriver with a laptop.

    B. Document and label screw locations.

    C. Refer to the manufacturer's instructions.

    D. Remove the keyboard before removing the motherboard.

7. You have just replaced faulty RAM in a desktop computer. You reboot the computer, and after a few seconds it beeps once. What does this indicate?

    A. The RAM is faulty.

    B. The motherboard needs to be replaced.

    C. The system BIOS detected an error in the POST routine.

    D. The system BIOS completed the POST routine normally.

8. You are troubleshooting a computer that has been randomly rebooting, and now it refuses to boot properly. Upon boot, you receive one long beep and three short beeps but no video on the screen. What tool should you use to troubleshoot the situation?

    A. Multimeter

    B. Power supply tester

    C. Loopback plug

    D. POST card

9. Over time, the hard drive performance of your computer has gotten slower. You believe that many of the files stored on the drive are fragmented, slowing down disk read and write speeds. What should you do to resolve this issue?

    A. Run Disk Defragmenter.

    B. Format the hard drive and restore the data.

    C. Delete the partition, create a new one, and restore the data.

    D. Run chkdsk.

10. A user's computer has failed. When you try to boot it up, you hear a loud, rhythmic clicking sound, and the system does not boot properly. What is most likely the issue?

    A. HDD failure

    B. SSD failure

    C. RAM failure

    D. Power supply fan failure

11. A laser printer you are working with consistently produces images with white streaks running down the page. What can you do to resolve this issue?

    A. Clean the transfer corona wires.

    B. Clean the EP drum.

    C. Clean the fusing assembly.

    D. Replace the toner cartridge.

12. The dot-matrix printer in your office recently started creasing papers and producing paper jams. Which of the following are likely to cause these problems? (Choose two.)

    A. Bits of paper in the paper path

    B. Paper tension settings

    C. Using the wrong paper

    D. Paper perforations

13. The monitor for your desktop computer will randomly shut down after long periods of use. What is the most likely cause of this problem?

    A. Video card failure

    B. Monitor overheating

    C. Improper video resolution

    D. Backlight failure

14. You power on a desktop computer, and you hear the fan spinning. However, you do not see any indicator lights or get a POST beep. Which component is likely causing the problem?

    A. CPU

    B. RAM

    C. PSU

    D. HDD

15. You have just replaced a toner cartridge in an HP Laser Jet printer. It is displaying "Error 14 No EP Cart." What should you do to resolve the issue?

    A. Turn the printer off and back on.

    B. Remove the toner cartridge and press the Reset button.

    C. Remove the toner cartridge and reinsert it.

    D. Remove the toner cartridge and replace it with a new one.

16. Your office uses an ink-jet printer. Recently, it started having problems picking up paper. Which component is likely to cause this problem?

    A. Transport rollers

    B. Pickup rollers

    C. Exit rollers

    D. Transmission rollers

17. Your office uses an old dot-matrix printer. Recently, the printer has started producing output that goes from dark to light when you look at the paper from left to right. What is causing this problem?

    A. A worn-out printer ribbon

    B. The ribbon-advance mechanism

    C. The print head

    D. The paper feed assembly

18. Your network uses 802.11n for all client computers. Recently, several users moved from one office space to another, increasing the users in the area from 20 to about 50. Now, both new and old users are reporting very slow network transfer speeds. What is most likely the cause of the problem?

   A. 802.11n can't support that many concurrent users.

   B. It's too far from the wireless access point.

   C. There are too many users for one wireless access point.

   D. The new users all have 802.11b network cards.

19. Your computer has been intermittently rebooting when you play an online video game. You install a hardware monitoring utility and notice in the log that the CPU temperature spikes before the system shuts down. Which action should you take first to help resolve the issue?

   A. Use the system BIOS to overclock the CPU.

   B. Replace the CPU and heat sink.

   C. Reseat the CPU heat sink.

   D. Replace the power supply.

20. Users in one section of your building report that wireless network service is spotty. Their workstations have slow connectivity and frequently drop the connection. Which tool should you use to test the problem?

   A. Wireless locator

   B. Fox and hound

   C. Loopback plug

   D. Packet sniffer

21. A technician has just replaced a faulty hard drive and created a partition on the new drive. Which utility should she use next to ready the drive for data storage?

   A. format

   B. bootrec

   C. chkdsk

   D. diskpart

22. You are troubleshooting a computer with a RAID-0 array using four disks. One of the disks fails. What can you do to recover the array?

   A. Rebuild the failed disk and restore from backup.

   B. Replace the failed disk and rebuild the array.

   C. Replace the failed disk and restore from backup.

   D. Remove the failed disk and rebuild the array.

23.   The laser printer in your office is about five years old. Recently, when you print, you will occasionally get low memory error messages. What should you do to fix the problem?

   A.   Stop and restart the print spooler.

   B.   Implement printing priorities for the most important users.

   C.   Upgrade the printer's memory.

   D.   Upgrade the printer's hard drive.

24.   You are troubleshooting a recently installed three-disk RAID array. The original technician left notes that he was concerned about creating multiple points of potential failure in the system. Which type of RAID array creates more points of potential failure than a single hard drive?

   A.   RAID-10

   B.   RAID-1

   C.   RAID-0

   D.   RAID-5

25.   A technician is troubleshooting a computer that is experiencing continuous reboots. He isn't sure where to begin diagnosing the problem, so he calls you for advice. Which tool should you tell him to use to try to identify the problem?

   A.   Multimeter

   B.   Power supply tester

   C.   Loopback plug

   D.   POST card

26.   Users are printing to a laser printer, but nothing is coming out. When you look at the print queue, you see several jobs backed up. The printer is online, has paper, and says Ready. What should you do to resolve the problem?

   A.   Turn the printer off and back on.

   B.   Stop and restart the print spooler.

   C.   Press the Reset button on the printer.

   D.   Use the printer's display to clear out the oldest job, take it offline, and put it back online.

27.   Your company has a plasma monitor that used to display conference room information in a common area. Recently, you repurposed the monitor in another area. Regardless of what is on the screen, you can still always see the conference room information template on the screen as well. What is this called?

   A.   Dead pixels

   B.   Overheating

   C.   Burn-in

   D.   Backlight failure

28. A user reports that his tablet computer will work on battery power for only about 20 minutes, even after the battery icon says it's full. She claims that it used to work on battery power for several hours. What is the most likely cause of the problem?

   A. The user is running too many apps.

   B. The user is constantly using the Wi-Fi connection.

   C. The battery needs to be charged longer.

   D. The battery is failing.

29. While troubleshooting a computer, you notice that the hard drive indicator light is constantly on. The system seems unresponsive. You reboot the computer, and a few minutes later the same problem happens. What should you do?

   A. Replace the hard drive.

   B. Replace the motherboard.

   C. Reinstall the operating system.

   D. Test the hard drive with a multimeter.

30. Your director's network cable has failed, and he needs network connectivity immediately. You are unable to find a spare patch cable, but you have a spool of CAT5e cable and some RJ-45 connectors. Which tool do you need to create a new cable?

   A. Crimper

   B. Wire strippers

   C. Punchdown tool

   D. Cable tester

31. You have just installed a second hard drive in your computer. When you boot up the computer, you get an error message that the operating system is not found. What should you try first?

   A. Check jumper settings on the hard drives.

   B. Run bootrec /fixmbr.

   C. Run dispart.

   D. Replace the new hard drive.

32. You are troubleshooting a computer that will not boot properly. When you power it on, it produces a series of long and short beeps. Which components are most likely to be causing this to happen? (Choose two.)

   A. BIOS

   B. Hard drive

   C. Network card

   D. RAM

33. You are working on a laptop that appears to be frozen. You press the Num Lock key several times, but the indicator light remains on. What can you do to try to resolve this issue?

    A. Push and hold the power button until the laptop turns off, and reboot.

    B. Remove the battery and disconnect the laptop from an AC power source, and reboot.

    C. Press and hold the Num Lock key until the light turns off.

    D. Press Ctrl+Alt+Del to reboot the laptop.

34. A user complains that when he turns his desktop computer on, nothing appears on the screen. It sounds like the computer's fan is running, and the user reported hearing one beep when the computer powered on. What is the first thing you should check?

    A. Is the monitor plugged into the video card?

    B. Did the computer complete the POST properly?

    C. Is the monitor turned on?

    D. Does another monitor work on this computer?

35. A user reports that her mobile phone is extremely hot and appears to be locked up. What should you instruct her to do?

    A. Plug the phone into a wall outlet or USB port to charge it.

    B. Turn the phone off and let it cool down.

    C. Perform a factory reset of the phone.

    D. Open the Power app and set the phone to operate on the low voltage setting.

36. The desktop computer you are troubleshooting will not retain the proper time and date. You set the time and date, power the system down, and power it back on. Again, the settings are incorrect. Which component is likely causing the issue?

    A. CMOS battery

    B. BIOS

    C. Hard drive

    D. RAM

37. You have an Android phone and it's running slowly. The problem seems to be isolated to one app in particular. You check and you have plenty of free memory. You have rebooted the phone several times and the app is still slow. What should you try next?

    A. Hold the power button and the Home button simultaneously for 10 seconds, and the phone will reset.

    B. Reset the phone to factory specifications.

    C. Uninstall and reinstall the app.

    D. Get a new phone.

38. A laser printer you are servicing has been producing ghosted images. That is, regardless of whatever prints, you can always see a faint copy of a previous image that was printed. What can be causing this? (Choose two.)

    A. Dirty charging corona wire

    B. Broken cleaning blade

    C. Broken fusing assembly

    D. Bad erasure lamps

39. You charged your laptop overnight, but in the morning, it will not power on. You remove and reinsert the battery, but still it will not power on. The system will power on when you use the wall adapter, and the battery icon indicates that it's full. What is the most likely problem?

    A. The battery is defective.

    B. The AC adapter is not properly charging the battery.

    C. The battery charging icon is not properly reading the battery life.

    D. The DC converter between the battery and the motherboard is defective.

40. A user reports that regardless of what is showing on his LCD desktop monitor, he can always see an outline of another image that never changes. What is the solution to this problem?

    A. Replace the video card.

    B. Degauss the monitor.

    C. Replace the monitor.

    D. Clean the screen.

41. A user claims that on his laptop, the mouse cursor will occasionally jump to different areas of the screen when he is typing. It is causing problems with his work because he ends up typing in different fields than he needs to. What can you suggest to help this issue?

    A. Disable the point stick.

    B. Replace the keyboard.

    C. Replace the motherboard.

    D. Disable the touch pad.

42. A user complains of a burning smell coming from her desktop computer. You instruct her to immediately shut the system down. What should be your next step?

    A. Replace the power supply.

    B. Replace the motherboard.

    C. Test the power supply with a multimeter.

    D. Inspect the inside of the computer for visible signs of damage.

43. The desktop computer in your office's lobby plays a welcome video for guests. Recently, the audio started intermittently failing. You replaced the speakers, and it still happens. What is the next step you should take in troubleshooting the issue?

A. Replace the motherboard.

B. Reseat the speakers.

C. Replace the sound card.

D. Reseat the sound card.

44. A user reports that her iPhone 5 is always overheating and constantly locks up. What should you advise her to do?

A. Replace the battery.

B. Open the Power app and set the phone to operate on the low voltage setting.

C. Turn off the phone and let it cool down.

D. Replace the phone.

45. You have just used administrative privileges to install a printer on a user's workstation. When the user tries to print to the printer, she gets an error message saying access denied. What is the cause of this problem?

A. The printer is offline.

B. The printer is out of memory.

C. The print spooler needs to be restarted.

D. The user does not have the security permissions to print.

46. You are using a CRT monitor at a kiosk. The colors on the monitor recently started looking wrong. What should you do to try to resolve the issue?

A. Replace the monitor.

B. Replace the video card.

C. Disconnect the monitor and plug it back in.

D. Degauss the monitor.

47. The ink-jet printer in your office jams a lot and produces many crinkled papers. What is the most likely cause of this?

A. Incorrect paper tension settings

B. Dirty print heads

C. Obstructed paper path

D. Paper that is too dry

48. A user reports that her Windows 7 computer will not boot. When booting, it gives the error message, "Operating System not found." Which utility can you use to attempt to fix this issue?

A. format

B. chkdsk

C. bootrec

D. diskpart

49. A technician is troubleshooting a computer configured for wired network connection that can't connect to the network. Given the unavailable resources including the Internet, he verified that the cable is plugged in, but there are no lights lit on the network card. The computer could connect yesterday, and no other users report an issue. Which of the following are most likely to be causing this problem? (Choose two.)

   A. Faulty network cable

   B. Faulty network card driver

   C. Incorrect TCP/IP configuration

   D. The cable is unplugged at the other end.

50. While replacing a toner cartridge in a laser printer, a technician spilled toner on and around the printer. What should he use to clean up the spill?

   A. A damp cloth

   B. Compressed air

   C. A toner vacuum

   D. Denatured alcohol

51. The AC adapter for your laptop has a green LED indicator on it. When you plug the adapter into a wall outlet, the light does not illuminate. What could be the reason for this? (Choose two.)

   A. The laptop is off.

   B. The wall outlet is defective.

   C. The AC adapter is defective.

   D. The voltage selector for the AC adapter is set incorrectly.

52. You are troubleshooting an ink-jet printer. Users report that the printer is printing in the wrong colors. The problem just started happening recently. What could be causing it? (Choose two.)

   A. Ink cartridges installed in the wrong spot

   B. Leaking ink cartridges

   C. Malfunctioning fusing assembly

   D. Malfunctioning stepper motor

53. You have installed an 802.11ac wireless access point for a company. To cut costs, the company wanted only one central access point in the building, which is about 150 feet long. Users at both ends of the building report intermittent wireless connectivity drops and slow access. What is most likely the cause of the problem?

   A. Low RF signal

   B. Oversaturated WAP

   C. SSID not found

   D. IP address conflicts

54. You are disassembling a defective laptop to replace the motherboard. Which of the following steps are recommended? (Choose two.)

    A. Place the screws in a multicompartment pill box and label where they go.

    B. Remove the hard drive before removing the motherboard.

    C. Label where the cables plug into the motherboard.

    D. Use needle-nose pliers to remove the motherboard from the spacers.

55. A user reports that his LCD monitor is flickering constantly. What is the easiest course of action to resolve this problem?

    A. Replace the video card.

    B. Replace the monitor.

    C. Remove external interference such as fans or motors.

    D. Degauss the monitor.

56. You are having problems printing to a networked printer from your Windows 8.1 workstation. Several jobs were sent, but none printed. You just tried to print a test page and nothing came out. What should you do?

    A. Check your connections and stop and restart the print spooler.

    B. Turn the printer off and back on.

    C. Use the printer's display to clear out the oldest job, take it offline, and put it back online.

    D. Press the Reset button on the printer.

57. A user reports that none of the keys on her laptop keyboard seem to work. She has rebooted the computer and the problem has not gone away. She needs to finish an important paper before lunch. What should you do next?

    A. Replace the keyboard.

    B. Check to ensure that the internal keyboard is still connected properly.

    C. Connect an external keyboard using the USB port.

    D. Clean under the keys of the keyboard with compressed air.

58. You are troubleshooting a Mac running MacOS. Intermittently, the computer will completely lock up and display a rotating pinwheel instead of the mouse cursor. Which component is most likely causing this problem?

    A. CPU

    B. RAM

    C. Motherboard

    D. Hard drive

59. A user reports that his CRT monitor will randomly produce a wavy image during the day. When you go to his desk to troubleshoot, it appears to be working normally. Later that afternoon, he reports it happening again. When you go back to his desk, what should you look for?

   A. Cell phones in use

   B. If the video connector is properly plugged in

   C. Motors or fans in use

   D. If the screen resolution is properly set

60. At random times, your computer will completely lock up, requiring a hard reboot. Which two components are most likely to cause this type of problem? (Choose two.)

   A. CPU

   B. RAM

   C. PSU

   D. GPU

61. A worker drove heavy machinery over a bundle of unprotected network cables, and now you are replacing them. You're in the wiring closet and need to attach the cables to a 110 block. Which tool will you use to do this?

   A. Crimper

   B. Wire strippers

   C. Punchdown tool

   D. Cable tester

62. You are consulting with a user who has a failed hard drive in a Windows 7 computer. The user needs to get critical data off the drive, but he did not make a backup. Are there any options for him to recover the data?

   A. There is no way to recover data from the failed drive.

   B. Use the Windows Disk Repair tool to create a backup and then restore the backup to a new hard drive.

   C. Use a file recovery service or software package to try to recover the data.

   D. Install a second hard drive of the same or larger size. During Windows installation, choose Recover Contents Of Hard Drive from the Advanced Options menu.

63. In the morning, a user calls from his desk and reports that his laptop will not connect to the wireless network. He has never had a problem connecting to the wireless network from that location. When you look at his wireless adapter, you notice that there are no lights illuminated. What is most likely the problem?

   A. He is not receiving a Wi-Fi signal.

   B. The SSID cannot be found.

   C. His wireless card is disabled.

   D. There is a conflict between his wireless card and his wired network port.

64. A user calls the help desk stating that the icons on her computer screen are huge. She can see only about six of them, and she can't see the Start menu. What most likely caused this issue?

A. Failing backlight

B. Incorrect video resolution

C. External interference, such as a fan or a motor

D. Incorrect video driver

65. A user calls you about a printer not working. The user is standing next to the printer while you are in the next building. What can the user do to be helpful in your diagnosing the problem?

A. Turn the printer off and on.

B. Read the printer error code.

C. Remove the jammed paper.

D. Check the network link light.

66. Your iPhone 6 has appeared to lock up. The touch screen is unresponsive. You press and hold the power button, but it does not turn off. What should your next step be?

A. Hold the power button and the sleep/wake button simultaneously for 10 seconds and the phone will reboot.

B. Use a paper clip to press the recessed reset button on the bottom of the phone to reset the phone.

C. Hold the power button and the up and down volume buttons simultaneously for 10 seconds and the phone will reset.

D. Get a new phone.

67. The laser printer in your office recently started producing images that are not completely set. When the images come out, people are smudging them as they pick them up. What is causing this problem?

A. Fusing assembly

B. Exit rollers

C. Drying assembly

D. Charging corona

68. You frequently need to carry your laptop around the building as you troubleshoot computer issues. In several places, you notice that the Wi-Fi connection drops completely. What is the most likely cause of this problem?

A. You are walking too fast for the Wi-Fi to stay connected.

B. Low RF signal

C. Oversaturated WAP

D. Failing Wi-Fi antenna in the laptop

69. You have just installed a printer on your client computer. When you print to the printer, the output is completely garbled characters. What is the most likely cause of this problem?

A. The print spooler

B. The printer's memory

C. The printer driver

D. The print queue

70. A user calls to report that he can't access the Internet or a corporate server. However, he is still able to print to a printer nearby. He has not received any error messages. Other users in his area are also unable to access the Internet. What is most likely the problem?

A. IP address conflict

B. Default gateway down

C. Incorrect subnet mask

D. Network card failure

71. A user's laptop computer does not display anything on the screen, although the power light and other indicator lights are on. You plug in an external monitor, and after you toggle the LCD cutoff switch, an image appears on the external monitor. Which components are most likely causing the problem? (Choose two.)

A. Video driver

B. Backlight

C. Screen

D. Video card

72. You have an Android phone and it's running very slowly. The apps aren't working as fast as they used to, but you still have plenty of free memory. You have rebooted the phone several times and it's still slow. What should you try next?

A. Hold the power button and the Home button simultaneously for 10 seconds, and the phone will reset.

B. Reset the phone to factory specifications.

C. Uninstall and reinstall all apps.

D. Get a new phone.

73. A technician is troubleshooting a RAID-5 array with four hard disks. One of the disks has failed. What can she do to recover the array?

A. Replace the failed disk and rebuild the array.

B. Replace the failed disk and restore from backup.

C. Rebuild the failed disk and restore from backup.

D. Remove the failed disk and rebuild the array.

74. The laser printer you are using has started producing all-black pages. What should you do to fix the problem?

   A. Use the display to initiate a self-cleaning cycle.

   B. Use a maintenance kit to clean the printer.

   C. Replace the toner cartridge.

   D. Turn the printer off and back on again.

75. You have installed an internal RAID controller and configured a RAID-5 array on it with four hard disks. It has been operating normally. Today when you boot up, you receive an error message saying, "RAID not found." Which component is likely causing this issue?

   A. One of the four hard disks

   B. The RAID controller

   C. The system BIOS

   D. The onboard hard drive controller

76. One of your friends complains that when he plays action games on his computer, the screen is slow to refresh and the motion is often jerky. What should he do to resolve this problem?

   A. Buy a newer monitor.

   B. Increase system RAM.

   C. Increase video memory.

   D. Lower the screen resolution.

77. You are troubleshooting a workstation that can't connect to websites by name. You need to check to see the IP address of the DNS server the host is trying to reach. Which command should you use?

   A. `ipconfig`

   B. `ipconfig /show`

   C. `ipconfig /display`

   D. `ipconfig /all`

78. You are troubleshooting a Windows 7 workstation that is having issues connecting to the Internet. Interestingly, the computer seems to be able to connect to websites beginning with `https://` but not `http://`. Other workstations can connect to all websites. You want to check to see whether this computer is making any TCP/IP connections on port 80. Which command should you use?

   A. `netstat`

   B. `nbtstat`

   C. `netdom`

   D. `net`

79. A user reports that her Samsung phone case has swollen. What does she need to do to fix the problem?

    A. Replace the phone.

    B. Open the Power app and set the phone to operate on the low voltage setting.

    C. Open the case of the phone and drain the excess electrolyte from the battery.

    D. Turn the phone off and let it cool down and then use it normally.

80. You have downloaded a scheduling app for your Android tablet. After two months of use, it will not load. You reboot your tablet, and the app still will not open. Other apps appear to work normally. What should you do?

    A. Reset the tablet to factory specifications.

    B. Reinstall the app.

    C. Ensure that the app is configured to run in Settings.

    D. Replace the tablet.

81. You have a Windows 8.1 desktop computer that does not produce an image on the screen when it boots. You hear a POST beep and normal indicator lights are on. The monitor is connected to the computer and the power light is on. What should be your next troubleshooting step?

    A. Try the monitor on another computer or another monitor on this computer.

    B. Replace the video card.

    C. Switch the monitor to another video connector on the video card.

    D. Replace the monitor.

82. A user shows you her mobile phone, and the screen is constantly flickering. She turns the device off and on again, and it still happens. Which component is likely causing the problem?

    A. Display

    B. Video card

    C. Backlight

    D. Converter

83. A user reports that the video on her desktop computer does not display properly. There are several places where the screen will not light up; those spots are always black dots. What is this a symptom of?

    A. Artifacts

    B. Dead pixels

    C. Backlight failure

    D. Overheating

84. You are troubleshooting a laptop computer that has a drifting mouse cursor. If nobody is moving the external mouse, the cursor will slowly drift up and to the right. You have tried a different external mouse and the problem still happens. What should you do to resolve the problem?

A. Replace the laptop keyboard.

B. Recenter the laptop's point stick.

C. Recenter the laptop's touch pad.

D. Replace the laptop motherboard.

85. You are troubleshooting network connectivity issues in one section of the building. After a few hours, you come to the conclusion that the network cables in the wiring closet must be mislabeled. Which tool is most appropriate to test your theory?

A. Multimeter

B. Cable tester

C. Punchdown tool

D. Tone generator and probe

86. You are upgrading a laptop with new memory. Which of the following disassembly processes should you follow? (Choose two.)

A. Remove the keyboard to access the memory sockets.

B. Use appropriate hand tools.

C. Leave the clamshell case open.

D. Document and label cable and screw locations.

87. A remote workstation can't connect to the network. You want to narrow down the problem to the UTP cable or the network card. Which tool can help you determine whether the cable is causing the problem?

A. Multimeter

B. OTDR

C. Cable tester

D. Crimper

88. You have just installed a new HP LaserJet printer on your network. You've plugged it directly into a CAT6a network cable. You try to install the printer on a client using the printer's IP address, but you are unable to connect. The printer is in Ready state. What should you do next?

A. Double-check the printer's IP configuration information.

B. Stop and restart the spooler service.

C. Take the printer offline and bring it back online.

D. Turn the printer off and back on to save the IP configuration information.

89. Your network has recently grown from 50 client computers to about 90. All workstations on the network are connected using CAT5e or better cabling, and all network devices support at least 100 Mbps data transfers. Users have been reporting very slow network speeds since the expansion, and complaints are now coming more frequently. Which of the following actions is most likely to help resolve the issue?

   A. Add another hub to the network.

   B. Upgrade all the cabling to at least CAT6a.

   C. Upgrade the existing router to support 10 Gbps data transfers.

   D. Add another switch to the network.

90. An iPhone 6 user just downloaded a new app that requires the use of GPS. It doesn't function properly. Another app she has on her phone also needs GPS and it also does not work. How does she configure the phone to let the new app work properly?

   A. Enable GPS under Settings ➤ Privacy.

   B. Enable Location Services under Settings ➤ Privacy.

   C. Enable GPS under Settings ➤ Location Services.

   D. Enable Location Services under Settings ➤ GPS.

91. A technician just replaced the toner cartridge in a laser printer. Now the printer only prints blank pages. What should you do to resolve the problem?

   A. Stop and restart the print spooler.

   B. Reinstall the printer driver.

   C. Replace the toner cartridge with a new toner cartridge.

   D. Remove the toner cartridge, remove the sealing tape, and then reinstall the cartridge.

92. You are troubleshooting a desktop computer that is prone to unexpected shutdowns. The user reports that no error messages appear before the computer shuts down. Which two things are most likely to cause this type of problem? (Choose two.)

   A. Failing hard drive

   B. Bad RAM

   C. BIOS misconfiguration

   D. Improperly seated chips

93. You are troubleshooting a workstation that can't connect to the network. Which tool should you use to test the functionality of the send and receive circuitry on the network card?

   A. Punchdown tool

   B. Loopback plug

   C. Ping

   D. `ipconfig`

94. You want to transfer files from your computer to a remote server. To do this, you want to connect to a shared directory on the server and copy the files. Which command-line utility will allow you to do this?

A. netstat

B. net

C. netshare

D. netdom

95. A user's Windows-based desktop computer always attempts to boot to the DVD-ROM drive. Where can she go to change the settings to boot to the hard drive?

A. Windows Control Panel

B. Windows Device Manager

C. Windows Disk Management

D. BIOS

96. A technician is troubleshooting a computer that occasionally will not read data from the hard drive. What should she try first?

A. Run Disk Defragmenter.

B. Run chkdsk.

C. Format the hard drive and reinstall the OS.

D. Replace the hard drive.

97. You are troubleshooting network connectivity issues from a Linux workstation. Which command should you use to check the computer's IP address and subnet mask?

A. ping

B. ipconfig

C. ifconfig

D. netstat

98. The finance group reports that its laser printer will not power up. It's plugged in, and the outlet has been verified as working. When testing the DC power supply with a multimeter, what voltage reading should you get from pin 1?

A. −5 V

B. +5 V

C. −24 V

D. +24 V

99. You are troubleshooting a Windows 10 computer that appears to be unresponsive. You press the Caps Lock key on the keyboard, but the Caps Lock light on the keyboard does not light up. What is most likely happening?

A. The keyboard has malfunctioned.

B. The system is waiting for a process to finish and will respond soon.

C. The motherboard has failed.

D. The system has locked up and needs to be rebooted.

100. You have replaced a failed hard drive and need to prepare it for data storage. Which utility will you use first?

    A. format

    B. diskpart

    C. chkdsk

    D. bootrec

101. You are troubleshooting a desktop computer and receive S.M.A.R.T. errors. To which component do these errors refer?

    A. SSD

    B. RAM

    C. CPU

    D. Network card

102. The desktop computer you are troubleshooting will not boot. When you push the power button, no status light indicators come on, and you do not hear a fan. You verify that the outlet is working and try a power cord that you know works, but it doesn't help. Which component is most likely causing the problem?

    A. RAM

    B. PSU

    C. CPU

    D. HDD

103. A user reports that his computer is running slowly. When you investigate, you notice that his free disk space is at 5 percent. What is the first solution to try?

    A. Add more RAM.

    B. Remove old files or applications.

    C. Format the hard drive and reinstall from backup.

    D. Replace the hard drive.

104. About a dozen network cables were unplugged from the patch panel, and none of them is labeled. You are at the one workstation that needs to be reconnected, and another technician is in the wiring closet. You want to set this computer to persistently check network connectivity so you know when he plugs in the right cable. Which command should you use?

    A. ping -t

    B. ping -p

    C. ping -l

    D. ping -n

105. You are troubleshooting a laptop, and some of the keys on the left side of the keyboard are constantly sticking. The user says that a little soda might have spilled on the keyboard. What should you do first to resolve the issue?

    A. Use a slightly dampened cotton swab to clean under the keys.

    B. Remove the keyboard and rinse it with soap and water in a sink.

    C. Replace the keyboard.

    D. Hold the keyboard upside down and shake it.

106. A user complains that sometimes his computer will not open files, and it happens in different programs. Which component is most likely to cause this problem?

    A. RAM

    B. CPU

    C. HDD

    D. Motherboard

107. You are troubleshooting a laptop with a no connectivity to the wireless network. The laptop does not have a wired network port. What can you do to quickly get the laptop back on the network?

    A. Reinstall the network card driver.

    B. Insert a USB wireless network card.

    C. Replace the wireless network card.

    D. Reboot the computer and reinitialize the wireless network card.

108. A user is upset because his Android tablet does not ring whenever he receives a phone call. What is the first thing you should have him check?

    A. If the tablet is configured to receive voice calls

    B. If the tablet is in Airplane mode

    C. If the tablet is set to silent mode

    D. If the tablet's speakers are working in another application

109. The LCD monitor you use with your desktop suddenly became very dim. You have attempted to adjust the brightness settings, but even on the highest setting the picture is still dim. What will most likely resolve the issue?

    A. Degauss the monitor.

    B. Replace the backlight.

    C. Replace the screen.

    D. Replace the inverter.

110. You are troubleshooting a Windows 7 desktop computer that boots into VGA mode. What is the first step to take in the troubleshooting process?

    A. Reinstall the video card driver.

    B. Replace the video card.

    C. Reset the video resolution to a lower setting and reboot.

    D. Replace the monitor.

111. The display on the HP LaserJet printer in your office has gone blank, but the power light is still on. You try to run a self-test, but nothing happens. You power it off and back on, but the problem persists. Which component has likely failed?

    A. DC controller

    B. The display

    C. HVPS

    D. LVPS

112. The office space you work in consists of several rows of small cubicles. The person sitting next to you has a fan on his desk, very close to your CRT monitor. What problems might this cause?

    A. Distorted image

    B. Distorted geometry

    C. Incorrect color patterns

    D. Artifacts

113. You have an iPhone 6 running iOS 9.3. One of your colleagues sends you an encrypted email with highly confidential information, but your device is unable to decrypt it. What do you need to do to resolve this problem?

    A. Upgrade to iOS 10.0 or newer.

    B. Install the Secure Mail app.

    C. Have the colleague resend the email unencrypted.

    D. Enable S/MIME.

114. You are troubleshooting a Windows 7 computer that has crashed. It displays a blank screen on bootup, with the error "UNEXPECTED_KERNEL_MODE_TRAP" on it. Which component most likely caused this problem?

    A. RAM

    B. CPU

    C. SSD

    D. PSU

115. A user reports that her screen image appears to be squeezed on her LCD monitor, and it does not go all the way to the edges like it used to. What is most likely the cause of the problem?

    A. External interference, such as a fan or a motor

    B. Incorrect video driver

    C. Failing backlight

    D. Incorrect video resolution

116. The lines of print on your ink-jet printer are unevenly spaced. Some are too close together, while others are too far apart. What is the most likely cause of this problem?

   A. Paper feed mechanism

   B. Exit rollers

   C. Print cartridge

   D. Stepper motor

117. While plugging in a VGA monitor, a user bent some of the pins on the connector. You attempted to straighten them, but two broke off. If you use this monitor, what will most likely happen?

   A. It will work properly.

   B. It will display incorrect colors.

   C. It will display a distorted image.

   D. It will produce dim or flickering images.

118. You are troubleshooting a Windows 10 workstation's connectivity issues on the local network. Another administrator suggests it could be a naming or group membership issue. Which command-line utility will let you check the workstation's name and group memberships?

   A. netstat

   B. netdom

   C. nbtstat

   D. net

119. The ink-jet printer in your office is producing consistently faded prints. What should you do to resolve the problem?

   A. Replace the paper feed mechanism.

   B. Turn up the color dithering.

   C. Replace the ink cartridge.

   D. Adjust the print head to be closer to the paper.

120. Your HP laser printer has recently started producing poor-quality images. What will your HP representative recommend you periodically do to resolve this issue?

   A. Blow out the printer with compressed air.

   B. Clean out old toner with a toner vacuum.

   C. Stop and restart the printer spooler.

   D. Apply a maintenance kit.

121. You are at a Windows server with a command prompt open. You believe that a user is improperly accessing files on a shared folder named docs. On the server, the D:\ userfiles folder is shared as docs. Which command will immediately stop the sharing of this folder?

    A. `net share D:\userfiles /delete`

    B. `net share D:\userfiles /stop`

    C. `net share docs /delete`

    D. `net share docs /stop`

122. You have sent several print jobs to a networked printer and nothing has printed. You do not have printer administrator access. What can you do to see whether your Windows 7 computer is communicating properly with the printer?

    A. Send the print job in RAW format.

    B. Stop and restart the print spooler.

    C. Print a test page.

    D. Print a blank document from Notepad.

123. You are troubleshooting a laptop with an integrated wireless networking card. The user reports that the laptop will not connect to the Internet. When you look at the network card, the connection and activity lights alternate blinking, in a steady pattern. What is the most likely cause of the problem?

    A. No network connection

    B. Incorrect TCP/IP configuration

    C. Failed network card

    D. Unable to reach a DNS server

124. You are troubleshooting a laptop that has a poor battery life. It will work for only about 30 minutes on a full charge. Which two things should you try first? (Choose two.)

    A. Replace the battery.

    B. Perform a battery calibration.

    C. Drain the battery completely and then charge it fully.

    D. Open the Power Management app and set the laptop to run on low energy mode.

125. The name resolution server on your local network does not appear to be resolving hostnames properly. Which command will allow you to verify the entries on this server?

    A. `dnslookup`

    B. `nslookup`

    C. `namelookup`

    D. `netlookup`

126. You have installed a PCIe RAID controller and want to create a RAID-5 array with three disks. You plug the disks in and boot up the computer. The RAID array is not detected. Where should you go to set up or troubleshoot the RAID array?

   A. Windows Device Manager

   B. Windows Disk Management

   C. The RAID controller's BIOS

   D. The system BIOS

127. A user complains of a loud whining noise coming from her computer. It occurs whenever the computer is on and is relatively constant. Which component is most likely to cause this problem?

   A. RAM

   B. SSD

   C. CPU

   D. PSU

128. You have just upgraded the RAM in a desktop computer. After you power on the computer, no video appears on the screen, and the computer produces a series of three long beeps. What does this indicate?

   A. The system BIOS detected an error in the POST routine.

   B. The system BIOS completed the POST routine normally.

   C. The RAM is faulty.

   D. The motherboard needs to be replaced.

129. You are troubleshooting a computer that will not boot up. When the computer powers on, the power supply fan spins, but the computer does not POST. You look at the motherboard and see that a capacitor has swollen and looks ready to burst. What should you do?

   A. Replace the motherboard.

   B. Replace the power supply.

   C. Replace the capacitor.

   D. Drain the excess electrolyte from the capacitor.

130. A user with an 802.11g network adapter is trying to join your 802.11n network. Her laptop is next to yours, which is connected to the network. However, she is unable to locate the SSID. What is the most likely cause of the problem?

   A. 802.11g is not compatible with 802.11n.

   B. SSID broadcasting is disabled on the wireless access point.

   C. The user is out of range of the wireless access point.

   D. The SSID has been changed.

131. A user just started having intermittent network access problems. While you're troubleshooting, a message pops up saying Windows has detected an IP conflict. Your network has a DHCP server. You open the user's TCP/IP properties and it's configured as shown here. What do you need to do to resolve the issue?

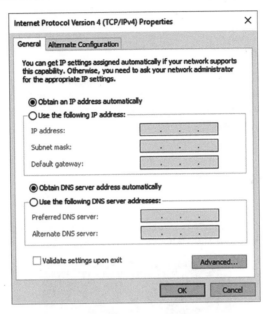

- **A.** On the DHCP server, exclude the user's IP address from the scope.
- **B.** On the user's computer, run `ipconfig /release` and `ipconfig /renew`.
- **C.** On the user's computer, set it to Use The Following IP Address and assign them a different address.
- **D.** Use a packet sniffer to determine the computer with the duplicate address, and change that computer to obtain an IP address automatically.

132. You are troubleshooting a laser printer that keeps producing vertical black lines running down the page. Which component is most likely causing this problem?

- **A.** Fusing assembly
- **B.** Pickup rollers
- **C.** Exit rollers
- **D.** EP drum

133. A user reports that the screen on his tablet computer is very dim and hard to see. He's adjusted it to the maximum brightness and it's still dim. Which component is likely causing the problem?

- **A.** Backlight
- **B.** Converter
- **C.** Display
- **D.** Video card

134. You have been troubleshooting a computer, and you believe the power supply has failed. Which of the following tools can you use to test the integrity of the power supply? (Choose two.)

- **A.** Power supply tester
- **B.** Loopback plugs
- **C.** POST card
- **D.** Multimeter

135. A user is trying to display a presentation on a projector, but nothing appears on the external screen. She tries toggling her LCD cutoff switch, and it doesn't help. Another user had just presented on the projector, and it worked fine. Which component is most likely causing the problem?

- **A.** Backlight
- **B.** Display
- **C.** Video card
- **D.** Inverter

136. A mobile phone user is unable to connect to his wireless headset to make hands-free calls. His iPhone screen is shown here. What is most likely the problem?

- **A.** His wireless headset is turned off.
- **B.** Bluetooth is disabled.
- **C.** AirPlay is disabled.
- **D.** Airplane mode is enabled.

137. A user calls to report that she can't access the Internet or any local resources, including no network shares, printers or her email. The IP address on her computer is 169.254.1.102. Which of the following is most likely to have caused this?

A. Unable to reach a DNS server

B. Unable to reach a DHCP server

C. Unable to reach the default gateway

D. Unable to read the local host configuration file

138. The day after an electrical thunderstorm, you are troubleshooting a computer. After you power it up, it flashes information briefly on the screen and then reboots. It continuously reboots itself after this. Which components are most likely to cause this problem? (Choose two.)

A. Hard drive

B. Power supply

C. Motherboard

D. CPU

139. Within the last five minutes, several users in one part of the building have called in to report that they have lost their network connection. It had been working earlier in the day. What is most likely the cause of the problem?

A. Faulty network card drivers

B. Incorrect TCP/IP configuration

C. Bad network cable

D. Faulty switch

140. All computers on your network are having intermittent Internet connectivity issues. Some websites work, while others do not. If you want to track the problem down by verifying the path to the problematic websites, which tool should you use?

A. ping

B. netstat

C. tracert

D. nslookup

141. A user reports that he cannot see his network shares or email, or even connect to the printer. But local applications are working fine. You ask what has changed since the last access, and he mentions cleaning his desk. What might be the problem?

A. User might not have logged in.

B. Printer, email, and file server could be offline.

C. Network cable may not be connected.

D. New group policy

142. During a meeting, the manager mentions the projector was giving her problems since the start of the meeting. She had tried the projector from a few laptops with no success. Multiple pop-ups were occurring, but it's unknown what the pop-up windows reported. What might be your next step?

- **A.** Open the log for information on failed jobs.
- **B.** Check the light source for failure.
- **C.** Verify that cables were attached.
- **D.** Allow the projector to cool down and try again.

143. A user reports the wireless Internet connection will randomly shut down in the afternoon. You check the Internet router by the window to find it still has power. What is the most likely cause of this problem?

- **A.** Network overloaded
- **B.** Printer queue full
- **C.** Wireless router overheating
- **D.** Workstation requires patching.

144. A technician is troubleshooting a desktop computer that he suspects has a network card problem. He has tested his theory to determine the cause of the problem. According to troubleshooting theory, which step should he take next?

- **A.** Conduct external or internal research based on symptoms.
- **B.** Document findings, actions, and outcomes.
- **C.** Verify full system functionality.
- **D.** Establish a plan of action to resolve the problem and implement the solution.

145. You are troubleshooting a laptop that you suspect was infected with malware. You have established your plan of action and implemented the solution. According to troubleshooting theory, which step should you take next?

- **A.** Test the theory to determine cause.
- **B.** Determine next steps to solve the problem.
- **C.** Verify full system functionality and, if applicable, implement preventive measures.
- **D.** Document findings, actions, and outcomes.

146. A technician is troubleshooting a suspected hard drive issue. He is following the troubleshooting theory. As part of identifying the problem, what should he do?

- **A.** If necessary, conduct external or internal research based on symptoms.
- **B.** Question the user and identify user changes to the computer.
- **C.** Document findings, actions, and outcomes.
- **D.** Determine next steps to resolve the problem.

147. You are troubleshooting a MacBook Pro and have identified the problem. According to troubleshooting theory, which step should you take next?

- **A.** Establish a theory of probable cause.
- **B.** Question the user and identify user changes to the computer.

    C. Test the theory to determine cause.

    D. Establish a plan of action to resolve the problem and implement the solution.

148. You are troubleshooting a Windows Vista desktop computer that appears to be having driver issues. According to troubleshooting theory, when is the appropriate time to perform backups of the system?

    A. After verifying full system functionality and implementing preventive measures

    B. Before making changes

    C. After documenting findings, actions, and outcomes

    D. Before identifying the problem

149. A technician is troubleshooting a Windows 7 laptop that won't boot properly. She has established a theory of probable cause. According to troubleshooting theory, what should she do next?

    A. Identify the problem.

    B. Test the theory to determine cause.

    C. Establish a plan of action to resolve the problem and implement the solution.

    D. Document findings.

150. You are troubleshooting a difficult network connectivity problem. You have tested your theory to determine cause and found that you were wrong. According to troubleshooting theory, you have two choices for next steps. What are they? (Choose two.)

    A. Tell the user that the problem has been fixed, and document it as such.

    B. Verify full system functionality and document findings, actions, and outcomes.

    C. Escalate the issue.

    D. Establish a new theory of probable cause.

151. You are about to begin troubleshooting a laptop with no display. According to troubleshooting theory, before you begin troubleshooting, what should you always consider?

    A. The user's feelings

    B. The cost associated with hardware replacement

    C. The implications of delivering bad news to management

    D. The corporate policies, procedures, and impacts before implementing changes

152. You are troubleshooting a laptop with a video problem. According to troubleshooting theory, there are two immediate steps you can take after testing the theory to determine cause. What are those two steps? (Choose two.)

    A. Determine next steps to resolve the problem.

    B. If necessary, conduct external or internal research based on symptoms.

    C. Question the user and identify user changes to the computer.

    D. Establish a new theory or escalate the problem.

153. You are troubleshooting a desktop computer that is exhibiting erratic behavior. As part of establishing a theory of probable cause, what step should you take, as part of the troubleshooting process?

   A. Question the user and identify user changes to the computer.

   B. Determine next steps to resolve the problem.

   C. Establish a plan of action to resolve the problem.

   D. If necessary, conduct external or internal research based on symptoms.

154. You need to troubleshoot a laptop computer that is having video problems. According to troubleshooting theory, what is the first step you should take?

   A. Establish a theory of probable cause.

   B. Establish a plan of action to resolve the problem and implement the solution.

   C. Identify the problem.

   D. Conduct external or internal research based on symptoms.

155. You get a service ticket that a user is having to constantly reset the system's time. What part of the system is likely at fault?

   A. RAM

   B. CPU

   C. Power

   D. BIOS

156. After a junior analyst rebuilt a system, the system now attempts to boot to incorrect device. What would be at fault in his scenario?

   A. RAM

   B. CPU

   C. Power

   D. Motherboard

157. A user reports that their system experiences intermittent device failure, with no particular pattern or predictable device. What might be the area causing the problem?

   A. CPU

   B. Power

   C. RAM

   D. Hard drive

158. A user calls you and tells you that his system's indicator lights are blinking, with no bootup. Additionally, he hears that fans running, but no power to other devices. What might be the problem? (Choose two)

   A. CPU

   B. RAM

C. BIOS

D. Power

159. What are some of the symptoms that point to when a hard drive begins to fail? (Choose two)

   A. System time losing an hour a week.

   B. Read/write failure

   C. OS not found

   D. Internet access is intermittent

160. The server indicates that the RAID array is in a degraded state, with no "spare" disk available. You learn that a system administrator has recently added a newer disk to the RAID array. Which of the following causes would cause this to happen?

   A. Failed cabling

   B. Incompatible RAID type

   C. Drive not recognized

   D. Overheating

161. The CEO brings you into the board room, pointing at the dark screen on the wall. The CEO's laptop display is fine. You try someone else's laptop and the projector displays onto the wall. What might be the issue?

   A. Projector has failed

   B. Video source has failed

   C. The laptop's RAID array has failed

   D. The CEO's laptop display has failed

162. The CEO brings you into the board room again, pointing to the CFO's laptop. The CFO's laptop display is dark and she mentions it recently turned off. As you pick up the laptop, you realize the laptop has been by the window sill. What symptom caused the CFO's laptop to stop displaying?

   A. The laptop is sticky

   B. No connectivity

   C. Read/write failure

   D. Laptop experienced an overheat shutdown

163. A user complains that apps are not loading on her mobile device. How would you proceed to troubleshoot the problem?

   A. Try unloading existing apps to free up memory

   B. Load the same application on your mobile device

   C. Check the mobile device's available storage

   D. Change the mobile device's service provider

Exam 220-1002

Chapter 6

Operating Systems

THE FOLLOWING COMPTIA A+ EXAM 220-1002 TOPICS ARE COVERED IN THIS CHAPTER:

✓ **1.1 Compare and contrast common operating system types and their purposes.**

- 32-bit vs. 64-bit
    - RAM limitations
    - Software compatibility
- Workstation operating systems
    - Microsoft Windows
    - Apple Macintosh OS
    - Linux
- Cell phone/tablet operating systems
    - Microsoft Windows
    - Android
    - iOS
    - Chrome OS
- Vendor-specific limitations
    - End-of-life
    - Update limitations
- Compatibility concerns between operating systems

✓ **1.2 Compare and contrast features of Microsoft Windows versions.**

- Windows 7
- Windows 8
- Windows 8.1
- Windows 10

- Corporate vs. personal needs
    - Domain access
    - Bitlocker
    - Media center
    - Branchcache
    - EFS
- Desktop styles/user interface

✓ **1.3 Summarize general OS installation considerations and upgrade methods.**

- Boot methods
    - USB
    - CD-ROM
    - DVD
    - PXE
    - Solid state/flash drives
    - Netboot
    - External/hot-swappable drive
    - Internal hard drive (partition)
- Type of installations
    - Unattended installation
    - In-place upgrade
    - Clean install
    - Repair installation
    - Multiboot
    - Remote network installation
    - Image deployment
    - Recovery partition
    - Refresh/restore
- Partitioning
    - Dynamic
    - Basic

- Primary
- Extended
- Logical
- GPT
- File system types/formatting
  - ExFAT
  - FAT32
  - NTFS
  - CDFS
  - NFS
  - ext3, ext4
  - HFS
  - Swap partition
  - Quick format vs. full format
- Load alternate third-party drivers when necessary.
- Workgroup vs. Domain setup
- Time/date/region/language settings
- Driver installation, software, and Windows updates
- Factory recovery partition
- Properly formatted boot drive with the correct partitions/format
- Prerequisites/hardware compatibility
- Application compatibility
- OS compatibility/upgrade path

✓ **1.4   Given a scenario, use appropriate Microsoft command-line tools.**

- Navigation
  - dir
  - cd
  - ..
- ipconfig

- ping
- tracert
- netstat
- nslookup
- shutdown
- dism
- sfc
- chkdsk
- diskpart
- taskkill
- gpupdate
- gpresult
- format
- copy
- xcopy
- robocopy
- net use
- net user
- [command name] /?
- Commands available with standard privileges vs. administrative privileges

✓ **1.5 Given a scenario, use Microsoft operating system features and tools.**

- Administrative
  - Computer Management
  - Device Manager
  - Local Users and Groups
  - Local Security Policy
  - Performance Monitor
  - Services
  - System Configuration

- Task Scheduler
- Component Services
- Data Sources
- Print Management
- Windows Memory Diagnostics
- Windows Firewall
- Advanced Security
- Event Viewer
- User Account Management
- MSConfig
  - General
  - Boot
  - Services
  - Startup
  - Tools
- Task Manager
  - Applications
  - Processes
  - Performance
  - Networking
  - Users
- Disk Management
  - Drive status
  - Mounting
  - Initializing
  - Extending partitions
  - Splitting partitions
  - Shrink partitions
  - Assigning/changing drive letters
  - Adding drives

- Adding arrays
- Storage spaces
- System utilities
  - Regedit
  - Command
  - Services.msc
  - MMC
  - MSTSC
  - Notepad
  - Explorer
  - Msinfo32
  - DxDiag
  - Disk Defragmenter
  - System Restore
  - Windows Update

✓ **1.6   Given a scenario, use Microsoft Windows Control Panel utilities.**

- Internet Options
  - Connections
  - Security
  - General
  - Privacy
  - Programs
  - Advanced
- Display/Display Settings
  - Resolution
  - Color depth
  - Refresh rate
- User Accounts
- Folder Options
  - View hidden files.
  - Hide extensions.

- General options
- View options
- System
  - Performance (virtual memory)
  - Remote settings
  - System protection
- Windows Firewall
- Power Options
  - Hibernate
  - Power plans
  - Sleep/suspend
  - Standby
- Credential Manager
- Programs and features
- HomeGroup
- Devices and Printers
- Sound
- Troubleshooting
- Network and Sharing Center
- Device Manager
- Bitlocker
- Sync Center

✓ **1.7 Summarize application installation and configuration concepts.**

- System requirements
  - Drive space
  - RAM
- OS requirements
  - Compatibility

- Methods of installation and deployment
    - Local (CD/USB)
    - Network-based
- Local user permissions
    - Folder/file access for installation
- Security considerations
    - Impact to device
    - Impact to network

✓ **1.8   Given a scenario, configure Microsoft Windows networking on a client/desktop.**

- HomeGroup vs. Workgroup
- Domain setup
- Network shares/administrative shares/mapping drives
- Printer sharing vs. network printer mapping
- Establish networking connections.
    - VPN
    - Dial-ups
    - Wireless
    - Wired
    - WWAN (Cellular)
- Proxy settings
- Remote Desktop Connection
- Remote Assistance
- Home vs. Work vs. Public network settings
- Firewall settings
    - Exceptions
    - Configuration
    - Enabling/disabling Windows Firewall
- Configuring an alternative IP address in Windows
    - IP addressing
    - Subnet mask

- DNS
- Gateway
- Network card properties
  - Half duplex/full duplex/auto
  - Speed
  - Wake-on-LAN
  - QoS
  - BIOS (on-board NIC)

✓ **1.9 Given a scenario, use features and tools of the Mac OS and Linux client/desktop operating systems.**

- Best practices
  - Scheduled backups
  - Scheduled disk maintenance
  - System updates/App Store
  - Patch management
  - Driver/firmware updates
  - Antivirus/Anti-malware updates
- Tools
  - Backup/Time Machine
  - Restore/Snapshot
  - Image recovery
  - Disk maintenance utilities
  - Shell/Terminal
  - Screen sharing
  - Force Quit
- Features
  - Multiple desktops/Mission Control
  - KeyChain
  - SpotLight
  - iCloud

- Gestures .
- Finder
- Remote Disc
- Dock
- Boot Camp
- Basic Linux commands
  - ls
  - grep
  - cd
  - shutdown
  - pwd vs. passwd
  - mv
  - cp
  - rm
  - chmod
  - chown
  - iwconfig/ifconfig
  - ps
  - su/sudo
  - apt-get
  - vi
  - dd
  - kill

1. You want to create a backup of your Windows 8.1 system configuration so you can restore it in the event of a system crash. What should you create?

    A. Restore point

    B. System restore

    C. Windows backup

    D. Shadow copy

2. You have a Windows 7 Professional computer with multiple printers installed. Which of the following administrative tools allows you to manage multiple print servers and printers from a single interface?

    A. Printers app in Control Panel

    B. Print Management

    C. Device Manager

    D. Services

3. Which of the following file systems was originally designed by Apple?

    A. NTFS

    B. HFS

    C. ext4

    D. NFS

4. You are talking with a vendor about configuration changes you need to make to several Windows 8 workstations. You decide you should take notes so you do not forget the instructions. What application comes with Windows and allows you to create and edit basic text documents?

    A. Word

    B. Notepad

    C. WordPad

    D. Command

5. You are working on a Windows 7 workstation and need to perform a management task. However, you can't remember the name of the utility that you need to use. Which management tool provides a list of other useful Windows management tools for you and lets you launch them by clicking their name?

    A. `MSCONFIG.EXE`

    B. `EVENTVWR.EXE`

    C. `TASKMGR.EXE`

    D. `CONTROL.EXE`

6. Which feature of Windows 7 allows all users (not just administrators) to encrypt files on an NTFS volume, even one file at a time, to increase data security?

    A. BitLocker

    B. EFS

    C. Shadow Drive

    D. OneDrive

7. You have a Windows 7 Professional computer set up in a workgroup, and you need to perform some routine management tasks on it. Which of the following can you configure through the Computer Management MMC? (Choose two.)

    A. Hard drives

    B. File permissions

    C. Windows Firewall

    D. Shared folders

8. You are at a Windows Vista command prompt. What command can you type to close the command prompt window?

    A. `quit`

    B. `exit`

    C. `close`

    D. `/x`

9. You are looking for general information about a Windows workstation's hardware resources. Which command do you need to type into the Run box to display the utility shown here?

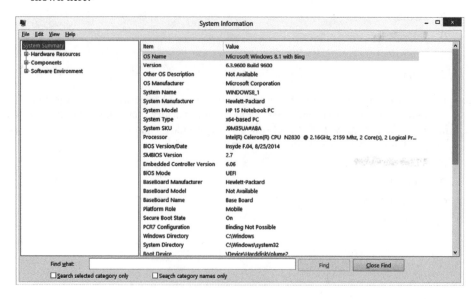

A. DXDIAG

B. COMPMGMT

C. MSINFO32

D. MMC

10. Your manager has asked you to investigate the possibility of installing a database on a Windows 8.1 computer. Which Windows administrative tool would you use to view the installed database drivers on the computer?

    A. Local Security Policy

    B. Component Services

    C. Device Manager

    D. Data Sources

11. You have recently made some configuration changes to a Windows 8.1 workstation, and now it's behaving erratically. You reboot the computer and enter the Windows Recovery Environment. What should you do to roll back those recent changes?

    A. Recover

    B. Refresh

    C. Reset

    D. Restore

12. One of your technicians needs to use the Task Manager utility. What are two ways she can open Task Manager? (Choose two.)

    A. Press Ctrl+Alt+Delete and then click Task Manager.

    B. Press Ctrl+Shift+T.

    C. Press Ctrl+Alt+T.

    D. Press Ctrl+Shift+Esc.

13. You are at a Windows 7 workstation command prompt. You want to know what the enforced set of Group and Local Policy settings are for a specific user. Which command can you use to understand this?

    A. gpedit

    B. gprefresh

    C. gpresult

    D. gpupdate

14. You have a Windows 7 workstation and need to configure programs to load upon startup. Which management tool should you use to do this?

    A. Task Scheduler

    B. System Configuration

    C. Computer Management

    D. Programs and Applications

15. You have chosen to install Windows 8 Pro on a workstation that is currently running Windows 7 Professional. You choose a Custom installation but do not format the hard drive. Which of the following statements is true regarding Windows 7 Professional?

- **A.** It is permanently removed from the hard drive.
- **B.** Its settings are migrated to Windows 8, and it is removed from the hard drive.
- **C.** It remains available as a dual-boot option for 28 days and then is removed from the hard drive.
- **D.** Its files are placed in a folder named `Windows.old` and retained for 28 days and then are removed from the hard drive.

16. Your manager has asked you to prepare for an unattended installation of 50 Windows 7 workstations, each with the same hardware. What type of installation will be most efficient for this task?

- **A.** Clean
- **B.** Upgrade
- **C.** Custom
- **D.** Image deployment

17. Which Windows 8 utility lets you view items in Category view or Classic view?

- **A.** Administrative Tools
- **B.** System Utilities
- **C.** Disk Management
- **D.** Control Panel

18. Which feature of Windows 8 allows you to write script files based on the Microsoft .NET programming framework?

- **A.** OneDrive
- **B.** Event Viewer
- **C.** PowerShell
- **D.** Task Scheduler

19. A user wants to ensure that his hard drive is encrypted for maximum data security. What are two commands you can have the user type into the Run box to see whether the BitLocker Drive Encryption Service is enabled? (Choose two.)

- **A.** `SERVICES.MSC`
- **B.** `PERFMON.EXE`
- **C.** `COMPMGMT.MSC`
- **D.** `BLDES.MSC`

20. You have a computer running Windows 7 Home Premium 64-bit and you want to upgrade to Windows 7 Ultimate 64-bit. What should you run to determine whether your computer can support the new operating system?

   A. Hardware Compatibility List

   B. Windows Upgrade Assistant

   C. Windows Upgrade Advisor

   D. Windows Easy Transfer

21. What feature of Windows allows you to place icons of your favorite apps on the Start menu, Windows Desktop, or Taskbar to get to them quickly?

   A. Sticking

   B. Pinning

   C. Posting

   D. Easy launch

22. You are at a Windows 7 command prompt. There is a directory named `d:\files` that you want to delete. It currently has six subdirectories and dozens of files in it. Which command should you use to delete `d:\files`?

   A. `del d:\files /s`

   B. `del d:\files /q`

   C. `rd d:\files /s`

   D. `rd d:\files /q`

23. Which Windows feature, introduced with Vista, allows you to place customizable programs on the Windows Desktop, such as a clock or the weather?

   A. Charms

   B. Widgets

   C. Gadgets

   D. Sidebar

24. You have just upgraded a Windows XP Home computer to Windows Vista Home Basic. A few days after the upgrade is complete, you reboot the computer and it tells you that you can use Windows Vista for only 25 more days. What must you do to remove this message?

   A. Purchase a full version of Windows Vista Home Basic.

   B. Upgrade to Windows Vista Home Premium.

   C. Register Windows Vista Home Basic.

   D. Activate Windows Vista Home Basic.

25. Which of the following are true statements about Windows To Go (WTG)? (Choose two.)

A. It does not support BitLocker.

B. It requires a USB 3.0 drive.

C. It does not support OS upgrades.

D. ~~It is available in Windows 7 and Windows 8/8.1.~~

26. What feature of Windows 7 provides anti-spyware protection?

A. Windows Defender

B. Windows Firewall

C. Windows Protector

D. Windows Action Center

27. You are at a Windows 8.1 command prompt, and the directory you are in has a Windows cabinet file in it. Which command do you use if you want to get a file out of that cabinet file?

A. extract

B. expand

C. unzip

D. excab

28. You believe that someone is trying to hack into a Windows 8.1 workstation using brute-force methods to guess the password. To deter the attacker, you want to lock out the account if there are five failed login attempts. Which management tool should you use to configure this?

A. SECPOL.MSC

B. COMPMGMT.MSC

C. SECMON.EXE

D. MSRA.EXE

29. Which feature available in Windows Vista and Windows 7 is used to create a snapshot of a file, even when the file is in use, for retrieval if the original file is accidentally deleted or overwritten?

A. Shadow Copy

B. Windows Backup

C. OneDrive

D. Easy Transfer

30. Sitting at a Windows 8.1 command prompt, you want to delete the read-only `doc.txt` file in the directory you are in. You do not want Windows to ask you for permission to delete the file. What is the syntax to delete the file?

    A. `del doc.txt /y /r`

    B. `del doc.txt /y /f`

    C. `del doc.txt /q /r`

    D. `del doc.txt /q /f`

31. You are preparing to make major configuration changes to a Windows 8.1 workstation. Before you begin, which command can you run to ensure that there is a current restore point for the workstation?

    A. `MSRA.EXE`

    B. `RSTRUI.EXE`

    C. `MSTSC.EXE`

    D. `COMPMGMT.MSC`

32. You need to check the integrity of key Windows system files on the `C:` drive, which are hidden from view by default. Which tool can you use to allow you to view hidden files?

    A. Computer Management

    B. System Configuration

    C. Local Security Policy

    D. Windows Explorer

33. Which of the following features were first featured in a Microsoft operating system with Windows 8? (Choose two.)

    A. Pinning

    B. Windows Store

    C. PowerShell

    D. Charms

34. You are creating a network for a small office with Windows 7 and Windows 8/8.1 workstations. They do not want centralized security, but they want it to be easy to share printers and files, including libraries. What type of network setup should you recommend?

    A. Workgroup

    B. HomeGroup

    C. Distributed

    D. Domain

35. A client wants to install a new video game, and he's read that the game requires DirectX 11. He's afraid that his Windows 8.1 computer doesn't support this version; which command should you tell him to run to see whether he's correct?

   A. MSTSC

   B. MSINFO32

   C. MMC

   D. DXDIAG

36. You need to install a copy of Windows 7 onto a PC with no current operating system. Which boot methods are acceptable to begin this installation? (Choose all that apply.)

   A. PXE

   B. CD-ROM

   C. USB

   D. Internal hard drive

   E. DVD

37. You are working on a Windows 8.1 workstation and want to view statistics for how busy the processor is and how much memory is in use. Which two of the following tools will easily allow you to do this? (Choose two.)

   A. CONTROL.EXE SYSTEM

   B. COMPMGMT.MSC

   C. SERVICES.MSC

   D. PERFMON.EXE

38. You are planning to install Windows 7 on several dozen computers that will join an existing Windows Server domain. What is the least powerful edition of Windows 7 you can install on these client computers?

   A. Windows 7 Enterprise

   B. Windows 7 Starter

   C. Windows 7 Professional

   D. Windows 7 Home Premium

39. What disk partition's usage is directly affected by how much RAM memory is installed in the system?

   A. The swap partition

   B. The root partition

   C. The third extended partition

   D. The /home partition

40. You have several Windows 7 and Windows 8.1 workstations on your network. Before any operating system patches get applied to your workstations, you want to review them. Which tool do you configure this setting in?

   A. Windows Patch Management

   B. Windows Update

   C. Computer Management

   D. System Configuration

41. You have recently connected your Windows 7 workstation to a cloud storage service. You want to ensure that the cloud-based service synchronizes with your Windows Desktop every morning at 2:30 a.m. Which Windows management utility should you use to enable this?

   A. Task Scheduler

   B. Event Viewer

   C. Component Services

   D. Data Sources

42. You are working on a Windows workstation and do not know what edition of Windows it is running. Which command can you type in the search box to determine the edition and display the information shown here?

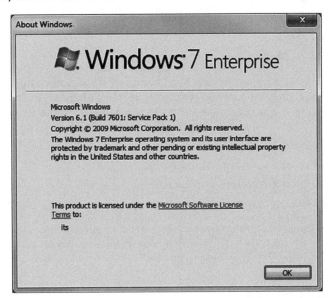

   A. wined

   B. winspec

   C. wininfo

   D. winver

43. You are installing Windows 7 Enterprise on a workstation. You want to format the hard drive with a file system that is also supported by Linux. Which file system should you choose?

   A. NTFS

   B. NFS

   C. ext3

   D. ext4

44. A user's Windows 8.1 workstation is getting "out of memory" errors. Upgrading the physical RAM is not an option, so you want to increase the amount of virtual memory available. Where do you do this?

   A. Control Panel ➤ Computer Management ➤ Advanced System Settings ➤ Performance

   B. Control Panel ➤ Memory ➤ Advanced System Settings ➤ Performance

   C. Control Panel ➤ Device Manager ➤ Advanced System Settings ➤ Performance

   D. Control Panel ➤ System ➤ Advanced System Settings ➤ Performance

45. Which Windows 8 feature provides an area for users to tap or click tiles to open applications, websites, files, and other items?

   A. Start screen

   B. App center

   C. Windows Store

   D. Windows Desktop

46. Your manager has a laptop running Windows 8.1. She wants to configure the laptop so that when she is on battery power, the display shuts off after five minutes of inactivity. When the laptop is plugged in, she wants the display to stay active for up to 45 minutes of inactivity. Where should she configure these settings?

   A. Control Panel ➤ Power Options

   B. Control Panel ➤ Computer Management

   C. Control Panel ➤ Performance Monitor

   D. Control Panel ➤ System Configuration

47. You have a Windows 7 Professional workstation configured in a workgroup. You want to configure the workstation to require users to reset their passwords every 90 days. Which management utility should you use to do this?

   A. Users and Groups

   B. System Configuration

   C. Local Security Policy

   D. Advanced Security

48. A Windows 7 workstation on your network has corrupted key operating system files. What is the most efficient way to repair this installation without losing the user's files?

   A. Boot to the Windows 7 DVD and perform a clean install.

   B. Boot to the network and perform a remote network installation.

   C. Boot into the Windows RE and repair the installation.

   D. Boot to the recovery partition and reset Windows 7.

49. The hard drive performance on your Windows 7 workstation has deteriorated over time. To attempt to help performance, you want to ensure that files on the hard drive are written in contiguous blocks. Which administrative tool should you use to make this happen?

   A. Disk Management

   B. Disk Defragmenter

   C. Disk Optimizer

   D. Device Manager

50. A member of your sales team wants to work from a remote location while traveling. The location he is going to does not have high-speed Internet, and he will be connecting to the network using a modem. When Windows Vista asks what type of networking connection he wants to establish, what should he choose?

   A. WWAN

   B. Wired

   C. Wireless

   D. Dial-up

51. What is the name of the user interface introduced with Windows 8?

   A. Aero

   B. Metro

   C. WinPE

   D. Windows Explorer

52. One of your workstations is running Windows 7 and has been occasionally crashing. You believe it's an OS issue and not a hardware issue. You decide to upgrade the computer to Windows 8.1; however, you want to avoid continuing to have errors if they were software related. What type of installation should you perform?

   A. Upgrade

   B. Unattended

   C. Migration

   D. Clean

53. You have a Windows 7 command prompt open. You are in the D:\users directory and want to copy all 20 of the files with a .doc extension into the D:\files directory. Which of the following statements is true?

    A. You need to copy the files one at a time.

    B. You can use the command copy *.doc d:\files.

    C. You can use the command copy all.doc d:\files.

    D. You can use the command copy .doc d:\files.

54. After you install Windows 8.1, you notice that an application called Windows Firewall is enabled. What is Windows Firewall designed to help protect your computer against?

    A. Viruses and worms

    B. Spyware

    C. Fires

    D. Malicious network traffic

55. A Windows Vista user uses a lot of memory-intensive applications and has been recently getting "out of memory" error messages. Her computer has 16 GB RAM and can't be upgraded any further. You want to ensure that her system has ample virtual memory as well; what is the minimum recommended size that her swap file should be?

    A. 8 GB

    B. 16 GB

    C. 24 GB

    D. 48 GB

56. You are going to install a Windows 8.1 workstation from an image located on a server. What does the workstation need to support to enable this installation?

    A. Netboot

    B. Unattended installation

    C. PXE boot

    D. USB boot

57. The ability to have a Windows Taskbar appear on multiple monitors was introduced with what version of Windows?

    A. Windows 8

    B. Windows 7

    C. Windows Vista

    D. Windows 8.1

58. You have chosen to install Windows 8 Pro on a workstation that is currently running Windows 7 Professional. You choose a Custom installation and format the hard drive. What type of installation are you performing?

    A. Migration

    B. Clean

    C. Upgrade

    D. Incremental

59. You are at a Windows 8 command prompt. Which command allows you to copy files and directories, copy NTFS permissions, and mirror a directory tree?

    A. copy

    B. xcopy

    C. robocopy

    D. copyall

60. You need to install Windows 7 onto several client computers that currently have no OS. You have created a PXE server and will perform the installation over the network. What is required to create the PXE environment?

    A. WinPE

    B. WinRE

    C. A flash drive

    D. Netboot

61. A user has poor eyesight and is having trouble reading the small fonts on his monitor, including Windows Desktop icons. What should you do to make everything on the Windows Desktop appear larger?

    A. Open Control Panel ➤ Appearance and Personalization and decrease the resolution.

    B. Open Control Panel ➤ Appearance and Personalization and increase the resolution.

    C. Open Control Panel ➤ Appearance and Personalization and decrease the refresh rate.

    D. Open Control Panel ➤ Appearance and Personalization and increase the refresh rate.

62. You are installing a Windows Vista workstation. When you're joining the network, it asks for the location of your computer. The choices are Home, Work, and Public. Which of the following statements about these choices is true?

    A. Home and Work have network discovery turned on, but Home has Windows Firewall turned off.

    B. Home has network discovery turned on and Windows Firewall turned off.

    C. Home and Work have network discovery turned on but Windows Firewall turned off.

    D. Home and Work have network discovery turned on.

63. A Windows 7 computer in your office is being used as a file server by the sales team. There is a folder on the D: drive named DailyReports where the sales team files their reports. The D: drive is now full. What is the easiest way to provide more capacity and not disrupt access to the folder?

A. Mount a new hard drive as a subfolder in DailyReports.

B. Extend the D: partition so it has more room.

C. Add another hard drive and create an array for the D: drive.

D. Split half of the data from the D: partition into a different partition.

64. A user's Windows 7 workstation is having memory issues. You want to look and find the user's virtual memory file to see how large it is and whether it has enough space on the hard drive. What is the name of the file you are looking for?

A. vmm32.sysVMM32.SYS

B. swapfile.sysSWAPFILE.SYS

C. pagefile.sysPAGEFILE.SYS

D. vmemory.sysVMEMORY.SYS

65. You are at a Windows Vista command prompt. You need to create a directory named files on the D: drive. What is the proper command and syntax to do this?

A. cd d:\files

B. cd files d:\

C. md d:\files

D. md files d:\

66. A user's Windows 7 workstation seems to be using an excessive amount of memory. Which management tool can you use to identify the application that is using the most memory?

A. Performance Monitor

B. Computer Management

C. Windows Memory Diagnostics

D. Task Manager

67. What command-line tool allows you to view the network configuration on a Windows system?

A. ipconfig

B. ifconfig

C. tracert

D. traceroute

68. A Windows 8 workstation appears to have an application that's locked up, but the keyboard is still responsive. Which system tool can you use to kill the application?

    A. Performance Monitor

    B. Task Manager

    C. Computer Management

    D. MSCONFIG

69. Which of the following file systems was not designed for hard drives but rather for optical media?

    A. CDFS

    B. ExFAT

    C. FAT32

    D. NFS

70. A junior technician is trying to troubleshoot a Windows 8.1 workstation, and he is having some problems. You go to help, and when you get there, he has opened the utility you see here. Which utility is he running?

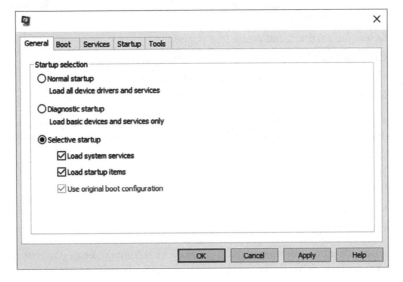

    A. TASKMGR.EXE

    B. CONTROL.EXE

    C. MSCONFIG.EXE

    D. MSINFO32.EXE

71. You are trying to troubleshoot a remote Windows 7 workstation and want to use Remote Assistance. However, the workstation will not allow you to connect. Where do you tell the user to go to enable Remote Assistance connections to her computer?

   A. Computer Management ➢ Remote

   B. Advanced Security ➢ Remote

   C. System Properties ➢ Remote

   D. Network and Sharing Center ➢ Remote

72. You need to establish a connection to a remote Windows Desktop. Which Windows system utility allows you to set up and configure this type of connection from the command line or through a graphical interface?

   A. MMC

   B. MSTSC

   C. RDPCON

   D. DXDIAG

73. Your Windows 7 workstation has one physical hard drive with one partition that takes up the entire drive. You want to create a second partition on the drive. What is the easiest way to accomplish this?

   A. Delete the partition and create two partitions.

   B. Create a secondary partition within the existing partition.

   C. Shrink the partition and create a second one in the empty space.

   D. Change the partition into a split partition.

74. You have a Windows 7 workstation, and you are planning system configuration changes. Which utility allows you to make a backup of your system configuration before making these changes?

   A. System Restore

   B. Windows Backup

   C. BitLocker

   D. OneDrive

75. You are at a Windows 8.1 command prompt. Which command can you type to see a list of system commands available to you?

   A. `dir`

   B. `list`

   C. `help`

   D. `cmd`

76. A Windows 7 workstation will not boot properly. Upon boot, you receive the error message, "Boot sector not found." You boot to the Windows installation CD and enter the Windows Recovery Environment. Which command should you use to fix this error?

A. `bootrec.exe /scanos`

B. `bootrec.exe /rebuildbcd`

C. `bootrec.exe /fixmbr`

D. `bootrec.exe /fixboot`

77. You need to format a hard drive so you can install Windows 7 on it. Which file system will you not be able to choose?

A. NFS

B. FAT32

C. ext4

D. NTFS

78. Which feature of Windows Vista, Windows 7, and Windows 8/8.1 allows you to use a removable drive as temporary cache space to speed up the system?

A. OneDrive

B. ReadyBoost

C. Shadow Copy

D. Windows Easy Transfer

79. You have purchased a dozen Windows 8.1 workstations from a computer vendor. The vendor has set aside space on the hard drive to hold an extra copy of key operating system files. What is this space called?

A. Restore partition

B. Recovery partition

C. Reinstallation partition

D. System image

80. You want to configure a Windows 8.1 workstation to boot from an external hard drive. Which of the following must be true for that to happen? (Choose two.)

A. The drive must be USB.

B. The computer's BIOS must support it.

C. BitLocker needs to be enabled.

D. The external drive must be listed in the BIOS boot order.

81. Which version of Windows was the first to feature side-by-side apps, where two applications can be snapped to the side of a widescreen display, each taking up half of the screen?

A. Windows Vista

B. Windows 7

C. Windows 8

D. Windows 8.1

82. The data storage partition on your Windows 7 workstation is nearly out of room. It's configured as a basic volume. What needs to be true for you to extend this partition? (Choose two.)

   A. You need to convert it to a dynamic volume.

   B. It must be formatted with NTFS.

   C. It must be extended into contiguous free space.

   D. It must be a primary partition.

83. You have a Windows 7 workstation configured in a workgroup. Before you reboot your computer to apply a change, you want to be sure that no one else is remotely connected to your workstation. Which administrative tool can you use to do this?

   A. Users and Groups

   B. Performance Monitor

   C. Control Panel ➤ Networking

   D. Task Manager

84. You are installing a new network for a small office. They are concerned about security and therefore want it managed by one computer. When installing the Windows computers, what type of network setup will you choose?

   A. Workgroup

   B. HomeGroup

   C. Distributed

   D. Domain

85. You are at a Windows 7 command prompt. A process has frozen and is making the computer slow to respond. What is the syntax used to find the process and how much CPU time it has used?

   A. tasklist /s

   B. tasklist /v

   C. tasklist /svc

   D. tasklist /c

86. You are migrating user files and applications for a few user accounts from Windows Vista to Windows 7. Which tool does Microsoft recommend you use to make this transfer?

   A. User State Migration Tool (USMT)

   B. Windows Easy Transfer (WET)

   C. Windows Migration Tool (WMT)

   D. User Accounts in Control Panel

87. You are at a Windows 8.1 command prompt, in the D:\users\jdoe\files directory. What command can you use to get to the D:\ directory?

A. cd\

B. cd..

C. cd/

D. cd:\

88. You have a Windows 7 workstation that you suspect has faulty memory. Which Microsoft tool should you use to check it?

A. Device Manager

B. Windows Memory Diagnostics

C. Task Scheduler

D. Computer Management

89. You have several important files on your computer that you can't afford to lose. Which Windows utility should you run to ensure that you have a replica of these files?

A. System Restore

B. Disk Management

C. Backup

D. Remote Desktop

90. You are at a Windows 8.1 command prompt. A remote Windows 7 workstation named Wanda is misbehaving and needs to be shut down and rebooted. What is the proper syntax to shut down this remote system?

A. shutdown /r /m \\wanda

B. shutdown /s /m \\wanda

C. shutdown /r /c \\wanda

D. shutdown /s /c \\wanda

91. You are preparing to install Windows 8.1 on a computer with a solid-state drive (SSD). What does Microsoft recommend you run to optimize performance on this drive?

A. WinSAT.exe formal

B. WinSAT.exe prepop

C. WinSAT.exe moobe

D. WinSAT.exe media

92. You are looking at a Windows 7 workstation's hard drives using the Disk Management utility. You want to find the partition that the computer boots from. What must the partition be marked?

A. Basic

B. Primary

C. Active

D. Bootable

93. You are at a Windows 10 command prompt. You believe that some of the Windows system files are corrupt. Which command should you use to scan and repair problematic system files?

    A. `sfc /scanfile`

    B. `sfc /scannow`

    C. `sfc /verifyfile`

    D. `sfc /verifyonly`

94. You have just configured an alternative IP address on a Windows 8.1 workstation. What is the purpose of configuring this alternative address?

    A. To allow the workstation to participate on multiple networks

    B. To allow the workstation to have an IPv4 and IPv6 address at the same time

    C. To provide an alternate address if the first choice is not available

    D. To mask the IP address and hide the workstation's identity

95. You are at a Windows command prompt. You remember the name of the command-line tool that you want to run, but you don't remember the switch you need to use with it. What switch can you use to show the context and switches used for that command? (Choose two.)

    A. `/help`

    B. `/?`

    C. `/*`

    D. `/#`

96. Which Windows feature, introduced with Vista, is designed to prevent unintentional or unauthorized changes to the computer by prompting for permission to continue?

    A. BitLocker

    B. PowerShell

    C. Security Center

    D. User Account Control

97. You are working at a Windows 7 command prompt. Which of the following commands require administrative privileges to run? (Choose two.)

    A. `chkdsk`

    B. `diskpart`

    C. `tasklist`

    D. `sfc`

98. A user reports that her Windows 8.1 workstation seems to be having issues with the operating system. You want to repair the installation but allow her to keep her personal files and apps. Which option should you choose in the Windows Recovery Environment?

  A. Reset

  B. Restore

  C. Recover

  D. Refresh

99. Users are sending jobs to a printer managed by a Windows 7 computer, but the jobs are not printing. The printer is online and connected. From your A+ test preparation, you know that you are supposed to stop and restart the print spooler. Where can you do this?

  A. Control Panel ➤ System

  B. Computer Management ➤ Device Manager

  C. Computer Management ➤ Services

  D. Control Panel ➤ Printers and Scanners

100. You are at a Windows 8 workstation and have a command prompt open. Which of the following commands is used to refresh Group Policy settings and force their changes to take effect?

  A. gpedit

  B. gpresult

  C. gprefresh

  D. gpupdate

101. You are training new technicians on network sharing. How do you tell them to identify administrative shares?

  A. They all start with the word admin.

  B. They all end with a dollar sign ($).

  C. They all end with an at symbol (@).

  D. They all end with a percent sign (%).

102. Which of the following describes the functionality of compatibility mode in Windows 7?

  A. It allows you to run 64-bit applications within a 32-bit operating system.

  B. It allows you to run 32-bit applications within a 32-bit operating system.

  C. It allows you to run programs designed for a different operating system than Windows.

  D. It allows you to configure programs to believe they are running on an older version of Windows.

103. You would like to configure a test workstation to be able to boot to Windows Vista, Windows 7, and Windows 8.1. Which of the following statements is true regarding installation of these operating systems?

   A. You can't install all three operating systems on one workstation.

   B. You should install the oldest operating system first and work toward the newest.

   C. You should install the newest operating system first and work toward the oldest.

   D. The order of operating system installation does not matter in this situation.

104. You are installing a Windows 8.1 client in a Windows Server 2012 R2 domain. The client computer will need to be able to implement file and share permissions. Which Windows-native file system best meets your needs?

   A. FAT32

   B. NFS

   C. NTFS

   D. ext4

105. You need the ability to remotely boot up computers on the network by sending a signal to their network cards. Which technology do you need to ensure that the network cards support?

   A. Remote Boot

   B. Network Boot

   C. Wake-on-LAN

   D. NetBIOS

106. You are at a Windows 7 command prompt, and you need to kill the process named winword.exe. What is the right context to kill this process?

   A. taskkill /IM winword.exe

   B. taskkill /PID winword.exe

   C. taskkill /S winword.exe

   D. taskkill /FI winword.exe

107. You have created a reference image for an unattended installation. Now you need to edit the image for customization of a few workstations. Which tool should you use to easily do this?

   A. Sysprep

   B. ADK

   C. MDT

   D. WIM

108. You are installing a Windows Vista workstation on a network. The network is small, and each user manages their own security. What type of network setup is most appropriate for this workstation?

   A. Workgroup

   B. Domain

   C. HomeGroup

   D. Localgroup

109. You are installing Windows 8.1 on a workstation and want to create a striped volume on its three hard disks. What type of partition do you need to create in Disk Management to allow this?

   A. Primary

   B. Extended

   C. Logical

   D. Dynamic

110. You have a desktop computer running Windows Vista Starter 64-bit. To which of the following operating systems can you do an in-place upgrade?

   A. Windows 7 Home Premium 32-bit

   B. Windows 7 Home Premium 64-bit

   C. Windows 7 Ultimate 64-bit

   D. None of the above

111. You have a workstation with a 64-bit processor and no operating system. When you install an operating system on the workstation, which of the following is true?

   A. You can only install a 64-bit operating system.

   B. You can only install a 32-bit operating system.

   C. You can install either a 64-bit or a 32-bit operating system.

   D. You can install a 64-bit operating system or a 32-bit operating system running in compatibility mode.

112. You are installing a second hard drive in a Windows 7 workstation. On the drive, you will need to create six different logical partitions. What type of partition should you create to enable this?

   A. Primary

   B. Extended

   C. Active

   D. Spanned

113.   You have a Windows 7 computer that you want to upgrade to Windows 8 Core. Which two operating systems can you upgrade to this version of Windows 8? (Choose two.)

    A. Windows 7 Starter

    B. Windows 7 Professional

    C. Windows 7 Enterprise

    D. Windows 7 Home Premium

114.   You have just installed Windows 8.1 on a workstation. After the installation is complete, the sound card does not work. It worked previously, and Device Manager appears to have detected the card. What step should you try to get the card working again?

    A. Reseat the sound card.

    B. Uninstall Windows 8.1 and reinstall the previous OS.

    C. Ensure that the MIDI port is enabled in Device Manager.

    D. Install an alternate third-party driver.

115.   You have a Windows Vista workstation with a built-in network card. The card is intermittently malfunctioning. You install a USB network card and want to permanently disable the internal card to avoid any conflicts. Which administrative tool should you use?

    A. Computer Management

    B. System Configuration

    C. Device Manager

    D. Services

116.   You have a workstation with a 32-bit processor and no operating system. When you install an operating system on the workstation, which of the following is true?

    A. You can only install a 32-bit operating system.

    B. You can only install a 64-bit operating system.

    C. You can install either a 64-bit or a 32-bit operating system.

    D. You can install a 32-bit operating system or a 64-bit operating system running in compatibility mode.

117.   You have installed a secondary hard drive into a Windows 8 workstation. The user asks you to create a logical partition. Which of the following is the defining characteristic of a logical partition?

    A. It spans multiple hard drives.

    B. It is active.

    C. It has a drive letter.

    D. It is created within an extended partition.

118. An application on a user's Windows 7 workstation has become corrupted. Where can you go in Control Panel to attempt to repair or reinstall the application?

  A. System

  B. Computer Management

  C. System Configuration

  D. Programs and Features

119. You are at a Windows Vista command prompt in the D:\files directory. You want to display all files that have the archive bit set. Which command should you use to do this?

  A. dir /b:a

  B. dir /d:a

  C. dir /q:a

  D. dir /a:a

120. You have just installed a new Windows 7 workstation. You want to ensure that all new operating system patches are installed automatically when they become available. Which administrative tool do you configure to do this?

  A. Performance Monitor

  B. System Monitor

  C. Advanced Security

  D. Windows Update

121. You want to create a Windows Desktop shortcut on your Windows 7 computer to a Windows management tool that gives you quick access to manage hard drives, user accounts, scheduled tasks, and Event Viewer. What should you create a shortcut for?

  A. PERFMON.EXE

  B. MSINFO32.EXE

  C. SERVICES.MSC

  D. COMPMGMT.MSC

122. Which Windows 7 utility allows you to review recent messages and resolve problems, see your computer's security status, and perform troubleshooting and maintenance steps?

  A. Control Panel

  B. Action Center

  C. System and Security

  D. Windows Defender

123. Several workstations in your office are running Windows XP Professional. You want to upgrade them to Windows Vista. To which versions of Vista can you upgrade Windows XP Professional? (Choose two.)

  A. Windows Vista Enterprise

  B. Windows Vista Home Premium

  C. Windows Vista Ultimate

  D. Windows Vista Business

124. You have just installed a Windows Vista workstation for a user. Company policy is that the user's TEMP folder should not be located on the system partition. Which administrative tool can you use to change the location of the user's temporary files folder?

   A. Computer Management

   B. Users and Groups

   C. Local Security Policy

   D. System Configuration

125. You are installing Windows Vista on an empty mechanical hard drive. When formatting the drive, you want to choose a file system that is lightweight. The user is not concerned about data security. Which file system best meets the user's needs?

   A. ExFAT

   B. NFS

   C. NTFS

   D. FAT32

126. You have a desktop running Windows Vista Home Basic 32-bit and want to upgrade your OS. To which of the following operating systems can you perform an in-place upgrade?

   A. Windows 7 Ultimate 32-bit

   B. Windows 7 Professional 32-bit

   C. Windows 7 Professional 64-bit

   D. None of the above

127. Which Windows Vista utility provides a single interface for configuring your firewall, getting automatic updates, and setting up malware protection?

   A. Action Center

   B. Security Center

   C. Windows Defender

   D. Windows Firewall

128. One of the developers in your organization has created a new software package for Windows 8.1 client computers. He wants to custom configure application-specific access permissions. Which administrative tool would he use to do this?

   A. System Configuration

   B. Advanced Security

   C. Component Services

   D. Users and Groups

129. Several workstations in your office are running Windows Vista Business. You want to upgrade them to Windows 8.1 Pro. Which of the following statements is true?

- **A.** There is no direct upgrade path from Vista to Windows 8.1. You must perform a clean install.
- **B.** You can upgrade Windows Vista Business only to Windows 8.1 Enterprise.
- **C.** You can upgrade Windows Vista Business only to Windows 8.1 Basic.
- **D.** When you begin the upgrade, choose Custom and then do not format the hard drive.

130. You want to format a hard drive with the NFTS file system. It's the `D:` drive on a Windows Vista computer. Which command do you use at the command prompt to do this?

- **A.** `format d: /fs:ntfs`
- **B.** `format d: /ntfs`
- **C.** `format d: /v:ntfs`
- **D.** `format d: /q:ntfs`

131. You are trying to update a Windows Vista workstation. After you make changes to the configuration, the system does not boot properly. Another technician suggests reverting the OS to the previous configuration settings. Which tool can you use to do this?

- **A.** Windows Update
- **B.** Computer Management
- **C.** System Restore
- **D.** System Configuration

132. A user reports that it seems like her network performance has recently become very slow. While investigating her network card properties, you notice that her network card is set to half duplex. What does this mean?

- **A.** That is the normal operating setting for a network card.
- **B.** The switch that she is connected to configured her network card to operate in this mode for backward compatibility.
- **C.** The card needs to be set to simplex mode for it to run faster.
- **D.** The card needs to be set to full-duplex mode for it to run faster.

133. You have recently deployed a custom application to several Windows workstations on your network. The application appears to have a bug, and the developer suggests you edit the Registry to fix it. Which administrative tool would you use to do this?

- **A.** `MSINFO32`
- **B.** `COMMAND`
- **C.** `REGEDIT`
- **D.** `NOTEPAD`

134. You will be installing several new resource-intensive applications on a Windows 7 workstation, and the user has concerns over system performance. You want to monitor memory and CPU performance and set up the workstation so that it logs performance over time. Which utility should you use to set this up?

    A. Resource Monitor

    B. Performance Monitor

    C. Task Manager

    D. Event Viewer

135. Which Windows 7 utility allows you to view error messages generated by applications or login failures?

    A. Action Center

    B. Windows Defender

    C. Message Center

    D. Event Viewer

136. A user with a Windows 8.1 workstation recently received a second hard drive. Another administrator created a partition on the hard drive, and it's ready for use. He will store the raw video files he creates on that drive and insists that it be called the R: drive. Which of the following statements is true?

    A. You can use Disk Management to change the drive letter to R:.

    B. You can use Disk Management to change the drive letter to R:, but only if it's a dynamic disk.

    C. You can use Disk Management to change the drive letter to R:, but only if it's in an extended partition.

    D. You will need to use Disk Management to delete the partition and re-create it as R:.

137. You have a Windows 8 workstation with corrupt files in the operating system. It will not boot properly. You need to boot the computer using its network card to connect to an image server to restore Windows. What is this boot process called?

    A. Netboot

    B. PXE boot

    C. The WinPE process

    D. The WinRE process

138. You need to format a blank SDXC card and transfer files to it. Which file system is ideally suited for this type of media?

    A. CDFS

    B. FAT32

    C. NTFS

    D. ExFAT

139. You have a Windows 8.1 workstation. You want to connect to a printer located on a Windows 7 workstation. What do you need to do?

   A. Right-click the printer, choose Printer Properties, and share the printer.

   B. Right-click the printer, choose Printer Properties, and map the network printer.

   C. Open the Add a Printer Wizard and share the printer.

   D. Open the Add a Printer Wizard and map the network printer.

140. You are installing Windows Vista on a computer. When you partition the hard drive, which type of partition is limited to having only one logical drive on it?

   A. Primary

   B. Basic

   C. Extended

   D. GPT

141. A laptop user has traveled to visit a client and forgot his power adapter. Before going to lunch with the client, he wants to conserve battery power, but he wants to enable the fastest possible startup when he gets back, with his applications already open. Which power mode will conserve battery life but enable the fastest startup?

   A. Shut down

   B. Sleep

   C. Hibernate

   D. Resting

142. You have just installed a second hard drive into a Windows 7 workstation. The drive is properly recognized by the BIOS when the system boots, but you are unable to see it in Windows Explorer. What do you need to do?

   A. Mount the drive.

   B. Assign a drive letter.

   C. Initialize the drive.

   D. Create an array.

143. Which Windows user interface was the first one to have translucent windows and provides the ability to create a three-dimensional stack of open windows for users to cycle through?

   A. Metro

   B. Aero

   C. WinPE

   D. Windows Explorer

144. You have a Windows 7 workstation with four hard disks. You want to take advantage of having multiple disks by creating a disk array. What types of arrays can you create in Windows that will combine the disks into one volume? (Choose two.)

    A. Simple

    B. Spanned

    C. Mirrored

    D. Extended

145. Which versions of Windows 7 support BitLocker? (Choose two.)

    A. Enterprise

    B. Professional

    C. Ultimate

    D. Home Premium

146. You are working on a Windows 8.1 workstation that you believe has cross-linked files. At a command prompt, you want to check for these files and automatically fix any problems. Which command should you run to do this?

    A. chkdsk /f

    B. chkdsk /c

    C. chkdsk /scan

    D. chkdsk /r

147. You are configuring a secondary hard drive using Disk Management in Windows Vista. When setting up basic storage, which two types of partitions can you create? (Choose two.)

    A. Primary

    B. Simple

    C. Extended

    D. Spanned

148. You are installing Windows 8.1 on a new workstation. Before you format the drive with NTFS, your manager tells you to perform a full format. Which of the following statements best describes what a full format does?

    A. Remove files from the partition, create a new file allocation table, and scan the hard disk for bad sectors.

    B. Remove files from the partition and create a new file allocation table.

    C. Create a new file allocation table and scan the hard disk for bad sectors.

    D. Delete the partition, re-create the partition, create a new file allocation table, and scan the hard disk for bad sectors.

149. You are at a Windows 8.1 command prompt. Which command should you use to create and manage partitions?

- **A.** fdisk
- **B.** diskpart
- **C.** sfc
- **D.** format

150. You need to install Windows 8.1 on 30 identical workstations. You do not want to manually input information into each of the workstations. What type of installation should you perform?

- **A.** Upgrade
- **B.** Unattended
- **C.** Deployment
- **D.** Clean

151. You are working at a Windows Vista command prompt. Which command should you use to copy directories and subdirectories but not empty directories?

- **A.** xcopy /e
- **B.** xcopy /s
- **C.** xcopy /h
- **D.** xcopy /a

152. You need to configure Internet connections on a Windows 7 workstation. In which tabs of Internet options do you set the home page and enable the pop-up blocker?

- **A.** Connections, Security
- **B.** General, Security
- **C.** General, Privacy
- **D.** Connections, Privacy

153. You have a user who just purchased a Windows Phone. He wants to know what the name of the virtual assistant is on his phone. What do you tell him?

- **A.** Windows Phone does not have a virtual assistant.
- **B.** Windy
- **C.** Siri
- **D.** Cortana
- **E.** Alexa

154. Which type of server on your network will utilize UDP ports 67 and 68 to communicate with other computers?

- **A.** Authentication server
- **B.** Print server
- **C.** DHCP server
- **D.** DNS server

155. Which Linux command is used to copy and convert files from one format to another?

 A. dd

 B. cp

 C. mv

 D. rm

156. You are consulting with a mobile phone company. You are told that for a new usage tracking program, the company wants to use the 15-digit number that identifies a user and their network. Which number is the company looking for?

 A. IMEI

 B. IMSI

 C. PRI

 D. PRL

157. What command-line utility allows you to check network connectivity by simply relaying a ICMP message to the IP address provided?

 A. netstat

 B. ping

 C. ifconfig

 D. nslookup

158. Which type of server maintains a database called a zone file, which it uses to provide clients with requested information?

 A. Authentication server

 B. DNS server

 C. DHCP server

 D. Proxy server

159. You have just joined a new network team, and one of your coworkers reports that he is frustrated from working on a legacy system. Which of the following might he be referring to? (Choose two.)

 A. The sales management software that was created in the 1980s

 B. The file server that runs on a Windows NT 4.0 server

 C. The accounting software that runs on a Linux server

 D. The graphic arts package that runs on an iMac

160. What command-line utility displays statistics related to the network interfaces?

 A. ping

 B. nbtstat

 C. nslookup

 D. netstat

161. On your MacBook Pro, what is the name of the utility used to browse through files and folders?

    A. SpotLight

    B. Remote Disc

    C. iCloud

    D. Finder

162. While using your mobile phone, you want to set up a secure connection over a Wi-Fi network. What type of connection do you need to enable?

    A. VPN

    B. IMEI

    C. IMSI

    D. PRI/PRL

163. A user is concerned that the connection to an external server seems to take a long time. The user asks if it is possible to identify the path through the network from her workstation to the end server. What command-line utility would be helpful here?

    A. netstat

    B. ping

    C. nslookup

    D. tracert

164. You need to start a new shell on a Linux workstation, with root permissions. Which command should you use to do this?

    A. su

    B. sudo

    C. vi

    D. dd

165. What command-line utility can help identify what DNS server the computer relies on?

    A. nslookup

    B. netstat

    C. ping

    D. tracert

166. In Linux, what is the name of the interpreter between the user and the operating system?

    A. Terminal

    B. Command prompt

    C. GUI

    D. Shell

167. A user types in her username and password into a workstation that is configured in a domain. Which type of server examines her information and determines whether she gets access to network resources?

A. Authentication server

B. Proxy server

C. File server

D. DHCP server

168. On your network, a few users have been accessing material on inappropriate websites. What type of server can you install to block content from a list of prohibited websites?

A. DNS server

B. Authentication server

C. Proxy server

D. Web server

169. Which type of server on a network is responsible for listening for inbound traffic on ports 80 and 443?

A. DHCP server

B. DNS server

C. Mail server

D. Web server

170. You are working on a Linux file server. Which command would you use to see the amount of free disk space on a volume?

A. fsck

B. df

C. du

D. vi

171. In your web browser, you type **www.google.com** and press Enter. Which type of server identifies the owner of that name and tells your computer the IP address of the server you want to communicate with?

A. Proxy server

B. DHCP server

C. DNS server

D. Authentication server

172. You wish to create a script that maps a drive. What command allows you to map a network drive to either a computer name or IP address?

A. net user

B. net use

C. netstat

D. mapdd

173. Which piece of software on a mobile phone manages all wireless communication for the phone?

    A. PRI

    B. PRL

    C. Baseband OS

    D. SIM OS

174. You have a MacBook running MacOS Yosemite on your network. You want to create a backup of critical operating system files in case the system crashes and is unable to locate the hard drive. What should you create?

    A. Recovery disk

    B. Image

    C. Snapshot

    D. Time Machine

175. A user recently left the company, and you need to change ownership of his files on the Linux server to a new user. Which command should you use to do this?

    A. chown

    B. chmod

    C. chperm

    D. cp

176. One of your network users has a MacBook Pro running OS X Yosemite. Where should this user go to see whether there are any OS updates available?

    A. Open the App Store and click Updates in the toolbar.

    B. Open Safari and click Updates in the toolbar.

    C. Open System Preferences and click Updates in the toolbar.

    D. Open iTunes and click Updates in the toolbar.

177. Which two commands are used in Linux to check or modify network configuration settings? (Choose two.)

    A. ipconfig

    B. ifconfig

    C. iwconfig

    D. inconfig

178. You want to enable data synchronization for your iPhone. Which two statements are true regarding Wi-Fi synchronization? (Choose two.)

    A. You must enable Sync over Wi-Fi within iTunes.

    B. You can sync to iCloud only over Wi-Fi.

    C. The iPhone should be plugged into a USB port.

    D. The iPhone and computer must be on the same network SSID.

179. In Linux, the command to add a user is `useradd`. What is the equivalent command-line utility on a Microsoft Windows platform? (Choose two)

    A. `adduser`

    B. `netadd user`

    C. `net user`

    D. `net users`

180. Which type of server will extensively use ports 25 and 143 in its communications with clients on the network?

    A. Print server

    B. Mail server

    C. DHCP server

    D. Authentication server

181. You are working on a Linux workstation. A file named docs needs to be renamed to newdocs. What is the right command to execute this?

    A. `ren docs newdocs`

    B. `mv docs newdocs`

    C. `cp docs newdocs`

    D. `rm docs newdocs`

182. You want to download applications for a device running iOS. Where will you download them from?

    A. Android Market

    B. Google Play

    C. App Store

    D. Windows Store

183. You are at a Linux workstation and need to search for text within several files. Which command should you use?

    A. `sudo`

    B. `grep`

    C. `cp`

    D. `ls`

184. One of your network users has a MacBook Pro running OS X Mavericks. She asks you about installing or updating antivirus software. What should you tell her?

    A. There are no viruses for Macs, so no antivirus software is needed.

    B. Use the free MacAntiVirus program that comes with the OS and set it to update automatically.

    C. Install a commercial antivirus program and set it to update automatically.

    D. Install a host-based firewall and set it to update automatically.

185. The MacBook you are using does not have a built-in DVD player, but you need to access some files stored on one. Which MacOS feature allows you to access the DVD player on another computer?

    A. Remote Disc

    B. Finder

    C. SpotLight

    D. iCloud

186. For most command-line utilities on a Microsoft Windows system, how does the user find out which command switches exist or which parameters are necessary for that command? (Choose two.)

    A. By typing: man `[command]`

    B. By typing: more `[command]`

    C. By typing: `[command]` /help

    D. By typing: man `[command]` /?

187. You are working on a MacBook Pro and need to search the computer for a document you wrote a few months ago. Which feature should you use to search the hard drive?

    A. KeyChain

    B. SpotLight

    C. Finder

    D. Siri

188. You have a MacBook Pro and need to run a critical application for work that is compatible only with Windows. Is there any way you can do this?

    A. Yes. Macs will run Windows applications natively.

    B. Yes. Use Boot Camp to install Windows and dual-boot.

    C. Yes. Use Dock to install Windows and dual-boot.

    D. No. You can't run the Windows application.

189. On a Linux workstation, which command do you use to display the contents of a directory?

    A. dir

    B. grep

    C. cp

    D. ls

190. You are configuring your tablet computer to connect to your corporate email server. Which ports do you need to set up if you want to use SMTP with SSL and IMAP4 with SSL?

    A. 25 and 143

    B. 465 and 993

    C. 465 and 995

    D. 587 and 993

    E. 587 and 995

191. Which command is used to change a file's permissions in Linux?

  A. chperm

  B. cp

  C. chown

  D. chmod

192. What type of update does your mobile phone need if you need to refresh the reference list the phone uses to connect to the proper cell phone tower when roaming?

  A. PRL

  B. PRI

  C. Baseband

  D. IMEI

193. Your network uses a Linux file server. It has four volumes, each formatted with ext4. You want to check the /ops/files volume for any filesystem errors and fix them. Which command should you use?

  A. fsck /ops/files

  B. du /ops/files

  C. df /ops/files

  D. chkdsk /ops/files

194. A network consultant recommended to your boss that you install an IPS. Which of the following statements best describes what an IPS does?

  A. It detects anomalies in network traffic, logs the activity, and takes actions to stop the activity.

  B. It detects viruses transmitted across the network, logs the activity, and deletes the network packets infected with the virus.

  C. It detects anomalies in network traffic, logs the activity, and sends an alert to the administrator.

  D. It allows or denies incoming network traffic based on a set of rules.

195. Which mobile operating system has versions named for types of candy or sweets?

  A. BlackBerry OS

  B. Android

  C. iOS

  D. Windows Phone

196. One of the designers on your network has an iMac running OS X El Capitan. Which of the following is not considered necessary with this workstation?

  A. Running scheduled backups

  B. Installing antivirus software

  C. Updating drivers and firmware

  D. Defragmenting the hard drive

197. Which type of server on your network could have its functionality replaced with NAS or a SAN?

    A. Mail server

    B. File server

    C. Print server

    D. Web server

198. You have a MacBook Pro and want to share files with a small group of Mac users. Because your team edits the files frequently, you want to make sure everyone has access to the same version of the files online. What storage solution should you use?

    A. iCloud

    B. Finder

    C. Remote Disc

    D. SpotLight

199. The Linux workstation you are using seems slow. You want to see what processes are running on the computer. Which command should you use?

    A. vi

    B. cp

    C. dd

    D. ps

200. You are working on an iMac, and about a dozen applications are open. Which feature allows you to easily see all of them and switch to your desired application?

    A. SpotLight

    B. KeyChain

    C. Mission Control

    D. Finder

201. You are configuring your Android phone to synchronize with your Windows 8.1 workstation. Which of the following types of data will not be synchronized between the devices?

    A. Passwords

    B. Bookmarks

    C. Email

    D. Social media data

202. Your manager asked you to find a device for network security. He wants it to be able to perform packet filtering, shut down network attacks, block spam, and prohibit access to inappropriate websites. What type of device should you look for?

    A. Firewall

    B. IPS

    C. IDS

    D. UTM

203. An intern working to be a system administrator is helping a user with his Windows desktop. Opening a command window on the Windows Desktop, the intern attempts to run the System File Checker (SFC) utility. However, the utility fails to run. What is likely the problem?

    A. SFC can run only from an administrator's system.

    B. SFC is not a Windows utility.

    C. SFC requires administrative privileges to run.

    D. SFC is not a command-line utility.

204. One of your users has a MacBook Pro, and an application appears to have crashed. What can she use to force the app to close?

    A. Task Manager

    B. Force Quit

    C. Shell/Terminal

    D. Time Machine

205. Where can a user find web and local credentials on a Windows 10 Desktop?

    A. Web credentials are never stored by Windows 10.

    B. No credentials are ever stored by Windows 10.

    C. Credentials can be managed in Credential Manager.

    D. Credentials can be managed in MSInfo32.

206. A user with an Android phone reports that it isn't properly detecting where she touches the virtual keyboard—it seems to be a bit off. What should she do to resolve the issue?

    A. Recalibrate the screen.

    B. Turn the phone off and back on again.

    C. Perform a reset to factory specifications.

    D. Purchase a new device.

207. You call your cell phone provider to do some troubleshooting, and it tells you it needs the phone's 15-digit serial number. What number is it looking for?

    A. PRI

    B. PRL

    C. IMEI

    D. IMSI

208. You are updating user accounts on a Linux workstation and need to change a user's password. Which command do you use to do this?

    A. chperm

    B. cp

    C. pwd

    D. passwd

209. A user wants to perform a backup on his MacBook running OS X El Capitan. Which software utility should he use to do this?

    A. Image Recovery

    B. Time Machine

    C. iBackup

    D. MacBackup

210. Which of the following mobile operating systems is an open-source OS?

    A. iOS

    B. Windows Phone

    C. BlackBerry OS

    D. Android

211. You are at a Linux workstation on your network with the terminal open. Which command can you issue to see the size of files and directories on this computer?

    A. fsck

    B. df

    C. du

    D. vi

212. You want to start the visual file editor on your Linux server. Which command is used to do that?

    A. cd

    B. ps

    C. vi

    D. cp

213. What feature in Windows 10 allows a user to synchronize files and folders between the local system and an offline location?

    A. MSTSC

    B. Credential Manager

    C. MSINFO32

    D. Sync Center

214. One of the workstations on your network runs Ubuntu Linux. Which command can you use to install patches to upgrade the operating system?

    A. apt-cache

    B. apt-get

    C. vi-get

    D. chown-get

215. What does the `taskkill` command do on a Windows system?

    A. Shuts down the machine without warning

    B. Shuts down the machine gracefully

    C. Kills all applications running at the time

    D. Kills a single process

216. Which of the following features are typically present in mobile operating systems by default but not in desktop operating systems? (Choose two.)

    A. SDK

    B. Power options

    C. Gesture-based interaction

    D. Emergency notifications

217. Which feature of MacOS allows others to see your screen and requires a Virtual Network Computing (VNC) connection?

    A. Remote assistance

    B. Shell/Terminal

    C. Image sharing

    D. Screen sharing

218. What operating system developed by Google is compatible with Android-based tablets?

    A. Ubuntu

    B. iOS

    C. Windows 10 Professional

    D. Chrome

219. What network optimization feature can run in distributed or hosted mode?

    A. LocalCache

    B. BranchCache

    C. CacheBypass

    D. CacheServe

220. What modern partitioning scheme replaces Master Boot Record and eliminates the need for an extended partition?

    A. Primary

    B. Dynamic

    C. GPT

    D. Basic

221. Which command-line tool allows an administrator to prepare and mount a Windows Desktop image?

    A. dism

    B. chkdisk

    C. diskpart

    D. netstat

222. Which disk management tool is used to pool together multiple hard drives?

    A. Diskpart

    B. Storage spaces

    C. MSTSC

    D. robocopy

223. Which Windows 10 networking option is available to permit connecting to the Internet using a cellular connection.

    A. VPN

    B. CAN

    C. WWAN

    D. LPAN

224. What policy would an administrator set to limit network bandwidth usage on a Windows Server 2016 system?

    A. Network Limit

    B. NBG

    C. DSCP

    D. QoS

225. What does KeyChain provide the user in MacOS?

    A. Password management

    B. Local file sharing

    C. Certificate management

    D. Screen protection

226. Compared to Windows or Apple workstations, what is a difference between those and a Linux workstation?

    A. Linux is more expensive to license

    B. Windows experiences fewer threats and exploits

    C. Linux is open source

    D. There is one Linux workstation operating system version

227. Comparing Apple Macintosh OS, Microsoft Windows and Linux, which rarely, if ever, announces an end-of-life date for their OS?

- **A.** Apple
- **B.** Microsoft
- **C.** Linux
- **D.** None - they all announce product end-of-life dates

228. What workstation operating system has update limitations per hardware form factor?

- **A.** Apple Macintosh OS
- **B.** Microsoft Windows
- **C.** Linux
- **D.** None

229. Which of the following Windows 7 editions cannot use domain access?

- **A.** Windows 7 Ultimate
- **B.** Windows 7 Professional
- **C.** Windows 7 Home
- **D.** Windows 7 Enterprise

230. Which of the following Microsoft Windows versions comes with Windows Media Center?

- **A.** Windows 7
- **B.** Windows 8
- **C.** Windows 8.1
- **D.** Windows 10

231. You need to install Windows 10 onto a few nearby systems currently with no OS or optical drive. What method suits your work best and even allow for unattended installation if needed? (Choose two)

- **A.** Solid state/flash drives with answer file
- **B.** CD-ROM with answer file
- **C.** External/hot-swappable drive with unattended file
- **D.** ISO image on DVD with unattended file

232. What type of partition does the Windows 10 version 1803 update create on Windows 10 installations?

- **A.** Factory recovery partition
- **B.** Pre-upgrade partition
- **C.** Command-line (no GUI) Windows partition
- **D.** Update storage partition

233. You are creating a boot drive for a Windows 8 system. What happens if it is not a properly formatted boot drive with the correct partitions/format? (Choose two)

    A. Boot drive will not boot

    B. Boot drive boots but cannot be seen

    C. Boot drive works, but cannot save

    D. Boot drive works fine. For Windows 8, the format is irrelevant

234. You have several older applications, some originally run on Windows 95. You suspect application compatibility issues may occur on Windows 10. What step can you take to continue using those old applications?

    A. Contact the application vendor for updated app versions

    B. Maintain older Windows systems for which applications were intended.

    C. Use Compatibility mode on Windows 10, set to Windows 95

    D. Replace older applications with modern day equivalents

235. As a systems administrator, you issued a policy update to the computer ABC1 using the command line utility gpupdate. Which of the following commands and switches would help ensure the policy changes are in effect?

    A. gpupdate /chk ABC1

    B. gpscan /v ABC1

    C. gpupdate /scan:ABC1

    D. gpresult /scope:ABC1

236. Which of the following scenarios involves User Account Management in Windows 10?

    A. Users ask for Internet access

    B. Multiple users request a network printer

    C. Users request their theme settings be synchronized together

    D. User requests you to wipe his extended partition

237. When using Windows Management Interface Command, what is the disk management command used to check the drive status?

    A. diskdrive get status

    B. disk status check

    C. diskdrive health

    D. drive status check

238. You purchased a new Windows 10 desktop, the drive for which came as a single partition. What is the least destructive method allowed in Windows 10 to create three partitions from the one large partition?

    A. Split the partition once, then again to create a third partition

    B. Create bootable installation media. Format and create the new partitions

    C. Install a second physical disk, which can be split into two partitions

    D. Package and return the new desktop. Request one with three partitions

239. A user needs a printer to print in color and legal size, but the user does not have the privileges to change printer settings. How do you proceed to make the changes for him?

   A. Walk to the printer and change the settings on its attached display panel

   B. Direct the user to a different printer

   C. Tell the user you need to take lunch first

   D. Adjust the printer's settings for the user in the Windows Control Panel

240. An HR manager mentions he can't hear any sound from his Windows 10 laptop watching a video of his son's soccer game. To fix the problem, where would you direct the HR employee to go?

   A. Suggest the manager go check the sound driver license

   B. Have the user adjust Sound settings under the Control Panel

   C. Calibrate the laptop speakers with a matching-sized magnet.

   D. Forward the video to try on the HR Director's laptop.

241. A user is frustrated with what seems to be a common problem. Unfortunately, you are unavailable for the next few hours. Despite the user having little technical knowledge, he is willing to hear any suggestions you have to fix it. What can you suggest the user try, to diagnose and even possibly fix the problem by himself?

   A. Have the user read the manual

   B. Suggest the Automated Serve and Protect tool in the Control Panel's Security section to troubleshoot the problem

   C. Direct the user to continue at a different desk for the remainder of the week

   D. Use the Troubleshoot tool in the Control Panel's Update and Security section to analyze the problem

242. A user asks for help with installing an application on their desktop. He wants to run Active Directory Domain Services to help with studying for a test. He confirms the desktop is powerful enough and has enough storage to meet the application's system requirements. but the application will not complete the installation. What could be the problem?

   A. Drive space is too limited

   B. Not enough RAM

   C. Conflicting with another application

   D. OS compatibility issue

243. When trying to install an application, the install process halts with a message about requiring access to the system directory. Which of the following actions would help the install process to complete?

   A. Install additional RAM

   B. Change the local user permissions

   C. Propose a different installation directory

   D. Verify the drive has sufficient free space available

244. The CEO asks the local IT administrator to copy the company's financial data to a second system for the sake of backup. The financial data is critical to the company's success. The administrator places a copy of the data on the company's public web server. What has the administrator failed to consider in fulfilling the CEO's request?

- **A.** Security considerations and impact to the device
- **B.** Performance considerations and capacity of the device
- **C.** Local user considerations and use of the device
- **D.** Availability considerations and backup of the device

245. The disk in a user's Mac OS desktop has fallen victim to ransomware, which encrypts all their data without chance to recover it. What best practice should the user adopt for their Mac OS desktop to prevent this issue from happening again?

- **A.** The user should begin doing scheduled disk maintenance
- **B.** The user should regularly perform drivers/firmware updates
- **C.** The user should regularly perform antivirus/anti-malware updates
- **D.** The user should regularly clean their screen

246. A user chose to install a different Linux desktop operating system. He was excited to finally install the distro image he had been saving for over a year. He soon noticed that certain applications were unable to run or install correctly. What best practice had the user likely failed to adopt for their Linux OS desktop?

- **A.** The user should perform patch management
- **B.** The user should a system update
- **C.** The user should update their antivirus/anti-malware
- **D.** The user should conduct scheduled backups

247. The hard drive on a user's Mac OS desktop has recently failed. The data is unrecoverable. What best practice should the user adopt to prevent losing their data again?

- **A.** The user should begin doing scheduled system updates
- **B.** The user should perform scheduled backups
- **C.** The user should regularly perform antivirus/anti-malware updates
- **D.** The user should regularly perform drivers/firmware updates

248. The hard drive on a user's Mac OS desktop seems to be performing quite slowly. Finally, after a few applications report lost or corrupted data, the user decides to ask the local IT person for help. What best practice does the IT person suspect is not being done?

- **A.** The user needs to begin doing scheduled disk maintenance
- **B.** The user needs to regularly perform drivers/firmware updates
- **C.** The user needs to regularly perform antivirus/anti-malware updates
- **D.** The user needs to regularly perform drivers/firmware updates

249. A user's Linux OS desktop was recently exploited by malware. What best practice should the user adopt for their Linux OS desktop to prevent this issue from happening again?

   A. The user should begin doing scheduled disk maintenance

   B. The user should regularly perform drivers/firmware updates

   C. The user should regularly perform scheduled backups

   D. The user should regularly perform patch management

250. After attaching the latest innovative gadget to their Mac OS desktop, a user is disappointed it doesn't seem to do what it's supposed to do. The user repeatedly installs the needed drivers and application. The application does give a message about system compatibility but the user is certain all hardware requirements are met. What best practice is the user not considering?

   A. The user needs to begin doing scheduled disk maintenance

   B. The user needs to regularly perform drivers/firmware updates

   C. The user needs to regularly perform antivirus/anti-malware updates

   D. The user needs to regularly perform drivers/firmware updates

251. A Mac OS desktop user needs to install a tool to create backups of their desktop. The user does not want to have to buy or install any extra applications. Which of the following tools would help this user?

   A. Timeshift

   B. Time Machine

   C. Time Warp

   D. Timer

252. A Linux Mint desktop user wants to install a tool to create restore/snapshots of their desktop. Which of the following tools would help this user?

   A. Timeshift

   B. Time Machine

   C. Time Warp

   D. Timer

253. A user new to having a Mac OS desktop wants to verify their desktop's connectivity to the network. The user knows about the command utility ping but does not know how to open it on a Mac OS without the DOS prompt. Which of the following tools would help this user?

   A. Terminal

   B. DOS box

   C. Pages

   D. Maps

254. A Mac OS desktop user wants to perform some disk maintenance. She needs a utility that can both check the health and format an external drive. Which of the following tools would satisfy her requirements?

    A. Disk Utility

    B. Timeshift

    C. Sophos Home for Mac

    D. VmStat

255. On the Mac OS desktop, what is the purpose of the tool called Sharing?

    A. File sharing

    B. Screen sharing

    C. Bluetooth sharing

    D. All the above

256. A user new to the Mac OS is asking if her desktop has any application for saving and managing her passwords. What is the native Mac OS tool for password management?

    A. MacinKey

    B. MacPass

    C. KeyChain

    D. Key Ring

257. A user knows her Mac OS desktop allows her to search for any file or document. But she recently noticed she can search by description, not just by name. What is the name of this Mac OS utility?

    A. Search

    B. SpotLight

    C. Spot

    D. Finder

258. Laptops with a touchpad can be customized to open a utility or application when users touch or swipe their touchpad in various ways. Choose the best answer to name this feature and the OS on which it is available.

    A. Fingex on Mac OS

    B. Gestures on Linux OS

    C. Fingex on Linux OS

    D. Gestures on Mac OS and Linux OS

259. The Linux commands kill and killall are used to kill running processes. Choose the correct answer that explains how they differ?

    A. kill uses a process name

    B. killall uses a process ID number

    C. killall can send specific signals, but killall cannot

    D. killall uses a process name

Chapter

7

Security

THE FOLLOWING COMPTIA A+ EXAM 220-1002 TOPICS ARE COVERED IN THIS CHAPTER:

✓ **2.1 Summarize the importance of physical security measures.**

- Mantrap
- Badge reader
- Smart card
- Security guard
- Door lock
- Biometric locks
- Hardware tokens
- Cable locks
- Server locks
- USB locks
- Privacy screen
- Key fobs
- Entry control roster

✓ **2.2 Explain logical security concepts.**

- Active Directory
  - Login script
  - Domain
  - Group Policy/Updates
  - Organizational Units
  - Home Folder
  - Folder redirection

- Software tokens
- MDM policies
- Port security
- MAC address filtering
- Certificates
- Antivirus/Anti-malware
- Firewalls
- User authentication/strong passwords
- Multifactor authentication
- Directory permissions
- VPN
- DLP
- Access control lists
- Smart card
- Email filtering
- Trusted/untrusted software sources
- Principle of least privilege

✓ **2.3   Compare and contrast wireless security protocols and authentication methods.**

- Protocols and encryption
  - WEP
  - WPA
  - WPA2
  - TKIP
  - AES
- Authentication
  - Single-factor
  - Multifactor
  - RADIUS
  - TACACS

✓ **2.4 Given a scenario, detect, remove, and prevent malware using appropriate tools and methods.**

- Malware
  - Ransomware
  - Trojan
  - Keylogger
  - Rootkit
  - Virus
  - Botnet
  - Worm
  - Spyware
- Tools and methods
  - Antivirus
  - Anti-malware
  - Recovery console
  - Backup/restore
  - End-user education
  - Software firewalls
  - SecureDNS

✓ **2.5 Compare and contrast social engineering, threats, and vulnerabilities.**

- Social engineering
  - Phishing
  - Spear phishing
  - Impersonation
  - Shoulder surfing
  - Tailgating
  - Dumpster diving
- DDoS
- DoS
- Zero-day

- Man-in-the-middle
- Brute force
- Dictionary
- Rainbow table
- Spoofing
- Non-compliant systems
- Zombie

✓ **2.6 Compare and contrast the differences of basic Microsoft Windows OS security settings.**

- User and groups
  - Administrator
  - Power user
  - Guest
  - Standard user
- NTFS vs. share permissions
  - Allow vs. deny
  - Moving vs. copying folders and files
  - File attributes
- Shared files and folders
  - Administrative shares vs. local shares
  - Permission propagation
  - Inheritance
- System files and folders
- User authentication
  - Single sign-on
- Run as administrator vs. standard user
- BitLocker
- BitLockerTo Go
- EFS

✓ **2.7 Given a scenario, implement security best practices to secure a workstation.**

- Password best practices
  - Setting strong passwords
  - Password expiration
  - Screensaver required password
  - BIOS/UEFI passwords
  - Requiring passwords
- Account management
  - Restricting user permissions
  - Logon time restrictions
  - Disabling guest account
  - Failed attempts lockout
  - Timeout/screen lock
  - Change default admin user account/password
  - Basic Active Directory functions
    - Account creation
    - Account deletion
    - Password reset/unlock account
    - Disable account
- Disable autorun
- Data encryption
- Patch/update management

✓ **2.8 Given a scenario, implement methods for securing mobile devices.**

- Screen locks
  - Fingerprint lock
  - Face lock
  - Swipe lock
  - Passcode lock
- Remote wipes
- Locator applications

- Remote backup applications
- Failed login attempts restrictions
- Antivirus/Anti-malware
- Patching/OS updates
- Biometric authentication
- Full device encryption
- Multifactor authentication
- Authenticator applications
- Trusted sources vs. untrusted sources
- Firewalls
- Policies and procedures
  - BYOD vs. corporate-owned
  - Profile security requirements

✓ **2.9 Given a scenario, implement appropriate data destruction and disposal methods.**

- Physical destruction
  - Shredder
  - Drill/hammer
  - Electromagnetic (Degaussing)
  - Incineration
  - Certificate of destruction
- Recycling or repurposing best practices
  - Low-level format vs. standard format
  - Overwrite
  - Drive wipe

✓ **2.10 Given a scenario, configure security on SOHO wireless and wired networks.**

- Wireless-specific
  - Changing default SSID
  - Setting encryption
  - Disabling SSID broadcast

- Antenna and access point placement
- Radio power levels
- WPS
- Change default usernames and passwords
- Enable MAC filtering
- Assign static IP addresses
- Firewall settings
- Port forwarding/mapping
- Disabling ports
- Content filtering/parental controls
- Update firmware
- Physical security

1. Your network has 20 Windows 10 workstations. When it comes to managing patches and updates, which of the following is the best practice?

    A. Apply patches and updates only after they have received good reviews on the Internet.

    B. Apply patches and updates once per month.

    C. Apply patches and updates immediately after they become available.

    D. Apply patches and updates only if they fix a critical security flaw.

2. You have a Windows 10 workstation and want to prevent a potential hacker from booting to a CD from the optical drive. What should you do to help prevent this?

    A. Require strong Windows passwords.

    B. Restrict user permissions.

    C. Set a BIOS/UEFI password.

    D. Disable autorun.

3. Which type of security solution generally functions as a packet filter and can perform stateful inspection?

    A. VPN

    B. DLP

    C. Antivirus/anti-malware

    D. Firewall

4. Which of the following are examples of physical security methods? (Choose two.)

    A. Biometric locks

    B. Multifactor authentication

    C. Privacy filters

    D. Firewalls

5. A user on your network reported that he got a telephone call from Diane in the IT department saying that he needed to reset his password. She offered to do it for him if he could provide her with his current one. What is this most likely an example of?

    A. The IT department needs to reset the user's password.

    B. A spoofing attack

    C. A social engineering attack

    D. A man-in-the-middle attack

6. Your corporate IT department has decided that to enhance security they want to draft a mobile device management (MDM) policy to require both a passcode and fingerprint scan to unlock a mobile device for use. What is this an example of?

    A. Authenticator application

    B. Biometric authentication

    C. Multifactor authentication

    D. Full device encryption

7. Several employees at your company have been tailgating to gain access to secure areas. Which of the following security methods is the best choice for stopping this practice?

A. Door lock

B. Entry control roster

C. Mantrap

D. ID badges

8. Robert has joined your company as a network administrator. His user account name is RobertS. What is the recommended way to give Robert the administrative privileges he needs?

A. Add the RobertS user account to the Administrators group.

B. Create an account called AdminRobertS. Add that account to the Administrators group. Have Robert use the RobertS account unless he needs administrative rights, in which case he should use the AdminRobertS account.

C. Copy the Administrator account and rename it RobertS.

D. Add the RobertS user account to the Power Users group.

9. You are designing a security policy for mobile phones on your network. Which of the following are common methods of biometric authentication used with mobile devices today? (Choose two.)

A. Fingerprint lock

B. Face lock

C. Swipe lock

D. DNA lock

10. You have a Windows 7 workstation with one volume, C:, that is formatted with FAT32. What is the easiest way to enable this volume to have file- and folder-level security permissions?

A. Reformat the volume with NTFS and restore all of the data from backup.

B. Enable file and folder permissions in System Properties.

C. At a command prompt, type **reformat c: /fs:ntfs**.

D. At a command prompt, type **convert c: /fs:ntfs**.

11. Luana is a member of the Dev group and the HR group. She is trying to access a local resource on an NTFS volume. The HR group has Allow Full Control permission for the payroll folder, and the Dev group has Deny Read permission for the same folder. What is Luana's effective access to the payroll folder?

A. Full Control

B. Read

C. Write

D. No Access

12. Which default Windows group was designed to have more power than normal users but not as much power as administrators?

   A. Superuser

   B. Standard Users

   C. Power Users

   D. Advanced Users

13. You have just transformed a Windows workgroup into a small domain and are configuring user accounts. Which of the following is considered a best practice for managing user account security?

   A. Require every user to log on as a Guest user.

   B. Allow all users Read and Write access to all server files.

   C. Follow the principle of least privilege.

   D. Place all user accounts in the Power Users group.

14. Someone has placed an unauthorized wireless router on your network and configured it with the same SSID as your network. Users can access the network through that router, even though it's not supposed to be there. What type of security threat could this lead to?

   A. Zombie/botnet

   B. Spoofing

   C. Noncompliant system

   D. Man-in-the-middle

15. A security consultant for your company recommended that you begin shredding or burning classified documents before disposing of them. What security risk is the consultant trying to protect the company from?

   A. Shoulder surfing

   B. Dumpster diving

   C. Social engineering

   D. Brute forcing

16. You have installed a Windows 8.1 workstation into a HomeGroup. Which of the following are recommended best practices for maximizing security regarding the Administrator account? (Choose two.)

   A. Disable the Administrator account.

   B. Rename the Administrator account.

   C. Remove the Administrator account from the Administrators group.

   D. Require a strong password.

17. Which digital security method makes use of encapsulation to transfer data across networks?

    A. VPN

    B. Firewall

    C. Email filtering

    D. DLP

18. Which of the following are advantages of using NTFS permissions over using Share permissions? (Choose all that apply.)

    A. NTFS permissions will override Share permissions if there is a conflict.

    B. NTFS permissions affect users at the local computer, but Share permissions do not.

    C. NTFS permissions are more restrictive in their access levels than Share permissions.

    D. NTFS permissions can be set at the file level, but Share permissions cannot.

19. Which type of security method is worn by employees and usually has a picture on it?

    A. Key fobs

    B. ID badges

    C. Smart card

    D. Biometrics

20. You and your family members all have iPhones. Someone generally forgets where they put their phone, and it would be nice to easily find it. In addition, you want to see where other family members are when they are around town. Which type of app will allow you to do this?

    A. Trusted source app

    B. Remote control app

    C. Locator app

    D. Firewall app

21. Which security mechanism specifies permissions for users and groups as well as the type of activities the users or groups can perform?

    A. ACL

    B. DLP

    C. AUP

    D. VPN

22. Which of the following statements are true regarding file attributes on a Windows 7 workstation? (Choose two.)

    A. File attributes are available only on NTFS volumes.

    B. Only members of the Administrators group can change file attributes.

    C. The `attrib` command modifies file attributes.

    D. Compression is enabled as a file attribute.

23. Several workstations on your network have not had their operating systems updated in more than a year, and your antivirus software is also out-of-date. What type of security threat does this represent?

    A. Noncompliant systems

    B. Zombie/botnet

    C. Zero-day attack

    D. Brute forcing

24. You have been hired to implement new network security practices. One of the things you need to do is create a document describing the proper usage of company hardware and software. What is this type of document called?

    A. DLP

    B. AUP

    C. ACL

    D. Least privilege

25. You have a Windows 7 Enterprise workstation and want to encrypt the entire hard drive, including startup files. Which technology best meets your needs?

    A. Windows 7 Enterprise does not allow for the encryption of startup files.

    B. BitLocker

    C. BitLocker To Go

    D. EFS

26. Software was installed on a laptop without the user's knowledge. The software has been tracking the user's keystrokes and has transmitted the user's credit card information to an attacker. What type of threat is this?

    A. Zombie/botnet

    B. Spoofing

    C. Spyware

    D. Ransomware

27. A new user named Jelica has joined your company as a network administrator. Which of the following statements is most correct regarding her network access?

    A. She should have just one user account, with administrator-level permissions.

    B. She should have just one user account, with standard user-level permissions.

    C. She should have two user accounts, one with user-level permissions and one with administrator-level permissions.

    D. She should have thee user accounts, one with user-level permissions, one with administrator-level permissions, and one with remote access administrator-permissions.

28. Which types of security threats are direct attacks on user passwords? (Choose two.)

    A. Brute force

    B. Zombie/botnet

    C. Dictionary attack

    D. Spoofing

29. You read corporate email on your iPhone and do not want others to access the phone if you leave it somewhere. What is the first layer of security that you should implement to keep others from using your phone?

    A. Multifactor authentication

    B. Full device encryption

    C. Screen lock

    D. Remote wipe software

30. You use your mobile phone for email and extensive Internet browsing. You want to add an additional level of security to always verify your identity online when accessing various accounts. Which type of app do you need?

    A. Authenticator app

    B. Trusted source app

    C. Biometric authentication app

    D. Account encryption app

31. You have instructed users on your network to not use common words for their passwords. What type of attack are you trying to prevent?

    A. Brute forcing

    B. Dictionary attack

    C. Social engineering

    D. Shoulder surfing

32. Which type of malware is designed to look like a different program and, when installed, create a back door for an attacker to access the target system?

    A. Trojan

    B. Spyware

    C. Virus

    D. Worm

33. You have been asked to dispose of several old magnetic hard drives. What is the name of the process of using a large magnet to clear the data off a hard drive?

    A. Overwriting

    B. Zero writing

    C. Degaussing

    D. Incineration

34. You recently noticed a change on your computer. Now when you open your web browser, no matter what you search for, you get a dozen unsolicited pop-up windows offering to sell you items you didn't ask for. What type of problem does your computer have?

  A. Spyware

  B. Ransomware

  C. Zombie/botnet

  D. Trojan

35. On a Windows 7 workstation, there is one volume formatted with NTFS. The Developers group has Modify access to the C:\dev directory. You copy the folder to the C:\operations folder, to which the Developers group has Read access. What level of permissions will the Developers group have to the new C:\operations\dev directory?

  A. Full Control

  B. Modify

  C. Read & Execute

  D. Read

36. Your office has recently experienced several laptop thefts. Which security mechanism is designed to protect mobile devices from theft?

  A. Security token

  B. USB lock

  C. Key fob

  D. Privacy filter

37. Which type of security device displays a randomly generated code that the user enters for access to computer resources?

  A. ID badge

  B. RFID badge

  C. Smart card

  D. Key fob

38. Which type of digital security needs to have constant updates to best protect your network or computer?

  A. Antivirus

  B. Firewall

  C. Access control list

  D. Directory permissions

39. You are at work and receive a phone call. The caller ID indicates it's coming from your manager's desk. You can see your manager's desk and no one is sitting there. What is likely happening?

   A. A zombie/botnet attack

   B. An impersonation attack

   C. A zero-day attack

   D. A phishing attack

40. Graham is working on a Windows 7 workstation. His user account is a member of the Managers group. He is trying to access a folder named `reports`, located on a different computer. The NTFS permissions for the `reports` shared folder on that computer for the Managers group are Read and Write. The folder's shared permissions for the Managers group is Read permission. What is Graham's effective permissions on the `reports` folder?

   A. Full Control

   B. Read and Write

   C. Read

   D. No access

41. A system administrator is concerned about Windows users inadvertently installing malware from CD- or DVD-ROMs that contain malicious code. What can she do to help prevent this from happening?

   A. Set restrictive user permissions.

   B. Enable BIOS/UEFI passwords.

   C. Disable autorun.

   D. Enable data encryption.

42. You are configuring NTFS and Share permissions on a Windows 8.1 workstation. Which of the following statements is true regarding permissions?

   A. NTFS and Share permissions apply only when you are accessing a resource on the local machine.

   B. NTFS and Share permissions apply only when you are accessing a resource across the network.

   C. NTFS permissions apply when you are accessing a resource on the local machine or across the network. Share permissions apply only when you are accessing a resource across the network.

   D. NTFS permissions apply only when you are accessing a resource across the network. Share permissions apply when you are accessing resources on the local machine or across the network.

43. Which type of malware will attempt to hide itself by encrypting parts of itself, therefore changing its signature, to avoid detection?

    A. Retrovirus

    B. Stealth virus

    C. Phage virus

    D. Polymorphic virus

44. Which type of security threat gains administrative-level access for an attacker to perform another attack and then hides its presence from system management tools?

    A. Virus

    B. Spyware

    C. Rootkit

    D. Ransomware

45. Venkat wants to encrypt a few files on the NTFS volume on his Windows 7 workstation. He does not have administrative rights to the computer. Which of the following statements is correct?

    A. He can't encrypt files without administrative rights.

    B. He can use BitLocker.

    C. He can use BitLocker To Go.

    D. He can use EFS.

46. Which type of digital security is designed to protect your network from malicious software programs?

    A. Firewall

    B. DLP

    C. VPN

    D. Anti-malware

47. You are examining shared folders on a Windows 7 workstation. You notice that there is a shared folder named c$ that you didn't create. What is the most likely explanation for this share?

    A. An attacker has compromised the workstation and is using the share to control it.

    B. It's a local share that all users have access to.

    C. It's an administrative share that requires administrative privileges to access.

    D. It's an administrative share that all users have access to.

48. You are configuring NTFS and Share permissions on a Windows 7 workstation. Which of the following statements is true regarding permissions?

   A. Both NTFS and Share permissions can be applied only at the folder level.

   B. NTFS permissions can be applied at the file or folder level, and Share permissions can be applied only at the folder level.

   C. NTFS permissions can be applied only at the folder level, and Share permissions can be applied at the file or folder level.

   D. Both NTFS and Share permissions can be applied at the file or folder level.

49. Fiona is trying to access a folder on an NTFS volume on her local computer. She is a member of the Dev group. The Dev group's NTFS permissions are Allow Read & Execute. The share permissions for the Dev group are Deny Full Control. What is Fiona's effective permissions to this folder?

   A. Full Control

   B. Read & Execute

   C. Read

   D. No access

50. Which of the following security methods is a physical device that users carry around that provides access to network resources?

   A. Security token

   B. ID badge

   C. Biometrics

   D. Privacy filter

51. A system administrator is concerned about workstation security. He wants to be sure that workstations are not compromised when users are away from them during the workday. What should he implement?

   A. Login time restrictions

   B. Screen lock/time-out and screensaver passwords

   C. BIOS/UEFI passwords

   D. Restrictive user permissions

52. You are responsible for physically destroying several old hard drives with confidential information on them. Which methods are acceptable? (Choose two.)

   A. Incineration

   B. Power drill

   C. Degaussing

   D. Drive wipe

53. A user needs to download a new video card driver for her HP laptop. She finds the driver on the HP site and asks if she can download it. The HP site is an example of what?

   A. Part of an access control list

   B. An authenticator website

   C. A trusted software source

   D. An untrusted software source

54. You are planning a wireless network for a small office. Which of the following is a good rule of thumb when considering access point placement?

   A. Place them in walls or ceilings for protection.

   B. Place them near metal objects so the signal will reflect better.

   C. Place them in the center of the network area.

   D. Place them at the edge of the network area and focus them in the proper direction.

55. On the Internet, you get a news flash that the developer of one of your core applications found a security flaw. They will issue a patch for it in two days. Before you can install the patch, it's clear that the flaw has been exploited and someone has illegally accessed your network. What type of attack is this?

   A. Zombie/botnet

   B. Noncompliant system

   C. Zero-day attack

   D. Brute forcing

56. You have just installed a new wireless router for a small office network. You changed the username and password and the default SSID. Which other step should you take to increase the security of the wireless router?

   A. Enable WPS.

   B. Assign static IP addresses.

   C. Update the firmware.

   D. Enable port forwarding.

57. Which of the following types of security threats are generally not detectable by anti-malware software and consequently difficult to stop?

   A. Ransomware

   B. Trojans

   C. Rootkits

   D. Zero-day attack

58. Which type of malware will attack different parts of your system simultaneously, such as your boot sector, executable files, and data files?

   A. Phage virus

   B. Polymorphic virus

   C. Multipartite virus

   D. Retrovirus

59. You are creating a BYOD policy for mobile phones at your company. Which of the following are typically included in such a policy?

   A. Limits of proper use and authorized users

   B. Limits of proper use, authorized users, and software and security requirements

   C. Limits of proper use, authorized users, software and security requirements, and procedures for termination of employment

   D. Limits of proper use, authorized users, software and security requirements, procedures for termination of employment, and reimbursement policies

60. A user is worried about others peering over her shoulder to see sensitive information on her screen. What should she use to help avoid this problem?

   A. Mantrap

   B. Email filtering

   C. Privacy filter

   D. Smart card

61. Your company's website has been hit by a DDoS attack, coming from several hundred different IP addresses simultaneously. What type of attack did the hacker run first to enable this DDoS attack?

   A. Brute forcing

   B. Zero-day attack

   C. Zombie/botnet

   D. Noncompliant system

62. Aadi is trying to access a folder named Projects on a local NTFS volume. His user account is in the Developers group. The Developers group has Read & Execute permissions to the folder, and Aadi's user account has Full Control. What is Aadi's effective access to the Projects folder?

   A. Full Control

   B. Read & Execute

   C. Read

   D. No access

63. Alexandra is working on a Windows 7 workstation, formatted with NTFS. Her user account is a member of the Finance group. The Finance group has Read and Write NTFS permissions on the D:\reports folder. The folder is shared, and the Finance group has Read permission. What is Alexandra's effective permissions on the D:\reports folder?

   A. Full Control

   B. Read and Write

   C. Read

   D. No access

64. A network administrator wants to block all incoming network traffic on port 80. On which security mechanism can she disable port 80 traffic?

- **A.** Firewall
- **B.** VPN
- **C.** DLP
- **D.** Anti-malware

65. Which type of security system uses physical characteristics to allow or deny access to locations or resources?

- **A.** ID badges
- **B.** Mantrap
- **C.** Biometrics
- **D.** Tokens

66. An administrator is transferring confidential files from one Windows 8 Pro workstation to another, using a flash drive. Policy dictates that he encrypt the files on the flash drive. Which technology should he use?

- **A.** BitLocker To Go
- **B.** BitLocker
- **C.** EFS
- **D.** Windows 8 does not allow for the encryption of files on a flash drive.

67. Which type of malware will directly attack your antivirus software, attempting to disable the software so it can infect the target system?

- **A.** Retrovirus
- **B.** Stealth virus
- **C.** Polymorphic virus
- **D.** Multipartite virus

68. You are disposing of used hard drives, and a network administrator recommends performing a low-level format. What is the difference between a low-level format and a standard format?

- **A.** Low-level formats are performed at the factory, and standard formats are performed using the `format` command.
- **B.** Standard formats are performed at the factory, and low-level formats are performed using the `format` command.
- **C.** A low-level format records the tracks and marks the start of each sector on each track. A standard format creates the file allocation table and root directory.
- **D.** A standard format records the tracks and marks the start of each sector on each track. A low-level format creates the file allocation table and root directory.

69. You are setting up a wireless router for a small office. They want to set up the network so only specific computers are allowed to join, and they will provide you with a list. What can you enable to achieve this?

A. WPS

B. Static IP addresses

C. Port mapping

D. MAC address filtering

70. Which type of malware is designed to replicate itself and spread, without the need for inadvertent user action to help it do this?

A. Virus

B. Worm

C. Trojan

D. Spyware

71. Your network has recently been hit with a significant amount of spam messages. What should you implement to help reduce this nuisance?

A. Firewall

B. Email filtering

C. Access control list

D. A trusted software source list

72. You want to grant LaCrea the ability to change permissions for others on the Equity folder, which is on an NTFS volume. Which level of NTFS permission do you need to grant her?

A. Modify

B. Read & Execute

C. Change Permissions

D. Full Control

73. You read an article on the Internet about a hacker who bragged about creating a program that can try to log in by guessing one million passwords per second. What type of attack is he attempting?

A. Dictionary attack

B. Zombie/botnet

C. Phishing

D. Brute forcing

74. Which of the following security methods will prove to be ineffectual when trying to prevent software-based attacks? (Choose two.)

A. Mantrap

B. Firewall

C. Anti-malware

D. Privacy filter

75. You have been instructed to destroy several old hard drives that contained confidential information, so you take them to a local company that specializes in this process. The IT director wants confirmation that the drives were properly destroyed. What do you need to provide him with?

A. Hard drive fragments

B. Photos of the destroyed hard drives

C. A notarized letter from the disposal company

D. A certificate of destruction

76. You have a corporate iPhone. Today, you notice that there is a new iOS update available for your device. For the best security, which of the following is recommended?

A. Wait until corporate IT approves the change before updating your OS.

B. Update your OS immediately.

C. Wait one week to ensure that the OS update has no issues and then update your device.

D. Ignore the update until you confirm with corporate IT that it's not a Trojan or other malware.

77. Larissa is trying to access the `Flatfiles` folder on a remote NTFS volume. She is a member of the Datateam group. The Datateam group has NTFS permissions of Allow Read & Execute. The folder is shared with the Datateam group, but there are no explicit Allow or Deny permissions checked. What is Larissa's access level to the `Flatfiles` folder?

A. Full Control

B. Read & Execute

C. Read

D. No access

78. Sue is an administrator on the network and is logged in with an account in the Users group but not the Administrators group. She needs to run SFC on the computer, which requires administrative privileges. What is the easiest way for her to do this?

A. Log off and back on again with an account that is part of the Administrators group. Then open a command prompt and run SFC.

B. Open a command prompt by choosing Run As Administrator and then run SFC.

C. Right-click the SFC icon in Control Panel and choose Run As Administrator.

D. Reboot the computer. Log on with an account that is part of the Administrators group. Then open a command prompt and run SFC.

79. Priscila is working at a Windows 8.1 workstation, formatted with NTFS. She is a member of the Dev group and the Ops group. The Dev group has Read access to the `projects` folder, and the Ops group has Write access. What is Priscila's effective permissions for the `projects` folder?

A. Full Control

B. Read

C. Read and Write

D. No access

80. Which type of security method allows you to get your security device in close proximity to a reader (but doesn't require touching) to validate access?

    A. PIN code

    B. Badge reader

    C. Security token

    D. Biometrics

81. Someone has configured an external server with an IP address that should belong to one of your sister company's servers. With this new computer, they are attempting to establish a connection to your internal network. What type of attack is this?

    A. Spoofing

    B. Man-in-the-middle

    C. Zombie/botnet

    D. Noncompliant system

82. Which type of security device often incorporates RFID technology to grant access to secure areas or resources?

    A. Smart card

    B. Security token

    C. Mantrap

    D. Key fob

83. You are configuring a wireless network for a small office. What should you enable for the best encryption possible for network transmissions?

    A. WPA2

    B. WEP

    C. WPA

    D. WPS

84. Which of the following prevention methods will best deter the usefulness of Dumpster diving for confidential materials?

    A. Document shredding

    B. Privacy filters

    C. Cable locks

    D. Firewalls

85. Which types of security threats involve the attacker attempting to directly contact a potential victim? (Choose two.)

    A. Spoofing

    B. Phishing

    C. Social engineering

    D. Brute forcing

86. Jennie uses her security badge to enter the building through a secured door. Tim tries to enter the building behind her before the door closes, without swiping a badge. What type of behavior is Tim demonstrating?

   A. Shoulder surfing

   B. Man-in-the-middle

   C. Brute force

   (D) Tailgating

87. After installing a wireless router, a technician notices that he is able to get a network signal in the parking lot. The manager is afraid of potential attackers performing war driving. What can the technician do to reduce the risk of this?

   A. Disable the SSID broadcast.

   (B.) Reduce the radio power level.

   C. Enable WPS.

   D. Assign static IP addresses.

88. You receive an email from one of your friends. In it, she includes a link telling you to click it to see some recent pictures she took of you. It's been several weeks since you've seen this friend, and you are suspicious. What could this be an example of?

   (A.) Spear phishing

   B. Zombie/botnet

   C. Social engineering

   D. Zero-day attack

89. You receive an email from an overseas bank notifying you that a relative has left you a large sum of money. You need to respond with your bank routing information so they can electronically transfer the funds directly to your account. What is this most likely an example of?

   (A) Phishing

   B. Ransomware

   C. Spoofing

   (D) Spear phishing

90. What type of physical security explicitly relies upon a security guard or other personnel to determine who can access the facility?

   (A) Entry control roster

   B. Mantrap

   C. ID badges

   D. Biometrics

91. Which user account on a Microsoft Windows workstation has the least restrictive permissions by default?

    A. Administrator

    B. Root

    C. Guest

    D. Standard User

92. Which type of malware will often cause critical files to disappear, often while displaying a taunting message, and requires user intervention (usually inadvertent) to spread from computer to computer?

    A. Worm

    B. Virus

    C. Trojan

    D. Rootkit

93. It appears as though someone is trying to log in to a user account by guessing the password. Which account management policy will help prevent this type of attack?

    A. Setting failed attempts lockout

    B. Disabling autologin

    C. Requiring strong passwords

    D. Setting password expiration

94. Dianne is typing her password in to her workstation and notices her co-worker Todd hovering nearby. When she glances up at him, it appears as though he was watching her type, and he quickly looks away. What is this an example of?

    A. Phishing

    B. Spoofing

    C. Tailgating

    D. Shoulder surfing

95. You are installing a small office wired network. The manager is concerned that employees will visit websites with objectionable material. Which feature should you look for in a router to help prevent such access?

    A. Content filtering

    B. Disabling ports

    C. VPN access

    D. Port forwarding/mapping

96. Your office is in a building with several other companies. You want to configure the wireless network so that casual users in the building are not able to easily see your network name. What should you do to configure this?

  A. Enable WPA2.

  B. Enable MAC filtering.

  C. Disable SSID broadcasts.

  D. Reduce radio power levels.

97. You have a Windows domain network and want to ensure that users are required to maintain strong passwords. What is the best way to implement this on the network?

  A. Use a firewall.

  B. Use a VPN.

  C. Use DLP.

  D. Use Group Policy.

98. You are planning security protocols for your company's new server room. What's the simplest way to help keep potential attackers away from your servers?

  A. Install a mantrap.

  B. Use cable locks.

  C. Lock the doors.

  D. Implement biometrics.

99. A user on your network reported that his screen went blank and a message popped up. It's telling him that his files are no longer accessible, and if he wants them back, he needs to enter a credit card number and pay a $200 fee. Which type of malware has infected his system?

  A. Rootkit

  B. Ransomware

  C. Trojan

  D. Spyware

100. You are setting up a new wireless router for a home office. Which of the following should you change when initially configuring the network? (Choose two.)

  A. The router administrator's username and password

  B. The default SSID

  C. The radio power level

  D. The WPS setting

101. You are configuring a router for a small office network. The network users should be able to access regular and secure websites and send and receive email. Those are the only connections allowed to the Internet. Which security precaution should you take to prevent additional traffic from coming through the router?

   A. Enable MAC filtering.

   B. Enable content filtering.

   C. Enable port forwarding/mapping.

   D. Use port security.

102. Your iPhone requires a passcode to unlock it. Because of recent phone thefts around your office, you want to set your phone so that all data is destroyed if incorrect passcodes are entered 10 times in a row. Which feature allows you to do this?

   A. Failed login attempts restrictions

   B. Screen locks

   C. Remote wipes

   D. Locator applications

103. On a Windows 8 workstation, there are two NTFS volumes. The Managers group has Modify access to the D:\mgmt directory. You move the folder to the D:\keyfiles folder, to which the Managers group has Read access. What level of permissions will the Managers group have to the new D:\keyfiles\mgmt directory?

   A. Full Control

   B. Modify

   C. Read & Execute

   D. Read

104. For users to log on to your network from a remote location, they are required to supply a username and password as well as a code from an RSA token. What type of security is this an example of?

   A. Using a firewall

   B. Using multifactor authentication

   C. Using an access control list

   D. Using the principle of least privilege

105. You want to recycle some hard drives that your company no longer uses but do not want other people to have access to the data. Which methods of removing the data are acceptable for your purposes? (Choose two.)

   A. Formatting the drive

   B. Using an overwrite utility

   C. Using a drive wipe utility

   D. Using electromagnetic fields

106. Which of the following file attributes are turned on by default for system files on a Windows 8.1 workstation? (Choose two.)

    A. Hidden

    B. Archive

    C. System

    D. Read-only

107. You have just installed a Windows 8.1 workstation. For better security, which user account should you disable?

    A. Default User

    B. Administrator

    C. Power User

    D. Guest

108. Which type of network attack involves an intermediary hardware device intercepting data and altering it or transmitting it to an unauthorized user?

    A. Man-in-the-middle

    B. Noncompliant system

    C. Zombie/botnet

    D. Spoofing

109. You are implementing new password policies for your network, and you want to follow guidelines for password best practices. Which of the following will best help improve the security of your network? (Choose two.)

    A. Require passwords to expire every 180 days.

    B. Require passwords to be at least 8 characters long.

    C. Require passwords to have a special character.

    D. Require passwords to be no more than 10 characters long.

110. What does NTFS use to track users and groups and their level of access?

    A. ACLs

    B. Tokens

    C. Badges

    D. Control rosters

111. An administrator has granted a user Read & Execute permissions to the `C:\files` folder. Which of the following statements are true regarding subfolders of `C:\files`? (Choose two.)

    A. The user will have no access to subfolders of `C:\files`.

    B. The user will have Read & Execute access to subfolders of `C:\files`.

    C. Explicit permissions assigned to `C:\files\morefiles` will override those set on `C:\files`.

    D. Explicit permissions assigned to `C:\files` files override those set on `C:\files\morefiles`.

112. Which type of digital security method would you use if you wanted to monitor who is using data and transmitting it on the network?

A. VPN

B. Firewall

C. Access control system

D. DLP

113. You have created a user account for a contract employee, who will be with the company for one month. Which user group should this user's account be placed in?

A. Power Users

B. Administrators

C. Standard Users

D. Guest

114. On your network, there are multiple systems that users need to access, such as a Windows domain, a Box (cloud) site for storage, and SAP. You want to configure the network such that users do not need to remember separate usernames or passwords for each site; their login credentials will be good for different systems. Which technology should you use?

A. EFS

B. BTG

C. SSO

D. DLP

115. You are disconnecting a Windows 10 workstation from your network due to being compromised by malware. With minimal time for investigating the scope of the malware's impact on the workstation, what would be your next step?

A. Backup and Restore

B. Emergency Repair Disk creator

C. System Recovery Options

D. Uninstall the suspect application through Control Panel.

116. A user discovers a strange text file at the root of her User directory. It contains everything she has typed over the past few days, including her credentials. What is the likely cause of the text file?

A. System auditing enabled

B. Keylogger installed

C. Email application in debug mode

D. Backup file

117. A user asks what can be done to keep his web browsing private. Which of the following would accomplish that?

   A. Software firewall

   B. SecureDNS

   C. Anti-malware

   D. Antivirus

118. What security solution would protect a user from unwanted network traffic probing her workstation?

   A. Software firewall

   B. SecureDNS

   C. Anti-malware

   D. Antivirus

119. A user is taking a flight tomorrow and intends on using his laptop while seated on the plane. The user asks what steps he can take protect his privacy from wandering eyes sitting next to them. What could you offer to install on their laptop?

   A. Software firewall

   B. Multifactor authentication

   C. Antivirus

   D. Privacy screen

120. What security concept helps to ensure non-repudiation (assurance that someone cannot deny something) when sending emails?

   A. Comprehensive email signature

   B. Digital signature using certificates

   C. Phoning immediately after email is sent

   D. Texting immediately after email is sent

121. The user wants to use multifactor authentication at her PC but does not want to carry a key fob and is strongly against biometrics. What method can you suggest?

   A. Second password

   B. Hardware token

   C. Software token

   D. Fingerprint reader

122. What wireless protocol compensates for the weak encryption of WEP?

   A. VLAN

   B. TKIP

   C. VPN

   D. DLP

123. Which of the following Active Directory concepts can help enforce security settings? (Choose two)

    A. DLP

    B. Group Policy/updates

    C. Port security

    D. Login script

124. What 128-bit block size encryption algorithm, originally named Rijndael, was designed to replace DES?

    A. VPN

    B. DES3

    C. Caesar

    D. AES

125. What protocol was designed to authenticate remote users to a dial-in access server?

    A. TKIP

    B. TACACS

    C. VPN

    D. RADIUS

126. Which of the following encryption protocols is older than RADIUS but was used for similar purposes?

    A. TACACS+

    B. TACACS

    C. Extended TACACS

    D. SNMP

127. Your datacenter recently experienced a theft of a server from the rack. Which security mechanism would protect servers from future theft?

    A. Security token

    B. Server lock

    C. Key fob

    D. Firewall

128. A user is complaining that he can no longer sign into his account because of too many bad attempts. What basic Active Directory function would help here?

    A. Account creation

    B. Account deletion

    C. Password reset/unlock account

    D. Disable account

129. What concept in Active Directory creates a directory subdivision within which may be placed users, groups and other objects?

    A. User

    B. Domain

    C. Home folder

    D. Organizational unit

130. Normally, a company places a users' profiles and folders on the local machine. Now, the organization would like a few users to be able to log in from other computers. What concept in Active Directory allows a user's profile folders to be placed in storage somewhere else on the network?

    A. Home folder

    B. Folder redirection

    C. Organizational unit

    D. VPN

131. Which command-line tool permits someone to make changes to the operating system without having to boot up Windows?

    A. NSLOOKUP

    B. Emergency repair disk

    C. System recovery options

    D. WinRE / Recovery Console

132. Rainbow tables are used for what purpose?

    A. To offer more color options for the desktop background

    B. To compare cryptographic hashes for cracking passwords

    C. To reverse polarity of the DVI video connector

    D. To provide seven times the network bandwidth of the NIC

133. A Windows server volume for the Finance department is formatted with NTFS. The folder C:\receipts is shared with Travel group. Both Travel and Finance groups have Modify access to the directory C:\receipts. You move the C:\receipts folder to be under the C:\bigmoney folder. The Finance group alone has only Read access to the directory C:\bigmoney. Also, the C:\bigmoney folder is set to not propagate its permissions to any descendant folders. After the move, who has what permissions with the C:\bigmoney\receipts folder?

    A. Finance group alone has only Read access

    B. Both Finance and Travel have Read access

    C. Both Finance and Travel have Modify access

    D. Finance has Read, but Travel has Modify

134. A Microsoft Windows mobile device has the ability to back up applications, settings, camera pictures and text messages. Backups can be saved locally or remotely. Which of the following remote backup applications is easiest and capable to save the listed data in the cloud?

　　A. No extra app needed for device to save all data remotely

　　B. Microsoft OneDrive

　　C. Microsoft Azure

　　D. Time Machine

135. Windows user profiles contain a user's settings and personal files. Profiles can be configured as either local, remote, mandatory or temporary, depending on user needs and company policy. Which of the following is the optimal user profile choice for a traveling sales engineer who may or may not have network access?

　　A. local

　　B. remote

　　C. mandatory

　　D. temporary

Chapter

8

Software Troubleshooting

**THE FOLLOWING COMPTIA A+ EXAM
220-1002 TOPICS ARE COVERED IN THIS
CHAPTER:**

✓ **3.1 Given a scenario, troubleshoot Microsoft Windows
OS problems.**

- Common symptoms
  - Slow performance
  - Limited connectivity
  - Failure to boot
  - No OS found
  - Application crashes
  - Blue screens
  - Black screens
  - Printing issues
  - Services fail to start.
  - Slow bootup
  - Slow profile load
- Common solutions
  - Defragment the hard drive.
  - Reboot.
  - Kill tasks.
  - Restart services.
  - Update network settings.
  - Reimage/reload OS.
  - Roll back updates.

- Roll back devices drivers.

- Apply updates.

- Repair application.

- Update boot order.

- Disable Windows services/applications.

- Disable application startup.

- Safe boot

- Rebuild Windows profiles.

✓ **3.2 Given a scenario, troubleshoot and resolve PC security issues.**

- Common symptoms

  - Pop-ups

  - Browser redirection

  - Security alerts

  - Slow performance

  - Internet connectivity issues

  - PC/OS lockup

  - Application crash

  - OS updates failures

  - Rogue antivirus

  - Spam

  - Renamed system files

  - Disappearing files

  - File permission changes

  - Hijacked email

    - Responses from users regarding email

    - Automated replies from unknown sent email

  - Access denied

  - Invalid certificate (trusted root CA)

  - System/application log errors

✓ **3.3 Given a scenario, use best practice procedures for malware removal.**

- 1. Identify and research malware symptoms.
- 2. Quarantine the infected systems.
- 3. Disable System Restore (in Windows).
- 4. Remediate the infected systems.
    - a. Update the anti-malware software.
    - b. Scan and use removal techniques (safe mode, pre-installation environment).
- 5. Schedule scans and run updates.
- 6. Enable System Restore and create a restore point (in Windows).
- 7. Educate the end user.

✓ **3.4 Given a scenario, troubleshoot mobile OS and application issues.**

- Common symptoms
    - Dim display
    - Intermittent wireless
    - No wireless connectivity
    - No Bluetooth connectivity
    - Cannot broadcast to external monitor
    - Touchscreen non-responsive
    - Apps not loading
    - Slow performance
    - Unable to decrypt email
    - Extremely short battery life
    - Overheating
    - Frozen system
    - No sound from speakers
    - Inaccurate touch screen response
    - System lockout
    - App log errors

✓ **3.5 Given a scenario, troubleshoot mobile OS and application security issues.**

- Common symptoms
  - Signal drop/weak signal
  - Power drain
  - Slow data speeds
  - Unintended WiFi connection
  - Unintended Bluetooth pairing
  - Leaked personal files/data
  - Data transmission over limit
  - Unauthorized account access
  - Unauthorized location tracking
  - Unauthorized camera/microphone activation
  - High resource utilization

1. Your network has 24 Windows 8.1 workstations. The office manager is concerned about spyware. What does Windows 8.1 come with, if anything, that will help thwart spyware?

    A. Windows 8.1 does not come with spyware protection.

    B. Windows Firewall

    C. Windows Defender

    D. Windows Anti-malware

2. An iPhone user calls to report that his phone has no wireless connectivity. What is the first thing you should tell him to do?

    A. Turn the phone off and back on.

    B. Perform a reset to the factory default.

    C. Check whether airplane mode is on.

    D. Adjust the Wi-Fi signal receptivity.

3. A Windows 7 workstation will not boot properly. Instead, there is an error message stating that there is no OS found. How do you fix this problem?

    A. Boot to the installation DVD, open a command prompt, and type **Startup Repair**.

    B. Boot to the installation DVD, open SFC, and choose Startup Repair.

    C. Boot to the installation DVD, open System Recovery Options, and choose Startup Repair.

    D. Boot to Safe Mode, open System Recovery Options, and choose Startup Repair.

4. You have a user with an iPhone, and the device appears to be locked up. You need to tell him how to perform a hard reset. What do you tell him?

    A. Press and hold the Sleep/Wake and Home buttons for at least 10 seconds until you see the Apple logo and then let go.

    B. Press and hold the Sleep/Wake button until the red slider appears and then drag the slider to power off the device.

    C. Use a paperclip or pen point to press and hold the indented reset button on the bottom of the phone until you see the Apple logo and then let go.

    D. Open iTunes or iCloud, log in with his account, and enter recovery mode.

5. Your company purchases a custom database software package from an outside vendor. You install the client software on a Windows 10 workstation, and it crashes when you try to open it. You remove the software and reinstall it, but it still crashes when you open it. What should you do next?

    A. Run an antivirus remediation on the workstation.

    B. Contact the vendor to see whether an update or patch is available.

    C. Delete and reinstall Windows.

    D. Enable Software Compatibility through Control Panel.

6. On your MacBook Pro, you use the Safari browser to surf the Internet. Yesterday a friend borrowed your laptop. Today, when you try to browse the web, no matter what site URL you type in to the address bar, you are sent to a different website. What is most likely happening to your computer?

   A. A practical joke by your friend

   B. Browser redirection

   C. Rogue antivirus

   D. It has been infected with spam.

7. A Windows 8.1 workstation boots with this error message: "Security Center service cannot be started." You try to start the service manually, but it still refuses to start. What should you do to try to fix the issue?

   A. Use Event Viewer to see whether it produced any error codes.

   B. Use automated system recovery to fix the service.

   C. Run REGSVR32 to fix the issue.

   D. Run SFC /SCANNOW to fix the issue.

8. A user has an iPhone and has forgotten the passcode. He has entered in the passcode several times, and it will not unlock. He turned the phone off and back on, and the passcode is still invalid. What can he do to unlock the phone?

   A. Perform a reset to the factory default.

   B. Crack the phone using a back door from Apple.

   C. Perform a hard reset.

   D. Perform a soft reset.

9. You want to display the contents of your iPad on a full-sized computer monitor. The monitor has a DVI connector. What do you need to do?

   A. Turn on video broadcast mode.

   B. Plug the monitor in to the iPad's DVI port.

   C. Purchase a USB to DVI adapter.

   D. Purchase a Lightning to DVI adapter.

10. An iPhone user reports that his phone will not connect to his wireless headset for hands-free phone calls. His headset is powered on and has worked previously. His iPhone screen is shown here. What is most likely the problem?

   A. The headset is not paired with the iPhone.

   B. Bluetooth is turned off.

   C. Wi-Fi is turned off.

   D. Airplane mode is turned on.

11. You are troubleshooting a Windows 10 workstation that could have malware on it. To follow the best practices for malware removal, what is the first step you should take?

   A. Quarantine the infected system.

   B. Update the anti-malware software.

   C. Enable system restore and create a restore point.

   D. Identify malware symptoms.

12. Recently, users on your company network have been flooded with unrequested emails trying to sell them goods and services. Which solution will most likely resolve this issue?

   A. Install anti-malware on all client computers.

   B. Install antivirus on all client computers.

   C. Install a spam filter on the email server.

   D. Renew the invalid certificate on the email server.

13. Your network has several dozen mobile device users. Several of them have reported that there are areas within your office where network access is very slow. What can you use to test wireless access?

   A. Wi-Fi analyzer

   B. Cell tower analyzer

   C. Data transmission analyzer

   D. Hot spot analyzer

14. You just installed a new sound card in a Windows 7 workstation. Now, the computer has crashed and given you a blue screen of death. You turn the computer off. What should you try to resolve the issue?

    A. Reinstall Windows.

    B. Boot to the Windows installation CD and start the Recovery Console.

    C. Boot to Safe Mode and uninstall the sound card driver.

    D. Remove the sound card from the computer and reboot.

15. An iPad user reports that when he is in a certain part of the building, his wireless connection intermittently drops. What are the two most likely causes of this? (Choose two.)

    A. Poor wireless buffering in the iPad

    B. Interference with the wireless signal

    C. Weak signal strength from the wireless access point

    D. Retracted Wi-Fi antenna on the iPad

16. A network user with an Android tablet wants to back up and synchronize her data with her phone. Which service should she use to perform these tasks?

    A. Google Sync

    B. Google Cloud

    C. Android Sync

    D. Android Cloud

17. A technician is troubleshooting a Windows 10 computer that is acting strangely, and she suspects that it's infected with a virus. She has followed the best practices for malware removal and remediated the computer. What should she do next?

    A. Schedule scans and run updates.

    B. Educate the end user.

    C. Enable system restore and create a restore point.

    D. Disable system restore.

18. You are training technicians on the shutdown methods of an iPhone. What are two key differences between a soft reset and a hard reset? (Choose two.)

    A. A hard reset will delete all data on the phone, and a soft reset will not.

    B. A hard reset will work if the touch screen is unresponsive, and a soft reset will not.

    C. A soft reset will keep the data of running applications, and a hard reset will not.

    D. A soft reset will not reset the password, and a hard reset will.

19. A Windows 8 workstation will not load properly. During the Windows 8 boot process, the MBR is responsible for loading which key Windows file?

    A. BOOTMGR

    B. NTLDR

    C. WINRESUME

    D. WINLOAD

20. You are training a class on the installation and repair of Windows 10. What is the purpose of the Windows PE? (Choose two.)

- **A.** Runs as an operating system on thin clients
- **B.** Collects information during a Windows 10 install
- **C.** Launches the Windows RE for troubleshooting
- **D.** Repairs system files if any become corrupted

21. A technician is working on a Windows 10 workstation. Which command should she use to scan and fix corrupted system files?

- **A.** SFC /SCANFIX
- **B.** SFC /OFFBOOTDIR
- **C.** SFC /VERIFYFILE
- **D.** SFC /SCANNOW

22. You believe that someone has been trying to hack into a Windows 7 workstation by guessing passwords. Another administrator suggests you check the log files to be sure. Which utility can you use to see log files?

- **A.** Event Viewer
- **B.** Recovery Console
- **C.** Security Console
- **D.** System Monitor

23. You power on your Windows 8.1 client computer, and Windows will not load. When you investigate, you notice that the BOOTMGR file has been renamed DASBOOTMGR. You were the last one to use this workstation. What is the most likely cause?

- **A.** Practical joke
- **B.** Rogue antivirus
- **C.** Malware infection
- **D.** Quarantined boot files

24. You are talking to a friend about purchasing a gift, and he recommends a website to purchase it. When you put the website's address into your browser, you receive a message stating that there is an invalid certificate. What should you do?

- **A.** Visit the website anyway; it's probably OK.
- **B.** Do not visit the website.
- **C.** Visit the secure version of the website by changing the address to start with HTTPS://.
- **D.** Visit the unsecure version of the website by changing the address to start with HTTP://.

25. A workstation will not load Windows 7 properly after a driver was recently installed. The troubleshooting guide says to boot into Safe Mode. How do you do this in Windows 7?

    A. During the boot process, press F1.

    B. During the boot process, press Ctrl+Alt+Del.

    C. During the boot process, press F8.

    D. During the boot process, press F10.

26. You are concerned about workstations on your network getting viruses. You configure each machine with antivirus software. How often should the antivirus software update its database?

    A. Once per year

    B. Once per month

    C. Once per week

    D. Only as new threats are discovered

27. A user reports that his iPhone will not decrypt email. What is the most likely cause of this problem?

    A. iPhones can't read encrypted email.

    B. There's a problem with the S/MIME certificate.

    C. The user has a corrupt Mail app.

    D. Low memory. Restart the phone.

28. A user reports that his mobile phone has been experiencing high resource utilization for about a week. What two things should you immediately suspect could be causing the problem? (Choose two.)

    A. Unauthorized root access

    B. Failing battery

    C. Excessive open apps

    D. Stuck sync operation

29. A Windows 10 workstation will not boot properly. Windows starts to load but never finishes. After troubleshooting, you find that devices are not initializing. Which file is responsible for checking for installed devices and initializing them?

    A. WINRESUME

    B. WINLOAD

    C. BOOTMGR

    D. NTDETECT.COM

30. You are using an iPhone. When is it generally necessary to close running apps on the iPhone? (Choose two.)

    A. When you receive out-of-memory errors

    B. When the phone begins to overheat

    C. When an app locks up

    D. When you are done using them for the day

31. While working on a Windows 7 workstation, a user receives a flashing pop-up message saying that her computer has been infected with a virus and she needs to download a virus scanner now to fix it. What will most likely happen when she clicks the button to download the recommended virus scanner?

    A. It will download a virus to her computer.

    B. It will download an antivirus program to her computer and remediate the virus.

    C. The antivirus program she downloads will scan her computer and find nothing because her company already uses an antivirus program.

    D. It will take her to a website that will allow her to purchase an antivirus program to remediate the virus.

32. A Windows 7 workstation will not boot properly. It shows the Windows logo upon boot and then appears to lock up. No changes have recently been made to the workstation. What is most likely causing the problem?

    A. A missing or corrupt NTLDR file

    B. A missing or corrupt BOOTMGR file

    C. A missing or corrupt DLL file

    D. A corrupt file system driver

33. You have 20 Windows 7 workstations on your network. You want to create a bootable CD that will allow you to fix Windows boot issues in the event that you do not have a Windows installation CD available. Where can you create such a disc?

    A. Backup And Restore

    B. Emergency Repair Disk creator

    C. System Recovery Options

    D. Recovery Console

34. You are training technicians on the creation and use of restore points. Which of the following is not a way in which restore points get created?

    A. Windows creates them automatically by default.

    B. Windows creates them before a system crash.

    C. You can manually create them.

    D. Some installation utilities will create them before installing a new program.

35. You have a Windows 8.1 workstation that is running very slowly. When you look at the hard drive, you notice that very little space is available. Which tool should you run to attempt to free up space?

   A. DEFRAG

   B. Disk Cleanup

   C. REGSVR32

   D. SFC

36. A user reports that a Word document he needs will not open. Other documents open as they should. He has not made a backup of this file. Which of the following statements is true?

   A. The file is probably corrupt, and its contents are lost.

   B. He can use a restore point to get the file back.

   C. He can reboot into the Last Known Good configuration and then open the file.

   D. He can use the Emergency Repair Disk to repair the file and then open it.

37. You have an iPhone that has been charging for an hour. When you unplug it from the charger, the phone feels very hot to the touch. What should your next step be?

   A. Replace the phone.

   B. Replace the phone charger.

   C. Turn the phone off and let it cool down.

   D. Turn on airplane mode.

38. You receive an email warning you of a new form of ransomware. It contains a link to receive more information on how to protect yourself from this terrible threat. What should you do next?

   A. Click the link to receive more information.

   B. Check to ensure that your system has a rogue antivirus installed.

   C. Check www.us-cert.gov for information on the threat.

   D. Forward the email to everyone in your contacts list.

39. A user just dropped his Android phone, and the screen now has a large crack in it. The touch screen is unresponsive. He is in the field and needs contact information from his phone so he can call his client. What is his best option to get the phone working again?

   A. None. He will need to replace the phone.

   B. Reboot the phone.

   C. Perform a force stop.

   D. Reset the phone to the factory default settings.

40. You are visiting a customer's office in a large city high-rise building. You need to make a call on your mobile phone, but you have only one bar. The call will not complete. What should you do?

A. Wait a few minutes and try again.

B. Perform a soft reset.

C. Perform a hard reset.

D. Step outside or near a window to see whether your signal improves.

41. An iPhone user brings you her phone, and it's completely frozen. Neither the touch screen nor the buttons respond. What should you try first to make the phone work again?

A. Soft reset

B. Hard reset

C. Close running applications.

D. Reset to the factory default.

42. The GPS app on your mobile phone has stopped responding. What should you do to resolve the issue?

A. Perform a hard reset.

B. Perform a force stop.

C. Perform a soft reset.

D. Uninstall and reinstall the app.

43. A Windows 8 user wants to see who has successfully logged in or failed to log in to her workstation. What is the name of the specific log she should look for?

A. Security

B. Login

C. System

D. Authentication

44. A technician is troubleshooting a Windows 7 workstation that has been infected with malware. He has disabled system restore. Following the best practices for removing malware, what should he do next?

A. Quarantine the infected system.

B. Remediate the infected system.

C. Schedule a malware scan and run updates.

D. Educate the end user.

45. Mobile device users on your network are required to use a VPN app to connect to the corporate network when they are out of the office. A user reports that the app will not open for her. She turned her tablet off and back on again, and the app still will not open. What should she try next?

   A. Perform a soft reset.

   B. Perform a hard reset.

   C. Uninstall and reinstall the app.

   D. Perform a force stop.

46. A user on your network is concerned about spyware. What should be installed to help stop this threat?

   A. Antivirus software

   B. Anti-malware software

   C. Firewall

   D. Proxy server

47. A user with a Linux workstation reported that she received an error that says "kernel panic." What should she do to resolve the issue?

   A. Close the program that caused the error and continue working.

   B. Reboot the workstation and see whether the issue persists.

   C. Reboot into Safe Mode and run Linux Diagnostics to determine the cause of the problem.

   D. Reinstall Linux.

48. Your Windows 10 workstation started running very slowly. Which of the following could cause that to happen?

   A. Rogue antivirus

   B. Malware

   C. Hijacked email

   D. Invalid certificate

49. You want to broadcast the contents of your iPhone screen to a computer monitor. What are two ways you can accomplish this? (Choose two.)

   A. Use Apple TV.

   B. Enable iBroadcast on the iPhone.

   C. Download an app that lets you broadcast wirelessly.

   D. Plug the computer monitor in to the iPhone's video port.

50. You install an updated video card driver, and your Windows 10 workstation crashes with a blue screen of death. What are the quickest two options for getting your system running again? (Choose two.)

 A. Reinstall Windows.

 B. Boot to the Windows installation CD and start the Recovery Console.

 C. Boot to Safe Mode and uninstall the video card driver.

 D. Boot to the Last Known Good configuration.

51. Your Windows 7 workstation is having problems at startup. Too many applications are loading, and it is slowing the system down considerably. Which tool should you use to disable programs from loading automatically at startup?

 A. REGEDIT

 B. REGSVR32

 C. MSCONFIG

 D. Safe Mode

52. A user just tried to boot his Windows 7 workstation, and Windows will not load. When you investigate, you notice that several key boot files for Windows have been deleted. What is this a sign of?

 A. Virus infection

 B. Ransomware infection

 C. Rogue antivirus

 D. OS expiration

53. You have one Linux workstation on your network. Another administrator gives you advice on how to enable an antivirus program, and she tells you that you need to type in the commands. What is the name of the interface where you do this?

 A. Shell

 B. Bash

 C. Cmd

 D. Terminal

54. You arrive at work in the morning to see that your inbox is full of automated replies and out-of-office messages. The subject line is for something you did not send. What is this a sign of?

 A. Ransomware

 B. Hijacked email

 C. Rogue email server

 D. Rogue antivirus

55. You are troubleshooting a Windows 8.1 workstation that has contracted a virus. According to the best practices for malware removal, which two steps are part of remediating the infected system? (Choose two.)

    A. Disable system restore.

    B. Schedule scans and run updates.

    C. Scan for and remove the virus.

    D. Update antivirus software.

56. You have a Windows 8 workstation that is not booting properly. You need to boot to the installation DVD to repair the installation. Where do you make the change to the boot settings?

    A. Recovery console

    B. Automated system recovery

    C. BIOS/UEFI

    D. `MSCONFIG`

57. You are visiting a website using Internet Explorer, and without you clicking anything, a new Internet Explorer window opens in front of it with an advertisement. Which of the following is the most likely explanation?

    A. Your computer has been infected with adware.

    B. Your computer has been infected with spyware.

    C. Your computer has been infected with a virus.

    D. The website is programmed to show a pop-up advertisement.

58. In the afternoon, you start receiving email responses from co-workers and friends. They want to know why you are trying to directly sell them electronics through a suspicious-sounding website. What is most likely the cause of this?

    A. Hijacked email

    B. Poisoned email server

    C. Rogue antivirus

    D. Invalid certificate

59. A technician is describing a situation he had yesterday where the workstation gave him a kernel panic error and locked up. What operating system was the technician most likely dealing with?

    A. Windows 8.1

    B. MacOS

    C. Windows 10

    D. Linux

60. You are working on your Windows 7 computer and a security alert pops up, as shown here. What should your next action be?

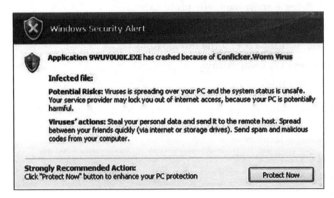

A. Click the Protect Now button.

B. Click the X in the upper-right corner to close the alert.

C. Shut down your computer. Reboot, and initiate a virus scan using your antivirus software.

D. Use System Restore to create a snapshot and then click the Protect Now button.

61. When booting a Windows 8.1 workstation, a user receives an error message about a missing DLL file. However, Windows still loads. Which utility should you use to attempt to fix the issue?

A. SFC

B. Recovery Console

C. REGSVR32

D. REGEDIT

62. The touch screen on a user's iPhone is not responding, and the phone is powered on. What should you recommend she do as a next step to get the phone working again?

A. Perform a hard reset.

B. Perform a soft reset.

C. Remove the battery to power it off. Reinsert the battery and turn it back on.

D. Perform a force stop.

63. On a Windows 7 workstation, you receive an error message that says "Security Center service cannot be started," but Windows still loads. What is the first step you should try in troubleshooting the problem?

A. Reinstall the service with SFC.

B. Reinstall the service with MSCONFIG.

C. Check to see whether the service is set to be started automatically in Services.

D. Check to see whether the service is set to be started automatically using REGEDIT.

64. An Android phone user just received a new Bluetooth headset for phone calls. She reports that it does not work with her phone. Both devices are powered on and appear to be operational. What is most likely the problem?

    A. Bluetooth is turned off on the Android device.

    B. Bluetooth is turned off on the mobile headset.

    C. The devices need to be paired.

    D. Airplane mode is on.

65. Your Windows 7 workstation performance has been slowing down, particularly when it comes to disk reads and writes. Which of the following tools is designed to help improve your hard disk performance?

    A. REGEDIT

    B. DEFRAG

    C. REGSVR32

    D. Event Viewer

66. You have a Windows 8.1 workstation that will not boot properly. After the POST, the screen displays a message saying "Operating System Not Found." What is most likely causing the problem?

    A. NTLDR

    B. BOOTMGR

    C. Boot.ini

    D. BCD

67. You are troubleshooting a Windows 7 workstation and believe it has malware. To follow the best practices for malware removal, after you identify the malware symptoms, which step should you take?

    A. Update the anti-malware software.

    B. Disable system restore.

    C. Quarantine the infected system.

    D. Scan for and remove the malware.

68. While driving through the remote countryside, you notice that your mobile phone battery has been quickly drained of power. What is the most likely cause of this?

    A. The battery needs to be replaced.

    B. The phone has been searching for a signal.

    C. You need to perform a soft reset.

    D. The phone needs to be replaced.

69. You have a workstation that dual-boots between Windows XP and Windows 8.1. When choosing to boot Windows XP, you receive an error message saying that NTLDR is missing. Which utilities will let you repair or replace this file? (Choose two.)

A. Recovery Console

B. REGSVR32

C. Repair disk

D. Safe Mode

70. An iPhone user is concerned about her privacy. She wants to ensure that others can't hack into her phone and track her location without her knowing about it. Which of the following actions will provide her with the least amount of protection to help prevent this from happening?

A. Install an iPhone anti-malware app.

B. Update iOS as soon as updates or patches are available.

C. Disable Location Services.

D. Enable sync with iCloud.

71. A user reports that the battery life on his iPhone is very short. It works for only about three hours before it needs to be recharged. What can you recommend he do to extend the battery life? (Choose two.)

A. Turn off unnecessary wireless connections.

B. Perform a reset to the factory defaults.

C. Set the screen to automatically dim.

D. Install an antivirus app.

72. You have just purchased an Android mobile phone and are concerned about security threats. Which of the following statements is true?

A. There are no viruses for Android-based mobile phones.

B. Android-based phones come with an automatically enabled antivirus app.

C. You should download and install an antivirus app.

D. As long as you automatically install OS patches, you will not get an Android virus.

73. A Windows 7 workstation has started exhibiting slow system performance. Where can you go in Windows to find tools to help you troubleshoot this problem?

A. Control Panel ➤ Performance Information And Tools

B. Control Panel ➤ System Tools

C. Control Panel ➤ Device Manager

D. Control Panel ➤ Configuration And Settings

74. You have an Android mobile phone. When you go outside, the screen of your phone is dim, and you can't see anything. What should you do to resolve the problem?

A. Power the device off and back on again.

B. Adjust the screen brightness settings.

C. Remove the screen protector.

D. Add an external battery pack.

75. Before you install a new antivirus program, a technician recommends that you manually create a restore point. What will the restore point do?

A. It will create a copy of the entire hard drive.

B. It will create a copy of system configuration data.

C. It will create a copy of the Users folder and system configuration data.

D. It will create a bootable disk with copies of key system files.

76. An employee with an iPhone quit, and you are giving his iPhone to a new employee. What should you do to the phone before giving it to the new user?

A. Perform a hard reset.

B. Perform a soft reset.

C. Reset to the factory default.

D. Adjust configurations/settings.

77. Your iPad is experiencing slow performance. What are the best two options to increase performance speed? (Choose two.)

A. Close open apps.

B. Perform a reset to the factory default.

C. Increase the RAM.

D. Perform a soft reset.

78. You are working on a Windows workstation. When it boots up, it produces an error message that says "Missing Boot.ini" and does not boot any further. What is the purpose of the Boot.ini file?

A. In Windows XP and older, it identifies where the boot files are for the operating system.

B. In Windows 7 and newer, it identifies where the boot files are for the operating system.

C. In Windows XP and older, it starts the bootstrapping of the operating system.

D. In Windows 7 and newer, it starts the bootstrapping of the operating system.

79. A user with an iPhone reports that almost immediately after she touches her touch screen, the screen becomes dark and hard to read. What should she do to fix this?

A. Remove the screen protector.

B. Replace the phone.

C. Adjust the settings to keep it from dimming so quickly.

D. Power the device off and back on again.

80. You have an Android tablet. The screen does not seem to accurately sense where you are touching on the touch pad. You reboot and the problem is still there. What should you do?

    A. Replace the tablet.

    B. Calibrate the screen.

    C. Disable the gyroscope.

    D. Remove the screen protector.

81. A Windows 10 workstation will not load Windows. Which file in the boot process is responsible for switching the system from real mode to protected mode?

    A. NTLDR

    B. BOOTMGR

    C. WINLOAD

    D. WINRESUME

82. You are working on a Windows 8.1 workstation that has dual monitors. For some reason, everything on the secondary monitor is upside down. What is the easiest solution to this problem?

    A. Turn the monitor over.

    B. Right-click the desktop, choose Screen Resolution, and change the monitor orientation.

    C. Reinstall the video card driver.

    D. Right-click the desktop, choose Video, and change the monitor orientation.

83. A Windows 7 workstation will boot only into Safe Mode. Even after multiple reboots, Windows will not load properly. Which tool should you use to scan for problems?

    A. REGEDIT

    B. MSCONFIG

    C. Event Viewer

    D. Recovery Console

84. A user with an Android phone reports that she is running out of memory on her phone. Which of the following will help resolve that issue?

    A. Uninstall apps.

    B. Perform a soft reset.

    C. Perform a hard reset.

    D. Perform a force stop.

85. On your mobile phone, you notice that you are connected to a Wi-Fi network that you don't recognize instead of your normal home network. What is a possible consequence of this unintended Wi-Fi connection?

A. More susceptible to hacking

B. Better Internet access speed

C. Battery drain

D. Network interference

86. You are training new users on proper mobile device usage. In the class, you suggest that they disable their Bluetooth connection unless they need it. What is the biggest risk caused by an unintended Bluetooth pairing?

A. Power drain

B. Security risk

C. Data transmission over-limit risk

D. High resource utilization risk

87. Your MacBook Pro appears to be unresponsive, and the cursor has changed to a rotating pinwheel. What should you do next?

A. Force a reboot of the system.

B. Wait for the problem to clear and then resume working.

C. Open Apple Diagnostics to see what the problem is.

D. Reboot the Mac into Safe Mode.

88. A network user with an iPad wants to back up her data. Which of the following are options for her to use? (Choose two.)

A. iSync

B. iPadPlus

C. iTunes

D. iCloud

89. You are training new company employees on the proper use of Windows 8.1 workstations. What are two problems that could likely arise from improperly shutting down a workstation? (Choose two.)

A. Data loss in important files

B. Corrupt DLL files

C. Corrupt device drivers

D. Windows may fail to start.

90. You use the most recent version of Internet Explorer to browse the Internet on your Windows 8.1 workstation. Today when you try to visit any website, you receive an error message that there is an invalid certificate. It happens regardless of the site you visit. What should you do?

    A. Check your computer's time and date.

    B. Refresh your certificate through Control Panel ➤ Security.

    C. Refresh your certificate through Control Panel ➤ Internet Options.

    D. In Internet Explorer, set the security level for the Internet zone to Low.

91. You are educating network users about software security challenges. A user asks what the best way to avoid spam is. What should you recommend to the group?

    A. Install an antivirus program on your computer.

    B. Install anti-malware on your computer.

    C. Only visit websites that have a secure site (that start with HTTPS://).

    D. Don't give your email address to websites.

92. Mobile device users on your network report that the network has very slow data speeds. Which of the following are likely contributors to this problem? (Choose two.)

    A. Low battery life

    B. Signal interference

    C. Unintended Wi-Fi connections

    D. Weak signal

93. A client has a Windows 8 computer with a virus on it. She has quarantined the system from the rest of her network. To follow malware removal best practices, what is the next step she should take?

    A. Identify malware symptoms.

    B. Disable system restore.

    C. Enable system restore.

    D. Update anti-malware software.

94. The GUI fails to load on a Windows 8.1 workstation. The Windows logo appears during boot and then disappears, and the workstation appears to hang. What should you do to resolve the issue?

    A. Boot to the installation DVD, open System Recovery Options, and choose Startup Repair.

    B. Boot to Safe Mode, open System Recovery Options, and choose Startup Repair.

    C. Boot to the installation DVD, open a command prompt, and type **Startup Repair**.

    D. Boot to the installation DVD, open SFC, and choose Startup Repair.

95. An iPad user reports that when he eats lunch in the garden next to the office building, he has intermittent wireless connectivity. What is the most likely cause of this?

A. Weak signal

B. Retracted antenna

C. The iPad's signal receptivity is set to low.

D. Low battery

96. On your network, you are concerned about mobile users accidentally granting unauthorized account access or root access. What step should you take to help prevent these security problems?

A. Apply patches and upgrades as soon as they are available.

B. Monitor resource utilization and remediate high usage.

C. Install mobile firewalls on all devices.

D. Disable location tracking, the camera, and the microphone.

97. A user with a new iPhone wants to know how she can change her wallpaper, notifications, and battery configurations. Where should she do this?

A. In iTunes or iCloud

B. Using the Configuration app on the iPhone

C. Using the Desktop, Messages, and Power apps on the iPhone

D. Using the Settings app on the iPhone

98. Client computers on your network connect to the Internet through a proxy server. Recently, a Windows 8.1 client was infected with adware and a browser redirector. You have removed the malware, and now the computer will not connect to the Internet. What should you do to resolve the problem?

A. Perform malware remediation again.

B. Disable the network card. Reboot and enable the network card.

C. Check the IP configuration to ensure it's pointing to the correct proxy server address.

D. Disable the proxy server configuration to connect directly to the Internet.

99. You use an iPad and an iPhone at work. Which of the following represents the greatest threats to leaking personal files or data? (Choose two.)

A. Unauthorized root access

B. Unintended Wi-Fi connections

C. Unauthorized location tracking

D. High resource utilization

100. You receive a notice from your wireless provider that you are about to exceed your data transmission limit for the month. What type of risk does this present?

   A. Your account may be deactivated.

   B. You may incur a security breach.

   C. You may have to pay high fees.

   D. Your phone may be locked.

101. Your favorite restaurant locator app on your iPhone won't load. You closed it and tried to reopen it a few times and it still doesn't work. What should you try next?

   A. Remove and reinstall the app.

   B. Perform a hard reset.

   C. Perform a force stop.

   D. Reboot the phone and try the app again.

102. A Windows 7 user's antivirus software has crashed. He reboots the computer and tries to open it again, and it crashes again. What should he do to solve the problem? (Choose two.)

   A. Look for a patch or update on the manufacturer's website.

   B. Delete the antivirus software.

   C. Delete and reinstall Windows.

   D. Repair the antivirus installation through Programs in Control Panel.

103. You have a Windows 8 workstation that is spontaneously shutting down and restarting. What should you do to troubleshoot and resolve the issue?

   A. Check the system BIOS to ensure that the boot order is set properly.

   B. Boot to the Windows installation CD and start the Recovery Console.

   C. Boot to Safe Mode and see whether the problem persists.

   D. Reinstall Windows.

104. An iPhone user reports that her device no longer makes sound, even when she is playing videos or receives a phone call. What is the first thing you should check?

   A. If airplane mode is on

   B. If too many applications are running

   C. If the phone has been put into silent mode

   D. If the connection to the speakers is still operational

105. You want to register some DLL files as command components in the Windows 8.1 Registry. Which command should you use?

   A. REGSVR32

   B. REGEDIT

   C. MSCONFIG

   D. REGDLL

106. You have a Windows 7 workstation that was infected with adware. You've removed the adware, but now the computer is unable to connect to the Internet. It is still able to print to a local printer. What is the most likely cause of the problem?

    A. The DNS server has been poisoned.

    B. The malware changed the computer's TCP/IP configuration to point to a fake DNS server.

    C. The malware is still on the computer and has infected the boot sector.

    D. The computer has a rogue antivirus.

107. You are dual-booting a workstation with Linux and Windows 8.1. One day when you boot up, you get a GRUB error message. What is the most likely cause of the problem?

    A. The Windows boot loader is missing.

    B. The Linux boot loader is missing.

    C. The MBR is missing or corrupted.

    D. The BIOS/UEFI is missing or corrupted.

108. You have a user with an iPhone 6, and the user needs to restart the phone. He asks you how to perform a soft reset. What do you tell him?

    A. Use a paperclip or pen point to press and hold the indented reset button on the bottom of the phone until you see the Apple logo and then let go.

    B. Press and hold the Sleep/Wake and Home buttons for at least 10 seconds until you see the Apple logo and then let go.

    C. Press and hold the Sleep/Wake button until the red slider appears and then drag the slider to power the device off.

    D. Press the Home button two times, and the Home screen will appear. Swipe up to initiate a soft reset.

109. A technician just updated the network card driver for a Windows 7 workstation. Now, the network card does not appear to work. She reboots the computer and logs back in, and it still does not work. What should she do next to resolve the issue?

    A. Reboot into Safe Mode and uninstall the network card driver.

    B. Reboot using the Last Known Good configuration.

    C. Reinstall Windows.

    D. Open Device Manager, find the network card, and roll back the driver.

110. On a Windows 8.1 workstation, the user has received a full-screen message saying that his computer has been locked because of illegal activity. The message also states that he can unlock his computer by paying a $300 fine to the government. He reboots and logs into Windows, and the message immediately reappears. What should he do to remove this message?

    A. Pay the fine.

    B. Open his anti-malware software and perform a remediation.

    C. Delete and reinstall Windows.

    D. Boot into Safe Mode and use System Restore to roll the system back to an older restore point.

111. You have recently installed new software on a Windows 7 workstation. When you try to open it, you receive an error message that the application is not compatible with Windows. What should you try first to resolve the issue?

    A. Right-click the application and choose Troubleshoot Compatibility.

    B. Run SFC /scannow to check for compatibility issues.

    C. Run MSCONFIG to see whether there are system configuration settings causing the issue.

    D. Delete and reinstall the application.

112. You are educating mobile users on best security practices. Which of the following are the biggest threats to network and data security? (Choose two.)

    A. Power drains

    B. Data transmission over-limit

    C. Unintended Wi-Fi connections

    D. Unintended Bluetooth connections

113. While working on a Windows 8.1 workstation, a user receives a pop-up message saying that his computer has been infected with a virus and he needs to download a virus scanner now to fix it. The window does not look like it comes from the antivirus software that your company uses. What is this an example of?

    A. Ransomware

    B. Spam

    C. Rogue antivirus

    D. Hijacked antivirus

114. You have been experiencing power drains on your mobile phone recently. Which of the following is not a common cause of power drains?

    A. Placement into airplane mode

    B. Long periods of usage

    C. Searching for cellular signal

    D. Too many open apps

115. You just installed a new driver on a Windows 7 workstation, and now the operating system will not load. The manufacturer's troubleshooting suggestion is to reboot and use the Last Known Good configuration. Where do you choose this from?

    A. System Recovery Options

    B. Recovery Console

    C. Emergency Repair Disk

    D. Safe Mode

116. You have a Windows 7 workstation that will not boot properly. You suspect that the boot sector on the hard drive is corrupt. Which command in the Windows RE will allow you to create a new boot sector?

    A. BOOTREC /FIXMBR

    B. BOOTREC /FIXBOOT

    C. BOOTREC /REBUILDBCD

    D. BOOTREC /REBUILDMBR

    E. BOOTREC /REBUILDBOOT

117. You have an Android mobile phone, and the resource usage has been unusually high lately. What can you do to see whether your phone has acquired malware?

    A. There is no malware for Android-based phones.

    B. Download security software and use an app scanner.

    C. Download security software and use a Wi-Fi analyzer.

    D. Install the latest Android patches and perform a soft reset. If there was a virus, this will remove it.

118. You use Internet Explorer to browse the web. Starting yesterday, whenever you try to search for anything on your favorite search engine, you are always sent to the same specific website trying to sell you stuff. This happens regardless of what you are searching for. Which two things are most likely to cause this to happen? (Choose two.)

    A. Your computer has an invalid certificate.

    B. Your computer has malware that is causing browser redirection.

    C. The DNS server has been poisoned.

    D. The search engines you use have been compromised.

119. A Windows 7 workstation on your network is exhibiting slow performance. Which of the following tools should be used to check for a potential problem causing the slowdown?

    A. Anti-malware software

    B. Event Viewer

    C. MSCONFIG

    D. REGSRV32

120. You are consulting for a high school that is deploying iPads to its students for in-school use. The iPads all need to have identical configurations. Which service should you use to configure these devices?

    A. iConfigure

    B. iPadPlus

    C. Apple Configurator

    D. Apple Installer

121. You have installed a new network card driver, and it's not working properly. According to the manufacturer's website, you need to edit a setting in the Windows configuration database. Which tool should you use to do that?

  A. WINCONFIG

  B. REGSVR32

  C. REGEDIT

  D. MSCONFIG

122. You are trying to apply Windows Updates to a Windows 8.1 client computer. The update fails with this message: "Failure configuring Windows updates. Reverting changes." What should you do next?

  A. Wait until changes are reverted. Reboot the computer and try the update again.

  B. Immediately turn off the computer. Reboot and try the update again.

  C. Ignore the update.

  D. Delete and reinstall Windows.

123. You installed a new anti-malware software package on a Windows 8.1 workstation. Now the system does not seem to run normally. It's very slow and seems to hang often, and the anti-malware program will not open. You want to roll the system back to a previous configuration to see whether that removes the problem. Where do you do this?

  A. System Restore

  B. Backup And Restore

  C. Windows RE

  D. Event Viewer

124. A network user with a Microsoft Phone wants to back up her device. Which service should she use to do this?

  A. Google Sync

  B. OneDrive

  C. Office 365

  D. Microsoft Mobile

125. A technician is fixing a Windows 7 workstation that has contracted a virus. He is following the best practices for malware removal and has enabled system restore and created a restore point. What is the next step he should take?

  A. Educate the end user.

  B. Disable system restore.

  C. Quarantine the infected system.

  D. Remediate the infected system.

126. A user reports an application has been crashing on his mobile device. He says an error pop-up window appears briefly, but he is unable to read it. What would you be your next step?

   A. Wait for the next crash to read the error pop-up yourself.

   B. Install and run a screen recorder to capture the next pop-up.

   C. Reinstall the application.

   D. Check the application log for error messages.

127. A user reports her PC crashed when she tried to start a new application. She says an error pop-up window appeared but she needed to close it to continue. How can you find that pop-up information?

   A. Start the new application yourself and hope for the crash.

   B. Right-click on application to look for any help.

   C. Check the system and application logs for errors.

   D. Check the application on another user's PC.

128. A user reports the printer was working fine yesterday but is no longer working. Last night, he updated the printer drivers assuming he should always have the most up-to-date drivers installed. What is the likely fix for this problem?

   A. Roll back device driver.

   B. Update the boot order.

   C. Update network settings.

   D. Kill the printer spooler task.

129. The company has recently made changes to infrastructure services such as DNS. The new DNS information is available but not yet propagated to all workstations. Since then, a number of users have reported they are no longer able to browse for internal servers. What should each affected user do? (Choose two)

   A. Disable their software firewall.

   B. Reboot.

   C. Update network settings.

   D. Safe boot

130. Your Windows 10 PC is acting poorly after you installed a few poorly written applications. Now the system will not function properly. You want to refresh your Windows installation but still keep your personal files. Where do you choose this from?

   A. System Recovery Options

   B. Recovery Console

   C. Emergency Repair Disk

   D. Safe Mode

131. A user reports the PC was fine until an OS update was installed. Believing that all updates are necessary, the user voluntarily updated the system himself. However, the update was not yet tested and is found to be incompatible with a needed business application. What is your next step?

    A. Roll back the update.

    B. Update the business application.

    C. Do nothing; have the user take awareness training.

    D. Kill the updated task.

132. A user reports that his Windows 10 Start menu looks wrong. You know the environment relies on roaming profiles. What is a reliable solution to the user's problem?

    A. Rebuild the desktop image.

    B. Rebuild the Windows user profile.

    C. Delete the Registry on the local machine.

    D. Reboot the machine.

133. While booting up a Windows 8 PC, you find it takes a long time at the Welcome screen. The message "Waiting for the User Profile Service" appears on an error message window. What might be the problem?

    A. Slow profile load

    B. Update service cannot start.

    C. A peripheral is not connected as expected.

    D. Screen resolution is not compatible with the user profile.

134. Besides a blue screen of death, what evidence of an operating system crash does Windows provide?

    A. Red X seen across the screen

    B. Black screen of death

    C. Blue error code across the desktop

    D. Green cursor

Chapter

9

Operational Procedures

THE FOLLOWING COMPTIA A+ EXAM 220-1002 TOPICS ARE COVERED IN THIS CHAPTER:

✓ **4.1 Compare and contrast best practices associated with types of documentation.**

- Network topology diagrams
- Knowledge base/articles
- Incident documentation
- Regulatory and compliance policy
- Acceptable use policy
- Password policy
- Inventory management
  - Asset tags
  - Barcodes

✓ **4.2 Given a scenario, implement basic change management best practices.**

- Documented business processes
- Purpose of the change
- Scope the change.
- Risk analysis
- Plan for change.
- End-user acceptance
- Change board
  - Approvals
- Backout plan
- Document changes.

✓ **4.3 Given a scenario, implement basic disaster prevention and recovery methods.**

- Backup and recovery
  - Image level
  - File level
  - Critical applications
- Backup testing
- UPS
- Surge protector
- Cloud storage vs. local storage backups
- Account recovery options

✓ **4.4 Explain common safety procedures.**

- Equipment grounding
- Proper component handling and storage
  - Antistatic bags
  - ESD straps
  - ESD mats
  - Self-grounding
- Toxic waste handling
  - Batteries
  - Toner
  - CRT
  - Cell phones
  - Tablets
- Personal safety
  - Disconnect power before repairing PC.
  - Remove jewelry.
  - Lifting techniques
  - Weight limitations
  - Electrical fire safety

- Cable management
- Safety goggles
- Air filter mask
- Compliance with government regulations

✓ **4.5   Explain environmental impacts and appropriate controls.**

- MSDS documentation for handling and disposal
- Temperature, humidity level awareness, and proper ventilation
- Power surges, brownouts, and blackouts
    - Battery backup
    - Surge suppressor
- Protection from airborne particles
    - Enclosures
    - Air filters/mask
- Dust and debris
    - Compressed air
    - Vacuums
- Compliance to government regulations

✓ **4.6   Explain the processes for addressing prohibited content/activity, and privacy, licensing, and policy concepts.**

- Incident response
    - First response
        - Identify.
        - Report through proper channels.
        - Data/device preservation
    - Use of documentation/documentation changes
    - Chain of custody
        - Tracking of evidence/documenting process

- Licensing/DRM/EULA
  - Open-source vs. commercial license
  - Personal license vs. enterprise licenses
- Regulated data
  - PII
  - PCI
  - GDPR
  - PHI
- Follow all policies and security best practices.

✓ **4.7 Given a scenario, use proper communication techniques and professionalism.**

- Use proper language and avoid jargon, acronyms, and slang, when applicable.
- Maintain a positive attitude/project confidence.
- Actively listen (taking notes) and avoid interrupting the customer.
- Be culturally sensitive.
  - Use appropriate professional titles, when applicable.
- Be on time (if late, contact the customer).
- Avoid distractions.
  - Personal calls
  - Texting/social media sites
  - Talking to coworkers while interacting with customers
  - Personal interruptions
- Dealing with difficult customers or situations
  - Do not argue with customers and/or be defensive.
  - Avoid dismissing customer problems.
  - Avoid being judgmental.
  - Clarify customer statements (ask open-ended questions to narrow the scope of the problem, restate the issue, or question to verify understanding).
  - Do not disclose experiences via social media outlets.

- Set and meet expectations/timeline and communicate status with the customer.

  - Offer different repair/replacement options, if applicable.

  - Provide proper documentation on the services provided.

  - Follow up with customer/user at a later date to verify satisfaction.

- Deal appropriately with customers' confidential and private materials.

  - Located on a computer, desktop, printer, etc.

✓ 4.8 Identify the basics of scripting.

- Script file types

  - .bat

  - .ps1

  - .vbs

  - .sh

  - .py

  - .js

- Environment variables

- Comment syntax

- Basic script constructs

  - Basic loops

  - Variables

- Basic data types

  - Integers

  - Strings

✓ 4.9 Given a scenario, use remote access technologies.

- RDP

- Telnet

- SSH

- Third-party tools

  - Screen share feature

  - File share

- Security considerations of each access method

1. You have a client who is looking to plug three workstations and monitors into a wall outlet that has only two plugs. He's looking for the least expensive solution available. What should you recommend he purchase?

   A. UPS

   B. Voltage conserver

   C. Surge protector

   D. Power strip

2. The company has recently installed a server with HR information on it. The server, as with most systems, possesses input/output (I/O) ports and disk bays and is connected by network cable to the local client network. However, since the datacenter was full, the new server is temporarily placed in the printer room. What should be a primary concern of the responsible administrator?

   A. Security considerations of each access method

   B. I/O transfer bottleneck

   C. Ambient noise from server fans

   D. Scalability of the server while in printer room

3. You are upgrading a video card in a desktop computer. You are following appropriate safety procedures. When you open the case, what is the most common danger that you should watch out for?

   A. Electrical shock

   B. Sharp edges

   C. Burns

   D. Flying debris

4. A user needs to send a file to a co-worker. The user has no working USB ports, disk drives, or network shares. The file is too large for e-mail. What third-party software feature is the user requiring?

   A. USB share

   B. Encryption

   C. File share

   D. VPN

5. You open a desktop computer case and discover some dust, particularly around the fans. What should you use to clean the fans out?

   A. Denatured isopropyl alcohol

   B. Demineralized water

   C. Computer vacuum

   D. Compressed air

6. You are performing an audit of trip hazards at work, and you notice several cables strung across a walking path. Which of the following solutions best resolves this problem?

    A. A cable guard

    B. Cable ties

    C. Duct tape

    D. Electrical tape

7. What feature of third-party software would allow a technician to demonstrate to a user how to use an application on the local desktop?

    A. File sharing

    B. SSH

    C. Browsing

    D. Screen sharing

8. For administrators concerned about the confidentiality of authentication credentials, what is the secure version of Telnet?

    A. RDP

    B. SSH

    C. HTTPS

    D. FTP

9. You are installing a new piece of software on your computer, and you do not agree with terms in the end-user license agreement (EULA). Which of the following statements is true?

    A. You can skip the EULA and continue the installation.

    B. You will not be able to install the software unless you agree to the terms in the EULA.

    C. You can click that you agree with the EULA and then provide notes to the parts you disagree with and will not be bound to those terms.

    D. You can install the software but will be provided with limited functionality.

10. Your company has a policy prohibiting illegal content on work computers. You have seized a workstation from an employee after finding illegal content. How do you ensure that the illegal material is managed in the correct way and that it is delivered to the proper authorities?

    A. Use documentation.

    B. Follow the chain of custody.

    C. Drive the computer to the proper law enforcement agency.

    D. Remove the hard drive and preserve it in a locked safe.

11. Select two ways that differentiate Telnet from RDP. (Choose two.)

    A. Telnet is less secure.

    B. Telnet is usable only on the Windows operating system.

    C. Telnet uses less bandwidth.

    D. Telnet uses more bandwidth.

12. You just got off a repair job at a customer's site, and it was difficult. To make matters worse, the customer was argumentative and difficult to work with. Which of the following should you not do?

    A. Document the situation in your work log.

    B. Try to put the experience out of your mind and focus on your next call.

    C. Call your manager and explain the situation.

    D. Post the experience on social media.

13. You recently purchased software that you installed on your laptop. It worked for 30 days and now tells you that you must activate the product. What will be required to activate the software?

    A. EULA

    B. DRM

    C. Product key

    D. Open-source code

14. You are fixing a broken printer on the second floor of your office building. When you get the printer running again, you notice that it's printing off employee paychecks. What should you do?

    A. Take pictures of the paychecks and post them on social media.

    B. Look to see how much everyone gets paid compared to what you get paid.

    C. Ignore the information and focus on making sure the printer is fixed.

    D. Text your friends and tell them that you make more than they do.

15. When you are working at a client's site, which of the following is the most appropriate behavior you should exhibit?

    A. Taking personal calls

    B. Taking notes and asking questions

    C. Visiting social media sites

    D. Talking to co-workers

16. You are in the field replacing a defective PCI network card in a desktop computer. You realize that you forgot your ESD strap. The computer needs to be fixed quickly. What is the best way to proceed?

    A. Practice self-grounding by bending down to touch the ground before working on the PC.

    B. Practice self-grounding by touching the plastic front of the case while working on the PC.

    C. Practice self-grounding by staying in contact with the computer's desk while working on the PC.

    D. Practice self-grounding by staying in contact with the metal part of the case while working on the PC.

17. What Microsoft protocol allows you to connect your local system to a different Microsoft client, complete with a graphical user interface?

    A. RDP

    B. Telnet

    C. SSH

    D. Visio

18. A technician is concerned that he fried some RAM with ESD. Another technician says to not worry about it if he didn't feel the shock. Which of the following statements regarding ESD is true?

    A. People can feel a shock of 300 volts, and it takes 3,000 volts to damage computer components.

    B. People can feel a shock of 3,000 volts, and it takes 300 volts to damage computer components.

    C. People can feel a shock of 3,000 volts, and it takes 10,000 volts to damage computer components.

    D. People can feel a shock of 10,000 volts, and it takes 3,000 volts to damage computer components.

19. When working with a customer, which of the following demonstrates proper communication technique and professionalism?

    A. Staring at religious artifacts hanging on the wall

    B. Imitating the client's accent when speaking to them

    C. Using the client's title when speaking to them

    D. Laughing at the client's choice of clothing

20. You are practicing appropriate safety procedures as you fix computers. Which of the following are times you should wear an ESD strap? (Choose two.)

    A. When working inside a desktop case

    B. When working inside a power supply

    C. When working inside a CRT monitor

    D. When working inside a laptop case

21. While cleaning out an old filing cabinet, you discover a box filled with discarded batteries. What is the proper way to dispose of them?

    A. Burn them.

    B. Throw them in the trash.

    C. Crush them.

    D. Recycle them.

22. Your company has a policy prohibiting illegal content on work computers. A user reports that another user has illegal content, and you are the first responder at the scene. What is the first step you should take as the first responder?

    A. Follow the chain of custody.

    B. Preserve the data or device.

    C. Identify the illegal content that violates policy.

    D. Ask the user to delete the material.

23. When communicating with customers, which of the following should you do?

    A. Use jargon and acronyms to prove your abilities.

    B. Interrupt and ask questions often to clarify.

    C. Use appropriate professional titles.

    D. Assume you know what the customer wants, even if it's not what they said.

24. You are transporting several sticks of RAM and a few video cards from one of your offices to another. Which safety device should you use to help avoid electrically damaging the components?

    A. Static shielding bags

    B. ESD strap

    C. ESD mat

    D. Rubber gloves

25. In the scripting language Python, what is the str() function?

    A. Strong print

    B. String

    C. Security trace

    D. Still trace

26. Your company has a policy prohibiting illegal content on work computers. You have identified illegal content on a user's computer, and the workstation has been removed from the user's desk. What is the right next step in the incident response process?

    A. Document the situation.

    B. Notify the proper authorities.

    C. Follow the chain of custody.

    D. Delete the illegal material.

27. You are working on-site and trying to fix a client's workstation. His computer has a defective video card, and it will take about three days to get a new one in. Which of the following is the best course of action for you to take?

   A. Tell him it will take three days for the video card to arrive and you will return then to replace it.

   B. Tell him that the video card is dead and it will take a week for the new one to arrive. Then when you replace it in three days, you will have overdelivered versus exceeded his expectations.

   C. Tell him it will take three days for the video card to arrive. Offer him a loaner computer that he can use in the meantime.

   D. Tell him his computer is dead, and you'll be back to fix it whenever you can fit it into your schedule.

28. You are troubleshooting a difficult problem that you have never seen before. Even after an hour, you're still not sure what is causing the problem. The customer asks what's wrong. What should you tell her?

   A. You have no idea, and it's a hard one. This is going to take a while.

   B. You're not sure yet, but you're confident that you'll get it figured out soon.

   C. It's bad. It's really bad. You're not sure if you will ever get it fixed or not.

   D. Not even your escalation line could figure it out, so you're about ready to just give up.

29. You are advising a startup that handles payment transactions to employ additional security controls on credit card information. What type of compliance affects how these security controls are implemented?

   A. PHI

   B. PCI

   C. GDPR

   D. DDS

30. You are working on an LCD monitor that has a flickering display. Which component inside the monitor poses the biggest risk for delivering an electrical shock?

   A. Backlight

   B. Capacitors

   C. Inverter

   D. Screen

31. Your office uses five HP laser jet printers. An administrator has placed used toner cartridges in boxes and stacked them in the storage room. Which of the following statements is true regarding toner cartridge disposal?

    A. Toner is not harmful, but because they contain plastic, they should be recycled.

    B. Toner is not harmful and the cartridges are made of biodegradable plastic, so they can be thrown away.

    C. Toner is a carcinogen, so cartridges should be taken to an authorized recycling center.

    D. Toner will make a mess if it gets out of the cartridge, so to avoid making a mess, cartridges should be burned.

32. A desktop computer you are working on has a failed power supply. Another technician suggests that it could just be a failed capacitor inside the power supply and you could fix it. What should you do?

    A. Open the power supply, and test the capacitors with a multimeter.

    B. Open the power supply, and test the capacitors with a voltmeter.

    C. Open the power supply, and test the capacitors with an electrical probe.

    D. Do not open the power supply; dispose of it properly.

33. You are having a conversation with your manager about corporate security best practices. She asks what the company should do if users are found to have adult content or content that advocates hate crimes on their workstations. How should you answer?

    A. Users should be allowed to keep it if it is for personal use only.

    B. The company should implement a policy that forbids such material and specifies consequences for violating the policy.

    C. The company should not condone adult or hate crime–related content but can't legally prevent users from having it.

    D. The company should ignore the content that users have on their workstations.

34. You are training a new group of technicians on power issues. One asks what the difference is between a brownout and a blackout. What should you tell him?

    A. A blackout is a complete power loss, and a brownout is a drop in power without power loss. Both can damage electrical components.

    B. A blackout is a complete power loss, and a brownout is a drop in power without power loss. Neither one damages electrical components.

    C. A brownout is a complete power loss, and a blackout is a drop in power without power loss. Both can damage electrical components.

    D. A brownout is a complete power loss, and a blackout is a drop in power without power loss. Neither one damages electrical components.

35. When dealing with a customer, which of the following demonstrates the communication technique for using proper language?

    A. Using jargon

    B. Using acronyms

    C. Using slang terms

    D. Using basic terms

36. You have downloaded open-source software onto your personal laptop. Which of the following statements are true regarding open-source licenses? (Choose two.)

    A. You can modify the application in any way you'd like.

    B. You do not need to pay for the application.

    C. You can make changes only to the applications that are approved by the originator.

    D. You pay a fee for every user of the application.

37. You want to install an electrical device that lets you plug in multiple devices at the same time. It should have a fuse in it so that if there is a power surge, the fuse will be blown and not the electronics plugged into it. It does not need a battery backup. What type of device do you need?

    A. UPS

    B. Power strip

    C. Voltage conserver

    D. Surge protector

38. You have several old CRT monitors that are collecting dust in a storage room. To clear out space, you decide to dispose of them. What is the proper way to do this?

    A. Throw them in a dumpster.

    B. Smash them to bits with a hammer and then throw them in the Dumpster.

    C. Burn them.

    D. Recycle them.

39. When dealing with a customer and demonstrating proper communication techniques, what is meant by actively listening?

    A. Taking notes and making eye contact

    B. Asking many questions and moving the customer on to the important information

    C. Walking to the computer with the problem and starting to open it while listening

    D. Answering texts while listening

40. You are troubleshooting a desktop computer that is prone to shorting out and rebooting. When you open the case, there is a layer of grime on all the internal components. When you remove the expansion cards and memory, what should you use to clean the metal contacts on the cards?

    A. Demineralized water

    B. Mild soap and water

    C. Denatured isopropyl alcohol

    D. Compressed air

41. You are installing a server for a small company. They want to be sure that the server can be shut down properly in the event of a blackout, so they don't lose data. Which device should you recommend they plug the server into?

    A. UPS

    B. Voltage conserver

    C. Surge protector

    D. Power strip

42. You need to upgrade the RAM in a desktop computer. Which of the following should you do before beginning the procedure?

    A. Leave the power running.

    B. Put the desktop into hibernate mode.

    C. Turn the power off.

    D. Put the desktop into standby mode.

43. You are moving computer equipment from an old office to a new office. Which of the following are good personal safety measures to follow to avoid injuries? (Choose two.)

    A. Bend at the knees and lift with your legs.

    B. Bend at the waist and lift straight up.

    C. Observe weight limitations and lift with a partner if needed.

    D. When lifting, lift objects as high as possible to avoid running into things.

44. You have opened a desktop computer case and will be upgrading the memory. To help prevent ESD, you put on an ESD strap. Where should you connect the other end?

    A. The RAM

    B. The motherboard

    C. The metal case

    D. The plastic table

45. You are purchasing new spreadsheet software for your company. Your manager has instructed you to ensure that you purchase enough licenses for everyone in the office to use the product. What type of license will you likely purchase, designed for large groups of users? (Choose two.)

    A. Corporate

    B. Single user

    C. Concurrent

    D. Shareware

46. You have several old computers that you want to dispose of. What should you do with them?

    A. Throw them in the trash.

    B. Remove the hard drives to avoid having someone steal confidential data and then throw them in the trash.

    C. Dispose of them in compliance with government regulations.

    D. Put them at the curb for someone to take for free.

47. What regulation dictates the privacy of all European Union residents?

    A. General Data Privacy Regulation

    B. General Data Protection Requirements

    C. General Data Protection Regulation

    D. General Data Personal Requirements

48. You fixed a customer's laptop about three days ago. Which of the following demonstrates proper communication techniques and professionalism?

    A. Call the customer to see whether she is satisfied with the repair.

    B. Post "Another satisfied customer!" on your social media sites with a picture of her office building.

    C. Provide an accurate bill for services provided.

    D. Call the customer and ask if she has additional work you can do.

49. You have taken an old CRT monitor into a television repair shop. The technician opens the back of the monitor and prepares to discharge the capacitors. What tool will he use to do this?

    A. High-voltage probe

    B. Multimeter

    C. Voltmeter

    D. ESD strap

50. You are troubleshooting problems in a client's office, and the client starts arguing with you as to what the problem is. What should you do?

    A. Avoid arguing and becoming defensive.

    B. Argue back to prove that you are correct.

    C. Tell the client that they are making you uncomfortable and leave immediately.

    D. Tell the client that if they know so much, they can fix it themselves. Then leave.

51. Your company has a policy prohibiting illegal content on work computers. You have identified illegal content on a company-owned workstation. What is your next step?

    A. Get a verifier.

    B. Report through proper channels.

    C. Ask the user to delete the material.

    D. Preserve the data or device.

52. You are going to be upgrading the RAM on several desktop computers. Which of the following environmental conditions increases the risk of ESD damaging computer components?

    A. High temperature

    B. Low temperature

    C. High humidity

    D. Low humidity

53. Your company has a policy prohibiting illegal content on work computers. You have found illegal content on a user's workstation. What is the proper way to preserve the data or device?

    A. Ask the user to not delete the data from the device.

    B. Take a picture of the illegal content and email it to your manager.

    C. Take a picture of the illegal content and email it to yourself.

    D. Immediately remove the data or device from the possession of the offending user and preserve it in a safe location.

54. Your company maintains a database of customer's names, vehicle license plate numbers, and driver's license numbers. What type of policy should your company have regarding this information?

    A. This information can't be used in any damaging way; therefore, no special policy is needed.

    B. This information is related to motor vehicle operation, and no special policy is needed.

    C. This information is public information, and no special policy is needed.

    D. This is PII and should be kept confidential and secure.

55. You are looking for a new software application for your company's finance users, but you have a limited budget. Which of the following types of software licensing would you expect to not have to pay for? (Choose two.)

    A. Corporate

    B. Open source

    C. Single user

    D. Freeware

56. You are setting up a repair shop for PCs. To reduce the risk of damaging computer components, which of the following devices should you use? (Choose two.)

    A. Magnetic screwdrivers

    B. ESD mats

    C. ESD straps

    D. A dehumidifier

57. You have chosen to use compressed air to clean away dirt and debris from the inside of a desktop computer case. What is the recommended safety gear you should wear?

    A. Safety goggles and an air mask

    B. Safety goggles and a respirator

    C. Safety goggles, a respirator, and a hair net

    D. A biohazard suit

58. What type of information likely needs access safeguards per regulatory requirements as it relates to an individual's medical records?

    A. PCI

    B. PHI

    C. DOB

    D. GDPR

59. You need to dispose of a chemical solvent but are unsure how to properly do so. Where will you find information on this as well as the potential dangers the solvent possesses?

    A. SDS

    B. OSHA

    C. Warning label

    D. Bottom of the container

60. You are discussing the placement of several new computers with one of your co-workers. Which of the following are the best places to put them? (Choose two.)

    A. In the corner of a room that is typically about 15 degrees warmer than room temperature

    B. In an open area at room temperature

    C. In the corner of a room that is typically about 15 degrees colder than room temperature

    D. In an enclosed kiosk so that no users can damage the system

61. A user's work area is littered with debris and crumbs, and he reports that keys on his keyboard stick or sometimes make a crunching sound. What should be his first option for cleaning his keyboard?

A. Denatured isopropyl alcohol

B. Demineralized water

C. Computer vacuum

D. Compressed air

62. You are performing a safety audit for your company and are examining the company's fire extinguishers. Which type of fire extinguisher is designed to put out electrical fires?

A. A

B. B

C. C

D. D

63. You have a set meeting time with a client to upgrade her computer. Your prior service call runs long, and you will be late to the meeting. What should you do?

A. Get to your meeting as soon as you can.

B. Take your time; you're already late and a few more minutes won't matter.

C. Don't show up. Call the client later and tell her you were sick.

D. Call the client, apologize for being late, and explain that your last call went over. You will be there as soon as possible or can reschedule if she would prefer.

64. You are asked to help a client who is unable to send or receive email. When you get to the client's desk, what should you do?

A. Tell him that this problem is nothing and you have dealt with far worse issues today.

B. Ask him what he did to break his email.

C. Tell him that you would rather be working on updating the server, but you suppose you'll deal with him first.

D. Clarify the scope of the problem and verify that you understand what isn't working.

65. You are running network cables to support 20 new workstations in an office area. Which of the following is the best way to handle cable management and avoid safety issues?

A. Run the cables along the floor next to the cubicle walls.

B. Run the cables across the floor and duct tape them down.

C. Run the cables through a raised floor or drop ceiling.

D. Run the cables across the floor and use a cable guard.

66. Which of the following small devices should not be disposed of at a normal landfill but instead regarded as containing toxic chemicals? (Choose two.)

A. Tablet

B. Phone packaging

C. Mini-trebuchet

D. Cell phone

67. While changing a laser printer toner cartridge, a technician spilled toner on a desk. What should she use to clean the mess up?

A. Compressed air

B. Mild soap and water

C. Toner vacuum

D. Denatured isopropyl alcohol

68. You are repairing a desktop PC and upgrading the memory. What is the most important reason that equipment grounding is an important safety procedure?

A. To prevent an electrical shock to the technician

B. To prevent an electrical shock from damaging components

C. To prevent fire from starting inside the case

D. To prevent the desktop PC from slipping off of the workspace

69. What type of script has the filename extension .ps1?

A. PowerShell

B. Perl

C. Java class file

D. Shell

70. What term describes strings that specify script information such as path, drive, and filename?

A. Container configuration

B. Environment variables

C. Configuration variables

D. Initialization

71. In what type of editor would you normally view a script with the filename extension .vbs?

A. Notepad

B. XLS

C. vi

D. emacs

72. Which of the following commands could you find in a .sh script?

    A. `echo "Hello, World!"`

    B. `pscreen "Hello, World!"`

    C. `print("Hello, World!")`

    D. `print "Hello, World!"`

73. What plain-text script file would run on the operating system DOS?

    A. `.js`

    B. `.sh`

    C. `.py`

    D. `.bat`

74. What programming language uses the `.js` file?

    A. JavaScript

    B. Java

    C. Juice

    D. Joomla

75. When writing a script, how do you declare comments from the scripting language?

    A. Using a semicolon (;) to start a comment

    B. Using an exclamation point (!) to start a comment

    C. Using two slashes (//) to start a comment

    D. Using appropriate comment syntax

76. What scripting constructs help execute a command or series of commands repeatedly?

    A. IF/THEN conditional statements

    B. Basic loops

    C. IF/ELSE conditional statements

    D. Variables

77. What scripting constructs are values or placeholders for the programmer to declare or fill during the script?

    A. Comment syntax

    B. Basic loops

    C. Environmentals

    D. Variables

78. What data type is restricted to being a series of digits?

    A. String

    B. Array

    C. Integer

    D. Variable

79. What best practice assists the administrator to track the boundaries and perimeters of data flow through the environment?

  A. Asset tagging

  B. Change management

  C. Password policy

  D. Network topology diagrams

80. What best practice helps the administrator keep track of the hardware found throughout the workplace?

  A. Asset tagging

  B. Knowledgebase articles

  C. Password policy

  D. Network topology diagrams

81. Which policy might lock a user out of a workstation if the wrong credentials were used too many times?

  A. Disaster recovery policy

  B. Acceptable use policy

  C. Password policy

  D. Change management policy

82. The operations manager wants to employ asset management but does not wish to spend funds on equipping all hardware with RFID tags. What is an appropriate but less expensive option?

  A. Sharpie

  B. Color coding

  C. Association to user by name and role

  D. Barcodes

83. What describes the best practice of documenting learned experience and helpful content to be shared with others?

  A. Brown bagging

  B. Knowledge base article writing

  C. Change board

  D. Scrolling

84. What change management detail is not necessary to document?

  A. Purpose of the change

  B. Scope of the change

  C. Applications unaffected

  D. Approval

85. In documenting an anticipated change, what highlights how the change will be received by a sample of the employees?

  A. Backout plan

  B. Plan for change

  C. Risk analysis

  D. End-user acceptance

86. A company recently experienced an incident involving ransomware, corrupting the contents of a shared network folder. What basic disaster prevention and recovery method should an administrator implement?

  A. Image level

  B. File level

  C. Employee level

  D. Backup testing

87. Due to policy, an administrator wrote and documented disaster prevention and recovery procedures. Finally, critical data was backed up as required. What should be done next before the implementation can be considered reliable?

  A. Backup testing

  B. Documenting a checklist

  C. End-user acceptance

  D. Approving the policy

88. Which of the following would most likely be included in the scope of disaster prevention and recovery?

  A. Users' home folders

  B. Physical entry logs

  C. Network diagram changes

  D. Critical applications

89. In a geographical area prone to tornados, what option for storing backups seems most sensible?

  A. Tape backups in the basement.

  B. Tapes distributed among offices

  C. Cloud storage off-site

  D. Storage on a server against an inside wall

90. During what type of recovery would someone typically answer security questions or provide a PIN code from a phone call or text?

A. Account recovery

B. File decryption

C. Expanding a zipped file

D. Screen saver unlock

91. When handling electrical or solid-state electronics, what is a common safety procedure that should be followed?

A. Remove shoes.

B. Remove jewelry.

C. Pray.

D. Remove antistatic and ESD packaging.

Practice Exams

Chapter

10

Practice Exam 1 (220-1001)

1. You are investigating computer specifications for a new desktop workstation. If the specifications include 256 KB of L2 cache, approximately how much L1 cache would it be reasonable to expect the computer to have?

   A. 64 KB

   B. 256 KB

   C. 512 KB

   D. 12 MB

2. You have installed a printer on your Windows 10 computer using TCP printing and configured it to use the RAW protocol. Which port number will you need to open in Windows Firewall for this to work successfully?

   A. 9100

   B. 721

   C. 515

   D. 443

3. A user reports that his iPhone will not make any sounds. He has turned the phone off and back on, and the problem is still there. You check his settings, and the phone is not on silent mode and the volume is set to maximum. What can you do to fix this problem?

   A. Reset the phone to factory specifications.

   B. Replace the speakers.

   C. Replace the sound card.

   D. Replace the phone.

4. You have a laptop with a dead hard drive. You want to replace it with a newer SSD but have a few concerns. What disadvantages do SSDs have versus HDDs? (Choose two.)

   A. They produce more heat.

   B. They are more expensive.

   C. They are more susceptible to damage.

   D. They have less capacity.

5. You purchased a new monitor that has a native resolution of 1920×1080. What aspect ratio is this, and is it compatible with widescreen television aspect ratios?

   A. 16:9, yes

   B. 16:9, no

   C. 16:10, yes

   D. 16:10, no

6. A laser printer you are working on is producing images that have vertical black streaks running the length of the page. Which of the following could be causing this? (Choose two.)

   A. Scratch in the EP drum

   B. Fusing assembly not heating up properly

   C. Worn exit rollers

   D. Dirty charging corona wire

7. You have installed an 802.11g Wi-Fi network. The network has three overlapping wireless access points. What channels should you set the access points to in order to avoid communications problems?

   A. 1, 5, and 9

   B. 1, 6, and 11

   C. 2, 7, and 12

   D. Any three different channels will work fine.

8. You are installing an ATX power supply. Which of the following is not a voltage provided by the power supply?

   A. –3.3 VDC

   B. +5 VDC

   C. +12 VDC

   D. –12 VDC

9. A user complains that his desktop computer randomly reboots. He does not see any error messages before it happens, and there is not a specific program that triggers the reboot. Which of the following components is most likely to be causing this problem?

   A. RAM

   B. Hard drive

   C. BIOS

   D. Network adapter

10. A user calls the help desk to report that she has no network connectivity. She had connectivity yesterday, but when she booted up her desktop computer this morning, she could not connect. She does not use the wireless network. No other users have reported issues. What is the first thing you should do?

   A. Check to see whether the network card driver is responding.

   B. Run `ipconfig` to see what her IP address is.

   C. Use a loopback plug to test the network card.

   D. Check to ensure that the network cable is plugged in.

11. A user calls to report that he can't access the Internet or a corporate server. However, he is still able to print to a local printer. He has not received any error messages. Other users in his area are able to access all network resources and the Internet. What is most likely the problem?

    A. Incorrect subnet mask

    B. Network card failure

    C. IP address conflict

    D. Default gateway is down

12. Which of the following statements are true regarding CPUs and operating systems? (Choose two.)

    A. A 64-bit OS can run on a 32-bit CPU or a 64-bit CPU.

    B. A 32-bit OS can run on a 32-bit CPU or a 64-bit CPU.

    C. A 32-bit OS can run only on a 32-bit CPU.

    D. A 64-bit OS can run only on a 64-bit CPU.

13. Which of the following wireless connection types generally has a functional communication distance of 10 meters?

    A. NFC

    B. IR

    C. Bluetooth

    D. Wi-Fi

14. The Southbridge on a motherboard is responsible for managing which type of communications?

    A. High-speed peripherals

    B. Slower onboard peripherals

    C. CPU to RAM

    D. CPU to HDD

15. In your company's lobby, there is a desktop computer with an LCD monitor that plays a continuous loop of a welcome video. The monitor is enclosed in a cabinet. Recently, the monitor will shut itself down near the end of the day, for no apparent reason. What is likely causing this problem?

    A. Backlight failure

    B. Incorrect video resolution

    C. Video card failure

    D. Monitor overheating

16. One of your network users develops software for multiple operating systems. He asks for a specialized computer that will allow him to run multiple operating systems at the same time in virtualized environments. Which two components should you optimize in his computer? (Choose two.)

   A. CPU

   B. RAM

   C. HDD

   D. GPU

17. The design of the micro-ATX motherboard makes which of the following statements true?

   A. It will fit in standard ATX cases.

   B. It will fit in standard ATX cases when used with a mounting adapter kit.

   C. It will fit in standard ATX cases but can't support full-length expansion cards.

   D. It will not fit in standard ATX cases.

18. A 32-bit PCI expansion bus will operate at one of which of the following two data rates? (Choose two.)

   A. 33 MBps

   B. 66 MBps

   C. 133 MBps

   D. 266 MBps

19. What is the maximum speed of an ExpressCard 2.0 card running in PCIe 2.0 x1 mode?

   A. 480 Mbps

   B. 2.5 Gbps

   C. 5.0 Gbps

   D. 6.0 Gbps

20. Which two TCP/IP protocols are designed to download email from mail servers? (Choose two.)

   A. SMTP

   B. POP3

   C. IMAP

   D. SMB

21. You are testing the power levels provided to the paper-transport motor inside a laser printer. What voltage does this motor require?

   A. +5 VDC

   B. −5 VDC

   C. +24 VDC

   D. −24 VDC

22. You are examining an existing coaxial cable installation and notice that the previous technician installed a splitter. Which of the following statements is true?

    A. The splitter will degrade the quality of the network signal.

    B. The splitter will cause the network connection to fail.

    C. The splitter will increase the distance the network signal will travel.

    D. The splitter will have no effect on the network signal.

23. Users on your network complain of poor wireless network access in a certain part of your building. They say that the connection is slow and disconnects frequently. You are using 802.11n wireless routers and access points. What tool should you use to troubleshoot the situation?

    A. Wi-Fi analyzer

    B. Protocol analyzer

    C. Tone generator and probe

    D. Multimeter

24. In which scenario would you use the Fn key and the F5 key shown here?

    A. To turn the screen brightness down

    B. To turn the screen brightness up

    C. To turn the speaker volume down

    D. To turn the speaker volume up

25. A desktop computer will not retain the system time or date. The user always needs to reset them after his system is powered off. What should you do to fix the problem?

    A. Flash the BIOS.

    B. Replace the BIOS chip.

    C. Replace the CMOS battery.

    D. Use the jumper on the motherboard to set the BIOS back to factory specifications.

26. What type of power connector is shown here, and what device does it provide power to?

  A. ATX, motherboard

  B. Molex, hard drive

  C. PCIe, PCIe adapters

  D. SATA, hard drive

27. You have just installed a new printer on a client's workstation. When you attempt to print, nothing but garbled characters appear on the paper. Which two things are most likely to cause a problem like this? (Choose two.)

  A. The print spooler

  B. The printer driver

  C. The formatter board

  D. The printer's memory

28. A user has turned in a tablet computer that has a swollen battery. What should you do to resolve the problem?

  A. Turn the tablet off, let it cool down, and then return it to the user.

  B. Order a new tablet for the user, drain the excess electrolyte from the battery, and then dispose of the defective one in the trash.

  C. Order a new tablet for the user and dispose of the defective one in the trash.

  D. Order a new tablet for the user and take the defective one to a recycling center.

29. You are troubleshooting a Windows 10 desktop computer that boots into VGA mode. You have tried changing the resolution and reinstalled the video driver, but it still will only boot into VGA mode. What should you do next?

  A. Replace the monitor.

  B. Replace the video card.

  C. Flash the system BIOS.

  D. Flash the video card BIOS.

30. You are troubleshooting a laptop computer that will not boot properly. When you power it on, there is nothing on the display, and you hear beeps in a pattern of 1-3-3. What two things could you use to troubleshoot the problem? (Choose two.)

   A. Manufacturer's website

   B. PCIe POST card

   C. USB POST card

   D. BOOT tester

31. When creating a custom computer configuration, what type of system will most benefit from high-end video cards and cooling systems?

   A. Thick client

   B. Gaming PC

   C. Home theater PC

   D. A/V editing workstation

32. Which RAM modules have 240 pins? (Choose two.)

   A. DIMM DDR2

   B. DIMM DDR3

   C. DIMM DDR4

   D. DDR4 SODIMM

33. Several Bluetooth devices are connected in an ad hoc network. Which acronym best describes this type of network?

   A. LAN

   B. WAN

   C. PAN

   D. MAN

34. Your motherboard supports up-plugging for PCIe adapter cards. Which of the following statements is true?

   A. You can't put an x8 card into an x16 slot.

   B. You can put an x8 card into an x16 slot, but it will run at x1 speed.

   C. You can put an x8 card into an x16 slot, and it will run at x8 speed.

   D. You can put an x8 card into an x16 slot, and it will run at x16 speed.

35. The AES security algorithm was introduced with which Wi-Fi encryption standard?

   A. WEP

   B. WPA

   C. WPA2

   D. TKIP

36. You need to create several UTP patch cables from a roll of bulk cable. Your company uses the T568A standard. What is the correct order for wires in the connectors?

    A. White/orange, orange, white/green, blue, white/blue, green, white/brown, brown

    B. White/orange, green, white/green, blue, white/blue, orange, white/brown, brown

    C. White/green, green, white/orange, blue, white/blue, orange, white/brown, brown

    D. White/green, green, orange, blue, white/blue, white/orange, white/brown, brown

37. You are troubleshooting wireless networking issues on a Windows 8.1 laptop. Which command should you use to check the laptop's IP address?

    A. ifconfig

    B. ipconfig

    C. ping

    D. netstat

38. Identify the connectors shown here.

    A. ST

    B. SC

    C. LC

    D. BNC

39. Which computer component is most likely to use a DB15 connector?

    A. Modem

    B. Hard drive

    C. Monitor

    D. Keyboard

40. Which of the following statements is true about the function of the laser in the exposing step of the laser printer imaging process?

    A. It increases the charge from +100 VDC to +600 VDC.

    B. It decreases the charge from +600 VDC to +100 VDC.

    C. It increases the charge from –100 VDC to –600 VDC.

    D. It decreases the charge from –600 VDC to –100 VDC.

41. Your co-worker needs to transfer files from a mobile device using a memory card reader and an SD memory card. He quickly finds out that his maximum capacity is only 2 GB. Which technology does he have?

     A. SD

     B. SDLC

     C. SDHC

     D. SDXC

42. You need to purchase new RAM for two computer systems, both of which have an FSB speed of 667 MHz. The computer specifications require DDR2. Which RAM modules should you purchase?

     A. PC2-667

     B. PC2-3200

     C. PC2-5300

     D. PC2-6400

43. After a lightning storm, the laser printer in your office will not power up. You are testing it with a multimeter. What voltage do you expect to see from pin 9?

     A. −24 V

     B. +24 V

     C. −5 V

     D. +5 V

44. You need to print documents containing sensitive information, but all the printers are in a shared workspace. Which technology will allow you to hold the print job until you enter a PIN on the printer?

     A. Virtual printing

     B. Safe printing

     C. Cloud printing

     D. Secure printing

45. A guest speaker plugs an external projector into her laptop, using the VGA port on the back of the laptop. The projector is on but just shows a blue screen instead of her presentation. What is the easiest way for her to fix this issue?

     A. Turn the projector off and back on to synchronize it with the laptop.

     B. Press the Fn key on her keyboard and toggle the projector backlight function key until the image appears.

     C. Press the Fn key on her keyboard and toggle the video output function key until the image appears.

     D. Press the Fn key on her keyboard and toggle the screen brightness function key until the image appears.

46. Which of the following IP addresses is not routable on the Internet?

   A. 192.168.1.1

   B. 192.169.1.1

   C. 168.192.1.1

   D. 169.192.1.1

47. A technician is troubleshooting a computer in the field and calls you to report that she is getting a S.M.A.R.T. error ID 188, Command timeout. Which component is likely to be causing this error?

   A. CPU

   B. RAM

   C. Motherboard

   D. HDD

48. A user reports that when he presses the L key on his laptop keyboard, the L character repeats across the screen and doesn't stop until he presses the L key several more times. When you look at the laptop, it does not appear that the key is physically sticking. What should you tell him to do next?

   A. Replace the keyboard.

   B. Replace the L key.

   C. Clean under the key with compressed air.

   D. Reboot the laptop.

49. A technician is configuring a wireless router for use on a small office network. If he wants to assign private IP addresses to client computers but still allow them to have Internet access from the ISP, what option does he need to configure?

   A. DHCP

   B. DMZ

   C. NAT

   D. UPnP

50. You are troubleshooting a computer with a RAID-10 array using four disks. One of the disks fails. What can you do to recover the array?

   A. Replace the failed disk and restore from backup.

   B. Remove the failed disk and rebuild the array.

   C. Rebuild the failed disk and restore from backup.

   D. Replace the failed disk and rebuild the array.

51. A technician has two hard drives and wants to increase the data access speed of her computer. Which of the following is her best option?

    A. Install both drives and configure them as separate volumes.

    B. Install both drives and implement RAID-0.

    C. Install both drives and implement RAID-1.

    D. Install both drives and implement RAID-5.

52. What type of converter requires power, either from its own source or from the interface it plugs into?

    A. DVI to HDMI

    B. PS/2 to USB

    C. Thunderbolt to DVI

    D. HDMI to VGA

53. During the charging step of the laser printer printing process, what charge is applied to the imaging drum?

    A. −100 VDC

    B. −600 VDC

    C. +600 VDC

    D. +100 VDC

54. Your laptop has an internal Mini PCIe expansion slot. The documentation for an expansion card says that it supports Mini PCIe USB 3.0 functionality. What speed does the expansion card run at?

    A. 480 Mbps

    B. 2.5 Gbps

    C. 5.0 Gbps

    D. 6.0 Gbps

55. You are purchasing a mobile device that requires the use of a stylus to input information; it does not respond to the touch of a finger. What type of touch screen technology does this device use?

    A. Tempered

    B. Resistive

    C. Capacitive

    D. Object-oriented

56. What is the maximum data throughput rate of a SATA 3 hard drive?

    A. 1.5 Gbps

    B. 3 Gbps

    C. 6 Gbps

    D. 10 Gbps

57. In a laptop computer, which component is responsible for providing the right kind of energy to light the display?

   A. Inverter

   B. LCD

   C. Backlight

   D. Screen

58. A user complains of a burning smell and smoke coming from his computer. After shutting it down, you notice that the motherboard has burn marks on it. You replace the motherboard. The next day, the user complains of more smoke, and you see this motherboard is burnt as well. What should you do next?

   A. Replace the motherboard.

   B. Replace the power supply.

   C. Replace the motherboard and power supply.

   D. Plug the computer into a different wall outlet.

59. What type of connector is shown here on the left?

By Techtonic (edited from USB types.jpg) [Public domain], via Wikimedia Commons

   A. USB micro

   B. USB mini

   C. USB type A

   D. Lightning

60. You have a network installation that requires transmission speeds of 10 Gbps at a distance of 85 meters. Among the UTP standards listed, which one is the oldest one that meets the requirements for this network?

   A. CAT5

   B. CAT5e

   C. CAT6

   D. CAT7

61. You are troubleshooting a Windows 10 computer and suspect that the hard drive has some bad sectors. Which utility should you use to scan the hard drive and attempt to fix the bad sectors?

    A. format

    B. bootrec

    C. diskpart

    D. chkdsk

62. Which of the following is not verified as part of the POST routine?

    A. BIOS integrity

    B. Hard drive integrity

    C. Size of primary memory

    D. System buses

63. A UTP cable just failed, and you need to replace it. You have a spool of cable and connectors but no premade cables. Which tool do you need to use to make a new cable?

    A. Cable stripper

    B. Punchdown tool

    C. Multimeter

    D. Crimper

64. You are installing and configuring DHCP on one of your servers. What port numbers are used by DHCP? (Choose two.)

    A. TCP 67

    B. TCP 68

    C. UDP 67

    D. UDP 68

65. You are contemplating purchasing either a tablet or an e-reader to read books and magazines. What are two advantages an e-reader has over a tablet? (Choose two.)

    A. Longer battery life

    B. Better color representation

    C. Easier to read in bright conditions

    D. More memory

66. A user reports having an error message pop up saying that Windows has detected an IP address conflict. Your network uses a DHCP server. What should you do to resolve the problem?

    A. On the user's computer, run ipconfig /release and ipconfig /renew.

    B. On the DHCP server, exclude the user's IP address from the scope.

    C. On the user's computer, ensure that it's set to Obtain An IP Address Automatically.

    D. On the user's computer, ensure that it's set to Use The Following IP Address.

67. A technician is troubleshooting a RAID-5 array with four hard disks. Two of the disks have failed. What can he do to recover the array?

A. Rebuild the failed disks and restore from backup.

B. Remove the failed disks and rebuild the array.

C. Replace the failed disks and rebuild the array.

D. Replace the failed disks and restore from backup.

68. You are at a Windows server with a command prompt open. You want to share the D:\corp\acctrec directory and have users connect to it with the name receipts. Which command is correct to do this?

A. `net share receipts=D:\corp\acctrec`

B. `net share D:\corp\acctrec=receipts`

C. `netdom share receipts=D:\corp\acctrec`

D. `netdom share D:\corp\acctrec=receipts`

69. MicroSD cards, often used in mobile phones, are the smallest memory cards commonly used. What is the size of a MicroSD card?

A. 25 20 mm

B. 21.5 × 20 mm

C. 15 × 11 mm

D. 11 × 8 mm

70. You are troubleshooting a laptop that will not power up while plugged into a wall outlet. You verified that the outlet works and have tried a second AC adapter, but it still won't power up when plugged in. If you unplug it from the wall, it will power up from the battery. What should you do to get it to power up while plugged into the wall outlet?

A. Replace the AC adapter.

B. Remove the battery, power it up, and reinsert the battery.

C. Drain the battery completely and then power it up.

D. Replace the battery.

71. When setting up your network, you configured your clients to obtain IP addressing information automatically from a DHCP server. Which of the following configuration items can the DHCP server provide?

A. IP address

B. IP address and subnet mask

C. IP address, subnet mask, and default gateway

D. IP address, subnet mask, default gateway, and DNS server address

72. Your office just increased from 20 to about 40 people. Everyone uses the same laser printer. When you print, jobs are often processed very slowly. Other than get a new printer, what can you do to help eliminate the problem?

    A. Upgrade the printer's memory.

    B. Upgrade the printer's processor.

    C. Stop and restart the print spooler.

    D. Implement printing priorities for the most important users.

73. A user with an 802.11g network adapter is trying to join your new 802.11ac network. Her laptop is next to yours, which is connected to the network. However, she is unable to locate the SSID. What is most likely the cause of the problem?

    A. SSID broadcasting is disabled on the wireless access point.

    B. The user is out of range of the wireless access point.

    C. The SSID has been changed.

    D. 802.11g is not compatible with 802.11ac.

74. During the transferring step of the laser printer imaging process, what charge is applied to the paper?

    A. −100 VDC

    B. −600 VDC

    C. +600 VDC

    D. +100 VDC

75. In which situation would you want to use the special function key F4, shown here?

    A. To turn off your laptop's Wi-Fi connection

    B. To turn off your laptop's Bluetooth connection

    C. To mute your laptop's speakers

    D. To mute your laptop's microphone

76. You have configured four 1 TB hard drives as a RAID-10 array. After the array is configured, how much usable storage space will you have for data?

   A. 1 TB

   B. 2 TB

   C. 3 TB

   D. 4 TB

77. A client has an older Windows 8.1 laptop with an integrated 802.11b network adapter. She wants faster wireless access, and the network access points all support 802.11n. What is the best way to upgrade her system?

   A. Remove the old card, and replace it with an internal 802.11n NIC.

   B. Leave the old card in the system, and add a new internal 802.11n Mini-PCIe NIC. The system will automatically disable the old card.

   C. Add a USB 802.11n NIC. If needed, disable the old card in Device Manager.

   D. Add a USB 802.11n NIC. If needed, disable the old card in System Manager.

78. You are troubleshooting a Windows 8.1 desktop computer that does not produce video when it boots. You tried a second monitor, one that you know works, on this computer and there still is no video. What should you do to fix the problem?

   A. Replace the monitor.

   B. Reinstall the video card driver.

   C. Replace the video connector on the video card.

   D. Replace the video card.

79. In the laser printer printing process, which step comes immediately before the fusing step?

   A. Transferring

   B. Developing

   C. Cleaning

   D. Exposing

80. On an IPv6 network, if you want to send a single message to a group of computers at the same time, what type of address class do you need to use?

   A. Multicast

   B. Anycast

   C. Unicast

   D. Broadcast

81. Which TCP/IP Internet layer protocol is responsible for resolving IP addresses to MAC addresses?

A. IP

B. ICMP

C. ARP

D. RARP

82. A technician on your team has been asked to replace memory in a laptop. She has removed the old memory and brought it to you; it's shown here. What type of memory does she need to replace this with?

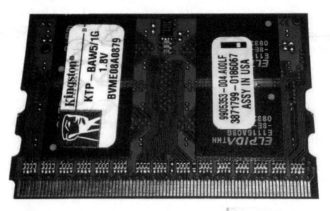

A. SODIMM

B. MicroDIMM

C. DIMM

D. Flash

83. In IPv6, which address range is the multicast range?

A. 2000::/3

B. FC00::/7

C. FE80::/10

D. FF00::/8

84. You are wearing a smart watch enabled with GPS and are hiking in the mountains. How many satellites must your watch communicate with for you to know your location and elevation?

A. One

B. Two

C. Three

D. Four

85. Data transfers for which wireless connection type will be interrupted if someone walks between the sending and receiving devices?

A. Bluetooth

B. Wi-Fi

C. RF

D. IR

86. You are configuring a wireless 802.11ac router for its first use. Which of the following configuration options is recommended?

A. Change the router's SSID.

B. Choose WPA as the encryption method.

C. Leave the administrator password as the default.

D. Enable the DMZ.

87. Which network device comes in two types: active, which is powered, and passive, which is not?

A. Bridge

B. Router

C. Switch

D. Hub

88. How much data throughput does a PCIe 1.1 x16 slot provide when operating bidirectionally?

A. 2 Gbps

B. 4 Gbps

C. 8 Gbps

D. 16 Gbps

89. You are purchasing a new LCD monitor for a small conference room. It will be viewed by people sitting at wide angles to the screen. Which technology should you purchase?

A. Fluorescent

B. LED

C. TN

D. IPS

90. A technician needs to choose an optical disc technology that provides the greatest storage space possible. Which technology will best meet her needs?

A. DVD+R DS, DL

B. BD-R SS, SL

C. BD-R DS, DL

D. CD SS

Chapter

11

Practice Exam 2 (220-1002)

1.   You are on-site fixing a client's laptop that will not load Windows 7. You are waiting to hear about your friend's awesome party that they are hosting this weekend, and your phone starts to vibrate. And it keeps vibrating. You're sure that all of your friends are texting information about the party. What should you do? (Choose two.)

   A.   Turn your phone off, and apologize to the client. Tell them that the phone was distracting you from your job, but it won't be a problem now.

   B.   Ignore your phone.

   C.   Text your friends back and tell them that you are working.

   D.   Call your friend and tell him to wait until after this job before planning all of the details because you want to help.

2.   A user is running an application that requires complex calculations and takes a lot of CPU power. He wants to set his Windows 10 workstation so that it gives the application priority over all non-system-critical programs. Which tool can he use to do this?

   A.   Task Manager

   B.   Application Manager

   C.   Performance Monitor

   D.   System Configuration

3.   You are planning on formatting a hard drive with NTFS to install Windows 8.1. Which of the following features are present in NTFS? (Choose two.)

   A.   Linux OS support

   B.   File compression

   C.   File security

   D.   Enhanced flash drive support

4.   You have a computer running Windows 8 Pro, and you want to upgrade to Windows 10 Pro. What should you run to determine whether your computer can support the new operating system?

   A.   Windows Easy Transfer

   B.   Hardware Compatibility List

   C.   Windows Update Advisor

   D.   Windows Update Assistant

5.   Which of the following statements best describes the purpose of a virtual private network?

   A.   It walls off one network from another, making it inaccessible.

   B.   It examines incoming network packets and forwards only those that match criteria in an access control list.

   C.   It makes network requests on behalf of a user, effectively masking the user's identity from the computer receiving the request.

   D.   It creates a private, secure network connection through a public network.

6. You are at a client's office and need to replace faulty memory but do not have an ESD strap. Which of the following describes the best way to practice self-grounding while replacing the RAM?

A. Leave the computer plugged in but powered off, and stay in contact with the plastic part of the case.

B. Leave the computer plugged in but powered off, and stay in contact with the metal part of the case.

C. Unplug the computer, and stay in contact with the plastic part of the case.

D. Unplug the computer, and stay in contact with the metal part of the case.

7. You have a Windows 10 workstation with an 802.11n network adapter. When you establish a network connection, which type of connection should you choose?

A. WWAN

B. Wireless

C. Wired

D. VPN

8. The police have come to you with a request for help. They have recovered a suspected criminal's iPhone and want to get information off of it, and they have a warrant. The suspected criminal will not give them the passcode, and therefore the system is locked out. What advice can you give them on how to retrieve data from the device?

A. They can perform a reset to factory defaults, which will reset the passcode. Then they can retrieve the data.

B. They can perform a hard reset, which will reset the passcode. Then they can retrieve the data.

C. There is no way to unlock the device and get the data without the appropriate passcode.

D. They can crack the phone using backdoor code from Apple.

9. You are logged into a Linux workstation with a regular user account. You need to execute a command with `root` permissions. Which command do you need to use?

A. su

B. sudo

C. vi

D. dd

10. A Linux user on your network has received an error message during boot that GRUB is missing, as well as an error number. What can you do to solve this problem?

A. Boot to the Linux installation CD or DVD, enter Linux rescue mode, and re-create the MBR.

B. Boot to the Linux installation CD or DVD, and reinstall Linux.

C. Boot to the Linux installation CD or DVD, enter Linux rescue mode, and mount the hard drive.

D. Boot to the Linux installation CD or DVD, enter Linux rescue mode, and overwrite the contents of the GRUB file.

11. A security consultant recommends that your secure facility implement biometrics as a form of building access control. What type of system is she most likely referring to?

    A. RFID badges

    B. Key fobs

    C. Retinal scanners

    D. Mantraps

12. You are looking online to find pictures to use as part of promotional materials your company wants to make. Which of the following statements is true regarding online content?

    A. Online content is considered open source; therefore, you may use whatever you find.

    B. Online content is protected through the use of DRM.

    C. Online content is protected through the use of EULA.

    D. Online content is protected through terms established in the Geneva Conventions.

13. In which type of security threat will someone try to gain access to a secure area without credentials by following someone else, who used their access rights, into the secured area?

    A. Brute forcing

    B. Tailgating

    C. Shoulder surfing

    D. Man-in-the-middle

14. A new law requires that you keep hard copies of all your workstations' system configurations. Which command can you use to easily gather this information for remote workstations and save a report as a text file?

    A. MSINFO32

    B. COMPMGMT

    C. MMC

    D. PERFMON

15. You are going to install Windows 10 Pro on a workstation that is currently running Windows 8.1 Professional. If you want to keep user accounts, data, and apps that are currently on the workstation, which type of installation should you perform?

    A. Migration

    B. Clean

    C. Upgrade

    D. Custom

16. You are configuring a wireless router for a home office. Which of the following changes will have the least impact on improving the security of the network?

   A. Enabling MAC filtering

   B. Disabling the SSID broadcast

   C. Configuring WPA2

   D. Changing the default username and password

17. Mobile device users on your network report unusually slow network access speeds when they use Wi-Fi. However, when they are using a cellular connection, the speeds seem fine. Which of the following is the least likely cause of slow data speeds in this case?

   A. Interference

   B. Weak signal

   C. Oversaturated access point

   D. Low battery

18. You are going to move a desktop computer from one office location to another. It's on the floor, underneath the desk. Which of the following are good personal safety procedures to follow? (Choose two.)

   A. Bend at the waist and lift straight up.

   B. Bend at the knees and lift with your legs.

   C. Tie back any loose jewelry, long hair, or neckties.

   D. Leave the computer plugged in to avoid ESD.

19. You have just installed a second and third hard drive into a Windows 8.1 workstation. Each drive is 500 GB. The user wants to combine her space into one 1 TB volume. What should you create to accomplish this and also give the user a disk read and write performance boost?

   A. A new simple volume

   B. A new spanned volume

   C. A new striped volume

   D. A new mirrored volume

20. Which feature of Windows 7 is designed to encrypt storage volumes, must be activated by an administrator, and can encrypt operating system startup files?

   A. BitLocker

   B. EFS

   C. OneDrive

   D. Shadow Drive

21. You want to set up your mobile phone to be able to pay for items at convenience stores simply by moving it close to the merchant's receiver. What type of mobile payment service is this?

 A. SMS or MMS

 B. NFC

 C. Direct mobile billing

 D. Mobile web payments

22. Which of the following statements best describes the functionality of privacy filters?

 A. To keep people from seeing inside the server room

 B. To keep a user from accessing another user's data on the server

 C. To prohibit the accidental release of personally identifiable information (PII)

 D. To keep people from seeing information on your computer screen

23. Your iPhone has been stolen. To ensure that the thief does not have access to your data, what should you do?

 A. Perform a remote backup.

 B. Enable full device encryption.

 C. Perform a remote wipe.

 D. Use a locator application.

24. You have installed a second hard drive in a Windows 10 workstation. In Disk Management, what type of partition can you create that will allow you to create an unlimited number of logical partitions in it?

 A. Extended

 B. Dynamic

 C. Logical

 D. GPT

25. You intend to recycle some older magnetic hard drives. You want to set all data on the drive to be nothing but 0s. What should you use to accomplish this?

 A. Overwrite

 B. format

 C. Degaussing

 D. diskpart

26. Your Windows 8.1 workstation just crashed, displaying a blue screen of death. You have not recently made any changes to the computer. What is the best way to restart Windows to see whether you can isolate the issue?

 A. Boot to the Windows installation CD and start the Recovery Console.

 B. Boot to Safe Mode.

 C. Boot to the Last Known Good configuration.

 D. Boot normally and see whether the error happens again.

27. A user reports that his Android phone will not turn on. When he hands you his phone, it is almost hot to the touch. He then admits that the phone had been in his locked car for most of the day, and it's summertime. What is the most likely cause of the problem?

    A. Overheating

    B. Frozen system

    C. System lockout

    D. Battery drain

28. The floor of a machine shop has several thin client computers on it. You want them to be able to boot a Windows 8 OS from a boot server on the network. What process will the thin clients need to use?

    A. PXE boot

    B. The WinPE process

    C. The WinRE process

    D. Netboot

29. You are at a Windows 10 command prompt. You need to terminate a process on a remote system named Sparky, and the process identifier is 14456. What is the right syntax to use to kill this process and any child processes started by it?

    A. `taskkill /S Sparky /PID 14456 /C`

    B. `taskkill /T Sparky /PID 14456 /S`

    C. `taskkill /S Sparky /PID 14456 /T`

    D. `taskkill /C Sparky /PID 14456 /T`

30. A workstation on your network is configured to dual boot between Windows 8.1 and Windows 10. Previously, the user would get a menu asking him which OS to choose. The user states he has not made any configuration changes, and you feel reasonably certain the initial boot process has completed. However, now that OS menu no longer appears. Which file is responsible for presenting the user with this menu?

    A. `WINRESUME`

    B. `WINLOAD`

    C. `BOOTMGR`

    D. `NTLDR`

31. A small business with two servers in a server closet wants you to find a solution to a problem. The business frequently has power outages and has lost important data on the servers as a result. The business wants some type of battery backup. What type of device should you install to protect against this problem?

    A. Surge protector

    B. Power strip

    C. UPS

    D. Voltage conserver

32. Which type of server on a network will be configured with a scope, which contains information the server will provide to clients who request it?

   A. DHCP server

   B. DNS server

   C. Proxy server

   D. Authentication server

33. You are working on a Windows 10 workstation that is operating very slowly. You want to quickly check system CPU and RAM usage to see whether anything appears amiss. Which two utilities can you use to do this? (Choose two.)

   A. Resource Monitor

   B. Performance Monitor

   C. Control Panel ➢ System

   D. Control Panel ➢ Device Manager

34. What Windows 10 edition allows for an in-place upgrade to Windows 10 Pro Education? (Choose two.)

   A. Home

   B. Pro

   C. Enterprise

   D. All of the above

35. You have a Windows 10 Professional workstation with a physically attached printer. You want others on the network to be able to use the printer as well. What do you need to do to enable this?

   A. Right-click the printer, choose Printer Properties, and share the printer.

   B. Right-click the printer, choose Printer Properties, and map the network printer.

   C. Open the Add A Printer Wizard and share the printer.

   D. Open the Add A Printer Wizard and map the network printer.

36. As the network administrator, you have set account lockout policies so that an account is locked out after five unsuccessful login attempts. What type of security threat will this deter?

   A. Shoulder surfing

   B. Brute forcing

   C. Zero-day attack

   D. Spear phishing

37. Occasionally when visiting websites using Google Chrome, you receive a pop-up window in front of your browser. Generally, it's an advertisement trying to sell you something. Which of the following actions will stop this from happening?

   A. Enable Chrome's pop-up blocker.

   B. Install an antivirus program.

   C. Install anti-malware software to stop the adware.

   D. Enable Windows Firewall.

38. You receive a notice from your wireless provider that you are about to exceed your data plan for the month. This month you have not used your phone often, so this surprises you. What could this be a sign of?

   A. The phone needs to be replaced.

   B. Unauthorized account access

   C. Rogue apps, such as a rogue antivirus

   D. High resource utilization

39. Which Windows 10 versions includes BitLocker, giving users the ability to encrypt data on their hard drive? (Choose all that apply.)

   A. Enterprise

   B. Education

   C. Home

   D. Professional

40. Your company works with confidential government files. It is illegal for employees to copy any files to flash drives. Where do you specify this as well as the penalties for not complying with the rule?

   A. AUP

   B. DLP

   C. ACL

   D. Employee handbook

41. A Windows 7 user reports that her computer just completely locked up. On her screen is a message saying that the person pictured has participated in an illegal activity. Her webcam turned on by itself, and she was pictured. The message also says she can resolve the charges against her by paying a $500 fine. She is understandably shaken by the incident. What should you do next?

   A. Tell her that if she performed an illegal activity with her work computer, her employment will be terminated.

   B. Boot to a recovery CD from your anti-malware provider, and run a remediation.

   C. Delete and reinstall Windows.

   D. Pay the fine.

42. One of your technicians just touched a plastic bottle containing chemicals you are not familiar with. His hand starts to feel like it's burning. Where can you find information on how to properly wash his hands without making the problem worse and how to dispose of the chemical?

   A. OSHA

   B. Bottom of the container

   C. Warning label

   D. MSDS

43. You want to protect mobile device users on your network from potentially leaked files or data. Which of the following should you do to help reduce this risk? (Choose two.)

   A. Disable network auto-connect.

   B. Enforce data transmission overlimits.

   C. Enable device encryption.

   D. Install mobile firewalls.

44. A network architect recommended that you install an IDS on your network. Which of the following statements best describes what an IDS does?

   A. It allows or denies incoming network traffic based on a set of rules.

   B. It detects anomalies in network traffic, logs the activity, and takes actions to stop the activity.

   C. It detects viruses transmitted across the network, logs the activity, and deletes the network packets infected with the virus.

   D. It detects anomalies in network traffic, logs the activity, and sends an alert to the administrator.

45. You are at a Windows 8 command prompt. The directory you are in has hundreds of files, so when you pull a directory listing, you want it to only show one page of files at a time. Which command should you use to do this?

   A. dir /p

   B. dir /o

   C. dir /s

   D. dir /d

46. You are installing virtualization on a network server. Which type of hypervisor should you install to minimize the amount of resources required by the physical machine hosting the virtual servers?

   A. Virtual machine manager

   B. Either Type 1 or Type 2 will function in the same way.

   C. Type 1

   D. Type 2

47. You have discovered that an outside attacker has gained control over several of your workstations and is remotely controlling them. It appears as though the attacker is using the systems to send spam to thousands of users. Which type of attack is this?

   A. Ransomware

   B. Zombie/botnet

   C. Noncompliant systems

   D. Spoofing

48. You have assigned the Finance group Modify permissions on the D:\MonthlyReports folder. You then create a folder named D:\MonthlyReports\January. What level of permissions does the Finance group have to the folder D:\MonthlyReports\January?

   A. No access, because no permissions were explicitly set

   B. Full control, because no permissions were explicitly set

   C. Modify, because the folder inherits permissions from its parent folder

   D. Modify, because the folder inherits permissions from its parent folder. Finance group members can also grant permissions to other users or groups for this folder.

49. A user has two monitors installed on his Windows 7 workstation. He wants his secondary monitor to be on the right side of his primary monitor. However, when he moves the mouse to the right on the primary monitor, the cursor stops at the edge of the screen. When he moves it to the left, the cursor then appears on the right side of his secondary monitor. Where can he go to change this setting?

   A. Right-click the Desktop and choose Screen Resolution.

   B. Right-click the Desktop and choose Mouse Alignment.

   C. Right-click the Desktop and choose Monitor Alignment.

   D. Right-click the Desktop and choose Display Settings.

50. The personal finance app on your Android phone will not load. You rebooted your phone and the app still does not work. What should you try next to get it to work?

   A. Perform a factory reset.

   B. Download an antivirus app and perform a virus scan.

   C. Remove and reinstall the app.

   D. Perform a force stop on the app and then open it again.

51. Your company has a policy prohibiting illegal content on work computers. You have identified and verified illegal content on a user's workstation. What is the next step you should take?

   A. Ask the user to delete the material.

   B. Delete the illegal material yourself.

   C. Document the situation.

   D. Report the incident through proper channels.

52. Your Windows 7 workstation is having intermittent video issues. The manufacturer's website suggests you install the latest driver. Which utility should you use to check the driver version installed on your computer?

- **A.** Display Settings
- **B.** Device Manager
- **C.** Services
- **D.** Computer Management

53. You are performing a large-scale migration to Windows 10 and need to migrate user accounts and settings. You prefer to do this by configuring a script instead of doing it manually. Which utility should you use?

- **A.** User Accounts in Control Panel
- **B.** Windows Easy Transfer (WET)
- **C.** Windows Migration Tool (WMT)
- **D.** User State Migration Tool (USMT)

54. On a MacBook Pro running MacOS, what is the name of the bar of icons that runs along the bottom of the screen, allowing you to open apps?

- **A.** Launcher
- **B.** Finder
- **C.** Spotlight
- **D.** Dock

55. You clicked a link in an email, and it took you to a site you were not familiar with. Later that day, you receive a pop-up message on your computer telling you that all the files on your hard drive have been encrypted, and you can no longer access any of your key documents. If you want the files to be decrypted, you need to pay a fee by entering a credit card number. What have you been infected with?

- **A.** Spyware
- **B.** Trojan
- **C.** Ransomware
- **D.** Worm

56. A Windows 7 workstation is not booting properly, and you believe it's a problem with system files. Which utility can scan and repair corrupt Windows 7 system files?

- **A.** MSCONFIG
- **B.** REGSVR32
- **C.** ERD
- **D.** SFC

57. An Android phone user reports that her phone can't connect to the Wi-Fi network but she has a cellular signal. What is the first thing to have her try?

  A. Check whether the phone is in airplane mode.

  B. Check whether the Wi-Fi connection is enabled.

  C. Adjust the Wi-Fi signal receptivity.

  D. Perform a hard reset.

58. You are instructing new technicians on safety procedures when fixing computers and monitors. As an exhibit, you have an old CRT monitor that has not been used in a few months. Which of the following are the biggest potential dangers if you were to open this monitor? (Choose two.)

  A. Broken glass

  B. Sharp edges

  C. High-voltage capacitors

  D. Burns

59. You are troubleshooting a Windows 8.1 workstation that has malware on it. Following the best practices for malware removal, you have gotten to the point where you've scheduled system scans and run anti-malware updates. What is the next step you should take?

  A. Educate the end user.

  B. Enable system restore and create a restore point.

  C. Disable system restore.

  D. Remediate the infected system.

60. You want to enable encryption on a Windows 10 Pro workstation. Which of the following statements are true? (Choose two.)

  A. Enabling EFS requires administrative access.

  B. Enabling BitLocker requires administrative access.

  C. EFS can encrypt an entire volume or single files.

  D. BitLocker can encrypt an entire volume or single files.

61. When configuring NTFS permissions on a Windows workstation, what is the recommended method?

  A. Grant permissions to user accounts.

  B. Put user accounts into groups. Grant folder permissions to groups and file permissions to users.

  C. Put user accounts into groups. Grant folder permissions to users and file permissions to groups.

  D. Put user accounts into groups. Grant permissions to groups.

62. You are installing client-side virtualization on a Windows 10 Enterprise workstation. The workstation will support two additional OSs. What is the recommended cost-effective way to ensure that each OS obtains proper network access to the rest of the physical network?

   A. Each OS will have a virtual NIC, which is connected to the physical NIC.

   B. Each OS will have its own physical NIC.

   C. Each OS will have a virtual switch connected to the physical NIC.

   D. Each OS will have a virtual NIC, connected to a virtual switch, which is connected to the physical NIC.

63. You are at a Windows 8.1 command prompt in the D:\users directory. You want to use the copy command to copy the D:\users\jdoe directory to the D:\files directory. Which of the following statements is true?

   A. You can't use the copy command to perform this task.

   B. You can use the command copy d:\users\jdoe*.* d:\files.

   C. You can use the command copy d:\users\jdoe d:\files.

   D. You can use the command copy d:\users\jdoe d:\files /y.

64. You would like to configure a test workstation to be able to boot to Windows 7, Windows 8.1, and Windows 10. Which of the following statements is true regarding installation of these operating systems?

   A. The location of operating system installation does not matter in this situation.

   B. You should install all the operating systems on the same partition.

   C. You should install each of the operating systems on its own partition.

   D. You can't install all three operating systems on one workstation.

65. A Windows 10 workstation has a corrupt BCD file. Which two commands can you use to fix this? (Choose two.)

   A. bootrec / fixmbr

   B. bootrec /fixboot

   C. bootrec /rebuildbcd

   D. bceedit

66. A technician is troubleshooting a driver issue on a Windows 8.1 workstation. She has verified full system functionality and implemented preventive measures. According to troubleshooting theory, what should she do next?

   A. Document findings, actions, and outcomes.

   B. Establish a plan of action to resolve the problem and implement the solution.

   C. Question the user and identify user changes to the computer.

   D. Perform backups of the computer.

67. You are working on your Windows 8.1 computer and a security alert pops up, as shown here. What should your next action be?

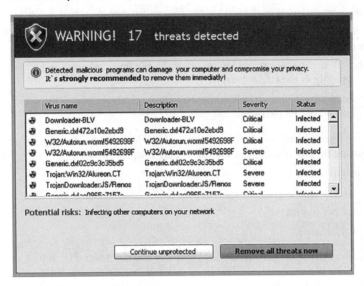

A. Click the Continue Unprotected button.

B. Click the Remove All Threats Now button.

C. Create a restore point and then click the Remove All Threats Now button.

D. Shut down your computer. Reboot, and initiate a virus scan using your antivirus software.

68. You are instructing a new Mac user on the features of MacOS. She asks if the system is capable of storing her passwords to various Internet sites. Which feature would she use for that?

A. Keychain

B. Wallet

C. Passport

D. Spotlight

69. You are troubleshooting a Windows 8.1 workstation that seems to have issues with its video card driver; it will display only 16 colors. You try to boot the system into Safe Mode, but the F8 option does not seem to work. Which management tool can you use to force the system to boot into Safe Mode when it reboots?

A. Task Scheduler

B. Computer Management

C. Task Manager

D. System Configuration

70. Which of the following is an advantage of using share permissions over using NTFS permissions?

    A. Share permissions will override NTFS permissions if there is a conflict.

    B. Share permissions apply when users access a resource across the network, but NTFS permissions apply only to local users.

    C. Share permissions are able to be set at the file level, whereas NTFS permissions can be set only at the folder level.

    D. Share permissions can be enabled to secure resources across the network that are not on an NTFS partition.

71. You have installed an antivirus program on your Windows 8.1 workstation. When configuring it, what should you set the update frequency to?

    A. Automatic

    B. Once per week

    C. Once per month

    D. Once per year

72. Your manager is concerned that your company could divulge PII. Which of the following types of data is not considered PII?

    A. First name

    B. Home address

    C. Family member names

    D. Employee ID number

73. A user reports that his Windows 8.1 installation keeps on crashing. He has installed numerous third-party apps on the computer, and you believe that some of these apps are causing the instability. After entering the Windows Recovery Environment, which option should you choose to repair Windows and delete all but the default apps?

    A. Recover

    B. Refresh

    C. Reset

    D. Restore

74. On a Windows 7 workstation, there are two NTFS volumes. The Managers group has Modify access to the `C:\mgmt` directory. You move the folder to the `D:\keyfiles` folder, to which the Managers group has Read access. What level of permissions will the Managers group have to the new `D:\keyfiles\mgmt` directory?

    A. Full Control

    B. Modify

    C. Read & Execute

    D. Read

75. You are training mobile users on potential security risks. Which of the following could make users more susceptible to a man-in-the-middle attack?

   A. Unintended Wi-Fi connection

   B. Unauthorized account access

   C. Unauthorized location tracking

   D. Unauthorized camera activation

76. The network you manage has a dozen Windows 7 workstations. You want to ensure that users do not have the ability to change the boot order, so they can't boot to an unauthorized device. Which step should you take?

   A. Set a BIOS/UEFI password.

   B. Disable autorun.

   C. Restrict user permissions.

   D. Enable a strong password policy.

77. A user needs to travel for a presentation and wants to be sure his laptop does not run off battery power, so he wants to turn it off. However, he wants to leave his files and applications running, so when he turns it back on, the applications are already open. Which of the following statements is true?

   A. The user will be unable to do this.

   B. The user should put his computer into standby mode.

   C. The user needs to activate the sleep power plan.

   D. The user should have his computer hibernate.

78. You are working on a Windows 7 workstation that will not properly load Windows. Another technician suggests using a snapshot to restore the system. Where do you do this from?

   A. Windows RE

   B. Windows pre-installation environment

   C. Safe Mode

   D. Backup and Restore

79. A user's NTFS permissions for the docs folder are Read & Execute. His share permissions are Full Control. What is his effective access when connecting to the resource across the network?

   A. No access

   B. Full Control

   C. Read & Execute

   D. Read only

80. You have a Linux server on your network. You want to back up all files in the /user/files volume without disrupting user access. What should you use to do this?

A. Time Machine

B. Linux Backup

C. Snapshot

D. Image recovery

81. You open a command prompt on a Windows 7 workstation and type in the sfc command. You receive an error message telling you that you need to be an administrator to run the command. What should you do next?

A. Run the sfc /admin command.

B. Run the sfc /elevate command.

C. Click Start ➤ All Programs ➤ Accessories; then right-click Command Prompt and choose Run As Administrator. Then run the sfc command.

D. Click Start ➤ All Programs ➤ Accessories; then right-click Command Prompt and choose Run With Elevated Privileges. Then run the sfc command.

82. You want to see events that your Windows 8.1 workstation has logged. Which of the following is not a type of log that is contained in Event Viewer?

A. Security

B. System

C. Login

D. Application

83. You want to grant a user the ability to make changes to files and run programs located in an NTFS folder. However, you do not want him to be able to delete files in the folder. Which level of access should you allow him?

A. Read & Execute, and Write

B. Modify

C. Full Control

D. Write

84. Your company has decided to stop purchasing commercial cloud services and enter into a cloud partnership with a sister company. What type of cloud will your company and the sister company create?

A. Public

B. Private

C. Hybrid

D. Community

85. You have a Windows 7 Professional workstation installed in a workgroup. There is no centralized security. Which tool should you use to help protect yourself against malicious network attacks?

A. Windows Firewall

B. Advanced Security

C. Local Security Policy

D. Computer Management

86. You are working on a client's desktop computer, and the video card is dead. You can get a warranty replacement, but it will take three days to arrive. Or you can replace it with a more expensive card today, but he would need to pay the difference. Which of the following is the best way for you to continue the service call?

A. Tell him that the video card is dead. It will take three days for the video card to arrive, and you will return then to replace it.

B. Tell him that the video card is dead. It will take three days for a warranty replacement to arrive (at no cost), or you can replace it with an upgraded model today if he wants to pay the difference in cost.

C. Tell him that the video card is dead. Offer to replace it today with a more expensive video card, and he can pay the difference in cost.

D. Tell him that he will be without a computer for three days, but then you will come back and fix it.

87. A friend is recycling his old computer and wants to be sure that no one can access his private information. He decides to format the hard drive and chooses a quick format. Which of the following statements is true?

A. His private information is safe because the old data has been permanently removed from the hard drive.

B. His private information is safe because once the file allocation table has been removed, none of the old data is accessible.

C. His private information is not safe because the quick format only writes a new file allocation table.

D. His private information is not safe because the quick format only removes the old operating system files.

88. When you begin synchronization of an iPhone to a desktop computer, what type of authentication occurs?

A. There is no authentication required for synchronization.

B. Both devices authenticate each other.

C. The iPhone authenticates the desktop computer.

D. The desktop computer authenticates the iPhone.

89. Which of the following types of threats are specific examples of social engineering? (Choose two.)

    A. Spoofing

    B. Viruses

    C. Shoulder surfing

    D. Spear phishing

90. You are attempting to update a Windows 10 workstation using Windows Update. The update fails with this message: "Failure configuring Windows updates. Reverting changes." You reboot and try again but receive the same error. What should you try next? (Choose two.)

    A. Wait until changes are reverted. Unplug removable media from your computer and try again.

    B. Wait until changes are reverted. Run a virus scan and try again.

    C. Wait until changes are reverted. Run the Windows Update Troubleshooter.

    D. Ignore the update.

Appendix

Answers and Explanations

Chapter 1: Mobile Devices

1. C. Smaller devices, such as tablets and phones, almost exclusively use LED backlighting, which is smaller and consumes less power than CCFLs.

2. B. Because of the much smaller space available for keys, some laptop keys are consolidated into special multifunction keys. These keys are accessed through the standard keys by using a special function (Fn) key. Video adjustments come in two varieties: changing the video output and dimming or brightening the screen. In this case, there is a large sun icon for brightening the screen. Some laptops will use a smaller sun to label the key for dimming and a larger sun to label the key for brightening, or they will use plus and minus signs or up and down arrows next to the suns. You may also see special function keys to turn network connections on or off or to play, fast forward, or rewind media.

3. A. Capacitive touch screens are a little less accurate than resistive touch screens but more responsive. They respond to changes in electrical current, and as such, the human fingertip works great as the facilitator of input.

4. C. Airplane mode turns off all wireless connections on a mobile device. It's common on phones and tablets, and some laptops have the feature as well.

5. A. Smart cameras have built-in wireless network connectivity for easy picture and video transfers. Many will include Wi-Fi, Bluetooth, and NFC.

6. B. Laptop processors generally are permanently attached to the motherboard. And motherboards are normally proprietary, meaning one from a certain model will not fit into a different case. Therefore, the best course of action is likely a laptop upgrade.

7. B. Because of the much smaller space available for keys, some laptop keys are consolidated into special multifunction keys. These keys are accessed through the standard keys by using a special function (Fn) key. Nearly every laptop has a video connector on the back or the side to plug in an external monitor or a projector. You will need to use the video toggle key to get this external port to work.

8. C. A USB to Wi-Fi dongle will allow your computer to use that wireless network connection to get back up and running. Once you are on the network again, you can send the file. Replacing a network card on a laptop generally means replacing the entire motherboard. You can also get USB to Ethernet adapters for wired networking.

9. A. Most e-readers use a technology called electrophoretic ink, or E Ink, which is a proprietary type of electronic paper. Although E Ink is available in color, many consider its best applications to be in grayscales or pure black and white. Additionally, E Ink uses almost no power to keep print on the page until the print is changed.

10. B. Tethering is connecting a device to a mobile hotspot. The term used to be reserved only for when you were connected via USB cable, as opposed to connecting via wireless. Some devices will not function as a mobile hotspot but will allow you to tether a mobile device to it with a USB cable so the mobile device can share the cellular Internet connection.

11.   B. Unlike many other smartphones, the BlackBerry smartphones are known for having a physical rather than an onscreen keyboard, although there are also some models that use the onscreen keyboard. Another feature unique to BlackBerry is the BlackBerry Messenger service.

12.   C. To physically secure your laptop, use a cable lock. Essentially, a cable lock anchors your device to a physical structure, making it nearly impossible for someone to walk off with it. LoJack is software that can help secure data but does not prevent physical theft. A protective cover will help protect your device from damage if it gets dropped (and some are waterproof too), but it won't stop someone from stealing it.

13.   C, D. SSDs have several advantages over magnetic HDDs. They include faster startup and read times, less power consumption, silent operation, and higher reliability because of lack of moving parts, and they are less susceptible to damage from physical shock and heat production.

14.   A. The Video Electronics Standards Association (VESA) introduced DisplayPort in 2008. It was designed to be an industry standard and to replace VGA and DVI. It's also backward compatible with VGA and DVI by using adapters. A display port is intended to be for video devices only, but like HDMI and USB, it can transmit audio and video simultaneously.

15.   D. OLED display illuminates each pixel individually. Conversely, LCD displays are backlit by an LED light.

16.   C. A digitizer is a device that can be written or drawn on and the content will be converted from analog input to digital images on the computer. Digitizers take input from a user's finger or a writing utensil, such as a stylus. Many touch screen devices have a digitizer built into them.

17.   D. Laptop motherboards are nearly always proprietary, meaning they are not interchangeable between manufacturers or even between models from the same manufacturer. When a laptop motherboard needs to be replaced, you most likely need a laptop motherboard from the same make and model.

18.   B. Traditional magnetic hard drives will have greater capacity than SSD (which are a type of flash memory) or hybrid drives.

19.   A. Near-field communication (NFC) is a wireless technology that uses radio frequency (RF) signals with limited range, about 4" (10 cm).

20.   B, C. Webcams are nearly universal on laptops today. The most common placement is right above the display on the laptop. Microphones are also often built into the display, next to the webcam.

21.   A. If you need to make mobile sales, you will need a credit card reader and an app to make the transactions. Many mobile credit card readers are small devices that plug into the speaker/headphone jack, like the PayPal Here shown here.

22. A. If you have a cellular-enabled device such as a smartphone, you may be able to turn that phone into a mobile hotspot. By doing so, you can share your cellular Internet connection with Wi-Fi enabled devices such as laptops and tablets.

23. D. Laptop motherboards are nearly always proprietary, meaning they are not interchangeable between manufacturers or even between models from the same manufacturer. When a laptop motherboard needs to be replaced, you most likely need a laptop motherboard from the same make and model.

24. A. The liquid crystal display (LCD) is the component that provides the backlight to the laptop's display.

25. D. Mobile devices often make use of small form factor memory cards, such as Secure Digital (SD), miniSD, or microSD cards. Higher-capacity versions of these cards are SDHC, SDXC, miniSDHC, microSDHC, and microSDXC. The standard versions can hold up to 2 GB in storage, HC up to 32 GB, and XC up to 2 TB.

26. C. Many companies choose to design their devices with a built-in micro USB or mini USB connector. Others modify the standard USB connector slightly, as Samsung has done with the connector for the S5 smartphone and other devices.

27. A. To save space, components of the video circuitry (and possibly other circuits as well) are placed on a thin circuit board that connects directly to the motherboard. This circuit board is often known as a riser card or a daughterboard.

28. C. A piconet is the name for a wireless Bluetooth network. Therefore, you need a USB to Bluetooth adapter.

29. B. A DC power adapter allows a user to plug the laptop into the DC power source (usually called an auxiliary power outlet) inside a car or on an airplane. AC power adapters are for plugging into standard wall outlets.

30. B. Mini PCIe cards running in PCIe 1.0 x1 mode have a maximum speed of 2.5 Gbps.

31. B. Common components to include in the display are the screen, Wi-Fi antenna, webcam, microphone, inverter, and digitizer.

32. B. A phablet is a device that blurs the line between a smartphone and a tablet. The term is not used much, but technically, a phablet is a smartphone with a display size between 5″ and 7″.

33. C. The Apple Watch uses Apple's WatchOS. Samsung watches use Tizen, Sony watches use Android Wear, and Pebble watches use Pebble OS.

34. C. Headsets are used for hands-free phone conversations and listening to music. Headsets can either plug into the speaker/headphone jack or be wireless. Most wireless headsets are Bluetooth.

35. A, B. You should choose an AC adapter rated for the same wattage as or higher wattage than the original. You must also pay special attention to the polarity of the plug that interfaces with the laptop. If the laptop requires the positive lead to be the center conductor, for instance, then you must take care not to reverse the polarity.

36. D. A docking station often replicates the functions of the ports on the back of a laptop so that peripherals such as monitors, keyboards, printers, and so on that don't travel with the laptop can remain connected to the dock and don't all have to be unplugged physically each time the laptop is taken away. This differs from a port replicator whose main function is to let the user connect several devices at once and doesn't require the laptop to be connected to offer that connectivity.

37. C. A docking port is usually located on the bottom of the laptop to connect to a docking station. The docking station often replicates the functions of the ports on the back of a laptop so that peripherals such as monitors, keyboards, printers, and so on that don't travel with the laptop can remain connected to the dock and don't all have to be unplugged physically each time the laptop is taken away.

38. D. As a rule of thumb, either you can access components from the bottom of a laptop, such as the memory and Mini PCIe card, or you're going to need to remove the keyboard to access the components from the top.

39. A. Airplane mode turns off all wireless connections on the mobile device. It's common on phones and tablets, and some laptops have the feature as well.

40. A, B. Mobile devices often make use of small form factor memory cards, such as Secure Digital (SD), miniSD, or microSD cards. Higher-capacity versions of these cards are SDHC, SDXC, miniSDHC, microSDHC, and microSDXC. The standard versions can hold up to 2 GB in storage, HC up to 32 GB, and XC up to 2 TB.

41. B. The iPhone 8 series and iPhone X series still use the proprietary connector called the Lightning connector.

42. A. ExpressCard/34 cards can have a variety of functions. However, they are too small to support expansion options such as 1.8 disk drives, card readers, and CompactFlash readers. For those devices, you will need ExpressCard/54.

43. C. GPS systems were designed to require multiple satellites. Receivers use a process called triangulation, which they use to calculate the distance between themselves and the satellites (based on the time it takes to receive a signal) to determine their location. They require input from four satellites to provide location and elevation or three to provide location.

44. C. There are two types of LCD technologies listed in the exam objectives: TN and IPS. Twisted nematic (TN) is the older of the two, and it is relatively inexpensive and low power. The issue with TN LCD screens is that when you start viewing them at wider angles, the picture quality suffers greatly. In-Plane Switching (IPS) LCD monitors provide better color representation as well as wider-angle viewing, but they tend to be a bit more expensive and have somewhat slower response times.

45. B. You need to stop the device first (this is good policy even for USB devices) using the Safely Remove Hardware icon in the system tray (it looks like a card and may have a green arrow or green check mark over it, depending on your version of Windows). Highlight the device and click Stop. Once it's stopped, you can unplug it.

46. C. The Apple Watch uses WatchOS. It's similar to iOS (used on iPads and iPhones) but was developed specifically for the watch. Its features are similar to iOS, but it includes features more tailored toward a smaller device.

47. B. A Universal ExpressCard host slot is wide enough to fit either an ExpressCard/54 or an ExpressCard/34 adapter; both of them have 26-pin connectors. (Slots designed for an ExpressCard/34 device cannot accommodate its wider cousins.) Universal ExpressCard slots also appear to be able to accept a CardBus adapter, but the card inserts not even an inch before stopping on the internal guide that ensures correct ExpressCard/34 insertion. ExpressCards can also be used to facilitate wireless and cellular connections.

48. D. The first version of Thunderbolt supported 10 Gbps data rates, which is fast. Thunderbolt 2.0 joins two 10 Gbps channels together for 20 Gbps throughput. But the fastest speed available today with Thunderbolt 3 is 40 Gbps.

49. B, C. Laptop hard drives will be one of two form factors (sizes): 1.8″ or 2.5″. Desktop computers have historically used 3.5″ hard drives.

50. A. Mini PCIe cards running in PCIe 1.0 x1 mode have a maximum speed of 2.5 Gbps. Mini PCIe cards running in USB 2.0 mode have a maximum speed of 480 Mbps, and those running in USB 3.0 or PCIe 2.0 x1 mode have a maximum speed of 5.0 Gbps.

51. A. A digitizer is a device that can be written or drawn on, and the content will be converted from analog input to digital images on the computer. Digitizers take input from a user's finger or a writing utensil, such as a stylus.

52. B. A fitness monitor is normally worn on the wrist, and it tracks a user's movements and heart rate. Some fitness monitors will be able to track sleep patterns and have a clock, alarm, and other features such as GPS. All fitness monitors have the ability to sync to a device such as a smartphone, laptop, or desktop.

53. A. Near-field communication (NFC) is a wireless technology that uses radio frequency (RF) signals with limited range, about 4″ (10 cm). To read an NFC tag in a poster, you would move your phone close to the tag, and the phone would generate a small RF field that would power the target. Data could then be read from the tag, which currently holds up to 8 KB of data.

54. D. A good game controller can make your mobile device feel a bit more like a gaming console. Most of the game pads will look like standard console controllers and connect via Bluetooth.

55. D. Thunderbolt was codeveloped by Apple and Intel as an offshoot of the DisplayPort technology. Apple added support for PCIe and launched it in 2011. In terms of versatility, it's really second only to USB. You will find video devices, hard drives (both HDD and SSD), printers, laptop docking stations, audio devices, and PCIe expansion enclosures that use Thunderbolt. Thunderbolt 3 is now compatible with USB-C.

56. A. An ExpressCard/34 slot is only 34 mm wide and will only accept a /34 card. There are no ExpressCard/22 cards or ExpressCard Universal cards (there is a universal slot), and the /54 card will be too wide to fit into the slot.

57. B. Near-field communication (NFC) is a wireless technology that uses radio frequency (RF) signals with limited range, about 4″ (10 cm). NFC can operate in card emulation mode, which lets the device act as a smart card. This is useful for making payments at the site of a merchant who uses NFC.

58. C. The job of the inverter is to store and convert energy; they have the potential to discharge that energy. They can be dangerous to technicians, so be careful when working with them.

59. B. Many laptops use shared video memory, meaning that system RAM is divided up for use between the processor and the video card. On these types of systems, the amount of RAM available for video is configured in the BIOS. Anything reserved for the video card is unavailable to the processor. In this case, subtracting half a gigabyte from 4 GB leaves the CPU with 3.5 GB.

60. D. Oculus VR specializes in virtual reality and alternate reality headsets (VR/AR headsets). Samsung and HTC, while manufacturing smartphones, also produce VR/AR headsets.

61. C. DDR3 SODIMMs have 204 pins. DDR and DDR2 SODIMMS have 200 pins each, and older SDDRAM has 144 pins.

62. B. The connector shown is the Apple Lightning connector used by iPhones since the iPhone 5.

63. A. A solid-state drive (SSD) uses the same memory technology found in other forms of flash memory. They are much faster than traditional magnetic drives or hybrid drives but generally don't have as much capacity.

64. A. When setting up a Bluetooth connection between a mobile device and an accessory, you will most often be required to connect the two devices logically in a process called pairing. Pairing is basically a discovery and authentication process that validates the communication link.

65. C. Tablet screen sizes typically fall anywhere between 7″ and 12″, although you can find much larger ones with 24″ displays.

66. B. The two center connectors are Thunderbolt connectors. They have the characteristic lightning bolt icon. Thunderbolt is an offshoot of DisplayPort technology and supports many types of peripherals.

67. D. Google Glass is a mobile technology that uses augmented reality. It projects a display onto a lens a few inches from the user's face that is equivalent to looking at a 25″ screen from about 8 feet away.

68. D. Laptops use either a fluorescent backlight (CCFL) or an LED backlight. LED backlights typically do not need an inverter.

69. B. A USB to RJ-45 dongle will allow your computer to participate on a wired network, provided that the network uses twisted-pair cabling. You can also get USB to Ethernet adapters for wireless networking.

70.   B. Mini PCIe cards come in two sizes. The full-size cards are similar in size to ExpressCard devices without the external cover, measuring 30 mm wide and 51 mm long. Half-size cards are 30 mm wide and 27 mm long.

71.   C. Most laptops don't have internal expansion room, so it will be impossible to install an internal component where one never existed. The best bet is to use an external DVD burner and attach it via a USB port. A DB-15 port is for VGA (video monitor) connections.

72.   C. Tablets are designed for mobile communication. As such, all tablets come equipped with Wi-Fi and Bluetooth, and many have cellular capabilities as well.

73.   D. The iPhone X series (and since the iPhone 5) use a proprietary connector called the Lightning connector.

74.   D. Many laptops use shared video memory, meaning that system RAM is divided up for use between the processor and the video card. On these types of systems, the amount of RAM available for video is configured in the BIOS.

75.   D. Because of the much smaller space available for keys, some laptop keys are consolidated into special multifunction keys. These keys are accessed through the standard keys by using a special function (Fn) key. Nearly every laptop has a video connector on the back or the side to plug in an external monitor or a projector. You will need to use the video toggle key to get this external port to work. Usually there are three or four states: laptop only, external output only, duplicate, or extend the desktop (some models won't extend the desktop).

76.   A, B. Most laptop motherboards have integrated components to provide different functions. It is common to have video, audio, and wireless networking circuitry built into the motherboard. Hard drives and memory are generally replaceable.

77.   B, C. To combat heat, you can either slow the processor down (run it at a lower speed) or give it less juice (run it at a lower voltage). Most of the time, this is configured in the system BIOS. For example, many Intel processors have SpeedStep technology to slow the processor down to produce less heat, and they may also have adaptive thermal management.

78.   C. If the integrated video card fails, you're looking at a motherboard replacement. Some laptops do have a replaceable video card. If it fails or if you choose to upgrade it, the procedure will probably resemble replacing system memory.

79.   A. Mini PCIe cards use a 52-pin connector. Cards are 30 mm wide.

80.   B, C. Google Glass has a touch pad on the side of the device that lets users scroll through menus and make selections. Other inputs can be made by voice command through a microphone or other built-in sensors such as the accelerometer, gyroscope, magnetometer, proximity sensor, and ambient light sensor.

81. B, D. Of the wireless communication methods, infrared (IR) and near-field communication (NFC) are the hardest to hack. IR communication is limited to about 1 meter, with a viewing angle of about 30 degrees. You would know if someone was trying to intercept the signal. NFC is limited to about 4" (10 cm). It would be pretty obvious if someone were trying to intercept that signal.

82. C. There are two types of LCD technologies listed in the exam objectives: TN and IPS. Twisted nematic (TN) is the older of the two, and it is relatively inexpensive and low power. The issue with TN LCD screens is that when you start viewing them at wider angles, the picture quality suffers greatly. In-Plane Switching (IPS) LCD monitors provide better color representation as well as wider-angle viewing, but they tend to be a bit more expensive and have somewhat slower response times.

83. A, D. Smart cameras have built-in wireless network connectivity for easy picture and video transfers. Many will include Wi-Fi, Bluetooth, and NFC.

84. B. The connector on the right is a USB mini connector.

85. D. If you are having problems with flickering screens or dimness, it's more likely that the inverter is the problem and not the backlight itself.

86. D. Infrared (IR) is a short-distance, line-of-sight, point-to-point communication method. It's usually used to transfer small amounts of data from one device to another. The maximum functional distance of IR in mobile devices is about 1 meter, with a viewing angle of about 30 degrees.

87. A. The overwhelming majority of Wi-Fi antenna connectors for indoor rated antennas found on the device are type SMA. On the device will be a SMA-female. What makes a connector "male" is the center pin and threads on the inside, while a "female" connector will have threads on the outside.

88. B. A port replicator is an attachment that provides the same ports or additional ports as a laptop. In addition, the port replicator does not require the laptop in order to offer the connectivity to the other devices.

89. C. Laptops with a rotating or removable screen allows the touch screen to function like a tablet. This would allow the warehouse manager to take notes with a tablet while keeping the laptop for her desk.

90. B. The IEEE standard 802.15.1 is commonly known as Bluetooth. The first step in using Bluetooth after enabling the protocol is finding a device with which to pair.

91. C. When pairing two Bluetooth devices, depending on the security settings, it is sometimes necessary to enter a Bluetooth PIN code. In security configuration menus, the PIN is sometimes referred to as the Bluetooth passcode or passkey.

92. D. Bluetooth connectivity was lost between the earpiece and the once-paired device, likely a phone. You will examine the phone and troubleshoot connectivity between the phone and the earpiece.

93. C. POP3, or Post Office Protocol 3, keeps emails stored on one device. This means both sent and received messages are stored on that one device, so all email is accessed from that device.

94. A. Internet Messaging Access Protocol, or IMAP, keeps emails on the server. This allows someone to view and work with their email from more than one device.

95. A. Secure/Multipurpose Internet Mail Extensions, S/MIME, is a protocol that allows someone to send a digitally signed email.

96. C. Apple's cloud service called iCloud is for users and subscribers to store their media, contacts, and so on.

97. B. Exchange Online is the cloud service version of Microsoft Exchange.

98. B. The port and SSL settings are used to first configure email on a device. The correct port will depend largely on whether you are using the IMAP or POP3 protocol. The SSL settings are not required but should be filled in to permit encrypted email.

99. A. The Preferred Roaming List (PRL) and Product Release Instructions (PRI) deal with how your phone connects to the correct mobile tower and network. Updates to this information on the phone are typically done over the air.

100. C. The International Mobile Station Equipment Identity (IMEI) is a unique number assigned to the physical phone. This unique identifier is hard-coded into the device.

101. B. The International Mobile Subscriber Identity (IMSI) is a unique number coded into the SIM card and identifies you, the user, to the cellular service.

102. D. A virtual private network (VPN) will keep his browsing confidential as well as bypass any local content blocking efforts.

103. A. Synchronization means to duplicate or back up the data from the device. Synchronization can be done to the local desktop, to the cloud service off premises, or even to an automobile.

104. C. When you synchronize bookmarks between devices, the website addresses are copied and readily available. The same synchronization can be done for several media types, such as videos, music, pictures, and documents.

105. A. Synchronizing calendars between devices and users is an easy and reliable option for ensuring that all parties have the same information.

106. A. Single sign-on is the authentication feature of users logging into their device, which in turn uses their authorization and credentials to authenticate to other systems or services. This is implemented through Active Directory or another centralized service that could store a user's privileges.

107. C. The user should definitely synchronize contact information between the desktop mail application and his mobile device.

108. B. Before installing a new application, it is highly recommended to verify software requirements needed to install the application on the PC.

Chapter 2: Networking

1. B. Because bridges work at the Data Link layer, they are aware of only hardware (MAC) addresses. They are not aware of and do not deal with IP addresses. Bridges are more intelligent than repeaters, but they are unable to move data across multiple networks simultaneously.

2. B. An Ethernet splitter will take the incoming signal on two pairs and then split it, so on the output end it produces two sets of signals using two pairs each. Because of this, Ethernet splitters are limited to 100 Mbps connections. It is not recommended that you use Ethernet splitters on a network. If you need to connect multiple computers using UTP, use a hub or a switch.

3. A. Cable testers are indispensable tools for any network technician. Usually you would use a cable tester before you install a cable to make sure it works. Of course, you can test them after they've been run as well.

4. C. Internet Message Access Protocol (IMAP) is a secure protocol designed to download email. It has several advantages over the older Post Office Protocol 3 (POP3). First, IMAP4 works in connected and disconnected modes. Second, it lets you store the email on the server, as opposed to POP3, which requires you to download it. Third, IMAP4 allows multiple clients to be simultaneously connected to the same inbox.

5. A. The Domain Name System (DNS) server is responsible for resolving hostnames, such as www.google.com, to IP addresses to enable communication. If it's not working properly or you can't connect to it, you won't be able to browse the Internet using friendly website names.

6. C. Single-mode fiber (SMF) can provide data throughput rates of 10 Gbps at a distance of 40 kilometers. Compare that to multimode fiber, which can reliably transmit 10 Gbps for only about 550 meters.

7. B. RG-59 network cable can run for about 228 meters (750 feet). The slightly thicker RG-6 has more insulation and can run for about 304 meters (1,000 feet). Transmission quality for RG-59 differs depending on the frequencies. RG-59 is good for baseband video, but at high frequencies the RG-59 does not do well over long distances.

8. B. Secure Shell (SSH) can be used to set up a secure Telnet session for remote logins or for remotely executing programs and transferring files. Because it's secure, it was originally designed to be a replacement for the unsecure telnet command.

9. B, C. Switches and bridges work at Layer 2. Switches are multiport bridges.

10. B. Computers are able to differentiate where the network ID ends and the host address begins through the use of a subnet mask.

11. B. Transmission Control Protocol (TCP) guarantees packet delivery through the use of a virtual circuit and data acknowledgments, and User Datagram Protocol (UDP) does not. Because of this, TCP is often referred to as connection oriented, whereas UDP is connectionless.

12. D. Telnet lets users log into another machine and "see" the remote computer in a window on their screen. Although this vision is text only, users can manage files on that remote machine just as if they were logged in locally.

13. C. A CIDR shorthand notation of /26 corresponds to the subnet mask 255.255.255.192.

14. C. 802.11g specifies a maximum of 54 Mbps transmissions in the 2.4 GHz frequency range.

15. C. Server Message Block (SMB) is a protocol used to provide shared access to files, printers, and other network resources. In a way, it functions a bit like FTP, only with a few more options, such as the ability to connect to printers and more management commands.

16. C. Telnet lets users log into another machine and "see" the remote computer in a window on their screen. Although this vision is text only, users can manage files on that remote machine just as if they were logged in locally. Telnet uses port 23.

17. D. A wireless locator, or a Wi-Fi analyzer can be either a handheld hardware device or specialized software that is installed on a laptop and whose purpose is to detect and analyze Wi-Fi signals. It can detect where signals are strong or weak to determine whether there are potential security issues.

18. C. Internet traffic is not encrypted by default. Websites that are secure and encrypt their transmissions will start with HTTPS:// rather than HTTP://. These sites can be trusted to encrypt the data, and their identity is verified.

19. A. The main Internet layer protocol is Internet Protocol (IP), and it's the workhorse of TCP/IP. Another key protocol at this layer is Internet Control Message Protocol (ICMP), which is responsible for delivering error messages. If you're familiar with the ping utility, you'll know that it utilizes ICMP to send and receive packets.

20. C. There are three types of addresses in IPv6: unicast, anycast, and multicast. A unicast address identifies a single node on the network. An anycast address refers to one that has been assigned to multiple nodes. A multicast address is one used by multiple hosts.

21. A. Of the wireless encryption methods listed, WPA2 is the newest and most secure. Some routers offer WPA2 Enterprise, which is a great choice as well.

22. B. A wide area network (WAN) covers large geographical areas and often supports thousands of users.

23. A. Developed by Microsoft, the Remote Desktop Protocol (RDP) allows users to connect to remote computers and run programs on them. When you use RDP, you see the desktop of the computer you've signed into on your screen. It's like you're really there, even though you're not.

24. B. Secure Shell (SSH) can be used to set up a secure Telnet session for remote logins or for remotely executing programs and transferring files. SSH uses port 22.

25. A. Private IP addresses are not routable on the Internet. The private IP address range for class A networks is 10.0.0.0/8.

26.   D. One of the key features of routers is that they break up broadcast domains. Broadcast traffic on one side of the router will not get passed to the other side, which greatly reduces network traffic.

27.   C. A loopback plug is for testing the ability of a network adapter to send and receive. The plug gets plugged into the NIC, and then a loopback test is performed using troubleshooting software. You can then tell whether the card is working properly.

28.   D. UTP cables are limited to 100 meters, so CAT5 and CAT7 will not work. You need fiber, and multimode fiber (MMF) can span distances of 300 meters.

29.   C, D. Simple Mail Transfer Protocol (SMTP, port 25), Post Office Protocol 3 (POP3, port 110), and Internet Message Access Protocol (IMAP, port 143) are all email protocols. SMTP is for sending email. POP3 and IMAP are for downloading email.

30.   A. Fiber-optic cabling uses pulses of light instead of electric voltages to transmit data, so it is immune to electrical interference and to wiretapping.

31.   D. Routers operate at the Network layer (Layer 3) of the OSI model. Because of this, they make their decisions on what to do with traffic based on logical addresses, such as an IP address.

32.   C. A firewall is a hardware or software solution that serves as your network's security guard. Firewalls can protect you in two ways: They protect your network resources from hackers lurking in the dark corners of the Internet, and they can simultaneously prevent computers on your network from accessing undesirable content on the Internet.

33.   D. The default gateway is the address to the network's router, which will allow the host to communicate with hosts not on the local network.

34.   D. The Remote Desktop Protocol (RDP) allows users to connect to remote computers and run programs on them. It uses port 3389.

35.   A. F-connectors are threaded and screw into place. The BNC connector locks by twisting one-quarter turn. SC and ST connectors are for fiber-optic cable.

36.   C. A personal area network (PAN) is a small-scale network designed around one person within a limited boundary area. The term generally refers to networks that use Bluetooth technology.

37.   D. At the Internet layer of TCP/IP, Address Resolution Protocol (ARP) resolves logical IP addresses to physical MAC addresses built into network cards. Reverse ARP (RARP) resolves MAC addresses to IP addresses.

38.   C. The 169.254.0.0/16 range in IPv4 is the APIPA range, used for automatic configuration if the host can't locate a DHCP server. The same task in IPv6 is accomplished with a link local address in the FE80::/10 range.

39.   D. Universal Plug and Play (UPnP) is a standard designed to simplify the process of connecting devices to a network and to enable those devices to automatically announce their presence to other devices on the network.

40. A, C. Addresses in the FE80::/10 range are link local unicast addresses. A link local address is assigned to each IPv6 interface but is not routable on the Internet. If this is the only address the host has, it will not be able to get on the Internet.

41. A. The File Transfer Protocol (FTP) is optimized for downloading files from servers. It uses port 21.

42. D. The Lightweight Directory Access Protocol (LDAP) is a directory services protocol based on the X.500 standard. LDAP is designed to access information stored in an information directory typically known as an LDAP directory or LDAP database. This often includes employee phone numbers and email addresses.

43. B. The default subnet mask for class B networks is 255.255.0.0, or written in shorthand, /16.

44. D. If you're working on a larger network installation, you might use a punchdown tool. It's not a testing tool but one that allows you to connect (that is, punch down) the exposed ends of a wire into wiring harnesses, such as a 110 block.

45. C. Fiber-optic broadband Internet offers fast speeds (often in the 1 Gbps range) but is also the most expensive.

46. C. Server Message Block (SMB) is a protocol used to provide shared access to files, printers, and other network resources. It uses TCP ports 137–139 and 445.

47. A, C. Each IPv6 interface can and often does have multiple addresses assigned to it. IPv6 is backward compatible with IPv4.

48. B, C. A hub is a device used to link several computers together. Hubs are simple devices that possess no real intelligence, and they work at Layer 1 of the OSI model. Extenders simply allow a signal to propagate for a longer distance, and they also work at Layer 1. Switches are Layer 2 devices, and routers work at Layer 3.

49. B. The Apple Filing Protocol (AFP) was developed by Apple as a file transfer protocol similar to FTP and Server Message Block (SMB). It was the default file transfer protocol on MacOS until Apple changed to SMB2 in 2013.

50. B. 127.0.0.1 is the loopback address, used to ping the local network interface. The IPv6 equivalent is ::1.

51. B. Port triggering allows traffic to enter the network on a specific port after a computer makes an outbound request on that specific port. For example, if a computer on your internal network makes an outbound Telnet request (port 23), subsequent inbound traffic destined for the originating computer on port 23 would be allowed through.

52. D. If you need to trace a wire in a wall from one location to another, a tone generator and probe is the right tool to use. It consists of two pieces: a tone generator and a probe. To use it, attach one end to one end of the cable, such as the end at the computer. Then go to the patch panel with the other end of the probe to locate the cable. These are lifesavers when the cables are not properly labeled.

53.   B. Dynamic Host Configuration Protocol (DHCP) dynamically assigns IP addresses and other IP configuration information to network clients.

54.   B. Switches work at Layer 2, as do bridges, and they provide centralized connectivity just like hubs. Switches examine the Layer 2 header of the incoming packet and forward it properly to the right port and only that port. Switches are multiport bridges.

55.   B. Email is pushed from clients to servers using the Simple Mail Transfer Protocol (SMTP). SMTP uses port 25.

56.   C. Of the Wi-Fi standards, 802.11n has the longest range by default, at roughly 70 meters indoors and 250 meters outdoors. 802.11ac is newer and faster than 802.11n, but it transmits exclusively in the 5 GHz range, which restricts its functional distance.

57.   C. Multimeters are versatile electronic measuring tools. A multimeter can measure voltage, current, and resistance on a wire.

58.   A. Simple Network Management Protocol (SNMP) gathers and manages network performance information. A management device called an SNMP server can be set up to collect data from these devices (called agents) and ensure that your network is operating properly.

59.   D. The cable/DSL modem is a popular choice for configuring Internet access for the small or home office environment. It utilizes existing phone lines and provides fairly reliable high-speed access. Most DSL subscriptions are asymmetrical, meaning they offer faster download speeds than upload speeds.

60.   B. Wi-Fi Protected Access (WPA) was the first Wi-Fi encryption standard to implement the use of the Temporal Key Integrity Protocol (TKIP). Whereas WEP used a static 40- or 128-bit key, TKIP uses a 128-bit dynamic per-packet key. It generates a new key for each packet sent.

61.   C. When setting up wireless access points, it's good practice to have their ranges overlap to ensure that there is no loss of communication when roaming in the network's area. However, to avoid problems, it's best to set up the access points with nonoverlapping channels.

62.   A. Simple Mail Transfer Protocol (SMTP), Post Office Protocol 3 (POP3), and Internet Message Access Protocol (IMAP) are all email protocols. SMTP is for sending email. POP3 and IMAP are for downloading email.

63.   A. Ethernet over power can make Ethernet connections by using electrical outlets. For it to work, both devices must be on the same electrical circuit.

64.   B. The 802.11g standard has an indoor range of approximately 40 meters. At a minimum, you will need three access points. Depending on coverage and indoor interference, such as thick walls, you might need more though.

65.   D. The cable can be any of the three major types, coaxial, twisted pair, or fiber, but it needs to be plenum rated. Normal cables have a PVC coating, which produces a poisonous gas when burned. Plenum-rated cables have a Teflon coating, which is not toxic when burned.

66. B. Power over Ethernet (PoE) allows you to power an Ethernet device (such as a switch) through one of the Ethernet ports. For it to work, the access point and the device it plugs into both need to support PoE. Further, both the access point and device need to be compatible with each other.

67. C. The private IP address ranges are 10.0.0.0/8, 172.16.0.0/12, and 192.168.0.0/16. The address 172.168.38.155 is outside the private IP address range and is a public address.

68. A. Quality of Service (QoS) is a strategy that allows an administrator to control resources to maintain a certain service level. By using QoS, an administrator can set different priorities for one or more types of network traffic based on different applications, data flows, or users.

69. D. To encrypt traffic between a web server and client securely, Hypertext Transfer Protocol Secure (HTTPS) can be used. HTTPS connections are secured using either Secure Sockets Layer (SSL) or Transport Layer Security (TLS). HTTPS uses port 443.

70. D. 802.11b/g transmit in the 2.4 GHz frequency, as does 802.11n, so they are compatible. The newer 802.11ac is a 5 GHz standard and therefore is not backward compatible with 802.11b/g. 802.11r is not a standard related to Wi-Fi speed and is not in the A+ exam objectives.

71. D. Integrated Services Digital Network (ISDN) is a digital, point-to-point network capable of maximum transmission speeds of about 2 Mbps, although speeds of 128 Kbps are more common.

72. D. Networks that are larger than a LAN but confined to a relatively small geographical area are metropolitan area networks (MANs). A MAN is generally defined as a network that spans a city or a large campus.

73. A. A subnet mask of 255.255.224.0 has eight bits in each of the first two octets set to on, and it has three bits in the third octet on. Therefore, it corresponds to /19 in shorthand.

74. B. To communicate on an IPv4 network, a host must be configured with a valid IP address and a subnet mask. A default gateway is needed only if the host will connect to a remote network. DNS servers are optional but useful, because they resolve hostnames to IP addresses.

75. A. Common Internet File System (CIFS) is a Microsoft-developed enhancement of the SMB protocol, which was also developed by Microsoft. The intent behind CIFS is that it can be used to share files and printers between computers, regardless of the operating system that they run. It's been the default file and print sharing protocol on Windows-based computers since Windows 2000.

76. D. All hosts on a network must have a unique IP address. The subnet mask should be the same for all computers on a local network. The network ID can't be set to all 1s; otherwise, it replicates the subnet mask. Default gateways, or router addresses, are needed only if hosts will communicate with hosts outside their local network.

77. D. Wired Equivalent Privacy (WEP) was one of the first security standards for wireless devices. It uses a static key; the keys are commonly 10, 26, or 58 hexadecimal characters long.

78. D. Simple Network Management Protocol (SNMP) is a noncritical service, so it uses UDP. It's assigned port 161. IMAP4 uses port 143.

79. B. Clients are unable to get to the DNS server, which resolves hostnames (or URLs) to IP addresses. DNS uses port 53.

80. D. Automatic Private IP Addressing (APIPA) is a TCP/IP standard used to automatically configure IP-based hosts that are unable to reach a DHCP server. APIPA addresses are in the 169.254.0.0/16 range. If you see a computer that has an IP address beginning with 169.254, you know that it has configured itself.

81. B. The fastest modems produced had a data rate of 56 Kbps. At the time, they were considered fast. Today, not so much.

82. C. Normal (unsecured) websites are accessed on port 80, which is the port that Hypertext Transfer Protocol (HTTP) uses. Shut it down, and no one will be able to access websites, except secure sites that use HTTPS, which is on port 443.

83. D. The Domain Name System (DNS) is responsible for resolving hostnames to IP addresses. This is used millions of times daily on the Internet; when someone types in a website name, such as www.sybex.com, DNS will resolve that to an IP address to enable communication.

84. D. Satellite Internet is not much like any other type of broadband connection. Instead of a cabled connection, it uses a satellite dish to receive data from an orbiting satellite and relay station that is connected to the Internet. Because it requires a clear line of sight between the transmitter and receiver, it can be referred to as "line of sight" wireless. For an installation far from civilization, it may be the only option.

85. C. The two host-to-host protocols are Transmission Control Protocol (TCP) and User Datagram Protocol (UDP). TCP guarantees packet delivery through the use of a virtual circuit and data acknowledgments, and UDP does not. Because of this, TCP is often referred to as connection oriented, whereas UDP is connectionless.

86. A. A local area network (LAN) is often defined as being contained in a single building, office, or home.

87. D. The Apple Filing Protocol (AFP) is a file transfer protocol developed by Apple. It uses port 548.

88. C, D. The only two options as Wi-Fi standards that provide greater than 100 Mbps throughput are 802.11n and 802.11ac. The 802.11g standard has a maximum throughput of 54 Mbps, and 802.11i is an encryption standard. Other standards not presented but that do provide throughputs over 100 Mbps are 802.11ah and 802.11ad.

89. C. NetBIOS over TCP/IP (NetBT) is for older applications still reliant on NetBIOS, the legacy network protocol intended for very small networks. NetBT lets such applications communicate over TCP/IP.

90. D. Service Location Protocol (SLP) enables a computer to discover local systems and other devices, if it is not already preconfigured with their location.

91. C. An unmanaged switch will simply perform the one task a switch should do: direct Layer 2 traffic out the correct destination port.

92. D. Migrating network configuration to the cloud would allow the network administrator to perform his duties without requiring travel.

93. B. The distance for Power over Ethernet (PoE) is limited by the maximum distance set by the Ethernet cabling: 100 meters. The power injector, the device that sources the electrical power to certain wires in the cable, can be as much as 100 meters from the powered device.

94. C. The end-user devices are configured to at least request a DHCP-assigned IP address or be preconfigured with a static IP, gateway and DNS information.

95. D. Unless an Internet of Things device (IoT) possesses an end-user accessible management interface, that device will likely connect by starting network connectivity using DHCP.

96. A. If the group of devices is small and rarely changes, a great way of defining only them as approved traffic sources is to use MAC filtering.

97. C. The whitelist is a defined list of approved applications to pass through the firewall.

98. B. Near-field communication (NFC) sets up connections between two devices that are within 2 inches, or 4 cm, of each other.

99. A. RFID uses radio frequencies and can be implemented to detect and read a "passive" (no power) tag that is essentially an antenna as it passes within a few feet in range.

100. D. The web server hosts and serves information available to the public (or internally as an intranet web server). Originally, files on the web server would be primarily HTML files, but today's web servers would also serve style sheets, scripts, and various media files.

101. C. The file server is a centralized repository for users, typically company employees.

102. B. Proxy servers act as a gateway or "middle-man," through which Internet access requests are handled, monitored, and, if need be, filtered.

103. A. The File Transfer Protocol (FTP) server hosts files for easy access, allowing users who are able to browse it to transfer and upload the files.

104. C. The print server provides centralized availability of print services to anyone on the network. The print server accepts print jobs from authorized users, and the documents are printed according to order of receipt or some configured priority.

105. B. If a user types www.sybex.com in a web browser, the domain name system (DNS) server will resolve the domain name to an IP address. Similarly, DNS servers will resolve a fully qualified domain named (FQDN) network directory resource on the network to make locating that resource possible.

106. D. The authentication server facilitates the challenge/response service for validating someone's credentials.

107. A. The Syslog server operates with the Syslog protocol, which is used by many different operating systems and devices. These system-generated messages vary from the mundane "System started" to critical alerts.

108. B. An intrusion detection system (IDS) will monitor and alert you on suspect behavior. The IDS can be a network-based device or host-based, meaning it runs as a process in the background.

109. D. The IDS will alert on suspect activity, but will not react or actively attempt to block the activity. The IPS, however, should attempt to block the activity.

110. C. Unified threat management (UTM) systems can be hardware network devices, virtual devices, or an off-premises service. The UTM's primary value is the integration of multiple security services into a singular device.

111. A. The end-point management server can be a policy-based or directory-based technique toward controlling access to network resources.

112. A. With many new systems added and already booted, it is likely that the DHCP reservation pool is now too small for the number of systems requesting IP addresses. Expand the DHCP reservation to solve the problem.

113. B. Virtual LANs, or VLANs, will segment your network into smaller broadcast domains. Traffic is isolated to only the paths determined by how you have identified VLANs on your managed switches.

114. A. A virtual private network (VPN) can encrypt your network traffic, keeping your data confidential along the wire.

115. C. Wireless mesh networks commonly have three types of nodes: a client, a router and a gateway.

116. B. The SC connector can be used for both single-mode and multimode, both in simplex and duplex. The RJ-11 is, of course, not a fiber connector.

117. C. RJ-11 accommodates two pair of wires and is the standard household or office wired telephone connection. RJ-45 is the four pair connector used for twisted-pair Ethernet. Coaxial is a type of network cable and would have a BNC connector (with a locking mechanism) or an F-connector.

118. D. T568B on both ends is a straight-through network cable. If you have a T568A on one end and a T568B on the other, that is a crossover cable.

119. C. While thermostats, light switches and door locks offer the feature of remote management, the security cameras would likely include continuous remote monitoring.

120. A, D. Any IoT device which is voice-activated or voice-enabled requires hardware capable of listening for external audio cues, such as a microphone.

121. D. The wireless networking protocol Z-wave is limited to just 232 total connected devices. By comparison, there is no concrete limit to how many devices Zigbee can connect. Long Term Evaluation (LTE) is a protocol stack, not a single wireless protocol.

122. C. The speed of wireless networking protocol 5G is expected to surpass 1 Gbps. The speed of 4G is considered reliable at 100 Kbps, only a tenth of 5G. Earliest of the options is 3G, which reaches speeds of 144 Kbps.

Chapter 3: Hardware

1.   B. FireWire 800 can span 100 meters when implemented over fiber-optic cable. Over copper cable, it's limited to 4.5 meters, like FireWire 400.

2.   A. A mini-ITX motherboard is a 6.7″ square. Nano-ITX motherboards are 4.7″ square, pico-ITX motherboards are 3.9″ × 2.8″, and mobile-ITX motherboards are 2.4″ square.

3.   A, C. A 32-bit OS can run on either a 32-bit or 64-bit processor, although you will not be able to fully utilize the 64-bit processor's capabilities with a 32-bit OS. A 64-bit OS will run only on a 64-bit processor.

4.   A, B, C. The DC power supply (DCPS) converts house current into three voltages: +5 VDC and –5 VDC for the logic circuitry and +24 VDC for the paper-transport motors.

5.   A. Three RCA-like connectors at the end of a cable indicate a component video cable.

6.   A. The TN will have the fastest response time for this list. The IPS is quick enough for someone interested in gaming, but the LED and plasma monitors would show significant blur or lag when pushed to their limits by fast-moving gameplay.

7.   A. A mini-DIN 6 connector is a round connector often called a PS/2 connector. It's historically used for a keyboard or a mouse. If you have only more modern USB peripherals, you can buy a PS/2-to-USB adapter to plug them into one of these ports.

8.   D. A hybrid hard drive is a combination of a conventional magnetic hard disk drive and solid-state storage. The goal is to increase access speed for commonly accessed data while still providing larger capacity similar to a conventional HDD.

9.   C. Thicker paper can cause paper jams, especially in printers with curved paper paths. Paper that is too thin may not get picked up by the printer rollers at all.

10. C. TCP printing allows clients with different OSs to send jobs directly to printers without worrying about intra-OS conflicts. Bonjour and AirPrint are both Apple services, and virtual printing allows you to print output to documents such as PDF files. Whenever sharing printers for remote printing, be sure to set proper user authentication on the print device.

11. B. A CAT6a cable is a network cable, and you are most likely to find an RJ-45 connector at the end of it. RJ-11 connectors are for phone lines. BNC connectors are network connectors but are typically used with coaxial cable. SATA connectors are hard drive connectors.

12. A. The connector shown is a DVI connector, used for digital video.

13. B. Thermal printers will often use a roll of paper as opposed to individual sheets. Fax machines may use thermal technology, but a fax machine in itself is not a printer technology.

14. A. Parity checking is a rudimentary RAM error-checking scheme that offers no error correction.

15. A, C, D. Laser printers need toner cartridges, impact printers need ink ribbons, and ink-jet printers use ink cartridges. Thermal printers heat up paper to produce images.

16. A. An imaging drum is a photosensitive drum that can hold a charge if it's not exposed to light. It is dark inside an EP printer, except when the laser scanning assembly shines on particular areas of the photosensitive drum.

17. B. A MicroATX motherboard is a 9.6″ square. ATX motherboards are 12″ × 9.6″, mini-ITX motherboards are 6.7″ × 6.7″, and pico-ITX motherboards are 3.9″ × 2.8″.

18. D. Resolution is the number of pixels used to draw a computer screen. Refresh rate determines how many times per second the screen can be redrawn. Frame rate tells you how many frames per second the original content was filmed in. Aspect ratio defines the dimensions (width × height) of an image.

19. B. In a RAID-5 array, each stripe places data on n–1 disks, and parity computed from the data is placed on the remaining disk. The parity is interleaved across all the drives in the array so that neighboring stripes have parity on different disks. Said differently, you lose the equivalent of one hard disk worth of storage to hold the parity information.

20. D. The disable execute bit allows for the CPU to set aside an area of memory and refuse to execute any code placed into that memory location. Oftentimes this serves as a buffer area. The result is that malicious buffer overrun attacks are less likely to succeed.

21. D. Cloud printing allows for printing to a remote device, one that is not necessarily located on your local network. Essentially, you are using the Internet to send the print job from your device to the printer from which you want the output to come, and the printer can be located practically anywhere in the world.

22. A. Heat sinks are often made of metal, with many fins on them to increase surface area and dissipate heat faster. Many modern CPU heat sinks will have both a fan (which requires power) and the finned metal heat sink.

23. A, C. VGA is an analog video connector, and RJ-11 connectors are used with modems. Modems receive a digital signal from the computer but then modulate that signal to analog to transmit over common phone lines.

24. B. Wi-Fi and Bluetooth can be used to connect a printer temporarily to a single computer (or mobile device), and the connection does not have permanent status. This type of configuration is known as an ad hoc network connection.

25. A, B. With up-plugging, you can put a smaller PCIe card into a larger slot, even though it does not fill it up completely. For example, you can insert an x8 card into an x16 slot. The x8 card won't completely fill the slot, but it will work at x8 speeds.

26. C. RAID-1 is called disk mirroring; it writes data simultaneously to both drives. If one drive fails, the other still has a working copy of the data. RAID-0 is disk striping and does not provide fault tolerance. RAID-5 is striping with parity and provides fault tolerance, but it requires three hard disks.

27. A. During the cleaning step, a rubber blade inside the toner cartridge scrapes any toner left on the drum into a used toner receptacle, and a fluorescent lamp discharges any remaining charge on the imaging drum. (Remember that the drum, being photosensitive, loses its charge when exposed to light.)

28. C. Plasma displays place electrodes in front of and behind sealed chambers full of inert gas (such as neon) and vaporized mercury. Current is run through the gas to ionize it and cause it to light up.

29. B. The audio connector on the front or top panel will use a round, 3.5 mm connector. You can plug speakers into it. Alternatively, you could plug a headset with a boom microphone into it for additional privacy.

30. D. With most dual-channel motherboards, RAM will work just fine if one module is installed. However, you will get better performance if you fill the entire bank.

31. D. There are four major versions of PCIe currently specified: 1.x, 2.x, 3.0, and 4.0. For the four versions, a single omnidirectional lane operates at a data rate of 250 MBps, 500 MBps, approximately 1 GBps, and roughly 2 GBps, respectively.

32. A, D. When installing or replacing a power supply, always make sure that it has enough wattage to power the components in the computer. In addition, it should have enough connectors to connect to all the components that require their own power. Dual rail and dual voltage are optional features.

33. D. Double-sided memory has chips on both sides of the RAM module instead of just on one side. It allows for doubling the amount of RAM on the module, so you get twice as much memory on one stick. This contrasts with "dual rank," a term seen when describing memory modules. The "dual rank" module may have two sets of chips but only one rank or channel is accessible by the system at one time.

34. A, B. Faster hard drives transfer more data than slower hard drives, but there is no specific correlation between hard drive speed and its life span. The downsides to faster hard drives can be increased battery usage and heat production.

35. A, B. PCI expansion buses operate at 33 MHz or 66 MHz (version 2.1) over a 32-bit (4-byte) channel, resulting in data rates of 133 MBps and 266 MBps, respectively, with 133 MBps being the most common, server architectures excluded.

36. C. Print servers need to have the appropriate drivers for all operating systems that will be clients. It's possible that this print server does not have the Mac driver installed.

37. D. A privacy filter is a panel that fits over the front of a display and, through a polarization affect, intentionally limits the viewing angle of the monitor.

38. B. The connector shown is USB Type B. It will plug into the USB peripheral device and is commonly used by printers.

39. B. Most digital monitors have a native resolution, which is a single, fixed resolution that they support. Attempting to change the resolution may result in distorted images, or the image may not display at all.

40. B, C. Liquid cooling systems are generally quieter than air-based systems that use fans, and they are more efficient at cooling the processor. However, they are more complex to install, and if the liquid were to leak out, that could cause damage to internal components.

41. C, D. Impact printers create images by impacting the paper, which can wear down the print head. Always check that. Also, impact printers most often use tractor feed mechanisms to load the paper, and they can wear down as well.

42. C. PCIe uses lanes. Each lane between any two intercommunicating devices comprises a separate pair of wires for both directions of traffic, which dramatically increases speed.

43. A. A thin client is any machine that divests itself of all or most local storage and varying levels of RAM and processing power without necessarily giving up all ability to process instructions and data.

44. C. The reset button, usually located on the front or top panel, allows a user to reboot the computer from a cold startup point without removing power from the components. This can be particularly helpful for dealing with software lockups.

45. B. The two most popular methods of manufacturing LCD panels are twisted nematic (TN) and in-plane switching (IPS). Of the two, IPS is regarded as having the best color representation in all angles, while TN is faster and less expensive. LED and plasma are not types of LCD panels.

46. B, C. A home server PC should be able to handle media streaming as well as file and printer sharing. A dedicated print server is not likely needed, though, as the operating system can function as a print server. A gigabit NIC will be helpful to manage the network traffic, and a RAID array can help protect against hard drive failure.

47. B. The x8 card won't completely fill the x16 slot, but it will work at x8 speeds if up-plugging is supported by the motherboard. Otherwise, the specification requires up-plugged devices to operate at only the x1 rate.

48. B. Secure Boot is an option enabled in system firmware. BIOS is not technically advanced enough to manage Secure Boot, but its successor UEFI is.

49. A. DDR has 184 pins, DDR2 and DDR3 have 240 pins, and SODIMMs can have 72, 100, 144, 200, or 204 pins. DDR4 has 288 pins, while DDR4 SODIMMs have 260 pins. Last, MicroDIMMs and MiniDIMMs have 240 pins.

50. D. Hyperthreading-capable processors appear to the operating system to be two processors. As a result, the operating system can schedule two processes at the same time on each physical core.

51. A. Dot-matrix printers are impact printers and typically require paper that always feeds at a consistent rate. To achieve this, the paper will have holes on the outside edges, which is fed into the printer using a tractor feed mechanism.

52. D. An embedded MultiMediaCard (eMMC) can be permanently embedded on the circuit board of a cheaper or smaller mobile device. All of the other flash memory standards, such as CompactFlash, xD, miniMMC, and microMMC, are designed to be removable.

53. A. ATX motherboards are common in desktop computers and measure 12″ × 9.6″. They are the largest motherboards commonly used in personal computers today.

54. D. The motor that makes the print head carriage move is also often called the carriage motor or carriage stepper motor. It has a belt attached to it, the carriage belt, which moves the print head carriage back and forth.

55. A, D. For an audio/video editing workstation, you should maximize the audio and video capabilities, including having at least two large monitors. Videos also take a lot of disk space, so significant storage space is required.

56. A, D. Intel's Virtualization Technology (Intel VT) is needed to support virtualization. It's enabled in the BIOS, not the operating system.

57. A. Graphic design (or CAD/CAM) workstations require solid CPU power, RAM, and a high-end video card. Hard drive storage is the least important upgrade for these types of users.

58. C. The most common analog video connector is a VGA connector.

59. A. Refresh rate defines the vertical scan frequency of a monitor and determines how many times, in one second, an image can be redrawn on the screen. Many LCD monitors have a fixed refresh rate.

60. D. Thunderbolt v1 and v2 both provide 20 Gbps of data bandwidth. In addition, Thunderbolt ports power the attached peripherals with 18 V and 9.9 W of power.

61. B. The fuser heats up to approximately 350° Fahrenheit (~175° Celsius). Do not touch it as it will cause burns.

62. B. A standard thick client is not really a custom configuration; it's the standard configuration on which custom configurations are based. In other words, a thick client is a standard client computer system.

63. C. The order of steps is processing, charging, exposing, developing, transferring, fusing, and cleaning.

64. B, C. PCI slots and adapters are manufactured in 3.3 V and 5 V versions. Adapters are keyed to fit in a slot based on their voltage requirements. Universal adapters are keyed to fit in slots based on either of the two voltages.

65. A. Trusted Platform Module (TPM) is an international standard for a dedicated security coprocessor, or cryptoprocessor. Coupled with a BIOS, it can be configured to boot the system only after authenticating the boot device.

66. A. The transfer corona assembly is given a positive charge, which is transferred to the paper, which in turn pulls the toner from the photosensitive imaging drum.

67. C. This is an eight-pin PCIe connector. They also come in 6-pin configurations.

68. D. After installing a new printer, it's good practice to print a test page to ensure functionality.

69. B. The high-voltage power supply (HVPS) provides the high voltages used by both the charging corona and the transfer corona during the laser printing process.

70. D. Wi-Fi (802.11a, b, g, n, or ac) and Bluetooth can be used to connect a printer temporarily to a single computer (or mobile device), and the connection does not have permanent status. This type of configuration is known as an ad hoc network connection. When Wi-Fi is used to connect printers to a network on a more permanent basis, it is known as infrastructure mode.

71. C. PCI-X version 2.0 introduced the current maximum bus speed, 533 MHz. With an 8-byte (64-bit) bus, this translates to a maximum throughput of 4266 MBps, roughly 4.3 GBps.

72. D. The power-on self-test (POST) is a series of system checks performed by the system BIOS. Checking the system memory is part of the POST routine.

73. C. RAID-10 (also known as RAID-1+0) provides fault tolerance to RAID-0 through the RAID-1 mirroring of each disk in the RAID-0 striped set. It requires four hard disks.

74. C. The image is of a SATA connector, commonly used for internal hard drives.

75. A. MiniSD and microSD cards are smaller than standard SD memory cards. Adapters are available to allow them to work in standard SD slots.

76. A. There are two backlight technologies for LCD monitors: LED and fluorescent. Of the two, LED produces higher-quality images. OLED and plasma are display technologies, not backlight technologies.

77. A. The Northbridge is responsible for managing high-speed peripheral communications. The Southbridge manages slower onboard peripherals. There is no Eastbridge or Westbridge in a motherboard chipset.

78. C. To use a second monitor on a desktop computer, you need to install a second video adapter or have one video adapter with two monitor interfaces. Laptops often have an external monitor interface and are capable of providing video to the built-in screen and an external monitor at the same time.

79. B, C. Buffered memory modules include specialized chips that act as buffers for signals from the memory controller. By buffering these signals, the electrical load placed on the controller is reduced because the memory controller communicates in series with the register, instead of in parallel with the memory chips. The register performs the parallel communication with the chips.

80. A. That capacity of module might not have been in existence when the motherboard's chipset was released. Sometimes flashing the BIOS is all that is required.

81. C. A modem allows computers to connect to a remote network (such as an ISP) via telephone lines. Modems were the most common Internet connection method in the 1990s but are uncommon today. NICs are expansion cards for network connections. USB and cellular are not expansion cards. Other types of expansion cards include video cards, sound cards, storage cards, TV tuner cards, and riser cards.

82. B, C. Touch screens, KVM switches, smart TVs, and set-top boxes are capable of both input and output. Digitizers are input devices, and printers are output devices. Multifunctional printers that have a scanner included can be classified as input and output devices, but a plain printer is output only.

83. A. DDR2 and DDR3 memory slots are both keyed, but the keys are in different places. Therefore, the memory will not fit into the slots on the motherboard.

84. C. During the transferring step, the positively charged paper pulls the negatively charged toner from the photosensitive drum at the line of contact between the roller and the paper.

85. C. The communications between the CPU and memory occur over what is known as the frontside bus (FSB), which is just a set of signal pathways connecting the CPU and main memory.

86. B. The user wants to make sure that the collate option is set properly. It will let her select whether she wants it to print pages in order (1, 2, 3. . . 1, 2, 3. . . and so on) or multiple copies of the same page at once (1, 1, 1. . . 2, 2, 2. . . and so forth). Other options you can often set up in the printer configuration settings are duplexing (printing on the front and back), orientation (portrait or landscape), and print quality (such as draft or high resolution).

87. A. The term *aspect ratio* refers to the relationship between the horizontal and vertical pixel counts that a monitor can display. For example, for a display that supports 4:3 ratios, such as 1600×1200, if you divide the first number by 4 and multiply the result by 3, the product is equal to the second number. Additionally, if you divide the first number by the second number, the result is approximately 1.3, the same as 4 ÷ 3.

88. D. Flashing the BIOS is the recommended way to upgrade a BIOS. It involves downloading the new BIOS and flashing software from the manufacturer and installing it on the computer. The worst-case scenario is replacing the motherboard (or in this case, the RAM, since that is what you upgraded).

89. A. CD-RW (re-writable compact disc) will be the least expensive of the optical solutions. In addition, CD-ROMs can store about 700 MB to 900 MB of data, depending on the standard used. This should be sufficient for the client.

90. C. A DVD-R double-sided dual-layer (DS, DL) will provide 17.1 GB of storage. BD-R single-sided dual-layer (SS, DL) will also work in this case, providing 50 GB of storage. (BD-R is a one-time recordable Blu-ray disc, and BD-RE is a re-recordable disc. Both have the same capacity.) A DVD-R SS, DL provides about 8.5 GB of storage, and DVD-R DS, SL provides about 9.4 GB of storage.

91. B. The connector shown is an RCA connector, which is often used for audio or video signals.

92. D. Lumens is the measure of brightness for a projector. For a well-lit business setting, you probably want a projector rated at 5,000–6,000 lumens.

93. C. Ink-jet printers typically use a reservoir of ink (also known as an ink cartridge), a pump, and a nozzle to print images.

94. D. The number designation of 1600 in DDR3–1600 indicates an FSB speed of 1600 MHz. To find the throughput, multiply the FSB speed by 8.

95. A. The refresh rate for plasma displays has always been in the 600 Hz range, which is 10 times the standard refresh rate of 60 Hz, thus ensuring fluid video motion. The result is a display that produces the state of the art in video motion fluidity.

96. C. DDR2, using a 100 MHz actual clock, transfers data in four operations per cycle (effective 400 MHz FSB) and 8 bytes per operation, for a total of 3200 MBps. DDR2 calls these modules PC2–3200.

97. D. The connector pictured is a four-pin FireWire (IEEE1394) port on a laptop.

98. B. iPads and iPhones can automatically detect AirPrint-enabled printers on their local network and print to them without requiring the installation of a driver.

99. B. To communicate with other computers on a network, you need a network interface card (NIC). A wireless access point (WAP) is a wireless hub that many wireless devices communicate with, and WPA is a wireless security standard. A KVM switch allows you to have multiple systems attached to the same keyboard, video, and mouse. Other types of expansion cards (that could use the same slot as a NIC) include video cards, sound cards, storage cards, TV tuner cards, and riser cards.

100. D. A 1920×1200 resolution is a 16:10 aspect ratio. If you take the second number (1200) and multiply it by 1.6, you get 1920.

101. B. The printer driver uses a page-description language (PDL) to convert the data being printed into the format that the printer can understand. The driver also ensures that the printer is ready to print.

102. D. The power supply fan is used to cool the power supply. In addition, this fan draws air from inside the case into vents in the power supply. This pulls hot air through the power supply so that it can be blown out of the case.

103. A. A solid-state drive (SSD) is the best choice for a hard drive when access speed is the most important characteristic. A conventional magnetic hard disk drive (HDD) is slower. Secure Digital (SD) is a memory card format, not a hard drive type. BD-R is a Blu-ray Disc format.

104. B. The Northbridge is responsible for managing high-speed peripheral communications. The Southbridge manages slower onboard peripherals such as PS/2, parallel, serial, and Serial ATA and Parallel ATA.

105. B. USB 1.0 supports 12 Mbps. In the following standards, USB 2.0 supports 480 Mbps, USB 3.0 supports 5 Gbps, and USB 3.1 Gen 2 supports 10 Gbps.

106. B. RAID-5 arrays require a minimum of three hard drives. Since the computer already has one, he therefore needs two more.

107. C. Any device that measures one or more physical or behavioral features of an organism is considered a biometric device. Biometric devices include fingerprint scanners, retinal and iris scanners, voice recognition devices, facial recognition devices, and others.

108. A. A processor that exhibits a multicore architecture has multiple completely separate processor dies in the same package. The operating system and applications see multiple processors in the same way that they see multiple processors in separate sockets.

109. B. All are digital video disc (DVD) technologies. A single-sided, single-layer (SS, SL) DVD provides about 4.7 GB of storage. A dual-sided (DS) disc will double that capacity to 9.4 GB. Adding a second layer, or dual-layer (DL), adds more capacity, but the technology does not double the capacity of a single layer. A single-sided, dual-layer (SS, DL) disc has capacity of about 8.5 GB.

110. D. Many power supplies have a two-position slider switch called a dual voltage switch. It can be set for 110–120 V or 220–240 V, depending on what local power specifications are.

111. D. MicroATX motherboards are a 9.6″ square, and mini-ITX motherboards are a 6.7″ square. Pico-ITX motherboards are 3.9″ × 2.8″, and mobile-ITX motherboards are 2.4″ square.

112. B, C. Daisy-wheel and dot-matrix printers use print heads that strike an ink ribbon, which presses up against the paper to make an image. Therefore, they are impact printers. Laser printers use a drum to create the image, and thermal printers use heat.

113. B. OLEDs create the image in an OLED display and supply the light source, so there is no need for a backlight with its additional power and space requirements, unlike in the case of LCD or plasma panels.

114. A. Although serial might sound slower than parallel, modern technology has made the serial bus much faster than parallel bus systems.

115. D. Only the most recently used data and code or that which is expected to be used next is stored in cache. Cache is much smaller and faster than RAM.

116. A, B. Sockets that support Intel processors are currently named starting with the letters LGA, such as LGA1156 and LGA2011. Socket names that start with AM or FM will support AMD processors and not Intel processors.

117. B. A standard hard disk drive (HDD) will provide her with the highest capacity of the four options and also give her immediate access. Network attached storage (NAS) speaks to its connection and availability, not capacity. If the client required file sharing as well, then using a NAS would be the proper choice. Secure Digital (SD) is a memory card format and does not offer the capacity or immediacy she needs. BD-R is a Blu-ray Disc format. It has good storage capabilities, but not the immediacy for editing.

118. A, C. A home theater PC (HTPC) needs to maximize the audio and video experience. It won't do a lot of processing or data management, so an upgraded processor or RAM is unneeded. Install a great sound card, a video card with multiple HDMI outputs, and a TV tuner card. (HDMI is capable of supporting 7.1 surround sound, so you may choose to buy one expansion card capable of handling both functions.) Some HTPCs come in a compact form factor, which is just a small case.

119. B, C. Digital monitors will have a digital interface, such as DVI-D, HDMI, or miniHDMI . Composite connectors are rarely used on monitors, and VGA is analog, not digital.

120. D. There is no need for laptops with LED displays to convert the DC power coming into the laptop to the AC needed to power traditional fluorescent backlights because LEDs operate on DC power just like the rest of the laptop. Therefore, systems with LED backlights have no inverter board.

121. A, B, D. The four virtual printing options are print to file, print to PDF, print to XPS, and print to image.

122. B. There are four major versions of PCIe currently specified: 1.x, 2.x, 3.0, and 4.0. For the four versions, a single omnidirectional lane operates at a data rate of 250 MBps, 500 MBps, approximately 1 GBps, and roughly 2 GBps, respectively. A bidirectional slot doubles the data rate.

123. D. Laser printers incorporate a fuser assembly, which uses two rollers that apply pressure and heat to fuse the plastic toner particles to the paper.

124. A. During the charging step, the charging corona uses a high voltage to apply a strong, uniform negative charge (around –600 VDC) to the surface of the imaging drum.

125. A. When installing dual-channel RAM, be sure that the RAM modules both have the same parameters. In some cases, you might even need to make sure they come from the same manufacturer.

126. D. Carriage motors are components in ink-jet printers. Laser printer components include a fuser assembly, imaging drum, transfer belt, transfer roller, pickup roller, separator pads, and a duplexing assembly.

127. A. A laser printer uses various high-voltage biases inside the case, and high voltages can create ozone.

128. D. The purpose of a KVM switch is to allow you to have multiple systems attached to the same keyboard, monitor, and mouse. You can use these three devices with only one system at a time, and the KVM switch will have a dial or buttons to allow you to switch between systems.

129. B. It sounds like this printer needs to manage its own print jobs; therefore, it probably needs to be its own print server. Installing an integrated print server with a network connection will probably do the trick.

130. B. Clean pickup rollers (and other rubber rollers) with mild soap and water and not alcohol. Alcohol can dry out the rollers, making them brittle and ineffective. A dry cloth will not remove the dirt or debris, and compressed air would just blow the debris into other internal printer components.

131. D. During the developing step, toner is attracted to areas of the drum where an image has been written by the laser. Those areas have a slight negative charge (–100 VDC) as opposed to unexposed areas of the drum and the developing roller (to which the toner is stuck), which each have a charge of –600 VDC.

132. C. The primary factor in determining data throughput for a magnetic hard drive is the spin rate. Higher spin rates will result in faster data reads and writes and increase data throughput.

133. B. LoJack, made by Absolute Software, allows you to remotely lock a computer if it has been stolen or compromised. It will also allow security teams to locate stolen laptops.

134. D. The white connector is a 20-pin ATX power connector. You will also see 24-pin versions, which have two rows of 12 pins each.

135. B. Motherboards support memory based on the speed of the frontside bus (or the CPU's QPI) and the memory's form factor. For example, if the motherboard's FSB is rated at a maximum speed of 1333 MHz, you should install memory that is rated at 1333 MHz.

136. C. To make information available to the rest of the computer more quickly, hard drive manufacturers increase the speed at which the hard drive platters spin.

137. A, B, C. The ATX, MicroATX, and mini-ITX motherboard form factors can all be mounted inside a standard ATX case. The mini-ITX will have only three of the four mounting holes line up with the case, but the rear interfaces are placed in the same location as those on ATX motherboards.

138. C. If memory supports ECC, check bits are generated and stored with the data. If one of the eight memory bits is in error, ECC can correct the error.

139. A, D. USB flash drives and SD cards are hot swappable. (In the case of USB, be sure that the flash drive does not contain key file system files needed for the computer to run!) Hybrid SSDs might or might not be hot swappable and are larger than USB and SD drives. PATA devices are generally not hot swappable.

140. C. This SLI-ready motherboard has three PCIe x16 slots (every other slot, starting with the top one), one PCIe x1 slot (second slot from the top), and two PCI slots (first and third slots from the bottom). Notice the latch and tab that secures the x16 adapters in place by their hooks.

141. B, D. Dual-channel motherboards have two banks of two RAM slots. They are color coded such that the two slots of the same color belong to the same channel. Sometimes the like-colored slots are adjacent to each other, but other times they alternate. For optimal performance, fill one channel completely.

142. C. Install an application that provides support for printing to .pdf. Then, when the user opens the print window, she can choose the PDF option.

143. A. The boot sequence of a computer is changed in the BIOS settings.

144. C, D. Typical front- or top-panel connectors include USB, audio, power button, power light, drive activity lights, and the reset button. Hard drives and optical disk players generally connect to the motherboard.

145. A. USB 3.0 has a cable length limitation of 3 meters. USB 2.0 cables can be up to 5 meters in length.

146. C. Printer firmware upgrades can offer newer features that are not available on previous versions.

147. D. PCI is a shared-bus topology, so mixing 33 MHz and 66 MHz adapters in a 66 MHz system will slow all adapters to 33 MHz.

148. B. In the exposing step, the image is written to the photosensitive imaging drum. Wherever the laser beam touches, the photosensitive drum's charge is severely reduced from –600 VDC to a slight negative charge (around –100 VDC). As the drum rotates, a pattern of exposed areas is formed, representing the image to be printed.

149. D. Passive cooling systems come in a variety of models, and some are very effective. The defining characteristic is that they do not use a fan or require a power source.

150. B. Compact discs have a capacity of approximately 700 MB. Other CD standards support capacities of 650 MB, 800 MB, and 900 MB.

151. A, C. The BIOS configures many hardware components and settings, such as system date and time, boot sequence, enabling and disabling devices, clock speeds, virtualization support, and BIOS security.

152. B, C. 64-bit SODIMMs come in 144-pin SDR, 200-pin DDR and DDR2, and 204-pin DDR3 varieties. DDR DIMMs have 184 pins, and DDR2 and DDR3 DIMMS have 240 pins.

153. A. The typical increasing order of capacity and distance from the processor die is L1 cache, L2 cache, L3 cache, RAM, and HDD/SSD. Currently, there is no L4 cache.

154. A. The picture shows a 20-pin ATX connector, which provides the motherboard with power.

155. A, D. A pin grid array (PGA) socket has holes to receive the pins that are on the CPU. The land grid array (LGA) is a newer technology that places the delicate pins on the motherboard instead of on the CPU.

156. C. To calculate the FSB speed from the RAM module name, divide by 8. In this case, that makes the FSB 1333 MHz (accounting for a bit of rounding).

157. C. Organic light-emitting diode (OLED) displays can be made to be flexible, whereas other displays cannot.

158. C. A duplexing assembly is used for two-sided printing. After the first page is printed, it's fed into the duplexing assembly, turned over, and fed back into the paper feed assembly.

159. C. The printer's logic circuitry and motors require low voltages, between +5 VDC and +24 VDC. The DC power supply (DCPS) converts house current into three voltages: +5 VDC and –5 VDC for the logic circuitry and +24 VDC for the paper-transport motors. This component also runs the fan that cools the internal components of the printer.

160. D. The top module is DDR3, and the bottom one is DDR2. Both have 240 pins and a single keying notch. The DDR3 notch is off-center.

161. D. Never ship a printer anywhere with a toner cartridge installed! The jostling that happens during shipping could cause toner to spill out of the cartridge and all over the inside of the printer. Remove the toner cartridge first. You can put it in a sealed, airtight bag to ship if needed.

162. D. Linear Tape-Open is the newest and highest-capacity tape storage technology. LTO 7, released in 2015, has an uncompressed capacity of 6 TB per tape. LTO 6 had an uncompressed capacity of 2.5 TB. QIC tapes can often store around 1 GB. DLT can store up to 800 GB, and DAT can store up to 300 GB.

163. A. Most internal video adapters today are PCIe cards. You might still find older PCI or AGP cards on the market as well. ISA is a legacy expansion slot type not used today. VGA and DVI are types of monitor connectors but not expansion slot types.

164. D. The order of steps is processing, charging, exposing, developing, transferring, fusing, and cleaning.

165. A, B. Apple created Bonjour and AirPrint.

166. D. Before you print to an ink-jet printer, you must ensure that the device is calibrated. Calibration is the process by which a device is brought within functional specifications. For example, ink-jet printers need their print heads aligned so that they print evenly and don't print funny-looking letters and unevenly spaced lines.

167. D. Desktop computers use dual inline memory modules (DIMMs), and laptops most commonly use small outline DIMMs (SODIMMs). Another potential laptop memory form factor is the Micro-DIMM.

168. C. Thermal printers use a heating element. It heats up spots on special waxy, heat-sensitive paper to form the image.

169. A. When a laser printer requests maintenance, it's because it has reached a certain page count. Apply a proper maintenance kit (one recommended by the manufacturer) and then clear the service message.

170. B. PCI-X slots are physically compatible with PCI adapters. Because all PCI-X slots support the 66 MHz minimum clock rate, PCI-X slots are compatible with 66 MHz PCI adapters.

171. C. There are dozens of peripherals on the computer market. Joysticks are used primarily to play video games. Chip readers will scan EMV chips, like on a credit card. Magnetic readers are for reading credit cards' magnetic stripes on the back. Smart TVs play television. Camcorders are another type of peripheral, used to record video.

172. B. The connectors pictured are BNC connectors. They are identifiable by their groove-and-notch fastening mechanism that locks by twisting one-quarter turn. F-connectors are easily identifiable because they are threaded. SC and ST connectors are for fiber-optic cable.

173. D. The connectors are a four-pin RJ-11, typically used for telephone installations, and an eight-pin RJ-45 connector, used on UTP and STP for network transmissions.

174. C. The connector shown is a type of mini form factor (MFF) fiber-optic connector called a local connector (LC). It's especially popular for use with Fibre Channel adapters, fast storage area networks, and Gigabit Ethernet adapters.

175. A. The correct order for a T568B cable is white/orange, orange, white/green, blue, white/blue, green, white/brown, brown.

176. A. Cable television installations typically use either RG-6 or RG-59 cable. RG-6 is slightly thicker, can run longer distances, and supports digital signals. RG-59 is suited only for analog TV signals.

177. D. RG-6 and RG-59 can, in many cases, be used interchangeably. RG-6 is a better choice because it supports digital signals and has a longer range (304 meters or 1000 feet). RG-59 can run up to 228 meters (750 feet). Both have impedance of 75 ohms, and both use BNC connectors or F-connectors.

178. A, D. Multimode fiber (MMF) and UTP CAT6 and newer support 10 Gbps transmission speeds.

179. D. Shielded twisted pair (STP) cabling has a foil shield surrounding the wire pairs to decrease electrical interference. Some STP cables also shield individual wire pairs. Unshielded twisted pair (UTP) does not have the shielding. Both types use RJ-45 connectors, can follow the T568A wiring standard, and can be produced as plenum-rated cable that does not produce poisonous gas when burned.

180. D. The connectors shown are ST connectors, which are used with fiber-optic cable. ST connectors are the most popular fiber connector, and they attach with a BNC-like locking mechanism.

181. B. The connector shown is a subscriber connector (SC), also known as a square connector because of its shape. It's a fiber-optic cable connector.

182. B. CAT5e cable can support speeds of 1 Gbps. CAT5 has a maximum of 100 Mbps. CAT6 and newer can support 10 Gbps, but no UTP cabling can currently support 20 Gbps.

183. B. The BNC connector locks by twisting one-quarter turn. F-connectors are threaded and screw into place. SC and ST connectors are for fiber-optic cable.

184. C, D. A crossover cable is one where the two devices being connected are similar, without using a hub or switch. The exception is when you are connecting a hub or switch with another hub or switch. If you are going to make a connection from hub to hub, switch to switch, router to router, hub to switch, or a computer directly to a router, you need a crossover cable. Otherwise, you need a regular patch cable. Lastly, if a networking device offers a medium dependent interface crossover (MDIX) port, then a straight-through cable can be used where a crossover cable would be correct.

185. A. F-connectors are threaded and screw into place. The BNC connector locks by twisting one-quarter turn. SC and ST connectors are for fiber-optic cable.

186. B. CAT5 UTP can transmit data at speeds up to 100 Mbps, for a distance of 100 meters.

187.   A. Most network cables are coated with a plastic PVC coating, which produces toxic gas when burned. Plenum-rated cables are coated with a Teflon-like material that is not poisonous when burned.

188.   B. In a crossover cable, pin 1 to pin 3 and pin 2 to pin 6 are crossed on one side of the cable only. This is to get the "send" pins matched up with the "receive" pins on the other side and vice versa.

189.   C. The 16-bit SCSI drives were connected by a molex connector, two rows of pins, totaling 68 pins.

190.   D. On small form factor devices like smartphones or tablets, the video out connector is the small version of HDMI: miniHDMI. It resembles a USB-C but is still tapered on one side.

191.   D. Lightning was introduced in autumn 2012 and was used by Apple for iPhone versions 5 through X.

192.   A. Thunderbolt 3 cables work as USB-C cables and are fully compatible. Thunderbolt 3 is capable of transferring at 40 Gbps, but USB 3.1 (on USB-C) can reach 10 Gbps.

193.   D. USB-C is the only one of these that can be inserted correctly both as you try the first time or flip over and try again. Micro-USB resembles USB-C but it is not "flappable"— one edge is slightly tapered.

194.   B. RS-232 was introduced in 1960 and was very common in 25-pin format for connecting printers and other peripherals as well as the 9-pin for connecting to network devices.

195.   C. DB9 was the "D" format, 9-pin connector type that was the standard format for keyboards, mice, and other small peripherals.

196.   D. Triple channel memory is achieved when three matching memory modules are installed, permitting data to be spread and memory accessed sequentially. The effect is lower memory latency, triple the access speed (compared to single channel), and triple the 64-bit communication path.

197.   D. M.2 is a solid-state hard drive format, measuring 22 mm wide. Its lengths vary between 30 mm, 42 mm, 60 mm, 80 mm, and 120 mm.

198.   D. Solid-state drives (SSDs) come in multiple form factors, such as, for example, a "stick" resembling a memory module or a 2.5″ box housed in metal. SSDs also come in 3.5″ form factor.

199.   C. Likely the friend forgot to connect the internal USB connector on the motherboard to the USB ports of the case.

200.   B. The system BIOS/UEFI settings include password protection to not allow system bootup unless someone enters a password. This would prohibit the OS from loading upon boot.

201.   A. Thermal paste is like a grease that ensures that the heat generated from the CPU is efficiently conducted away and into the heatsink. Lowering the CPU speed might result in less heat generated, but it would obviously also result in degraded performance.

202.   A. A USB expansion board would utilize an expansion slot on the motherboard to provide two to four additional USB ports. Not included as an option, but a USB hub is a cost-effective fix as well.

203. B. Under Windows Settings, you choose Devices, then click Touchpad. Under Taps, there is a pull-down menu named Touchpad Sensitivity.

204. D. You do require a Microsoft account in order to synchronize your settings across multiple devices. Under Windows Settings is Account. After you sign into the account, the option Sync Your Settings is available.

205. B. The 3D printer can be attached locally or, if allowed by the manufacturer, accessible by shared network. A smart card reader is used to integrate smart cards as an authentication factor for your system. A VR headset is used for experiencing virtual reality.

206. B. A signature pad is a peripheral device that is essentially a small touch-sensitive pad on which someone re-creates a signature.

207. A. The standards 568a and 568b are wiring standards. The difference between the two wiring standards is small but significant: the green and orange wires are switched. Unless both cable ends are terminated the same, mixing 568a and 568b standards will cause problems.

208. C. DVI-I cable sends both analog and digital. A DVI-D cable, however, is only capable of sending digital signals.

209. B. An Integrated Drive Electronics (IDE) cable typically connects a hard drive or optical drive to the motherboard.

210. D. M2 drives can use either the SATA or the PCIe bus, while a SATA SSD only uses the SATA interface. Magnetic hard drives spinning at 15,000 rpm are obviously not solid-state drives, while both the M2 and SATA 2.5 are solid-state drives.

211. A. While clearly different lengths, the 2.5 is also thinner and shorter. Generally, the 2.5 inch drives are used in laptops, whereas the 3.5 inch drives are installed in desktops. Both 2.5 and 3.5 can be found using the older IDE connectors or the SATA connectors, using a smaller data cable and a wider power cable.

212. D. IDE drives use a 40 pin connector. Serial ATA uses a 15 pin connector. M2 solid state drives plug into the motherboard like a RAM chip.

213. A. AIBs stands for video graphic add-in board (AIB).

214. B. A barcode scanner/QR scanner can quickly look over a tagged or marked item for easy identification without physically touching the item.

215. A. When connecting a new power supply, especially one from a different country, you must check the voltage the supply expects to receive as input from the power source. Most power supplies will have a small switch to toggle between 115V vs 220V input.

216. A, C. Integrated circuits and phones use 5V, while fans and hard drive motors will require 12V. Not all drive storage needs 12V. For example, any SSD will need only 5V.

217. C. When configuring a laptop or mobile device for employees expected to travel, they likely rely on remote access and VPN services.

218. B. Often, when the display no longer responds correctly, the user or technical staff much calibrate the screen.

219.   A. Device sharing the wired USB printer is the cost-efficient fix to this problem. There is no need to purchase additional equipment. Create accounts on one system causes the first employee to stop working.

220.   C. A device converting RS232 communication to RJ45 might allow someone connect the printer's serial port to the wired network.

221.   A. Employing user authentication on the device directly contributes toward confidentiality. Backups, a surge protector and a strong device case help toward availability of the data.

222.   B. Likely the security analyst's recommendation is focused on the data privacy aspect of disabling hard drive caching, which could possibly be accessed through exploitation.

223.   B, C. Printer heads can get clogged which causes poor quality, dim or no printing. And the cartridge may be near empty or performing badly. Clearing a jam is the right action when paper does not eject or partially ejects; likely a paper-crunching sound accompanies the issue. No paper coming out can also be a sign to replace or refill paper in the paper tray.

224.   A. When text is skewed or faded bars appear, then the calibrating the printer should be your first step to take. However, if there were black lines or smudging occurring, then that is a sign that the heating element has gone bad or the print heads are clogged. Debris may need to be removed if something which doesn't belong is obscuring the print job.

225.   B. In a 3d printer, a plastic filament is pulled though it's print head, a nozzle. This process contrasts to how ink is pushed through a paper printer's print head.

Chapter 4: Virtualization and Cloud Computing

1.   A. CompTIA refers to this as two words (One Drive), but Microsoft refers to it as one (OneDrive). Either way, it is the online/cloud storage account that comes with your Microsoft account. You can save files there from applications or move them there (and back again) using File Explorer (previously called Windows Explorer). There is a limited amount of storage given to each account for free, and you can purchase more as you need it.

2.   B. Companies can purchase virtualization software to set up individual clouds within their own network. That type of setup is referred to as a private cloud. Running a private cloud pretty much eliminates many of the features that companies want from the cloud, such as rapid scalability, and eliminates the need to purchase and manage computer assets. The big advantage, though, is that it allows the company to control its own security within the cloud. A hybrid model would be the scenario providing benefits of both public and private clouds. The community model is something akin to a shared private cloud, with responsibilities and benefits collaboratively shared among more than one organization.

3. B. Let's say that your company needs extra network capacity, including processing power, storage, and networking services (such as firewalls), but doesn't have the money to buy more network hardware. Instead, you can purchase Infrastructure as a Service (IaaS), which is a lot like paying for utilities—you pay for what you use. Of the four, IaaS requires the most network management expertise from the client side. In an IaaS setup, the client provides and manages the software.

4. A. The traditional type of cloud that usually comes to mind is a public cloud, like the ones operated by third-party companies such as Microsoft, Google, HP, Apple, Netflix, and Amazon with its Amazon Web Services (AWS). These clouds offer the best in scalability, reliability, flexibility, geographical independence, and cost effectiveness. Whatever the client wants, the client gets. For example, if the client needs more resources, it simply scales up and uses more.

5. A. The Task Scheduler (which may appear as Schedule Tasks in Windows 8.x Administrative Tools) allows you to configure an application to run automatically or at any regular interval. A number of terms are used to describe the options for configuring tasks: action (what the task actually does), condition (an optional requirement that must be met before a task runs), setting (any property that affects the behavior of a task), and trigger (the required condition for the task to run).

6. C. Platform as a Service (PaaS) adds a layer to IaaS that includes software development tools such as runtime environments. Because of this, it can be helpful to software developers; the vendor manages the various hardware platforms. This frees up the software developers to focus on building their application and scaling it. The best PaaS solutions allow for the client to export its developed programs and run them in an environment other than where they were developed.

7. D. The highest of the four levels of cloud service is Software as a Service (SaaS), which handles the task of managing software and its deployment, and it includes the platform and infrastructure as well. This is the model used by Google Docs, Microsoft Office 365, and even storage solutions such as Dropbox.

8. B. In most cases, clients can get more resources instantly (or at least quickly or on-demand), which is called rapid elasticity. For the client, this is a great feature because they can scale up without needing to purchase, install, and configure new hardware. Ubiquitous access refers to clients being able to access the cloud ubiquitously, or from anywhere, anytime. Resource pooling, particularly when a cloud provider deals with multiple tenants, refers to the provider effectively saving money by not duplicating available capacity. Finally, when service provided to those tenants is monitored and paid for according to their use, it's measured service.

9. A. When configuring a mobile email client to access a commercial email provider, you typically just need your username and password to establish connectivity. Examples include Google, Yahoo, `Outlook.com`, and iCloud.

10. D. In a non-domain-based environment, it is possible to use your Microsoft account (MSN, Hotmail, Outlook, and so forth) username and password to log into your Windows 8–based PC. This is intended to serve as a single sign-on, allowing you not only to interact with the OS but also to download apps from the Windows Store, sync files with OneDrive, and so on.

11. B. A Type 2 hypervisor sits on top of an existing operating system, called the host OS. This is most commonly used in client-side virtualization, where multiple OSs are managed on the client machine as opposed to on a server. The hypervisor is also called a virtual machine manager (VMM).

12. A. If presented with a scenario for installing multiple operating systems on a computer running client-side virtualization, just add the minimum hardware requirements (or recommendations) together. Treat it as if each OS needs its own minimum (which it does) and they are just sharing the available physical hardware (which they are). Also, each OS needs its own virtual network card to participate on the network and needs its security to be individually configured based on OS requirements and user needs. Treat it as though it is a separate computer.

13. C. If each client has been promised 16 GB RAM, then the server must have enough RAM to give each client their allotment. This means 64 GB in this case. The assumption is that the hypervisor will require no RAM on its own. In reality, it probably will require a little but not much. Resource pooling, when a cloud provider deals with multiple tenants, refers to the provider having additional capacity available but saving money by sharing that availability.

14. C. The major feature of virtualization is breaking down that one-to-one hardware and software barrier. The virtualized version of a computer is appropriately called a virtual machine (VM). Thanks to VMs, it is becoming far less common to need dual-boot machines today than in the past. VMs allow computers to do things like run five instances of an OS or one instance of several different OSs.

15. B. The ability to run applications in Windows XP Mode (XPM) is included with Windows 7 Professional, Enterprise, and Ultimate. This is a virtual client (emulating Windows XP Professional with Service Pack 3), and you must download and install Windows Virtual PC to use it. XPM was discontinued in Windows 8/8.1, but Virtual PC is still Microsoft's latest virtualization program for home-based platforms. Hyper-V can be used on business-end Microsoft platforms, including Windows 10 Professional, Education, and Enterprise.

16. B, D. Microsoft's hypervisor role, Hyper-V, runs on x86-64 variants of their operating system editions from Windows 8 and later. This would include Windows 8 Education and Windows 10 Professional.

17. C. Metered services is synonymous with pay as you use. The resources are available, but payment is calculated according to the actual usage. This is a common model for enterprise environments, especially during the early "migration of services" period.

18. D. Your supervisor probably prefers you are not on Twitch but has little actual impact on the site's performance. The Wi-Fi connection would be sufficient. The company likely has a policy against watching streaming applications or against particular websites like Twitch. However, the data retention policy is not relevant. Instead the firewall is the reason behind the streaming being denied.

19.   D. Windows 10 allows users to create multiple desktops with simple switching between them. This feature is called virtual desktops, where each desktop might be used for unique work functions or projects.

20.   B. The creation of virtual machines would alleviate the issue of space, power, and most of the hardware costs associated with maintaining bare-metal systems. Virtual machines can provide much of the same services, at a fraction of the costs. Control and management of the machines would not change.

21.   B. Shared resources are those resources made available to multiple employees or users on the network. Shared resources might also describe the cloud infrastructure shared among clients of a cloud provider.

22.   A. Internal assets would be under local network control and local security management, while external assets are very likely managed by an external cloud provider.

23.   C. For a company needing additional cloud resources as it needs it, the company requires on-demand cloud service.

24.   C. Measured service is cloud service based on the monitored use of resources such as storage, CPU utilization, or network bandwidth.

25.   D. From the business need, it seems the sales manager requires that the laptop files stay synchronized with the cloud. The sales manager should investigate synchronization apps.

26.   C. Deciding to virtually stream an application that is normally run on a desktop permits users to use that application from any desktop, from any location. Virtual application streaming desktop applications can greatly increase portability and productivity.

27.   A. Virtual streaming allows an organization to make a needed application available across multiple devices or form factors. This might apply to any platform the organization needs, be it a desktop computer or a mobile device.

28.   B. Virtual desktop moves the desktop icons, files, and folders to a server instead of the desktop originating from the local machine. When the desktop experience is hosted on a centralized server location, the icons, files, and folders are the same.

29.   C. A virtual network interface card (NIC) connects the virtual or guest machine to its local virtual network and any external networks.

30.   A. Before purchasing hardware of a host system to support a number of virtual systems, it is wise to consider the resource requirements of those virtual systems.

31.   A. Network requirements dictate the need for and configuration of virtual local area networks (VLANs). A VLAN is a network design feature that isolates network traffic by the switch port.

32.   D. When wanting to maintain confidentiality, integrity, and availability, security requirements must first be defined.

33.   B. Emulator requirements should be as small as possible in order to keep resources free for use by the host and guest operating systems.

Chapter 5: Hardware and Network Troubleshooting

1. D. Failure to boot at all likely means the drive is dead. But first, do your due diligence and reseat the connections and make sure the BIOS recognizes the drive before replacing it. Most BIOSs today auto-detect the hard drive. If that auto-detection fails, it's bad news for the hard drive unless there's a cable, connection, or jumper issue. If the internal hard drive is indeed dead, you might be able to get by temporarily by plugging in one that's in an external enclosure.

2. B. The system BIOS contains the boot sequence for a system. Most systems probably boot to the first hard drive, but they can also be configured to boot from a secondary hard drive, the optical drive, or the network. This setting is configured in the BIOS.

3. D. If a laptop does not display any video, it could be the screen or the video card. To test it, plug in an external monitor (that you know works) and use the function keys on the laptop to switch to external video output. If that doesn't work, it's likely that the video card is defective.

4. A. Try cleaning the fan before replacing any parts. The power supply fan has a protective grid covering it, and you won't really be able to get to it with a computer vacuum or a damp cloth. Using compressed air to blow it out is your best option.

5. C. If the battery won't charge while the laptop is plugged in, try removing the battery and reinserting it. If it still won't charge, you might want to replace the battery.

6. B, C. When repairing laptops, you should always document and label screw and cable locations, organize parts, refer to manufacturer instructions, and use appropriate hand tools. Power screwdrivers can be used. In some cases, but not all, you might need to remove the keyboard to remove the motherboard. Refer to the manufacturer's instructions.

7. D. Every computer has a diagnostic program built into its basic input/output system (BIOS) called the power-on self-test (POST). When you turn on the computer, it executes this set of diagnostics. If the computer doesn't perform the POST as it should, one way to determine the source of a problem is to listen for a beep code. This is a series of beeps from the computer's speaker. A successful POST generally produces a single beep.

8. D. This computer is giving you a beep code during the POST routine. One way to troubleshoot this is to use a POST card. This is a circuit board that fits into an expansion slot (PCI or PCIe) in the motherboard and reports numeric codes as the boot process progresses. Each of those codes corresponds to a particular component being checked. If the POST card stops at a certain number, you can look up that number in the manual for the card to determine the problem.

9. A. When files are written to a hard drive, they're not always written contiguously or with all of the data in a single location. As a result, file data is spread out over the disk, and the time it takes to retrieve files from the disk increases. Defragmenting a disk involves analyzing the disk and then consolidating fragmented files and folders so that they occupy a contiguous space, thus increasing performance during file retrieval.

10. A. A rhythmic clicking sound can be made only by components with mechanical parts, such as a conventional hard drive. A power supply fan failure will usually result in a whining sound or no sound at all because the fan doesn't work, but it will not cause a system boot failure.

11. A. Vertical white lines running down all or part of the page is because of foreign matter (more than likely toner) caught on the transfer corona wire. The dirty spots keep the toner from being transmitted to the paper (at those locations, that is), with the result that streaks form as the paper progresses past the transfer corona wire. Clean the transfer corona wires.

12. A, C. Printer jams and creased paper happen when something prevents the paper from advancing through the printer evenly. There are generally three causes of printer jams: an obstructed paper path, stripped drive gears, and using the wrong paper.

13. B. The most likely explanation is that the monitor is overheating. It could possibly be a backlight issue (if it's an LCD monitor), but backlights usually dim or flicker if they are failing.

14. C. This is most likely a problem with the power supply. Test it with a power supply tester or a multimeter.

15. C. The error message indicates that the printer does not detect the toner cartridge. That can happen if the toner cartridge isn't seated properly. Remove it and reinsert it, and the problem should go away.

16. B. If your printer fails to pick up paper, it could indicate that the pickup rollers are too worn. They press up against small rubber or cork patches known as separator pads. These help to keep the rest of the paper in the tray so that only one sheet gets picked up at a time. A pickup stepper motor turns the pickup rollers.

17. B. If your dot-matrix printer prints lines that go from dark to light as the print head moves across the page, it's the printer ribbon-advance gear slipping. Replace the mechanism.

18. C. It's recommended that no more than 30 or so client computers use one wireless access point (WAP) or wireless router. Any more than that can cause intermittent access problems. Too many users can easily result in slow network speeds.

19. C. If the CPU is overheating, it may be that the heat sink is not functioning properly or is not connected properly to the CPU. After the system cools down, try reseating the heat sink. Overclocking will only make the processor run hotter. If reseating the heat sink does not work, you might need to replace the processor.

20. A. Tools for locating Wi-Fi networks and analyzing their traffic are indispensable today. A wireless locator or a Wi-Fi analyzer can be either a handheld hardware device or specialized software that is installed on a laptop and whose purpose is to detect and analyze Wi-Fi signals.

21. A. The format command is used to wipe data off disks and prepare them for new use. Before a hard disk can be formatted, it must have partitions created on it.

22. C. If you are using RAID-0 (disk striping), you actually have more points of failure than a single device, meaning that you're at a greater risk of failure versus using just one hard drive. One drive failure will cause the entire set to fail. To recover it, replace the failed disk and restore from backup.

23. C. If print jobs are processed very slowly or if you are continually seeing "low memory" error messages, it might be a good time to upgrade the memory in the printer.

24. C. If you are using RAID-0 (disk striping), you actually have more points of failure than a single device, meaning that you're at a greater risk of failure versus using just one hard drive. One drive failure will cause the entire set to fail.

25. D. A failing motherboard or CPU may cause continuous reboots. A POST card may be helpful in narrowing down the exact component that is faulty.

26. B. If jobs aren't printing and there's no apparent reason why, it could be that the print spooler has stalled. To fix the problem, you need to stop and restart the print spooler. This is done through your operating system.

27. C. With artifacts, no matter what you have on your screen, you can still see the outlines of a different image. That image has been "burned" into the monitor (sometimes simply referred to as burn-in) and isn't going away. The only solution is to replace the monitor.

28. D. As batteries get older, they are not able to hold as much of a charge, and in some cases, they are not able to hold a charge at all. It might be time for a new tablet.

29. A. A hard drive indicator that is constantly on is generally not a good sign; it could indicate that the hard drive is constantly busy or that the system is frozen, either of which is bad. If the problem persists, it's likely a problem with the hard drive, and the drive should be replaced.

30. A. A crimper is a handy tool for helping you put connectors on the end of a cable. Most crimpers will be a combination tool that strips and snips wires as well as crimps the connector onto the end.

31. A. When you have multiple hard drives on the same controller, one needs to be set to master and the other to slave. Most drives today will do this automatically, but they have jumpers on them to configure this as well. The requirement to designate the master/slave arrangement is characteristic to Parallel ATA (PATA), where drives are connected by one cable. The alternate (and much faster) option is Serial ATA (SATA), where drives are connected by their own cable.

32. A, D. Every computer has a diagnostic program built into its basic input/output system (BIOS) called the power-on self-test (POST). When you turn on the computer, it executes this set of diagnostics. The steps include checking the CPU, checking the RAM, checking for the presence of a video card, and verifying basic hardware functionality. An error in the BIOS or one of the checked components can cause a beep code.

33. A. If the laptop is locked up, the only way to reboot it is with a hard boot. Although removing all the power sources would work, it's not necessary to do so. Simply hold down the power button for about five seconds, and the laptop will power off. If that does not work, then you might need to remove power sources.

34. C. Check the easy stuff first. It might seem silly, but be sure that the monitor is plugged in and powered on. Check to see if its power light is on.

35. B. If a mobile device is overheating, turn it off to let it cool down. It could be from overuse, or perhaps it was left in a hot environment or did not have proper ventilation.

36. A. A fairly common issue with the BIOS is when it fails to retain your computer's settings, such as time and date and hard drive configuration. The BIOS uses a small battery (much like a watch battery) on the motherboard to help it retain settings when the system power is off. If this battery fails, the BIOS won't retain its settings. Simply replace the battery to solve the problem.

37. C. If the phone is really slow but isn't completely locked up, isolate the issue. Is it one app or overall performance? It could be that apps are running in the background and need to be closed. Shutting down those apps or powering the device off and then back on is a good step. You can also check to see how much memory is available. If it's one app that's giving you problems instead of the entire device, look for updates to the app, or delete and reinstall the app. Finally, if none of these steps works, perform a restore to factory settings. If the problems persist, it's time for a new device.

38. B, D. Ghosting is caused by one of two things: a broken cleaning blade or bad erasure lamps. A broken cleaning blade causes old toner to build up on the EP drum and consequently present itself in the next printed image. If the erasure lamps are bad, then the previous electrostatic discharges aren't completely wiped away. When the EP drum rotates toward the developing roller, some toner sticks to the slightly discharged areas.

39. A. If the laptop works while it's plugged in but not while it's on battery power, the battery itself may be the culprit. As batteries get older, they are not able to hold as much of a charge, and in some cases, they are not able to hold a charge at all.

40. C. With artifacts, no matter what you have on your screen, you can still see the outlines of a different image. That image has been "burned" into the monitor (sometimes simply referred to as burn-in) and isn't going away. The only solution is to replace the monitor.

41. D. When users are typing, their palm might rest on the touch pad, causing erratic pointer behavior. This is referred to as a ghost cursor because it seems like the cursor just randomly jumps all over the screen. The touch pad can be turned off through Control Panel. Depending on the OS, you disable the touch pad under Settings.

42. D. If you smell an odd odor or see smoke coming from a computer, shut it down immediately. Open the case and start looking for visible signs of damage. Things to look for include melted plastic components and burn marks on circuit boards. If components appear to be damaged, it's best to replace them before returning the computer to service.

43. D. One potential cause of intermittent device failures is chip creep, which happens when components such as expansion cards start to creep out of their socket. This can be caused by heating and cooling. Reseat the card (and screw it into the case!) and see whether that resolves the issue. If not, you may need to replace the sound card.

44. D. If overheating is persistent, you have a few options. The first is to test or replace the battery, as that's the most likely culprit. With mobile phones, though, the battery is not designed to be field replaceable. In this case, she may have to replace the device.

45. D. In a networked environment, users need the proper permissions both to install and to print to the printer. Not having permission will result in denied access.

46. D. Seeing incorrect colors is most likely a monitor issue, and you can always confirm it by switching monitors. On CRTs, you can use a process called degaussing (decreasing or eliminating an unwanted magnetic field), which is done through a utility built into the menu on the monitor, to try to fix the problem. If that doesn't make the problem go away, it's probably time to replace the monitor.

47. C. Printer jams (aka "the printer crinkled my paper") happen when something prevents the paper from advancing through the printer evenly. There are generally three causes of printer jams: an obstructed paper path, stripped drive gears, and using the wrong paper.

48. C. This error message indicates that the master boot record (MBR) on the hard drive is missing or damaged. The bootrec utility can be run in Windows 10, Windows 8/8.1, Windows 7, or Windows Vista to interact with the Master Boot Record (MBR), boot sector or Boot Configuration Data (BCD) store. To run the tool, you must boot from the installation disk, choose the Repair Your Computer option, and enter the System Recovery Options. Choose Command Prompt from System Recovery Options and then type **BOOTREC.EXE**.

49. A, D. If the network card doesn't have any lights, it doesn't have a connection. It could be that the cable is bad or that it's not plugged in on the other side, or it could also be a problem with the NIC or the connectivity device on the other side. If nobody else in the same area is having the same problem, that points to an issue with this computer or cable.

50. C. Most of the time if you have dust or debris in a printer, you can go ahead and use compressed air to blow it away. Don't do that with toner, though, because it will make a huge mess. If you have a toner spill, use a specialized toner vacuum to pick it up. Also, never use a damp cloth to try to clean up a toner spill. If a cloth is needed, use a dry one.

51. B, C. Many laptop power adapters have a light on them indicating that they're plugged in. If there's no light, check to make sure that the outlet is working or switch outlets. Also, most laptops have a power-ready indicator light when plugged into a wall outlet as well. Check to see whether it's lit. If the outlet is fine, try another power adapter. They do fail on occasion.

52. A, B. Sometimes, when you print a color document, the colors might not be the same colors that you expected based on what you saw on the screen. A few different issues could cause this problem. First, ink could be bleeding from adjacent areas of the picture, causing the color to be off. A leaking cartridge can cause this, as can using the wrong type of paper for your printer. Second, the ink cartridges could be installed in the wrong spot. Third, it could be a dirty print head. Try running the self-cleaning routine.

53. A. The most common reason that users on wireless networks experience intermittent connectivity issues is distance. The farther away from the WAP the user gets, the weaker the signal becomes. When the signal weakens, the transfer rates drop dramatically. Ways to fix a low RF signal range from using a more powerful transmitter, using a larger antenna, focusing the signal toward where it is needed, or moving the users closer.

54. A, C. When repairing laptops, you should always document and label screw and cable locations, organize parts, refer to manufacturer instructions, and use appropriate hand tools. In some cases, but not all, you might need to remove the hard drive to remove the motherboard. To remove the motherboard, use appropriate tools recommended by the manufacturer as each system can be different.

55. B. In an LCD monitor, dimness or flickering is most commonly caused by the backlight starting to fail. In those cases, replace the backlight or the monitor.

56. A. If your printer isn't spitting out print jobs, it may be a good idea to print a test page and see whether that works. The test page information is stored in the printer's memory, so there's no formatting or translating of jobs required. It's simply a test to make sure that your printer hears your computer. If nothing happens, double-check your connections and stop and restart the print spooler. If garbage prints, there is likely a problem with the printer or the print driver.

57. C. If a laptop keyboard is not responding, you can always plug in an external keyboard and use that. It might not be an ideal long-term solution, but it will generally get a user back up and running.

58. B. Memory problems can cause applications to fail and produce error messages such as general protection faults (GPFs). Memory issues can also cause a fatal error in your operating system, producing the infamous blue screen of death (BSOD) in Windows or the rotating pinwheel in MacOS.

59. C. Distorted images can be a problem with CRT monitors if they are near a motor or other device that produces a magnetic field. Sometimes, the image will be wavy, and at other times it might look like it is getting stretched to one side of the screen. If your office is a cubicle farm, desk fans can be a major culprit.

60. A, B. The most likely components are the processor and the memory. Try reseating the chips or testing them. If the problems persist, you may need to replace those components. It could also be the motherboard.

61. C. If you're working on a larger network installation, you might use a punchdown tool. It's not a testing tool but one that allows you to connect (that is, punch down) the exposed ends of a wire into wiring harnesses, such as a 110 block (used many times in connectivity closets to help simplify the tangled mess of cables).

62. C. If your hard drive fails completely and you need to get critical data off it, there are third-party companies that provide file recovery software and services. These services are generally very expensive. (And you should have been backing up the drive in the first place!)

63. C. If your wireless networking isn't working, check to make sure that the LEDs on your network card are functioning. If there are no lights, it could indicate a problem with the card itself or, on some cards, that there is no connection or signal. Considering he received a signal in that location previously, it's most likely something to do with the card. First, make sure the wireless card is enabled through the OS.

64. B. Oversized images and icons are related to screen resolution; it usually means that your resolution is set too low for the monitor or projector you are using. Increase the resolution and the issue should disappear.

65. B. Without knowing the printer's problem, it would be most helpful if the user can tell you the error code seen on the printer's display. The error code might signify a paper jam or no connectivity, but knowing the error code will save the guesswork and possibly avoid creating more problems.

66. A. If an iPhone is entirely frozen, all you really can do is power it off and then back on. You might need to hold the power button down for several seconds to force the device to power off. If the power button does not work, you can reset an iPhone by pressing and holding the power button and the sleep/wake button simultaneously for about 10 seconds. The Apple logo will appear, and the phone should reset.

67. A. The fusing assembly heats up the toner, and the toner melts into the paper. If the fuser isn't heating properly, images can smudge.

68. B. The most likely cause of this intermittent Wi-Fi issue is a low RF signal. If you get too far from a WAP, the signal will be too weak and the Wi-Fi will disconnect.

69. C. The correct printer driver needs to be installed for the printer and operating system. For example, if you have an HP LaserJet III and a Windows 10 computer, then you need to install an HP LaserJet III driver made for Windows 10. If this is not done, you will get garbage out of the printer.

70. B. You can immediately rule out client-side hardware issues because the user can connect to some resources. You just need to figure out why he can't connect to others. This is most likely caused by one of two things: a configuration issue or a connectivity device (such as a router) problem. Since it's affecting multiple people, it's probably something to do with the router.

71. B, C. If a laptop does not display any video, it could be the screen or the video card. To test it, plug in an external monitor (that you know works), and use the function keys on the laptop to switch to external video output. If that doesn't work, it's likely that the video card is defective. If the external monitor works, you know it's a problem with the display on the laptop. The backlight (or inverter) could be dead or it could be the screen.

72.   B. If the phone is really slow but isn't completely locked up, isolate the issue. Is it one app or overall performance? It could be that apps are running in the background and need to be closed. Shutting down those apps or powering the device off and then back on is a good step. You can also check to see how much memory is available. If it's one app giving you problems instead of the entire device, look for updates to the app or delete and reinstall the app. Finally, if none of these steps works, perform a restore to factory settings. If the problems persist, it's time for a new device.

73.   A. If you're using RAID-5 (disk striping with parity), a single drive failure usually means that your data will be fine, provided you replace the failed drive. If you lose multiple drives at the same time, you will need to restore from backup.

74.   C. All-black pages happen when the charging unit (the charging corona wire or charging corona roller) in the toner cartridge malfunctions and fails to place a charge on the EP drum. Because the drum is grounded, it has no charge. Anything with a charge (like toner) will stick to it. As the drum rotates, all of the toner is transferred to the page and a black page is formed. Replace the toner cartridge. Other possible causes not listed include a defective DC Controller PCA or a defective high voltage power supply.

75.   B. If the system had been operating normally but now tells you RAID not found, it's likely something is wrong with the RAID controller. Double-check to ensure that the RAID controller BIOS is configured properly and everything is connected as it should be.

76.   C. Certain unacceptable video-quality issues (such as jerky refresh speeds or lags) can be remedied by adding memory to a video card. Doing so generally results in an increase in both quality and performance. If you can't add memory to the video card, you can upgrade to a new one.

77.   D. On a Windows workstation, the `ipconfig` command will show the TCP/IP configuration information. To see information beyond the address, subnet mask, and default gateway, use `ipconfig /all`.

78.   A. The `netstat` command is used to check out the inbound and outbound TCP/IP connections on your machine. It can also be used to view packet statistics, such as how many packets have been sent and received and the number of errors.

79.   A. This issue sounds like a swollen battery. If you have a swollen battery, turn the device off immediately and make sure that it's not plugged into a charger. It may be possible to remove the battery, but swollen batteries are more prone to explosions than normal ones because the casing is already compromised. The best course of action is to purchase a new device.

80.   B. Sometimes you will tap on an app and nothing happens. Most likely, this means that something has corrupted the app, but it could possibly be a memory issue. Try powering the device off and back on again and then try the app once more. If that doesn't resolve the problem, simply uninstall and reinstall the app.

81.   A. Try another monitor or try this monitor on another computer. That will narrow it down pretty quickly. Remember, if it's not the monitor, it's probably the video card.

82.   C. Dim or flickering displays on mobile devices are usually caused by a faulty backlight in the display panel. A failing inverter can cause these problems too.

83.   B. Dead pixels are spots on the screen that never "fire," or light up. You can check for these by setting the background to white and seeing whether any spots don't light up.

84.   B. Pointer drift is the mouse cursor slowly drifting in one direction even though you are not trying to make it move. This issue is generally related to the point stick not centering properly after it's been used. If you have pointer drift, try using the point stick and moving it back and forth a few times to get it to recenter itself. You can also try rebooting. If the problem persists, either disable or replace the point stick.

85.   D. If you need to trace a wire in a wall from one location to another, a tone generator and probe (or toner probe) is the tool for you. It consists of two pieces: a tone generator and a probe. Because it's so good at tracking, you will sometimes hear this referred to as a "fox and hound."

86.   B, D. When upgrading or repairing laptops, you should always document and label screw and cable locations, organize parts, refer to manufacturer instructions, and use appropriate hand tools. In some cases, but not all, you might need to remove the keyboard to upgrade the memory. Refer to the manufacturer's instructions.

87.   C. Cable testers are indispensable tools for any network technician. Usually you would use a cable tester before you install a cable to make sure it works. Of course, you can test them after they've been run as well.

88.   A. For network-enabled laser printers, no connectivity can be a sign of improperly configured IP settings such as the IP address. While each printer is somewhat different, you can manually configure most laser printers' IP settings through the LCD control panel.

89.   D. On a wired network, if you run into slow speeds or intermittent connectivity, it's likely a load issue. There's too much traffic for the network to handle, and the network is bogging down. Solutions include adding a switch, replacing your hubs with switches, and even creating virtual LANs (VLANs) with switches. If you want to upgrade the cabling or connectivity infrastructure to combat a speed issue, you should do all of it and not just cables or a router.

90.   B. The iPhone and iPad use the term *Location Services* to refer to GPS. Android devices will call it *Location*, *Location Services*, or *Location Reporting*. On an iPhone, you enable Location Services under Settings ➤ Privacy. In Android, location access settings are configured under Settings ➤ Location.

91.   D. One problem occurs with toner cartridges when someone installs a new toner cartridge and forgets to remove the sealing tape that is present to keep the toner in the cartridge during shipping. The solution to this problem is fortunately quite easy: Remove the toner cartridge from the printer, remove the sealing tape, and reinstall the cartridge.

92.   B, D. Unexpected shutdowns are difficult to troubleshoot, as are all intermittent issues. The first thing to check is to ensure that all socketed chips are seated properly; in fact, reseating them is a good option. If that does not resolve the issue, test the RAM or replace it if possible.

93. B. A loopback plug is for testing the ability of a network adapter to send and receive. The plug gets plugged into the NIC, and then a loopback test is performed using troubleshooting software. You can then tell whether the card is working properly.

94. B. Depending on the version of Windows you are using, net can be one of the most powerful commands at your disposal. While all Windows versions include a net command, its capabilities differ based on whether it is used on a server or workstation and the version of the operating system. Commonly, net share is used to create shared folders, and net use is used to connect to shared folders over the network.

95. D. The system BIOS contains the boot sequence for a system. Most systems probably boot to the first hard drive, but they can also be configured to boot from a secondary hard drive, the optical drive, or the network. If a computer can't find the right boot device, it could be that it's attempting to boot from the wrong device. This setting is configured in the BIOS.

96. B. It's possible that the hard drive has some bad sectors, so run chkdsk to scan the drive and attempt to repair them. If that doesn't work, formatting is the second option, and replacing the drive is the third.

97. C. The ifconfig command is used in Linux, Unix, and MacOS to check a computer's IP configuration information. ipconfig is used in Windows.

98. B. A laser printer's DC power supply provides three different DC voltages to printer components. Using the multimeter, you should find the following voltages: pin 1 +5 V, pin 5 –5 V, pin 9 +24 V.

99. D. Most keyboards will have status lights for the Caps Lock and Num Lock keys. If you believe a system is locked up, try pressing the Caps Lock or Num Lock key on the keyboard to see whether the lights change. If they don't, that's a sign that the system is unresponsive. Reboot the computer.

100. B. The diskpart utility shows the partitions and lets you manage them on the computer's hard drives. Because of the enormous power it holds, membership in the Administrators local group (or equivalent) is required to run diskpart.

101. A. Nearly every hard drive is built with Self-Monitoring, Analysis, and Reporting Technology (S.M.A.R.T.) software installed on it, which monitors hard drive reliability and theoretically can warn you in the event of an imminent failure.

102. B. If you try to power on the system but get no lights or fan, first check the obvious things. Is it plugged in? Does the cord work? If those all check out, then it's probably the power supply.

103. B. If a hard drive is too full and has less than 10 percent free space, it can slow down dramatically. The first solution to try is to remove files and free up space. If that doesn't work, you may need to format and reinstall, or potentially replace, the hard drive.

104. A. The ping command is one of the most useful commands in the TCP/IP protocol. It sends a series of packets to another system, which in turn sends back a response. This utility can be extremely useful for troubleshooting problems with remote hosts. The ping -t command sets a persistent ping, which does not stop until you cancel it.

105.   A. If the key physically sticks, you can try blowing out underneath the key with compressed air or use a cotton swab slightly dampened with water (or rubbing alcohol) to clean underneath the key. Make sure to clean the entire surface underneath the sticking key. If none of this resolves the issue, you might need to replace the keyboard.

106.   C. Failure to open files means that the computer can't properly read those files. In most cases, this indicates an issue with the hard drive.

107.   B. Laptops have USB ports, and they can come in handy in situations like this. Plug in an external USB NIC, and the user should be able to get on the network.

108.   C. There's probably a simple explanation for this one. The device may be in silent or vibrate mode. Most mobile devices will have a switch on the side that sets them to silent or vibrate mode, and that will mute the device from making a noise when it receives a call or a message. If that doesn't resolve the problem, it might also be a good idea to check his volume settings.

109.   B. In an LCD monitor, dimness or flickering is most commonly caused by the backlight starting to fail. In those cases, replace the backlight or the monitor.

110.   C. When your system refuses to boot into anything other than VGA mode, it indicates one of two problems. Either the video card is set to a resolution that it can't handle or the video card driver isn't loading properly. When in VGA mode, reset the video resolution to something you know the card can handle and reboot. If that doesn't solve it, reinstall the driver. If it still doesn't work, replace the video card.

111.   D. The screen assembly on a laser printer needs several components to work properly, including the formatter board, engine controller board, and cables connecting the display to each. If any of those components have failed, you could end up with a blank display. It could also be a failed low-voltage power supply (LVPS). If there is no output from the engine self-test, then you have a problem with the power supply.

112.   A. Distorted images can be a problem with CRT monitors if they are near a motor or other device that produces a magnetic field. Sometimes, the image will be wavy, and at other times it might look like it is getting stretched to one side of the screen. If your office is a cubicle farm, desk fans can be a major culprit.

113.   D. You could have your colleague resend the email unencrypted, but if it has highly confidential information in it, that's probably not a good idea. If you can't decrypt email, it is most likely because S/MIME settings are not properly enabled on your email account, which means installing a certificate (and by extension, your private security key) on your mobile device.

114.   A. Memory problems can cause applications to fail and produce error messages such as general protection faults (GPFs). Memory issues can also cause a fatal error in your operating system, producing a blank screen on bootup.

115.   D. Older, square CRT monitors had a 4:3 aspect ratio, and newer widescreen HD displays are either 16:9 or 16:10. If you set your resolution such that it doesn't match the monitor's geometry, you may get distorted geometry problems. When this happens, the screen will look stretched or squeezed, depending on how you set it. Just choose the proper resolution and the problem should go away.

116. D. Stepper motor problems on ink-jet and dot-matrix printers will look similar to each other. If the main motor is damaged, lines of print will be unevenly spaced, and if the print head motor goes bad, characters will be scrunched together.

117. B. A monitor can display incorrect colors if the pins on the connector are damaged or if the connector isn't plugged all the way in.

118. C. nbtstat is a command that shows NetBIOS over TCP/IP information. While not used as often as other command-line network troubleshooting tools, it can be useful when trying to diagnose a problem with NetBIOS name resolution.

119. C. Faded prints generally mean the printer is out of ink. Replace the ink cartridge and the problem should disappear.

120. D. Performing periodic preventative maintenance on your laser printers can help eliminate many potential problems before they happen. Preventative maintenance includes cleaning the printer and using manufacturer-recommended maintenance kits.

121. C. The net share command is used to share folders on a network as well as stop sharing folders. (And net use will allow users to connect to them.) The proper syntax to share a folder is net share <share_name>=<drive_letter>:<path>. To stop sharing, use net share <share_name>/delete.

122. C. If your printer isn't spitting out print jobs, it may be a good idea to print a test page and see whether that works. The test page information is stored in the printer's memory, so there's no formatting or translating of jobs required. It's simply a test to make sure that your printer hears your computer.

123. A. Some wireless cards will have their connection and activity lights alternatively blink if there is no network connection. If the card had failed, there likely would be no lights on it at all.

124. B, C. Small devices sometimes suffer from an extremely short battery life. If it's a laptop, you can try to perform a battery calibration. For all mobile devices, you can try to drain the battery completely and then charge it fully before turning the device back on. If these options don't work, then it's likely that the battery needs to be replaced.

125. B. nslookup is a command that enables you to verify entries on a DNS server.

126. C. Nearly all PCIe RAID controllers will have their own BIOS for setup, configuration, and troubleshooting. Some will have utilities available for use within an operating system as well.

127. D. The power supply is the only component listed with moving parts and therefore is the most likely component to cause a whining sound. It's more than likely a fan. Either it needs to be cleaned (desperately) or replaced. Power supplies that are failing can also sound louder and quieter intermittently because a fan will run at alternating speeds.

128. A. Every computer has a diagnostic program built into its basic input/output system (BIOS) called the power-on self-test (POST). When you turn on the computer, it executes this set of diagnostics. If the computer doesn't perform the POST as it should, one way to determine the source of a problem is to listen for a beep code. This is a series of beeps from the computer's speaker. A successful POST generally produces a single beep. If there's more than one beep, the number, duration, and pattern of the beeps can sometimes tell you what component is causing the problem. Check the documentation to determine the specific issue.

129. A. Many motherboards have capacitors on them, which store electricity. They are short cylindrical tubes. Sometimes, when capacitors fail, they will bulge, and brownish-red electrolyte residue may seep out of the vents in the top. These are called distended capacitors. If a capacitor fails, the best option is to replace the motherboard.

130. B. The most likely cause is that the router is configured to not broadcast SSIDs. 802.11g and 802.11n are compatible, and she is within range if your computer is connected.

131. D. The most common cause of an IP conflict is if someone configures a computer with a static IP address that's part of the DHCP server's range. The DHCP server, not knowing that the address has been statically assigned somewhere, doles out the address, and now there's a conflict. Rebooting the computer won't help, and neither will releasing the address and getting a new lease from the DHCP server—it's just going to hand out the same address again because it doesn't know that there's a problem. As the administrator, you need to track down the offending user. A common way to do this is to use a packet sniffer to look at network traffic and determine the computer name or MAC address associated with the IP address in question.

132. D. A groove or scratch in the EP drum can cause the problem of vertical black lines running down all or part of the page. Because a scratch is lower than the surface, it doesn't receive as much (if any) of a charge as the other areas. The result is that toner sticks to it as though it were discharged. The groove may go around the circumference of the drum, so the line may go all the way down the page.

133. A. Dim or flickering displays on mobile devices are usually caused by a faulty backlight in the display panel. A failing inverter can cause these problems too.

134. A, D. If you're curious as to the state of your power supply, you can buy hardware-based power supply testers or multimeters to test it.

135. C. If the laptop won't output a screen image to an external monitor or projector, it means one of two things (assuming you know that the monitor or projector works): Either the external VGA port is shot or the function keys aren't working. In either case, you likely need to replace the motherboard if you want the display to appear on an external device.

136. B. Most wireless headsets use a Bluetooth connection. The first thing to check is that the Bluetooth is enabled, which also means double-checking that Airplane mode is not turned on. In this case, Bluetooth is off.

137. B. The address shown is an APIPA/link local address, if your computer is set to receive an IP address from the Dynamic Host Configuration Protocol (DHCP) server and that server doesn't respond. You can always tell an APIPA/link local address because it will be in the format of 169.254.*x.x*.

138. C, D. A failing motherboard or CPU may cause continuous reboots.

139. D. If the problem affects multiple users, chances are that it's an issue with the central connectivity device. Suspect an issue with the hub or switch that the computers are plugged into.

140. C. tracert (trace route) is a Windows-based command-line utility that enables you to verify the route to a remote host. Execute the command tracert *hostname*, where *hostname* is the computer name or IP address of the computer whose route you want to trace. Tracert returns the different IP addresses the packet was routed through to reach the final destination.

141. C. Given he recently cleaned his desk, it is likely cables were moved. The first thing to check would be the network cable.

142. A. Opening the projector's log to review for relevant information is a good step to take. From the description, it doesn't sound like the culprit was loose cables, lighting, or overheating.

143. C. The most likely explanation is that the wireless router is overheating. If it randomly shuts down in the afternoon, being in the sun may contribute to overheating.

144. D. Troubleshooting theory for the A+ exam consists of six steps: identify the problem; establish a theory of probable cause; test the theory to determine cause; establish a plan of action to resolve the problem and implement the solution; verify full system functionality and, if applicable, implement preventive measures; and document findings, actions, and outcomes.

145. C. Troubleshooting theory for the A+ exam consists of six steps: identify the problem; establish a theory of probable cause; test the theory to determine cause; establish a plan of action to resolve the problem and implement the solution; verify full system functionality and, if applicable, implement preventive measures; and document findings, actions, and outcomes.

146. B. Part of identifying the problem is to question the user, identify user changes to the computer, and perform backups before making changes. One could argue that doing external or internal research is part of identifying the problem as well, but in A+ troubleshooting theory, that step is part of establishing a theory of probable cause. Troubleshooting theory for the A+ exam consists of six steps: Identify the problem; establish a theory of probable cause; test the theory to determine cause; establish a plan of action to resolve the problem and implement the solution; verify full system functionality and, if applicable, implement preventive measures; and document findings, actions, and outcomes.

147. A. Troubleshooting theory for the A+ exam consists of six steps: Identify the problem; establish a theory of probable cause; test the theory to determine cause; establish a plan of action to resolve the problem and implement the solution; verify full system functionality and, if applicable, implement preventive measures; and document findings, actions, and outcomes. Questioning the user and identifying user changes is part of the first step of identifying the problem.

148. B. According to troubleshooting theory, backups should be made before making changes. This is part of the first step, which is identifying the problem. In reality, it does make a lot of sense to perform backups before making major changes to a system. Just in case.

149. B. Troubleshooting theory for the A+ exam consists of six steps: identify the problem; establish a theory of probable cause; test the theory to determine cause; establish a plan of action to resolve the problem and implement the solution; verify full system functionality and, if applicable, implement preventive measures; and document findings, actions, and outcomes.

150. C, D. When troubleshooting an issue, a technician should never leave it unresolved. If the technician's first attempt at solving the problem failed, there are two acceptable next steps, depending on the situation and available resources. The first is to establish a new theory and test it. The second is to escalate the issue to a more experienced technician who may be able to solve it.

151. D. It's always good to consider the feelings of the user, such that you don't make them feel worse for a situation that they likely already feel bad about. But, the right answer is to consider corporate policies, procedures, and impacts before implementing changes. Perhaps considering user feelings should be part of the corporate policies and procedures for technicians.

152. A, D. When testing your theory, there are two logical outcomes. One is that your theory is correct and you can determine the next steps to solve it. The other is that you are incorrect and you need to establish a new theory or escalate the issue to someone better equipped to handle the situation. Troubleshooting theory for the A+ exam consists of six steps: identify the problem; establish a theory of probable cause; test the theory to determine cause; establish a plan of action to resolve the problem and implement the solution; verify full system functionality and, if applicable, implement preventive measures; and document findings, actions, and outcomes.

153. D. Part of establishing a theory of probable cause is to perform external or internal research based on symptoms. One could argue that you might also do this at any time during the troubleshooting process. Troubleshooting theory for the A+ exam consists of six steps: identify the problem; establish a theory of probable cause; test the theory to determine cause; establish a plan of action to resolve the problem and implement the solution; verify full system functionality and, if applicable, implement preventive measures; and document findings, actions, and outcomes.

154. C. Troubleshooting theory for the A+ exam consists of six steps: identify the problem; establish a theory of probable cause; test the theory to determine cause; establish a plan of action to resolve the problem and implement the solution; verify full system functionality and, if applicable, implement preventive measures; and document findings, actions, and outcomes.

155. D. The BIOS, with the help of a small, CMOS battery, maintains the proper time. Windows picks this up and displays it. If the CMOS battery may need to be changed.

156. D. The motherbard contains the BIOS, which controls the order in which bootup tries the devices available. On bootup, this device order is used to search for an operating system to launch.

157. B. When a system experiences intermittent device failure, it's most likely the power supply is delivering with intermittent voltage or current. If the RAM were faulty, you might see problems such as data corruption and system errors. If the CPU were faulty, the problems range from the operating system is likely to fail or crush a variety of ways, such as OS freezing or a "blue screen of death." Additionally, the system CPU may overheat.

158. A, D. For these symptoms, the problem could easily be either a CPU which has failed entirely or the power supply fails to deliver some voltages and is providing others, e.g. 12V is fine, while the 5V has failed.

159. B, C. A failing hard drive will produce a range of issues, with the most common being read/write failures or, in more unfortunate cases, the OS not found.

160. C. Most likely, the system administrator has inserted a drive that is, for some reason, incompatible. The RAID array fails to rebuild properly since the drive is not recognized.

161. B. Troubleshooting steps show the projector works fine with someone else's laptop. It is likely the CEO's laptop video output is failing.

162. D. From the information provided, it appears likely the laptop experienced an overheat shutdown. When computer equipment is exposed to direct sunlight or near heating equipment, the computer cooling component fails to operate efficiently.

163. C. In troubleshooting you should try the least invasive step first. Checking the device's available storage for new apps is a good step toward testing a likely cause, without unloading applications or possibly causing your own device's problems.

Chapter 6: Operating Systems

1. A. A restore point is a copy of your system configuration at a given point in time. Restore points are useful for when Windows fails to boot but the computer appears to be fine otherwise or when Windows doesn't seem to be acting right and you think it was because of a recent configuration change. Restore points are created in the System Restore utility.

2. B. Print Management allows you to manage multiple printers and print servers from a single interface. It is not available for Windows 7 in any edition lower than Windows 7 Professional. In all other editions, you must manage individual printers using the Printers applet in Control Panel, and you are limited in what you can manage.

3. B. Apple developed the Hierarchical File System (HFS) as the file system for its Apple computers, starting in 1998. The successor HFS+ was the file system for Mac OS X until 2017 when Apple File System (APFS) was released. NTFS was developed by Microsoft. The file system ext4 is found in most Linux-based systems. Finally, Sun Microsystems developed NFS.

4. B. Notepad is a simple Windows program, and it comes standard with all versions of Windows. Both Word and Notepad are used to create and edit documents, but Word is far more configurable and powerful. It's also not a free Windows application; you must purchase it separately.

5. A. The System Configuration Tools tab shows you a short list of available administrative tools. System configuration (MSCONFIG.EXE) has five tabs: General, Boot, Services, Startup, and Tools.

6. B. Encrypting File System (EFS) is available in the Professional, Enterprise, and Ultimate editions of Windows 7. It allows for the encryption/decryption of files stored in NTFS volumes. EFS can be used by all users, whereas BitLocker can be turned on only by administrators. EFS can encrypt just one file, if so desired, while BitLocker encrypts the whole volume and whatever is stored on it.

7. A, D. The Computer Management MMC allows you to configure several aspects of your computer. It includes Task Scheduler, Event Viewer, Shared Folders, Performance Monitor, Device Manager, Disk Management, and Services and Applications. You can't set file permissions; those are configured through Windows Explorer. You can enable or disable Windows Firewall, but it's configured through its own utility.

8. B. The exit command will get you out of the windows or processes that you are currently in. For example, if you are running a batch script, it will exit that batch script. If you are in the command interpreter, it will close the command interpreter.

9. C. The MSINFO32 tool shown in the picture displays a thorough list of settings on the machine. You cannot change any values from here, but you can search, export, and save reports.

10. D. The Data Sources app allows you to interact with database management systems. Database drivers that are added to the system will show up here and can be shared between applications.

11. D. When a problem pops up with the Windows 8 operating system, you can boot into the Windows Recovery Environment (Windows RE) and repair it by choosing to refresh, reset, or restore it. Refreshing it keeps personal files and settings along with the default apps and those that you installed from the Windows Store. Resetting reinstalls Windows and deletes all but the default apps (meaning that you lose your personal files and settings). Restoring allows you to just undo recent system changes.

12. A, D. Task Manager lets you shut down nonresponsive applications selectively in all Windows versions. There are three easy ways to get to Task Manager. You can press Ctrl+Alt+Delete and click the Task Manager button or option, you can right-click an empty spot in the Taskbar and choose it from the pop-up menu that appears, or you can press Ctrl+Shift+Esc.

13. C. The gpresult command is used to show the Resultant Set of Policy (RSoP) report/ values for a remote user and computer. Bear in mind that configuration settings occur at any number of places; they are set for a computer, a user, a local workstation, the domain, and so on. Often one of the big unknowns is which set of configuration settings takes precedence and which is overridden. gpresult will tell you which settings apply.

14. B. The System Configuration tool allows you to set up programs to boot automatically at startup, using the Startup tab. System configuration (MSCONFIG.EXE) has five tabs: General, Boot, Services, Startup, and Tools.

15. D. When you install Windows 8 and choose Custom, you can choose whether to format the hard disk. If you choose not to format the hard disk, the old operating system is placed in a folder named `Windows.old` to allow you to attempt to return to the old operating system if needed. After 28 days, any files placed in the `Windows.old` folder are automatically deleted. After Windows begins installing, you will have the option of configuring time, date, region, and language settings.

16. D. The heart of an unattended installation is utilizing image deployment, which is sort of like copying an ideal image over from one machine to another.

17. D. In Windows 8, when you first open Control Panel, it appears in Category view. Control Panel programs have been organized into different categories, and this view provides you with the categories from which you can choose. However, you can change this view to Classic view (or Small/Large Icons in Windows 7 and Windows 8), which displays all of the Control Panel programs in a list, as in older versions of Windows.

18. C. Windows PowerShell (one word per Microsoft and two per CompTIA) has been around for several years and was available with previous versions of Windows as well. It can be thought of as a greatly enhanced command interface where you can write script files based on the .NET programming framework.

19. A, C. There are several ways to see what services are running and to enable and disable services. They include the Services MMC, Computer Management, and Task Manager. Performance Monitor does not show running services, and there is no `BLDES.MSC`.

20. C. The easiest way to see whether your current hardware can run another version of Windows is to download the utility that Microsoft creates for checking what you have. For Windows 7, this was called Upgrade Advisor. For Windows 8 and Windows 8.1, it has been renamed Upgrade Assistant.

21. B. If you have favorite apps, you can "pin" (add) them to the Start screen or the Windows Desktop so that you can get to them quickly or see updates to their tiles at a glance.

22. C. The `cd`, `md`, and `rd` commands are used to change (or display), make, and remove directories, respectively. They're shorthand versions of the `chdir`, `mkdir`, and `rmdir` commands. The `rd` command will only delete empty directories by default. With `rd`, the `/s` switch will remove all subdirectories and files. The `/q` switch is quiet mode, and `rd` will not ask if it's OK to remove all of the files with the `/s` switch. The `del` command is for deleting files.

23. C. Gadgets are mini-programs, introduced with Windows Vista, which can be placed on the Windows Desktop, allowing them to run quickly and personalize the PC (clock, weather, and so on). Windows 7 renamed these Windows Desktop Gadgets but they were discontinued shortly after due to security vulnerabilities. Gadgets were replaced by apps thereafter.

24. D. To curb software piracy, Microsoft requires that each copy of Windows be activated after installation. Activation is the validation of the product key. Without activation, you can run the operating system, but only for a limited number of days. During that period of time, Windows will frequently remind you to activate the product.

25. B, C. Microsoft created Windows To Go (WTG) to allow Windows 8/8.1 to be installed on any USB-bootable device, such as a flash drive or external hard drive. WTG works with both USB 2.0 and USB 3.0 ports, but it requires USB 3.0 drives. WTG does not support OS upgrades, but it is compatible with BitLocker.

26. A. Windows Defender can identify spyware, and it is included with all versions of Windows from Windows Vista onward. As with similar programs, for Windows Defender to function properly, you need to keep the definitions current and scan on a regular basis.

27. B. The expand command is used to extract compressed files from a cabinet file.

28. A. You want to use the Local Security Policy tool, which is SECPOL.MSC. It allows you to set the default security settings for the system. This includes password settings, lockout policies, audit policy, and other security settings.

29. A. The Volume Shadow Copy Service creates copies from which you can recover should a file be accidentally deleted or overwritten. Windows 7 adds to Vista by including an interface for configuring storage used by volume shadow copies. The Properties dialog box for a file contains a Previous Versions tab that can be used to return to another version of the file.

30. D. The del command, short for delete, is used to delete files. The /q switch is for quiet mode. It will not ask for confirmation to delete the file. The /f switch forces deletion of read-only files. /y and /r are not valid switches for the del command.

31. B. Restore points are created and managed in the System Restore utility (RSTRUI.EXE). A restore point is a copy of your system configuration at a given point in time. Restore points are useful for when Windows fails to boot but the computer appears to be fine otherwise, or when Windows doesn't seem to be acting right and you think it was because of a recent configuration change.

32. D. Some of the more important files that you will need to work on are hidden by default as a security precaution. To make certain folders or files visible, you need to change the display properties of Windows Explorer. This is generally done by going to Folder Options and deselecting Hide Protected Operating System Files. The display properties of Windows Explorer also let you hide file extensions and set general folder options and has options to view the folders in different ways.

33. B, D. The Windows Store and charms were introduced with Windows 8. The Windows Store is an online site from which you can download apps, games, software, and so on. Charms are controls that are available on the side of the screen for every Windows Store app. They consist of Search, Share, Start, Devices, and Settings.

34. B. The purpose behind a HomeGroup is to simplify home or small office networking and, more specifically, the sharing of files and printers. Windows 7 Starter can only join a HomeGroup, while all other editions of Windows 7 can both join and create a HomeGroup. The location from which you network must be set to Home. Shared files can include libraries, which is a big feature of Windows 7. All computers participating in the HomeGroup must be running Windows 7 or Windows 8/8.1 (but not Vista), and the network cannot extend outside the small group.

35.   D. DirectX is a collection of application programming interfaces (APIs) related to multimedia. A great utility is the DxDiag (DirectX Diagnostic) tool, which allows you to test DirectX functionality. When you start it, you can also verify that Microsoft has signed your drivers.

36.   A, C, E. Windows 7 can be installed from three sources: PXE (over the network), DVD, or USB. Windows 7 does not come on CD-ROM. In this instance, the computer has no operating system, so the internal hard drive is not bootable.

37.   B, D. The Computer Management console (COMPMGMT.EXE) contains Performance Monitor, which allows you to view hardware performance statistics. PERFMON.EXE is the executable command for Performance Monitor in its own Microsoft Management Console (MMC) window. You can also use Task Manager and Resource Monitor to check CPU and memory usage statistics.

38.   C. Windows 7 Professional, Enterprise, and Ultimate can join a Windows Server domain. The Starter and Home Premium editions cannot.

39.   A. In a Linux system, one may find all of these partitions, but the swap partition is the one affected by the amount of RAM memory installed. The swap partition is mounted and used when the RAM is fully utilized but the system requires additional space.

40.   B. Windows Update manages the download and installation of Windows updates and patches. Most administrators choose to have patches applied automatically, which is a safe choice. You can also tell Windows Update to download patches but not apply them until the administrator manually approves them.

41.   A. The Task Scheduler (which may appear as Schedule Tasks in Windows 8.x Administrative Tools) allows you to configure an application to run automatically or at any regular interval. A number of terms are used to describe the options for configuring tasks: action (what the task actually does), condition (an optional requirement that must be met before a task runs), setting (any property that affects the behavior of a task), and trigger (the required condition for the task to run).

42.   D. If you don't know what edition of Windows is running on a particular machine, you can click Start and type **winver** in the search box. The screen that is returned will identify the edition as well as the service pack installed.

43.   B. NFS was created by Sun Microsystems a number of decades ago, and it was widely used in Unix and now also in Linux environments. Starting with Windows 7, Microsoft includes support for NFS with Windows 7 Ultimate and Enterprise. The ext3 and ext4 file systems are supported by Linux but not natively by those two versions of Windows 7.

44.   D. Virtual memory uses what's called a swap file or paging file. For Linux and Unix systems, it's called a swap partition. A swap file is hard drive space into which idle pieces of programs are placed while other active parts of programs are kept in or swapped into main memory. When the application needs the information again, it is swapped back into RAM so that the processor can use it. This generally speeds up system performance and is configured from the System applet in Control Panel. The System applet also lets you configure remote settings and system protection.

45.   A. The Windows Start screen, introduced in Windows 8, is the central location where you can access your most commonly used data and sites.

46. A. She needs to create a power plan with her desired settings. This is done in the Power Options applet of Control Panel. Different plans, such as hibernate or standby, can be configured for when the laptop is on battery power versus when it's plugged in.

47. C. Local Security Policy allows you to set the default security settings for the system. This includes password settings, lockout policies, audit policy, and other security settings.

48. C. When a problem pops up with the Windows 7 operating system, you can boot into the Windows Recovery Environment (Windows RE) and repair or restore it. Repairing it keeps personal files and settings along with the default apps and those that you installed from the Windows Store. Restoring allows you to just undo recent system changes.

49. B. When files are written to a hard drive, they're not always written contiguously or with all the data in a single location. Defragmenting a disk involves analyzing the disk and then consolidating fragmented files and folders so that they occupy a contiguous space (consecutive blocks), thus increasing performance during file retrieval. The executable for Disk Defragmenter is DEFRAG.EXE.

50. D. If you are using a modem to connect to the Internet, then the type of connection you are establishing is a dial-up connection. Internet access will be slow and painful!

51. B. Microsoft came up with a new user interface for Windows 8. This was originally called the Metro interface, but the name was changed after its release to the new Windows UI (or the Windows 8 UI).

52. D. The best plan in this scenario is to format the hard drive, which by definition makes it a clean installation.

53. B. The copy command makes a copy of a file in a second location. (To copy a file and then remove it from its original location, use the move command.) One useful tip is to use wildcards. For example, the asterisk (*) is a wildcard that means *everything*. So, you could type **copy *.exe** to copy all files that have an .exe filename extension, or you could type **copy *.*** to copy all files in your current directory. The other popular wildcard is the question mark (?), which does not mean everything but instead replaces one character. The copy abc?.exe command would only copy exe files with four-letter names of which the first three letters are abc.

54. D. Windows 7 incorporates Windows Firewall, which can be used to stop incoming and outgoing network traffic. Traffic is allowed or denied by specific rules that are part of an access control list (ACL). By default, Windows Firewall blocks incoming traffic. One example of custom configuration is to create exceptions, where you can specify the incoming traffic you want to allow through.

55. C. In general, the swap file should be at least 1.5 times the amount of RAM in the machine. You should place the swap file on a drive with plenty of empty space. As a general rule, try to keep 20 percent of your drive space free for the overhead of various elements of the OS, like the swap file. Do not set the swap file to an extremely small size. If you make the swap file too small, the system can become unbootable, or at least unstable.

56. C. An install can be started many ways—with a USB drive, a DVD, and so on—and an image and setup files can also be located on and installed from a network, thus saving you from having to keep all the files on the local machine. Often called a PXE-initiated boot (for Pre-boot Execution Environment), it allows the workstation involved in the installation to retrieve the files from the network, as needed, and configure variables accordingly.

57.   A. Multiple monitors have been available with Windows for some time, but not until Windows 8 has it been possible to have a Taskbar appear in each monitor.

58.   B. Whenever you format the hard drive, the old operating system is removed. Therefore, it is a clean install.

59.   C. The robocopy utility (Robust File Copy for Windows) is included with recent versions of Windows and has the big advantage of being able to accept a plethora of specifications and keep NTFS permissions intact in its operations. The /mir switch, for example, can be used to mirror a complete directory tree.

60.   A. You can boot a PC over the network (rather than from a DVD, USB, or hard disk) with the Windows Preinstallation Environment (WinPE), which is a stub operating system that creates a Pre-boot Execution Environment (PXE). Netboot is the process of booting the OS from the network, such as from a thin client.

61.   A. The screen resolution determines the number of pixels that go across and down to make up the screen image. Decreasing the resolution in effect makes each pixel bigger, thereby making images on the screen larger. Resolution, color depth, and refresh rate are set in Display or Display Settings in Control Panel.

62.   D. Both the Home and Work settings for Windows Vista and Windows 7 have network discovery on by default. This means that you can see other computers and other computers can see you. If you choose Public, network discovery is turned off. None of the options affects Windows Firewall.

63.   A. By mounting a drive, you can map a folder or subfolder to empty space on another hard drive or partition. For example, if the computer has a second hard drive with a partition that has space, you can create a folder there and then mount it as a subfolder of the DailyReports folder on the D: drive.

64.   C. Virtual memory uses what's called a swap file, or paging file. A swap file is hard drive space into which idle pieces of programs are placed while other active parts of programs are kept in or swapped into main memory. In Windows, the swap file is called pagefile .sys, and it's located in the root directory of the drive on which you installed the OS files. By default, the swap file is a hidden file.

65.   C. The cd, md, and rd commands are used to change (or display), make, and remove directories, respectively. They're shorthand versions of the chdir, mkdir, and rmdir commands.

66.   D. Task Manager is a multifunctional tool that shows you applications that are running as well as their individual CPU and memory usage. In addition, it lets you see network usage and connected users.

67.   A. The command-line utility ipconfig will display network configuration information, including the current adapters' IP address (IPv4 and/or IPv6), subnet masks, and default gateway. Command switches such as /all will present much more detailed information. The command ifconfig is the equivalent for Linux and Unix-based systems.

68. B. Task Manager is a multifunctional tool that shows you applications that are running as well as their individual CPU and memory usage. You can also use Task Manager to force applications or processes to shut down.

69. A. While not a file system that can be used on a hard drive, CDFS is the file system of choice for CD media, and it has been used with 32-bit Windows versions since Windows 95. A CD mounted with the CDFS driver appears as a collection.

70. C. The utility shown is the System Configuration tool. You can identify it because of the five tabs: General, Boot, Services, Startup, and Tools.

71. C. The Remote Assistance feature is turned on in System Properties, on the Remote tab.

72. B. MSTSC (Remote Desktop Connection) is used to configure remote Windows Desktop connections. It offers a glut of options and can be started from the command line, or it can be configured through the graphical interface.

73. C. With Windows Disk Management, you can shrink a partition. Then with the empty space, you can create a new partition. Remember that you can have a maximum of four partitions if on an MBR drive. Drives partitioned as dynamic disks do not have the four partition rule.

74. A. Restore points are created in the System Restore utility. A restore point is a copy of your system configuration at a given point in time. Restore points are useful for when Windows fails to boot but the computer appears to be fine otherwise, or when Windows doesn't seem to be acting right and you think it was because of a recent configuration change.

75. C. The `help` command does what it says: It gives you help. If you just type **help** and press Enter, your computer gives you a list of system commands that you can type. To get more information, type the name of a command that you want to learn about after typing `help`. For example, type **help rd** and press Enter, and you will get information about the rd command.

76. D. The `bootrec.exe` utility can be run in Windows 8/8.1, Windows 7, or Windows Vista to interact with the Master Boot Record (MBR), boot sector, or Boot Configuration Data (BCD) store. The options for `bootrec` are `/fixboot` (to write a new boot sector), `/fixmbr` (to write a new MBR), `/rebuildbcd` (to rebuild the BCD store), and `/scanos` (to scan all disks for installations the Boot Manager menu is not listing).

77. C. The ext3 and ext4 file systems are supported by Linux but not natively by Windows Vista, Windows 7, or Windows 8/8.1.

78. B. ReadyBoost allows you to use free space on a removable drive (usually USB) as virtual memory and speed up a system. For the option even to be possible, at least 256 MB of space must be available on the removable media. ReadyBoost is configured from the ReadyBoost tab of the Properties dialog box for the removable media device.

79. B. A recovery partition is an area of the hard drive set aside to hold files that can be used to recover the operating system in the event of a failure. You can copy the information from this partition to another location (usually a USB drive) to use in the event that the partition fails.

80. B, D. Rather than booting from an internal drive, it is possible to install and boot Windows from an external drive if your BIOS supports it (and looks for the external drive in the boot order). As silly as it sounds, bear in mind when taking the exam that an external drive will not boot if it is not found at startup.

81. C. Windows 8 was the first to feature side-by-side apps. Snapped applications will take up half of the screen by default. On larger screens, up to four apps can be snapped. Windows 7 does allow vertical or horizontal stacking of application displays by right-clicking on the Taskbar and choosing to show the windows stacked. Not exactly the same, but similar.

82. B, C. In Windows Vista and newer, you can extend existing partitions to give them more space, provided of course that the hard disk has unpartitioned space available. To extend a basic volume, it either needs to be raw or formatted with NTFS, and you can only extend it into contiguous disk space. Both primary and extended partitions can be extended. Only dynamic disks can be extended into noncontiguous space.

83. D. Task Manager's Users tab provides you with information about the users connected to the local machine. You'll see the username, ID, status, client name, and session type. You can right-click the name of any connected user to perform a variety of functions, including sending the user a message, disconnecting the user, logging off the user, and initiating a remote-control session to the user's machine.

84. D. A domain is a group of computers that are tightly connected or associated and share a common domain name. It has a single authority (called a domain controller) that manages security for all of the computers. All users will log in to the Windows domain using their centrally created user account.

85. B. The `tasklist` utility is used at the command line to see a list of all the running processes (and their process ID number), similar to what you see in the GUI by using Task Manager. By default, it shows the processes on the current machine, but the `/s` switch can be used to see the processes on a remote machine. `/svc` will show the services hosted in each process, and you can use `/u` if you need to run the command as another user. The `/v` switch is for verbose mode, which will show details such as CPU time and memory usage. `/c` is not a valid `tasklist` switch.

86. B. If you are migrating only a few accounts, Microsoft recommends Windows Easy Transfer (WET) instead of USMT. You don't need to use either one if you chose the Upgrade option and are doing an inplace upgrade because user files and applications are preserved.

87. A. The `cd`, `md`, and `rd` commands are used to change (or display), make, and remove directories, respectively. They're shorthand versions of the `chdir`, `mkdir`, and `rmdir` commands. To get back to the root directory, use `cd\`; the `cd..` command will take you up one directory.

88. B. The Windows Memory Diagnostics tool can be used to check a system for memory problems. For the tool to work, the system must be restarted. The two options that it offers are to restart the computer now and check for problems or to wait and check for problems on the next restart.

89. C. An important aspect of disk management is backing up the data on your drives. Toward that end, Windows has a built-in backup feature called Backup. The Backup utility in each of the different versions of Windows has different capabilities, with newer versions having greater capabilities. In general, you can either run a wizard to create a backup job or manually specify the files to back up. You can also run backup jobs or schedule them to run at specific times at a specific interval.

90. A. The shutdown command can be used to shut down and restart computers, either the system you are on or a remote one. The /s switch is used to shut down a computer, and /r is used for a full shutdown and reboot. The /m switch followed by the computer name is used to specify the remote computer. The /c switch is for comments.

91. A. Just as Windows 8 can run from USB, internal, and external drives, it can also run on solid-state drives (SSDs), as long as they meet the standard minimum requirements for size (a minimum of 16 GB, in this case). Microsoft recommends that WinSAT .exe formal be used to optimize Windows for the SSD. The command reduces the number of write operations that Windows makes.

92. C. The partition from which the operating system boots must be designated as active. Only one partition on a disk may be marked active.

93. D. The command switch "/scannow" will scan for corrupted, changed or missing Windows system files. Where System File Checker finds wrong files, it replaces with the correct versions. The "/verifyfile" and "/verifyonly" switches will not replace or repair file. The switch "/scanfile" will scan and, if necessary, replace, a specific referenced file.

94. C. Windows 7, Windows Vista, and Windows 8/8.1 all allow the use of an alternate IP address. This is an address that is configured for the system to use in the event the first choice is not available. For an alternate configuration to be set, the first choice has to be dynamic—the tab becomes visible only when the General configuration is set to Obtain An IP Address Automatically, and the alternate is used only if the primary address cannot be found/used, such as when the DHCP server is down.

95. A, B. Conventionally, the forward slash followed by a question mark provides the full list of possible switches with a brief explanation of how to use them. For most commands, the forward slash followed by help will return the same menu.

96. D. The User Account Control (UAC) is intended to prevent unintentional/unauthorized changes to the computer by either prompting for permission to continue or requiring the administrator password before continuing. It has the sole purpose of keeping the user from running programs that could potentially pose a threat by requiring escalating privileges for many actions.

97. B, D. Because of the power they possess, the disk partitioning (diskpart) and system file checker (sfc) commands require administrative privileges.

98. D. When a problem pops up with the Windows 8 operating system, you can boot into the Windows Recovery Environment (Windows RE) and repair it by choosing to refresh, reset, or restore it. Refreshing it keeps personal files and settings along with the default apps and those that you installed from the Windows Store. Resetting reinstalls Windows and deletes all but the default apps (meaning that you lose your personal files and settings). Restoring allows you to just undo recent system changes.

99. C. The print spooler is a Windows service; therefore, it is managed through the Services applet in Computer Management. You can also open Services by typing **services.msc** into the Windows Run box.

100. D. The gpupdate tool is used to update Group Policy settings. It refreshes, or changes, both local and Active Directory–based policies and replaces some of the functionality that previously existed with secedit.

101. B. Administrative shares are created on servers running Windows on the network for administrative purposes. These shares can differ slightly based on which OS is running, but they end with a dollar sign ($) to make them hidden. There is one for each volume on a hard drive (C$, D$, and so forth) as well as admin$ (the root folder—usually C:\WINDOWS), and print$ (where the print drivers are located). These are created for use by administrators and usually require administrator privileges to access.

102. D. Program Compatibility is included with various versions of Windows to configure programs to believe that they are running with an older version of Windows. To enable it for Windows 7, for example, choose Start ➢ Control Panel ➢ Programs and then click Run Programs Made For Previous Versions of Windows.

103. B. If there is sufficient space on a machine and the hardware will support it, you can have more than one operating system and choose which one to run when you boot. A rule of thumb from Microsoft is that you should always install older operating systems first and then work forward (have Windows Vista on before installing Windows 7 and then Windows 8, for example).

104. C. Introduced along with Windows NT, NTFS is available with all current versions of Windows. NTFS is a much more advanced file system in almost every way than all versions of the FAT file system. It includes such features as individual file security, compression, and RAID support as well as support for extremely large file and partition sizes and disk transaction monitoring. It is the file system of choice for higher-performance computing.

105. C. Wake-on-LAN is an Ethernet standard implemented via a network card that allows a "sleeping" machine to awaken when it receives a wakeup signal.

106. A. The taskkill command is used to terminate processes, just as you can do in Task Manager in Windows. To kill a process by its name, use the /IM switch. If you know the process ID, use the /PID switch. The /S switch is used to specify a remote system, and the /FI switch applies a filter to a set of tasks.

107. A. For an unattended installation, you create a reference image for deployment to the physical machines. Once it's created, you can edit this image with the System Preparation Tool (Sysprep) and create a Windows Imaging (WIM) file to roll out.

108. A. When configuring Windows, the three types of networks from which you can choose are workgroup, HomeGroup, and domain. A workgroup is a loosely associated group of computers, each of which is its own security authority, that share a common workgroup name. Domains have centralized security. Only Windows 7 and newer computers can join a HomeGroup.

109. D. Windows supports both basic and dynamic storage. Basic storage can only have primary and extended partitions. Dynamic partitions can be simple, spanned, or striped volumes. Sometimes you will hear of a logical partition as one that spans multiple physical disks, as in this scenario. However, Disk Management does not allow you to create something called a logical partition.

110. D. Windows Vista Starter versions are not upgradeable to Windows 7. You can still buy Windows 7 and install it, but you will need to do a clean installation instead (in other words, you won't be able to keep your existing files unless you back them up and restore them).

111. C. With a 64-bit processor, you can install either a 32-bit or a 64-bit operating system. Installing a 32-bit operating system will waste some of the 64-bit processor's capabilities, though.

112. B. With basic storage, Windows drives can be partitioned with primary or extended partitions. The difference is that extended partitions can be divided into one or more logical drives, and primary partitions cannot be further subdivided. Each hard disk can be divided into a maximum of four total partitions, either four primary partitions or three primary partitions and one extended partition.

113. A, D. When the upgrade is done without removing the existing operating system (the norm), this is known as an in-place upgrade. The versions of Windows 7 that can be upgraded in-place to Windows 8 Core are Windows 7 Starter, Windows 7 Home Basic, and Windows 7 Home Premium. Windows 7 Professional and Windows 7 Ultimate can be directly upgraded to Windows 8 Pro, and Windows 7 Enterprise can only be upgraded to Windows 8 Enterprise.

114. D. If hardware that should work stops working when you change the OS, loading alternate third-party drivers can be a solution to the problem. (And remember that it is preferred that those drivers be signed.) Each OS needs its own driver for hardware to work properly.

115. C. Device Manager has been present in every version of Windows since Windows 95. It allows you to manage all of your hardware devices, including updating drivers and disabling the device. It is found within the Computer Management console.

116. A. With a 32-bit processor, you can only install a 32-bit operating system. A 32-bit processor is not capable of running a 64-bit OS or 64-bit software.

117. C. A logical partition is any partition that has a drive letter. Often, you will hear a partition that spans multiple physical disks referred to as a logical partition. For example, a network drive that you know as drive H: might actually be located on several physical disks on a server. However, this is not what defines a logical partition.

118. D. All installed applications in Windows will appear under Control Panel ➤ Programs and Features. Here you can add, remove, or repair applications.

119. D. The dir command shows a directory listing. The /a switch displays only files with specified attributes.

120. D. Windows includes Windows Update, a feature designed to keep Windows current by automatically downloading and installing updates such as patches and security fixes. By default, Windows Update will run automatically when any administrator user is logged in. If you want to run it manually, however, you can always do so.

121. D. One Microsoft management tool allows you to manage hard drives, users and groups, scheduled tasks, and Event Viewer, and that tool is Computer Management. The executable file for Computer Management is COMPMGMT.MSC.

122. B. Available in Windows 7 and Windows 8, Action Center (Control Panel ➤ System and Security ➤ Action Center) is a central dialog for dealing with problems, security, and maintenance.

123. C, D. Windows XP Professional can be upgraded only to Windows Vista Business or Windows Vista Ultimate. Windows Vista Enterprise is typically installed as a clean install. It can be installed only as an "upgrade" to Windows Vista Business.

124. B. The user's TEMP directory is a user environment variable and is accessed through Users and Groups (or User Accounts).

125. D. FAT32 is lightweight and relatively fast. It allows for 32-bit cluster addressing, which provides for a maximum partition size of 2 terabytes (2,048 GB). It also includes smaller cluster sizes to avoid wasted space. FAT32 support is included in current Windows versions. FAT32 does not have individual file security permissions.

126. A. Windows Vista Home Basic is upgradeable to Windows 7 Home Premium or Windows 7 Ultimate but not Windows 7 Professional.

127. B. In Vista, Windows Security Center provides a single interface for firewall settings, automatic updating, malware protection, and other security settings. In Windows 7, other options were added, and it was renamed to Action Center.

128. C. Component Services is an MMC snap-in in Windows 7 that allows you to administer, as well as deploy, component services and configure behavior such as application-specific security. If you hear the terms *DCOM* or *COM+* mentioned in conjunction with Windows, Component Services is the tool needed for their management.

129. A. There is no direct upgrade path from Windows XP or Vista to Windows 8/8.1. You must do a clean installation. You can upgrade from Windows Vista to Windows 7 and then upgrade Windows 7 to Windows 8/8.1.

130. A. The format command is used to format hard drives. Before you format any drive, be sure that you have it backed up or are prepared to lose whatever is on it. The /fs:[filesystem] switch specifies the file system.

131. C. To revert to a previous configuration, you need to apply a restore point. Restore points are created and managed in the System Restore utility. A restore point is a copy of your system configuration at a given point in time. Restore points are useful for when Windows fails to boot but the computer appears to be fine otherwise, or when Windows doesn't seem to be acting right and you think it was because of a recent configuration change.

132. D. Duplexing is the means by which communication takes place. With full duplexing, the network card can send and receive at the same time. The main advantage of full-duplex over half-duplex communication is performance. NICs can operate twice as fast in full-duplex mode as they do normally in half-duplex mode.

133. C. Windows configuration information is stored in a special configuration database known as the Registry. This centralized database also contains environmental settings for various Windows programs. To edit the Registry, use the REGEDIT tool. Be careful, though, because an incorrect Registry change can render a system inoperable.

134. B. There are three tools that quickly show you CPU and memory usage in Windows. They are Resource Monitor, Performance Monitor, and Task Manager. The only one that lets you set up logs is Performance Monitor. It will collect counter information and then send that information to a console or event log.

135. D. Event Viewer is the Windows tool that allows you to view application error logs, security audit records, and system errors. It's available in most versions of Windows.

136. A. In Windows Vista and newer, you can reassign or change a drive letter by using the Disk Management utility.

137. B. Booting from a network card is referred to as a PXE (Pixie) boot. Netboot is the process of booting the entire OS from a network server, such as from a thin client.

138. D. Microsoft created ExFAT, and it is a proprietary file system of choice for flash drives where NTFS cannot be used (because of overhead), and FAT32 is not acceptable (because of file system limitations). It is ideal for SD cards that hold a lot of information, and it is supported in all current versions of Windows.

139. D. To connect to a printer over the network, you map a network printer. If the printer is on your local computer and you want others to use it, you need to share the printer. You do this by right-clicking the printer, choosing Printer Properties, and then going to the Sharing tab. Check the box to share the printer.

140. A. Windows supports both basic and dynamic storage. Basic storage can have a primary and an extended partition, while dynamic storage can be simple, spanned, or striped. In basic storage, Windows drives can be partitioned with primary or extended partitions. The difference is that extended partitions can be divided into one or more logical drives, and primary partitions cannot be further subdivided.

141. B. While in sleep mode, the computer uses very little power. When you turn it back on, all the applications you left open will still be open. Sleep uses a little more power than hibernate but also boots up faster. Shutting down will save the most battery life but will also take the longest to reboot. There is no resting power mode in Windows, but some configurations will offer a standby power mode.

142. C. New hard drives appear as not initialized in Windows. To use the disk, go into Disk Management and initialize the disk. Then you can create partitions, assign drive letters, and perform other disk management tasks.

143. B. An acronym for Authentic, Energetic, Reflective, and Open, Aero differs from previous GUIs in that its windows are translucent and it provides the ability to create a 3D stack of open windows and cycle through them (known as Flip 3D).

144. B, C. There are three types of volumes you can create in Disk Management: simple, spanned, striped, and mirrored. Simple volumes are on one disk. Spanned, striped, and mirrored will be made up of multiple physical disks.

145. A, C. BitLocker is available only for Windows 7 in the Enterprise and Ultimate editions.

146. A. You can use the Windows chkdsk command to create and display status reports for the hard disk. chkdsk can also correct file system problems (such as cross-linked files) and scan for and attempt to repair disk errors. The correct switch to automatically fix any issues is /f.

147. A, C. Windows supports both basic and dynamic storage. Basic storage can have a primary partition and an extended partition, while dynamic storage can be simple, spanned, or striped.

148. A. When formatting a hard drive, you can usually choose between a quick format or a full format. With a quick format, a new file table is created on the hard disk, but files are not fully overwritten or erased from the disk. A full format removes old files, creates a new file allocation table, and scans the hard drive for bad sectors. The scan is what takes so long.

149. B. The diskpart utility shows the partitions and lets you manage them on the computer's hard drives. Because of the enormous power it holds, membership in the Administrators local group (or equivalent) is required to run diskpart. diskpart replaced the older fdisk.

150. B. An unattended installation, as the name implies, is one in which you don't need to be sitting in front of the machine to complete the operation. The heart of an unattended installation is utilizing image deployment, which is sort of like copying an ideal image over from one machine to another.

151. B. The xcopy command is a more powerful version of copy. It lets you copy directories and also will copy file ownership and NTFS permissions. The /s switch is used to copy directories and subdirectories, except for empty ones. To copy those as well, use /e. The /h switch copies hidden and system files, and the /a switch copies only files with the Archive attribute set.

152. C. The Internet options in the Windows Control Panel utility allow you to configure Internet connections. It has six tabs: General, Security, Privacy, Connections, Programs, and Advanced. (Some versions of Windows also have a Content tab.) The home page is set from the General tab, and the pop-up blocker is enabled on the Privacy tab. Proxy settings are configured here as well, in the Connections tab.

153. D. Nearly all mobile operating systems now come with a virtual assistant. Cortana is the name of the Windows Phone (and Windows 10) virtual assistant. Windy is not currently the name of one. iOS uses Siri, and Amazon devices use Alexa.

154. C. DHCP servers provide TCP/IP configuration information to client computers. Clients will broadcast, searching for the DHCP server. The server will respond and provide the client with its IP address, subnet mask, default gateway, and other information. DHCP uses UDP ports 67 and 68.

155. A. The dd (data definition) command is used to copy files and can also be used to convert files from one format to another. It can also be used to copy blocks of data from a file and to back up the boot sector of the hard drive. The cp command will copy files but is not used for file conversion.

156. B. The International Mobile Subscriber Identity (IMSI) is a unique 15-digit identifier that describes a specific mobile user and their network. It's composed of three elements: a mobile country code, a mobile network code, and a mobile station identifier. The International Mobile Equipment Identity (IMEI) is also a 15-digit serial number, but it identifies the specific phone.

157. B. The command-line utility ping will send a short ICMP packet to the destination IP address you designate. Assuming the endpoint accepts and responds to the ICMP ping request, the source machine will receive a ping response. This in effect helps verify network connectivity.

158. B. DNS has one function on the network, and that is to resolve hostnames to IP addresses. For a computer or phone to open a website, it needs to know the IP address of that website. Each DNS server has a database, called a zone file, which maintains records of hostname to IP address mappings.

159. A, B. Legacy means that the system is old and hopelessly outdated by today's computing standards. Legacy systems are usually defined as those using old technology in one or more of the following areas: hardware, software (applications or OS), or network protocols.

160. D. The command-line utility netstat presents statistics related to the installed network interfaces. By default, on a Windows machine, running the command will display a list of connections and the associated protocol, the source and target address, and the current state of that connection.

161. D. To use an analogy, Finder is to MacOS what Windows Explorer is to Windows 7. It lets you browse through folders and find files, disks, apps, and so on. You can change the view to see the entries with images, a list view, a column view, and so on.

162. A. A virtual private network (VPN) is a secured network connection made over an unsecure network. For example, if you wanted to connect your phone to your corporate network over the Internet in order to read email but you also wanted to secure the connection, you could use a VPN. IMEI and IMSI are identifier numbers, and PRI and PRL are configuration lists the phone uses.

163. D. The utility tracert would list the path by successive connections or hops through the network.

164. A. The su command (switch user, substitute user, or super user) is used to start another shell on a Linux computer. Without specifying the username, it's assumed you are trying to start a shell with super user (or root) authority.

165. A. The utility `nslookup` will query the DNS server the computer is currently configured to use. The utility can be used to perform a variety of DNS queries.

166. D. The shell is the interpreter between the user and operating system. The most popular shell for Linux today is Bash (an acronym for Bourne Again Shell), but csh (C-shell), ksh (Korn shell), and a number of others are also in use. The terminal is used to enter commands and interface with the shell.

167. A. An authentication server is a device that examines the credentials of anyone trying to access the network, and it determines whether network access is granted. Said another way, they are gatekeepers and critical components to network security. A common term that you will hear in the Microsoft world is domain controller, which is a centralized authentication server.

168. C. A proxy server makes requests for resources on behalf of a client. Proxy servers are known for three things. One, the proxy server can cache the information requested, speeding up subsequent searches. Two, the proxy can act as a filter, blocking content from prohibited websites. Three, the proxy server can modify the requester's information when passing it to the destination, blocking the sender's identity and acting as a measure of security; the user can be made anonymous.

169. D. Whenever you visit a web page, you are making a connection from your device (the client) to a web server. To be more specific, a connection is requested by your Internet software (generally a web browser) using the Hypertext Transfer Protocol (HTTP) of the TCP/IP protocol suite. Your client needs to know the IP address of the web server, and it will make the request on port 80. Secure web connections are made using Hypertext Transfer Protocol Secure (HTTPS) and port 443.

170. B. The `df` (disk free) command is used to show free and used disk space on a volume. The `du` (disk usage) command is used to show disk usage per directory.

171. C. DNS has one function on the network, and that is to resolve hostnames to IP addresses. For a computer or phone to open a website, it needs to know the IP address of that website. The URL `www.google.com` means nothing to it. When a user enters the URL, the computer needs to figure out what the address is. The DNS server provides the answer, "That is 72.14.205.104." Now that the computer knows the address of the website that the user wants, it's able to go find it.

172. B. Mapping a network drive can be done at the command prompt by using the `net use` command.

173. C. Most mobile phones have three operating systems. The first is the primary OS, such as iOS or Android. Second, there is the baseband OS that manages all wireless communication, which is actually handled by a separate processor. Third, a subscriber identity module (SIM) OS manages all data transfers between the phone and the SIM chip, which is a small memory chip that stores user account information, phone identification, and security data, and it is generally tied to a specific carrier. Some people will call the wireless communications chips in a mobile phone the radio or the modem. Consequently, you might hear about radio firmware, a radio firmware update, or a modem update. The last two terms are interchangeable with baseband update, which simply means an update of the baseband OS.

174. A. Mac OS X Yosemite has the ability to create a recovery disk using the Recovery Disk Assistant. This can be used to boot the system in the event of a hard drive problem and to attempt to recover the hard drive.

175. A. The chown (change owner) command is used to change ownership of files in Linux.

176. A. Updates to MacOS Yosemite can be found at the App Store. Open it, and click Updates in the toolbar to see which updates are available. There will be an Install button to begin the installation. In System Preferences, there is generally a Software Update icon to help with updates as well.

177. B, C. The ifconfig command is used to view and change network settings, whereas iwconfig is used to view and change wireless network settings. The ipconfig command is used in Windows.

178. A, D. There are two ways to sync an iPhone: using Wi-Fi and using a USB connection. If you are going to use Wi-Fi, it must first be enabled in iTunes. The device should not be plugged into a USB port because that will take precedence over the Wi-Fi connection. Both devices must be on the same network SSID.

179. C, D. Both the commands net user and net users will perform the function to add or remove a user account on a Microsoft Windows system.

180. B. Email is critical for communication, and mail servers are responsible for sending, receiving, and managing email. There are three primary email protocols used today: SMTP (port 25), POP3 (port 110), and IMAP4 (port 143).

181. B. In Linux, the mv (move) command is used to rename files. The cp command copies a file, but that is a different process than moving it. rm is short for remove, and it deletes files. ren is a DOS or Windows command to rename files.

182. C. Apple produces iOS, and all of its apps can be found on the App Store. Google Play is used for Android-based devices, and it replaced Android Market. Windows Phone apps are found at the Windows Store.

183. B. The grep command (short for the impossibly long "globally search a regular expression and print") does just what it says it does: It searches for a string of text and then displays the results of what it found.

184. C. It's a fairly common myth that there are no MacOS viruses out there. The reality is that every operating system can be affected by malware. Because of this, it is imperative to have protection on every machine. Additionally, this protection—in the form of definition files—must be kept current and up-to-date. The best way to do that is to set the software to automatically update.

185. A. The Remote Disc feature lets you access files on a CD or DVD installed in one machine on a remote machine. This is handy if you need to retrieve files from a disc and the workstation at which you are sitting does not have a built-in drive.

186.   C, D. By appending the forward slash and question mark to nearly all commands at a Windows command prompt, you will be provided the expected usage and available options. For most commands now, the forward slash and *help* will also provide available options. By appending other words, it is also likely the command will fail with "Bad option" and display available options, too.

187.   B. The search feature within MacOS is Spotlight, and a magnifying glass icon in the upper-right corner of the menu bar represents it (or you can press Command+spacebar from any app). Spotlight can search for documents, images, apps, and so on.

188.   B. As great as MacOS is, there are times when you need Windows—for compatibility purposes with apps, legacy data, and many others. Because of this, you can use Boot Camp to install Windows on a Mac computer and then choose between operating systems as you boot. The Mac computer must be Intel-based, you need to have a 64-bit version of Windows, and you need a minimum of 30 GB of free disk space for it to work.

189.   D. The ls (list) command is used in Linux to show the contents of a directory.

190.   B. SMTP uses port 25, and IMAP4 uses port 143. However, when they run over SSL, SMTP uses port 465, and IMAP4 uses port 993. SMTP over TLS uses port 587, and POP3 over SSL or TLS uses port 995.

191.   D. The chmod (change mode) command is used in Linux to change file permissions.

192.   A. The Preferred Roaming List (PRL) is the reference guide the phone uses to connect to the proper cell phone tower when roaming. Product Release Instruction (PRI) contains settings for configuration items on the device that are specific to the network that it's on. Both PRI updates and PRL updates normally happen when the primary OS on the phone is updated, but your carrier may let you update them manually.

193.   A. The fsck (file system check) command is used to examine volumes for errors as well as attempt to fix them. The command is analogous to the chkdsk command for Windows-based computers. Be sure that the volume is unmounted before using fsck, to avoid corrupting data.

194.   A. An intrusion prevention system (IPS) is an active device. It monitors network traffic, and when it detects an anomaly, it can take actions to attempt to stop the attack. For example, if it senses suspicious inbound traffic on a specific IP port, it can shut the port down, block the sender, or reset the TCP connection.

195.   B. Android started off as its own company and was purchased by Google in 2005. Like Google's Chrome OS, Android is Linux-based. It's primarily installed on smartphones, but it is also found on specialized television, automobile, and wristwatch devices. Versions of Android are named after candy, such as Ice Cream Sandwich, Jelly Bean, KitKat, and Lollipop.

196.   D. Macs use the HFS+ file system, which Apple states does not require defragmentation as FAT or NTFS do. Therefore, disk defragmentation is not generally necessary. Regardless of the operating system, you should always back up data (unless you don't mind losing it), install and update antivirus software, and keep drivers and firmware current.

197. B. File servers provide a central repository for users to store, manage, and access files on the network. Networks can also use network attached storage (NAS) devices, which are stand-alone units that contain hard drives, come with their own file management software, and connect directly to the network. If a company has extravagant data storage needs, it can implement a storage area network (SAN). A SAN is basically a network segment, or collection of servers, that exists solely to store and manage data.

198. A. One of the best ways always to have the latest version of files, regardless of the device that you are using to access them, is to have them stored/accessed remotely. iCloud is Apple's answer to remote storage, and you can configure your Apple devices to place files there automatically or use it for backup.

199. D. The ps (process status) command in Linux is used to show currently running processes.

200. C. On a Mac, it's possible to run a large number of things at one time, whether those things in question are apps or Windows Desktops. Apple's Mission Control is an easy way to see what is open and switch between applications. To access Mission Control, you can press the Mission Control key on an Apple keyboard, click the Mission Control icon in Dock (or Launchpad), or swipe up with three or four fingers on a trackpad.

201. A. Passwords are not synchronized between devices. Types of data that are synchronized include contacts, programs, email, pictures, music, videos, calendar, bookmarks, documents, location data, social media data, and e-books.

202. D. The goal of unified threat management (UTM) is to centralize security management, allowing administrators to manage all of their security-related hardware and software through a single device or interface. A UTM device can generally provide the following types of services: packet filtering and inspection, intrusion protection service, gateway anti-malware, spam blocking, malicious website blocking, and application control.

203. C. SFC is a command-line utility that requires administrative privileges to run.

204. B. When an app hangs inside the Mac OS, you can use Force Quit to force it to close. Most devices, whether running Mac OS or iOS, offer similar options. You get to Force Quit by looking at the Apple menu or by pressing Command+Option+Esc, which is analogous to pressing Ctrl+Alt+Del on a PC.

205. C. On a Windows 10 Desktop, a user can manage his credentials by opening Credential Manager, which is found in under Control Panel.

206. A. Some mobile devices give you the option to improve the ability of the computer to recognize how you personally actuate the sensors. For example, many phones allow you to recalibrate (or retrain) the onscreen touch keyboard. That would be the first thing to try in this situation.

207. C. The International Mobile Equipment Identity (IMEI) is a 15-digit serial number that is unique to each phone. If a phone is reported stolen, the IMEI will be declared invalid. The IMEI can be displayed on most phones by dialing *#06#. AT&T and T-Mobile were the first networks to use IMEI. The International Mobile Subscriber Identity (IMSI) is also a unique 15-digit identifier, but it describes a specific mobile user and his network.

208. D. The `passwd` command is used in Linux to change user passwords. The similar-looking `pwd` command displays the current directory.

209. B. The backup software for all current versions of MacOS is called Time Machine. It allows users to back up and restore files just like any other commercial backup software.

210. D. Google offers the Android operating system to the mobile community under an open-source license. Apple and Microsoft keep their mobile OSs closed source, and they manage all the development and marketing of their operating systems. BlackBerry OS was closed source as well. Apps for mobile operating systems are created using a free software development kit (SDK). Android apps are installed using an Android application package (APK).

211. C. The du (disk usage) command will show how much disk space is being used. By default, it shows usage in disk blocks, which isn't very reader-friendly. Use the -h option to show it in kilobytes, megabytes, and so on, and use the -a option to show all files and directories. To use both together, the syntax would be du *-ah/[volume_name].*

212. C. The `vi` command (shortened from `visual`) is used to open a window-oriented text editor in Linux. The `cd` command is for change directory, `ps` lists processes, and `cp` is copy.

213. D. Sync Center in Windows 10 (from Windows 7 and after) allows users to select a folder or particular files and maintain synchronization between the local system and an offline location, such as, for example, on a network server.

214. B. Depending on the variant of Linux you are running, `apt` (Advanced Package Tool) can be useful in getting the patches from a repository site and downloading them for installation. The most common command used with this tool is `apt-get`, which, as the name implies, gets the package for installation.

215. D. The `taskkill` command is a command-line command, which typed with a task ID number, will kill that process. The command must be done with a command prompt window with administrative privileges.

216. C, D. To interact with a mobile operating system, people can use gesture-based interaction, or gestures. Mobile devices also have emergency notifications built-in, for Amber alerts or government-declared emergencies. Software development kits (SDKs) are available for nearly all OSs, as are power options.

217. D. Screen sharing is a MacOS feature that allows you to share your screen with others. It requires a Virtual Network Computing (VNC) connection.

218. D. Chrome OS was designed by Google, and may be installed on tablets, smartphones, laptops and desktops alike.

219. B. BranchCache is a network optimization feature found in the Windows OS, from version 8 onward. Network bandwidth is optimized as web content from a WAN connection and is cached locally. Local machines then fetch the web content from one or more servers (hosted mode) or from other local clients (distributed).

220.   C. GUID Partition Table (GPT) does not require an extended partition as needed by MBR. MBR is also limited to 2 TB drives, while the more modern GPT has no such limitation.

221.   A. Deployment Image Servicing and Management (dism) is used to prepare and mount a Windows Desktop image. The chkdisk tool identifies damaged disk sectors, while the diskpart tool will clean and format a disk partition. The netstat tool provides various network statistics.

222.   B. Storage spaces will pool together multiple hard drives, similar to creating a RAID set. Disk management also provides this feature.

223.   C. Wireless WAN (WWAN) is an option in Windows 10, provided it is enabled by the hardware, likely in the BIOS. WWAN provides Internet connectivity via cellular use.

224.   D. Quality of Service is not a networking technology just in Windows; in Windows Server 2016, an administrator can define a QoS policy to limit network bandwidth. The Differentiated Services Code Point (DSCP) is not a stand-alone policy but one of the values in configuring QoS.

225.   A. Remembering the passwords for various websites is easily managed in MacOS with Keychain.

226.   C. Indeed, Linux is open source, meaning a user has the choice to alter the underlying code as it suits their needs, then recompile for use. Clearly, Windows is more expensive and is the more popular target for exploits. There are several Linux OS varieties.

227.   A. Apple almost never gives a date to formally declare an OS version as end-of-life. Microsoft routinely announces a product's end-of-life, but also often provides extensions for business. Linux varieties do announce end-of-life, particularly those commercially managed, such as Red Hat.

228.   A. Unlike Microsoft Windows or Linux, the Apple Macintosh OS is typically issued updates specific to the type of workstation or device family. For example, an OS update may be developed for the 2018 Touch Bar MBP one day, while the 2018 MacBook Air update will be distributed separately a few months later.

229.   C. Windows 7 Home is not capable of joining a domain. In the configuration dialog box for joining as a member a domain or workgroup, the Windows 7 Home edition has domain grayed out. The other three editions offer you to join either a domain or workgroup.

230.   A. Windows Media Center was discontinued by Microsoft in 2009 in Windows 7. Microsoft offered it for Windows 8 and 8.1 only as a Media Center Pack add-on. Windows 10 does not support WMC at all.

231.   A, C. Both solid state/flash drives or external/hot-swappable drives can be set up as Windows installation media relatively easily. And once started, installation can be automated with an answer/unattended file. The DVD or CD-ROM cannot be used since the systems are without optical drives.

232.   A. The Windows 10 version 1803 update creates its "OEM partition," or what's known as a factory recovery partition. This assists with recovering from a corrupted operating system. The created partition is typically about 450MB in size.

233.   A. USB boot drives are typically formatted as NTFS. However, Windows 8 is a UEFI system, cannot boot from a NTFS formatted device. A boot drive for Windows 8 must formatted as FAT32. In this scenario, the boot drive will not boot.

234.   C. Compatibility mode is for this purpose and can be set as far back as Windows 95. Relying on vendors for updated versions or identifying a modern replacement is uncertain at best. Maintain a series of older systems is a security risk, assuming end-of-life has passed.

235.   D. The command line utility gpresult. The switch /scope displays results for either user or computer results. Values for the /scope switch can be either a user or a computer. Without the /scope switch, gpresult shows both user and computer settings.

236.   C. User account management is performed in Windows 10 for a variety of predictable actions such as create or delete a user, grant or deny privileges, change a password. Also included is the ability to sync Windows settings like theme, language preference and Internet Explorer settings across users. However, Internet access over the network is likely granted at a perimeter network device. Getting a printer involves procurement, while wiping a partition involves disk management.

237.   A. To check drive status, type wmic at a command prompt. At the WMIC prompt, type diskdrive get status. The command's response is (hopefully) Status OK. If a drive is failing, you will see a different response, for example "Pred Fail," which generally points to many bad sectors.

238.   A. Splitting partitions means to create two partitions from one. To split a partition, you first shrink the partition, then create a new, second partition from the unallocated space. No need for more destructive measures or returning the system.

239.   D. Given your escalated privileges, you can adjust the printer for the user's print job within the Windows Control Panel. Right-clicking on the particular printer, you open "Printing Preferences" to make the change. Not all printers have a display panel for adjusting settings. Even so, other users do not want the changed settings to apply to their print jobs. Delaying or directing a user elsewhere are simply unacceptable options, give your capacity to help.

240.   B. The Sound settings are under Control Panel, under Hardware. While forwarding the video to try on a different laptop is sound troubleshooting, it's unlikely a silent video is the cause.

241.   B. After the tool finishes its analysis, the tool issues a Troubleshooting report listing both "Issues Found" and "Potential issues that were checked."

242.   D. The user confirmed the desktop has enough drive space and RAM. The likely problem is the user's desktop is running a desktop OS, such as Windows 10, but trying to install an application intended for a server OS, such as Windows Server 2019. The desktop fails to meet OS requirements and is an OS compatibility issue.

243.   B. If the installation process fails with a message about the system directory, it's likely the local user does not have permissions or privileges to install the application. The message said nothing about hardware requirements and proposing a different installation directory would not stop the installation requiring access to the system directory.

244.   A. The IT administrator should not copy company critical data to a public facing server. This is a security concern and poses a high risk to the data. The other options may be legitimate but are hardly as significant as the security risk.

245.   C. If the user had regularly updated antivirus/anti-malware updates, ransomware might have been caught and quarantined or deleted before encrypting the user's data.

246.   B. Knowing the user installed an older distro image suggests incompatibility issues between the distro and installed applications, assumed newer. The user should have used a new version of the distro and after installing, ran commands such as `apt-get update` or `apt-get dist-upgrade`.

247.   B. Had the user been regularly performing backups on a backup server, the data would be recoverable.

248.   A. Given the information provided, the hard drive seems to be having performance or corruption issues. If the user had adopted the best practice of doing scheduled disk maintenance, its likely issues would have been avoided or identified earlier.

249.   D. If the user had regularly done patch management, the malware likely would not have been to exploit their system.

250.   D. Given the information provided, it seems the user could consider updating the desktop's firmware.

251.   B. Time Machine is a native Mac OS application installed on all Mac OS systems. Time Machine is used for creating backup images. You can exclude particular files or folders. The backup files are stored on an external drive, but you can also create snapshots and save them locally.

252.   A. Timeshift is a popular application used to maintain Linux file system files and settings. Timeshift is not the application used to back up your personal files or documents.

253.   A. Terminal is the tool that most resembles the command box in Windows or the Linux terminal. For the Mac OS, Terminal is actually a terminal emulator, which is just as capable for browsing the file system or running utilities like ping.

254.   A. The application Disk Utility is native to every Mac OS desktop and can perform on both local and external drives. Timeshift is a Linux OS tool for system file backup and recovery. Sophos Home for Mac is an antivirus tool. VmStat monitors statistics on virtual memory, CPU activity and other system data, but it is for Linux systems. Mac OS has a similar tool named vm_stat.

255.   D. Unlike any single tool for Microsoft Windows, Mac OS has a tool which offers a diverse range of sharing capabilities. The tool Sharing is used for sharing the screen, files, peripherals, Bluetooth, and Internet access as well as a variety of remote management capabilities.

256.   C. Keychain is the password management tool that's native to Mac OS, meaning it comes pre-installed with the desktop OS.

257.   B. Spotlight indexes files and folders, beginning to show resuls as you type in the search box, located at the top right of any Finder window, the file explorer application.

258.   D. Gestures is a feature that allows you to customize multi-finger gestures on the touchpad to then launch an application. Gestures is available on both Mac OS and Linux OS.

259.   D. The commands kill and killall are used to terminate running processes. The biggest difference is, the kill command is followed by the process ID number. The killall command can terminate a named process.

Chapter 7: Security

1.   C. Patches and updates should be applied regardless of the severity of the issue. In addition, they should be applied immediately. Use Windows Update to manage the process for you.

2.   C. A strong Windows password will help protect Windows but does not protect the computer in general. If a user can get into the BIOS, then he can change the boot sequence, boot to a CD, and do some damage to the system. The way to protect against this is to implement a BIOS/UEFI password.

3.   D. Firewalls are among the first lines of defense in a network. The basic purpose of a firewall is to isolate one network from another. Firewalls function as one or more of the following: packet filter, proxy firewall, or stateful inspection firewall.

4.   A, C. Biometric locks and privacy filters are physical security methods. Multifactor authentication may require a physical device (for example, something you have) but not necessarily. Firewalls can be hardware devices but can also be software packages.

5.   C. Social engineering is a process in which an attacker attempts to acquire information about your network and system by social means, such as talking to people in the organization. A social engineering attack may occur over the phone, over email, or in person. The intent is to acquire access information, such as user IDs and passwords.

6. C. Anytime there is more than one authentication method required, it's multifactor authentication. In this case, it does involve using biometrics, but the passcode is not a biometric factor. Multifactor authentication usually requires two of the following three types of inputs: something you know (password), something you have (smart token), or something you are (biometrics).

7. C. Tailgating refers to being so close to someone when they enter a building that you are able to come in right behind them without needing to use a key, a card, or any other security device. Using mantraps, which are devices such as small rooms that limit access to one or a few individuals, is a great way to stop tailgating.

8. B. Adding RobertS to the Administrators group will certainly work, but it's not the recommended approach. Since members of the Administrators group have such power, they can inadvertently do harm (such as accidentally deleting a file that a regular user could not). To protect against this, the practice of logging in with an Administrators group account for daily interaction is strongly discouraged. Instead, system administrators should log in with a user account (lesser privileges) and change to the Administrators group account (elevated privileges) only when necessary.

9. A, B. Biometric authentication requires identification of a physical feature of the user, such as a fingerprint or facial scan. DNA is considered a form of biometric authentication, but it's not commonly used today with mobile devices. (Imagine your phone needing to collect blood or saliva to authenticate you—no thanks!)

10. D. If you're using FAT32 and want to change to NTFS, the convert utility will allow you to do so. For example, to change the E: drive to NTFS, the command is convert e: / fs:ntfs.

11. D. When there are conflicting NTFS permissions, generally they are combined, and the most liberal is granted. The exception to that is when there is an explicit Deny. That overrides any allowed permissions.

12. C. Microsoft wanted to create a group in Windows that was not as powerful as the Administrators group, which is how the Power Users group came into being. The idea was that membership in this group would be given Read/Write permission to the system, allowing members to install most software but keeping them from changing key operating system files. However, after Windows 7, the Power Users group now assigns permissions equivalent to the Standard user Users Group.

13. C. When assigning user permissions, follow the principle of least privilege; give users only the bare minimum that they need to do their job. Assign permissions to groups rather than users, and make users members of groups (or remove them from groups) as they change roles or positions.

14. D. An unauthorized router with a seemingly legitimate configuration is specifically known as an evil twin. Those can lead to man-in-the-middle attacks, which involve clandestinely placing something (such as a piece of software or a rogue router) between a server and the user, and neither the server's administrator nor the user is aware of it. The man-in-the-middle intercepts data and then sends the information to the server as if nothing is wrong. The man-in-the-middle software may be recording information for someone to view later, altering it, or in some other way compromising the security of your system and session.

15. B. Companies normally generate a huge amount of paper, most of which eventually winds up in dumpsters or recycle bins. Dumpsters may contain information that is highly sensitive in nature, and attackers may seek it out by practicing dumpster diving. In high-security and government environments, sensitive papers should be either shredded or burned.

16. B, D. You should rename the default account and always require strong passwords. In Windows, you are unable to disable the Administrator account or remove it from the Administrators group.

17. A. A virtual private network (VPN) is a private network connection that occurs through a public network. VPNs make use of tunneling, which sends private data across a public network by placing (encapsulating) that data into other packets. Even though a VPN is created through the Internet or other public networks, the connection logically appears to be part of the local network.

18. B, D. NTFS permissions affect users regardless if they are at the local computer or accessing the resource across the network. They can also be applied to individual files, whereas Share permissions can be applied only to folders. One set of permissions is not inherently more restrictive than the other, as either type can be used to deny access in a given situation (at least when accessing across the network).

19. B. An ID badge is worn by employees to identify them. Some companies use different colored badges to indicate different functions or security privileges. Most ID badges have a picture of the user on them to prevent unauthorized use.

20. C. A locator app is what you need. Apple supplies a free app called Find My iPhone that, together with iCloud, allows multiple mobile devices and Macs to be located if powered on and attached to the Internet (via 4G, 3G, Wi-Fi, Ethernet, and so on). The app allows the device to be controlled remotely to lock it, play a sound (even if audio is off), display a message, or wipe it clean.

21. A. File systems such as NTFS, and security devices such as firewalls, can track security in access control lists (ACLs). ACLs can hold permissions for local users and groups, and each entry in the ACL can also specify what type of access is given. This allows a great deal of flexibility in setting up a network.

22. C, D. The four common file attributes are Read-only, Archive, System, and Hidden (remember the acronym RASH). They can be implemented on FAT32 or NTFS volumes and changed by anyone with proper access. On NTFS volumes, you can also compress or encrypt files as part of Advanced attributes. At a command prompt, the `attrib` command is used to change attributes. In Windows, right-click the file, choose Properties, and look for Attributes on the General tab.

23. A. The systems are not up-to-date and therefore are more vulnerable to attacks. These systems are considered noncompliant systems. It's a violation of security best practices to fail to keep all software on your network up-to-date.

24. B. Acceptable use policies (AUPs) describe how the employees in an organization can use company systems and resources, both software and hardware. This policy should also outline the consequences for misuse. In addition, the policy (also known as a use policy) should address the installation of personal software on company computers and the use of personal hardware such as USB devices.

25. B. BitLocker Drive Encryption allows you to use drive encryption to protect files—including those needed for startup and logon. This is available only with Windows 10 Professional and Enterprise versions, Windows 8 (Pro and Enterprise), and Windows 7 (Enterprise and Ultimate). For removable drives, BitLocker To Go provides the same encryption technology to help prevent unauthorized access to the files stored on them.

26. C. Spyware differs from other malware in that it works—often actively—on behalf of a third party. Rather than self-replicating, like viruses and worms, spyware is spread to machines by users who inadvertently ask for it. The users often don't know they have asked for it but have done so by downloading other programs, visiting infected sites, and so on. The spyware program monitors the user's activity and responds by offering unsolicited pop-up advertisements (sometimes known as adware), gathers information about the user to pass on to marketers, or intercepts personal data such as credit card numbers.

27. C. Jelica should have a non-administrative account to use for day-to-day tasks. And Jelica also needs an account with administrative privileges to perform the administrative duties. When creating user accounts, follow the principle of least privilege: Give users only the permissions they need to do their work and no more. This is especially true with administrators. Those users should be educated on how each of the accounts should be used.

28. A, C. Password attacks occur when an account is attacked repeatedly. This is accomplished by using applications known as password crackers, which send possible passwords to the account in a systematic manner. Two types of password attacks are brute-force and dictionary attacks.

29. C. All the options will increase the security of an iPhone. For just the basic level of security, though, enable a screen lock. A user will need to enter a code to gain access to the device. It's typically enough to thwart casual snoops and would-be hackers.

30. A. An authenticator app can help securely verify your identity online, regardless of the account you want to log into. Different apps work in different ways, but the general procedure is that the app will generate a random code for you to type in along with your username and password. The random code helps identify you and tells the site you are logging into that you really are who you say you are.

31. B. A dictionary attack uses a dictionary of common words to attempt to find the user's password. Dictionary attacks can be automated, and several tools exist in the public domain to execute them. As an example of this type of attack, imagine guessing words and word combinations found in a standard English-language dictionary. The policy you have recommended could also help thwart those who may try to look over a shoulder to see a user's password, but they can still see it whether it's a common word or not.

32. A. Trojan horses are programs that enter a system or network under the guise of another program. A Trojan horse may be included as an attachment or as part of an installation program. The Trojan horse can create a back door or replace a valid program during installation. It then accomplishes its mission under the guise of another program.

33. C. A large electromagnet can be used to destroy any magnetic media, such as a hard drive or backup tape set. The most common of these is the degaussing tool. Degaussing involves applying a strong magnetic field to initialize the media (this is also sometimes referred to as disk wiping). This process helps ensure that information doesn't fall into the wrong hands.

34. A. Spyware differs from other malware in that it works—often actively—on behalf of a third party. Rather than self-replicating, like viruses and worms, spyware is spread to machines by users who inadvertently ask for it. The users often don't know they have asked for it but have done so by downloading other programs, visiting infected sites, and so on. The spyware program monitors the user's activity and responds by offering unsolicited pop-up advertisements (sometimes known as adware), gathers information about the user to pass on to marketers, or intercepts personal data such as credit card numbers.

35. D. When a file or folder is copied on NTFS volumes, the new file or folder will inherit its permissions from its new parent folder. The old permissions will be discarded. However, when files and folders are moved, versus copying them, the original permissions are retained at the new location.

36. B. Users should never leave a company notebook computer, tablet computer, or smartphone in a position where it can be stolen or compromised while they are away from the office. USB locks or cable locks should be used to keep notebook computers securely in place whenever users are not near their devices.

37. D. Key fobs are named after the chains that used to hold pocket watches to clothes. They are security devices that you carry with you; they display a randomly generated code that you can then use for authentication. This code usually changes very quickly (every 60 seconds is probably the average), and you combine this code with your PIN for authentication. RSA is one of the most well-known vendors of key fobs. These may also be called security tokens.

38. A. Antivirus software is an application that is installed on a system to protect it and to scan for viruses as well as worms and Trojan horses. Most viruses have characteristics that are common to families of viruses. Antivirus software looks for these characteristics, or fingerprints, to identify and neutralize viruses before they impact you. Antivirus software needs to be constantly updated to ensure that it can detect the most current viruses.

39. B. Impersonation is an attempt by someone or something to masquerade as someone else. You might think of impersonation attacks as affecting network systems, but they can affect phone systems as well.

40. C. Because Graham is accessing the NTFS-based resource over the network, both NTFS and Share permissions are applied. If there is a difference between the two of them, the most restrictive permissions are used. Therefore, Graham has Read access only.

41. C. It is never a good idea to put any media in a workstation if you do not know where it came from or what it is. The simple reason is that said media (CD, DVD, USB) could contain malware. Compounding matters, that malware could be referenced in the autorun.inf file, causing it to be summoned when the media is inserted in the machine and requiring no other action.

42. C. NTFS permissions can affect users logged on locally or across the network to the system where the NTFS permissions are applied. Share permissions are in effect only when the user connects to the resource via the network.

43. D. Polymorphic (literally, many forms) viruses change form to avoid detection. These types of viruses attack your system, display a message on your computer, and delete files on your system. The virus will attempt to hide from your antivirus software. Frequently, the virus will encrypt parts of itself to avoid detection. When the virus does this, it's referred to as mutation. The mutation process makes it hard for antivirus software to detect common characteristics of the virus.

44. C. Rootkits are software programs that have the ability to hide certain things from the operating system; they do so by obtaining (and retaining) administrative-level access. With a rootkit, there may be a number of processes running on a system that don't show up in Task Manager, or connections that don't appear in a Netstat display may be established or available—the rootkit masks the presence of these items.

45. D. Encrypting File System (EFS) is available in most editions of Windows, and it allows for encryption/decryption of files stored in NTFS volumes. All users can use EFS, whereas only administrators can turn on BitLocker. It does not require any special hardware, while BitLocker benefits from having the Trusted Platform Module (TPM). As an additional distinction, EFS can encrypt just one file, if so desired, while BitLocker encrypts the whole volume and whatever is stored on it.

46. D. Anti-malware software will help protect computers from malicious programs. Typically, anti-malware does everything that antivirus software does as well as identify threats beyond just viruses. A lot of anti-malware software is marketed as antivirus software.

47. C. Administrative shares are created on servers running Windows on the network for administrative purposes. These shares can differ slightly based on which OS is running, but they always end with a dollar sign ($) to make them hidden. There is one for each volume on a hard drive (c$, d$, and so on), as well as admin$ (the root folder—usually c:\winnt) and print$ (where the print drivers are located). These are created for use by administrators and usually require administrator privileges to access.

48. B. NTFS permissions are able to protect you at the file level as well as the folder level. Share permissions can be applied to the folder level only.

49. B. Since the user and the volume are on the same computer, only NTFS permissions are in effect. Share and NTFS permissions are both consulted only when accessing an NTFS resource across the network. Then, the most restrictive permission set between the two is applied.

50. A. Security tokens are anything that a user must have on them to access network resources, and they are often associated with devices that enable the user to generate a one-time password authenticating their identity. SecurID, from RSA, is one of the best-known examples of a physical security token. ID badges can have security mechanisms built in, but not all do.

51.　B. Users should lock their computers when they leave their desks, but there should also be a screen lock/time-out setting configured on every workstation to prevent them from inadvertently becoming an open door to the network. A password should be required before the user can begin their session again.

52.　A, B. If your intent is to physically destroy the drive, you have a few options. They include shredders (not the paper kind but ones that can handle metal), a drill or hammer, and incineration. Although these methods can be fun, they can also be dangerous, so be sure to use adequate safety measures.

53.　C. There are trusted software sources that you know and work with all the time (such as Microsoft or HP) and there are untrusted sources, and you should differentiate between them. Don't use or let your users use untrusted software sources. Generally, common sense can be your guide, but there are "safe lists" of trusted software vendors from authoritative watchdog companies such as Comodo.

54.　C. There isn't any one universal solution to wireless access point placement; it depends a lot on the environment. As a general rule, the greater the distance the signal must travel, the more it will attenuate, but you can lose a signal quickly in a short space as well if the building materials reflect or absorb it. You should try to avoid placing access points near metal (which includes appliances) or near the ground. They should be placed in the center of the area to be served and high enough to get around most obstacles. Note that of all current 802.11 standards, only 802.11ac offers directional antennae. All other standards are omnidirectional, meaning that the signal transmits in all directions.

55.　C. When a hole is found in a web browser or other software and attackers begin exploiting it the very day it is discovered by the developer (bypassing the one- to two-day response time that many software providers need to put out a patch once the hole has been found), it is known as a zero-day attack (or exploit).

56.　C. Changing the default username, password, and SSID are all good measures to take when installing a new router. Another good step is to update the firmware. It's possible that new firmware was introduced while your device was sitting on a shelf somewhere, and it's always smart to be up-to-date.

57.　D. When a hole is found in a web browser or other software and attackers begin exploiting it the very day it is discovered by the developer (bypassing the one- to two-day response time that many software providers need to put out a patch once the hole has been found), it is known as a zero-day attack (or exploit). Because the vulnerability is so new, developers have not had a chance to patch the issue, and anti-malware software will not yet be updated to detect the attack signature.

58.　C. A multipartite virus attacks your system in multiple ways. It may attempt to infect your boot sector, infect all your executable files, and destroy your application files. The hope on the part of the attacker is that you won't be able to correct all the problems and will allow the infestation to continue.

59.　D. BYOD policies are becoming more common in corporate environments. Be sure to have a policy in place to clearly spell out security requirements and user expectations before the employees bring their own devices. Most companies require employees to sign the agreement to acknowledge that they have read it and understand it.

60. C. Privacy filters are either film or glass add-ons that are placed over a monitor or laptop screen to prevent the data on the screen from being readable when viewed from the sides. Only the user sitting directly in front of the screen is able to read the data.

61. C. Software running on infected computers called zombies is often known as a botnet. Bots, by themselves, are but a form of software that runs automatically and autonomously and are not harmful. *Botnet*, however, has come to be the word used to describe malicious software running on a zombie and under the control of a bot-herder. Denial of service attacks—DoS and DDoS—can be launched by botnets, as can many forms of adware, spyware, and spam (via spambots).

62. A. When there are conflicting NTFS permissions, generally they are combined, and the most liberal is granted. This holds true for conflicting permissions between groups or between a user's account and group memberships.

63. B. Since Alexandra is sitting at the computer, only NTFS permissions are in effect. Share permissions apply only when accessing the shared resource over the network. Therefore, her effective permission level is Read and Write.

64. A. A firewall operating as a packet filter passes or blocks traffic to specific addresses based on the type of application and the port used. The packet filter doesn't analyze the data of a packet; it decides whether to pass it based on the packet's addressing information. For instance, a packet filter may allow web traffic on port 80 and block Telnet traffic on port 23. This type of filtering is included in many routers.

65. C. Biometric devices use physical characteristics to identify the user. Biometric systems include fingerprint/palm/hand scanners, retinal scanners, and soon, possibly, DNA scanners. To gain access to resources, you must pass a physical screening process.

66. A. BitLocker allows you to use drive encryption to protect files—including those needed for startup and logon. This is available only with more complete editions of Windows 10 Professional and Enterprise versions, Windows 8 (Pro and Enterprise), and Windows 7 (Enterprise and Ultimate). For removable drives, BitLocker To Go provides the same encryption technology to help prevent unauthorized access to the files stored on them.

67. A. A retrovirus attacks or bypasses the antivirus software installed on a computer. You can consider a retrovirus to be an anti-antivirus. Retroviruses can directly attack your antivirus software and potentially destroy the virus definition database file. When this information is destroyed without your knowledge, you would be left with a false sense of security. The virus may also directly attack an antivirus program to create bypasses for itself.

68. C. What is known as a low-level format now is drastically different than it was years ago. The intent is the same, though, and that is to erase all data on the hard drive so it's not recoverable. Technically, the low-level format needs to happen first. Think of it as laying out walls for a building. Once the walls are laid out, the standard format can come along and decide what goes where.

69. D. When MAC address filtering is used, the administrator compiles a list of the MAC addresses associated with the users' computers and enters them. When a client attempts to connect, an additional check of the MAC address is performed. If the address appears in the list, the client is allowed to join; otherwise, they are forbidden from so doing. Many consider this a form of security, but when used by itself, it's pretty weak. Someone with a packet sniffer could spoof a MAC address and join the network.

70. B. A worm is different from a virus in that it can reproduce itself, it's self-contained, and it doesn't need a host application to be transported. Many of the so-called viruses that have made the news were actually worms. Worms can use TCP/IP, email, Internet services, or any number of possibilities to reach their target.

71. B. Email filtering, as the name implies, involves filtering email before passing it on. This can be done with messages intended both to enter and to leave the network, and it can head off problems before they can propagate. One of the simplest filters is the spam filter included with most email programs.

72. D. The Full Control permission gives the user all the other permissions and the ability to change permissions for others. The user can also take ownership of the directory or any of its contents. There is no Change Permissions standard NTFS permission.

73. D. A brute-force attack is an attempt to guess passwords until a successful guess occurs. Because of the nature of this attack, it usually occurs over a long period of time, but automated programs can do it quickly. In this situation, you might have been tempted to choose a dictionary attack, but the defining characteristic of those attacks is the use of common words, which was not part of this question. (Brute force can be combined with dictionary attacks as well.)

74. A, D. A mantrap and privacy filters are physical security methods. They will not prevent software-based attacks. Firewalls can block malicious network traffic, and anti-malware can block malicious software such as viruses and worms.

75. D. A certificate of destruction (or certificate of recycling) may be required for audit purposes. Such a certificate, usually issued by the organization carrying out the destruction, is intended to verify that the asset was properly destroyed and usually includes serial numbers, type of destruction done, and so on.

76. B. The best rule of thumb is that if your OS vendor provides an update, you should install it as soon as possible. Some companies do want their corporate IT groups to vet the update first, but it's still always a best practice to update sooner rather than later.

77. B. Share and NTFS permissions are both consulted when accessing an NTFS resource across the network. The most restrictive permission set between the two is applied. If there are no explicit Allow or Deny share permissions set, though, then only the NTFS permissions apply.

78. B. If you attempt to run some utilities (such as SFC) from a standard command prompt, you will be told that you must be an administrator running a console session in order to continue. Rather than opening a standard command prompt, choose Start ➤ All Programs ➤ Accessories and then right-click Command Prompt and choose Run As Administrator. The UAC will prompt you to continue, and then you can run SFC without a problem.

79. C. When users are granted NTFS permissions from multiple groups, their effective permissions are cumulative, or the most liberal of the permissions assigned. In this case, Write also gives the ability to Read; therefore, the user has both.

80. B. A smart card is a type of badge or card that gives you access to resources, including buildings, parking lots, and computers. It contains information about your identity and access privileges. A protected computer or area has a badge reader in which you insert your card. In the case of using Radio Frequency Identification (RFID), the reader is a wireless, no-contact technology and the user does not need to touch the card to the reader.

81. A. A spoofing attack is an attempt by someone or something to masquerade as someone else. This type of attack is usually considered an access attack. The most popular spoofing attacks today are IP spoofing, ARP spoofing, and DNS spoofing. This is an example of IP spoofing, where the goal is to make the data look as if it came from a trusted host when it didn't (thus spoofing the IP address of the sending host).

82. A. A smart card is a type of badge or card that gives you access to resources, including buildings, parking lots, and computers. It contains information about your identity and access privileges. Each area or computer has a card scanner or a reader in which you insert your card. Radio Frequency Identification (RFID) is the wireless, no-contact technology used with these cards and their accompanying reader.

83. A. There are generally three wireless encryption methods available. From least to most secure, they are WEP, WPA, and WPA2. Always go with WPA2 unless strange circumstances prevent you from doing so.

84. A. Companies normally generate a huge amount of paper, most of which eventually winds up in dumpsters or recycle bins. Dumpsters may contain information that is highly sensitive in nature, and attackers may seek it out by practicing dumpster diving. In high-security and government environments, sensitive papers should be either shredded or burned.

85. B, C. Social engineering is a process in which an attacker attempts to acquire information about your network and system by social means, such as talking to people in the organization. When this is done via email or instant messaging, it's called phishing.

86. D. Tailgating refers to being so close to someone when they enter a building that you are able to come in right behind them without needing to use a key, a card, or any other security device. Using mantraps, which are devices such as small rooms that limit access to one or a few individuals, is a great way to stop tailgating. Revolving doors can also help prevent tailgating.

87. B. On the chance that the signal is actually traveling too far, some access points include power level controls that allow you to reduce the amount of output provided.

88. A. This is an example of spear phishing, which is a specific form of social engineering. With spear phishing, the attacker uses information that the target would be less likely to question because it appears to be coming from a trusted source (when, in reality, the attacker in this case has hacked a friend's email account). Because it appears far more likely to be a legitimate message, it cuts through your standard defenses like a spear, and the likelihood that you would click this link is higher.

89. A. Social engineering is a process in which an attacker attempts to acquire information about your network and system by social means, such as talking to people in the organization. A social engineering attack may occur over the phone, by email, or in person. When the attempt is made through email or instant messaging, it is known as phishing, and it's often made to look as if a message is coming from sites where users are likely to have accounts (banks, eBay, and PayPal are popular).

90. A. If you have an open-access building but then need people to access a secured area, one way to provide security is through a guard. An access list or entry control roster should then exist to identify specifically who can enter and can be verified by the guard or someone with authority.

91. A. The Administrator account is the most powerful of all: It has the power to do everything from the smallest task all the way up to removing the operating system. Because of the power it wields, you should rename the account and assign it a strong password.

92. B. Many viruses will announce that you're infected as soon as they gain access to your system. They may take control of your system and flash annoying messages on your screen or destroy your hard disk. When this occurs, you'll know that you're a victim. Other viruses will cause your system to slow down, cause files to disappear from your computer, or take over your disk space. Many viruses today are spread using email. The infected system attaches a file to any email that you send to another user. The recipient opens this file, thinking it's something that you legitimately sent them. When they open the file, the virus infects the target system.

93. A. Configure user account settings so that there are a limited number of login attempts (three is a good number) before the account is locked for a period of time. Legitimate users who need to get in before the block expires can contact the administrator and explain why they weren't able to give the right password three times in a row, and illegitimate users will go away in search of another system to try to enter.

94. D. One form of social engineering is shoulder surfing, and it involves nothing more than watching someone when they enter their sensitive data. They can see you entering a password, typing in a credit card number, or entering any other pertinent information. The best defense against this type of attack is simply to survey your environment before entering personal data.

95. A. Content filtering is the process of blocking objectionable content, from either websites or email. Many routers and firewalls will provide content filtering services. In many cases, a reference service is used to block websites, and filters can be implemented to scan emails for prohibited content.

96. C. One method of "protecting" the network that is often recommended is to turn off the SSID broadcast. The access point is still there and can still be accessed by those who know of it, but it prevents those who are looking at a list of available networks from finding it. This should be considered a weak form of security because there are still ways, albeit a bit more complicated, to discover the presence of the access point besides the SSID broadcast.

97. D. In a Windows domain, password policies can be configured at the domain level using Group Policy objects. Variables that you can configure include password complexity and length and the time between allowed changes to passwords.

98. C. Sometimes the obvious solutions are the best ones! A key aspect of access control involves physical barriers. One of the easiest ways to prevent those intent on creating problems from physically entering your environment is to lock your doors and keep them out.

99. B. With ransomware, software—often delivered through a Trojan horse—takes control of a system and demands that a third party be paid. The "control" can be accomplished by encrypting the hard drive, by changing user password information, or via any of a number of other creative ways. Users are usually assured that by paying the extortion amount (the ransom), they will be given the code needed to revert their systems to normal operations. Even among malware, ransomware is particularly nasty.

100. A, B. When configuring a new wireless router, always change the username and password first. This prevents would-be hackers from having easy access to the router. Then change the default SSID.

101. D. Disable all unneeded protocols/ports. In this case, ports 80 and 443 are needed for HTTP and HTTPS access, and ports 25, 110, and 143 may be needed for email. That's it. If you don't need them, remove the additional protocols, software, or services or prevent them (disable them, or block them, as the setting is typically called on a router) from loading. Ports not in use present an open door for an attacker to enter.

102. A. Failed login attempt restrictions will destroy all local data on the phone if incorrect passcodes are entered 10 times in a row. While this is recommended for users with phones that contain sensitive data and that are frequently taken into public venues or placed in compromising positions, the casual user should not turn on this feature unless they can be sure there will always be a recent backup available in iTunes.

103. B. When you move a file or folder on the same NTFS volume, it will keep its original permissions. If you copy it or move it to a different volume, it will inherit permissions from its new parent directory.

104. B. When users log on to a computer or network, they are generally required to provide credentials such as a username or password. In multifactor authentication, the user is required to provide two or more items. These items are generally from two of three categories: something they know (such as a password), something they have (such as a code from a security token), or something they are (biometric screening).

105. B, C. The best methods are either overwrite or drive wipe. Overwriting the drive entails copying over the data with new data. A common practice is to replace the data with 0s. Drive wipes do a similar thing. Formatting the drive does not guarantee that others can't read the data. Using electromagnetic fields (or degaussing) isn't reliable and can damage the hard drive. (Not to mention it won't work at all on SSDs!)

106. A, C. System files are critical to the operating system working properly and should not be changed or deleted. By default, the Hidden and System attributes are set. Some are also set to Read-only, but not all. For example, the virtual memory file (pagefile.sys) is a system file but is not Read-only.

107. D. When Windows is installed, one of the default accounts it creates is Guest, and this represents a weakness that can be exploited by an attacker. While the account cannot do much, it can provide initial access to a system, and the attacker can use that to find another account or acquire sensitive information about the system. To secure the system, disable all accounts that are not needed, especially the Guest account, which is disabled by default.

108. A. Man-in-the-middle attacks clandestinely place something (such as a piece of software or a rogue router) between a server and the user, and neither the server's administrator nor the user is aware of it. The man-in-the-middle intercepts data and then sends the information to the server as if nothing is wrong. The man-in-the-middle software may be recording information for someone to view later, altering it, or in some other way compromising the security of your system and session.

109. B, C. Setting strong passwords is critical to network security. They should be as long as possible. Eight or 10 characters is a good minimum. Users should also need to use a combination of uppercase and lowercase letters, a number, and a special character such as #, @, &, or others. Passwords should also expire, but 180 days is too long. Having a 42-day or 90-day requirement would be better.

110. A. With NTFS, each file, directory, and volume can have its own security. NTFS tracks security in access control lists (ACLs), which can hold permissions for local users and groups, and each entry in the ACL can specify what type of access is given—such as Read & Execute, List Folder Contents, or Full Control. This allows a great deal of flexibility in setting up a network.

111. B, C. Inheritance is the default behavior throughout the permission structure, unless a specific setting is created to override it. For example, a user who has Read and Write permissions in one folder will have that in all the subfolders unless a change has been made specifically to one of the subfolders. Explicit permissions at a more granular level will apply instead of those set at a higher level of the directory tree.

112. D. Data loss prevention (DLP) systems monitor the contents of systems (workstations, servers, and networks) to make sure that key content is not deleted or removed. They also monitor who is using the data (looking for unauthorized access) and transmitting the data. DLP systems share commonalities with network intrusion prevention systems.

113. D. The Guest account is created by default (and should be disabled) and is a member of the Guests group. For the most part, members of Guests have the same rights as Users except they can't get to log files. The best reason to make users members of the Guests group is to access the system only for a limited time. There is no group named Standard Users by default. There is a Users group, Administrators, Power Users, Guests, and a few others.

114. C. One of the big problems larger systems must deal with is the need for users to access multiple systems or applications. This may require a user to remember multiple accounts and passwords. The purpose of single sign-on (SSO) is to give users access to all the applications and systems that they need when they log on. Some of the systems may require users to enter their credentials again, but the username and password will be consistent between systems.

115. A. If you want to recover your computer and bring it back to the point where it was when it was new (minus any files that you added since purchasing the machine), you can use the recovery CD set or DVD. In Windows, you can create a system repair disc from the Backup And Restore interface (beneath the Control Panel options for System And Security).

116. B. A keylogger seems to be running on the system, monitoring and copying all that is typed on the keyboard. Obviously, this malware needs to be removed and incident response steps taken.

117. B. SecureDNS, specifically DNS over HTTPS, would enable a person to browse while keeping the DNS queries private.

118. A. A software-based firewall on the workstation would be able to stop unwanted network traffic, including port scans and probes.

119. D. Privacy screens fitted on a display can shield the display content from anyone not sitting at the correct angle to the display.

120. B. Digital signatures can be used for non-repudiation. Digital signatures are done with digital certificates. A phone call or text might offer some assurance, but not to the degree as the email being digitally signed. Email signatures are simply your contact information and offer no true assurance.

121. C. The software token is stored on a general-purpose device, such as the PC. The hardware token option would involve carrying an added key fob or device. A fingerprint reader would be unacceptable as it involves biometrics. A second password defeats the benefit of using multifactor authentication.

122. B. Temporal Key Integrity Protocol (TKIP) is an encryption protocol for wireless connections that's intended to replace WEP's weak encryption.

123. B, D. Group Policy/updates and login scripts are common ways to push and enforce security settings on Active Directory objects.

124. D. Advanced Encryption Standard (AES) was originally named Rijndael, designed by Joan Daemen and Vincent Rijmen to replace the obsolete DES.

125. D. Remote Authentication Dial-In User Service (RADIUS) was originally designed to authenticate remote users to a dial-in access server but is now used in several authentication situations.

126. B. Terminal Access Controller Access Control System (TACACS) is the older encryption protocol here. The other two variants of the name, TACACS+ and Extended TACACS, are actually different protocols altogether. SNMP is not an encryption protocol.

127. B. It's a bold move to try to steal a server. But a server lock or locks on the rack door would stall future theft attempts.

128. C. Resetting the password or unlocking the account would give the user back the opportunity to sign in. Creating a new account or deleting his account would not help in this situation. Disabling the account might be the next step if you find out the account has been compromised.

129. D. The organizational unit is a subdivision within which may be placed users, groups, more organizational units, and other objects.

130. B. Folder redirection allows users' profile folders to be stored off of a local machine and instead placed in a more centralized location on the network.

131. D. The Windows Recovery Environment (Windows 8, 10) is a replacement for the Recovery Console, both of which are a command-line tool that allow the administrator the ability to copy or remove directories, enable or disable services, write a new Master Boot Record (MBR), format volumes, and much more.

132. B. Rainbow tables are tables of cryptographic hash values, against which an attacker can compare a captured password hash. A match tells the attacker what was the original password string to compute that matching hash.

132. B. Rainbow tables are tables of cryptographic hash values, against which an attacker can compare a captured password hash. A match tells the attacker what was the original password string to compute that matching hash.

133. C. When files and folders are moved (not copied) on a NTFS volume, the original permissions are retained at the new location, as is done in this case. However, when files or folders are copied, the new file or folder will inherit its permissions from its new parent folder. The old permissions would be discarded. In this case, there was no permission propagation.

134. A. Microsoft's mobile OS is capable to save applications, settings, camera pictures and text messages to the cloud without having to install any backup application.

135. A. In this situation where the sale engineer may not have network access when travelling, the local profile is best. A local profile keeps settings and files on the laptop. Generally, since remote user profiles keep settings and files centralized on a company server, it is preferred. That requires travelers to have network access. Mandatory enforces settings from the administrator, but changes to the local laptop are lost at logoff. Temporary profiles are also means any file changes are lost when the user disconnects.

Chapter 8: Software Troubleshooting

1. C. There are many other forms of malware in addition to viruses. While a true antivirus program will scan for viruses, anti-malware programs are a superset of virus scanners and will look for more than just traditional viruses. One program included with Windows that falls into this category is Windows Defender, which is mainly a spyware detector (and incorporates Microsoft Security Essentials, or MSE, with it as of Windows 8 and later).

2. C. A common cause for lack of wireless connectivity is for a device to be in airplane mode. Make sure the device is not in that mode, and do a hard reboot if necessary.

3. C. If the operating system is missing, it could be due to a bad or corrupt boot sector on the hard drive, or the operating system may indeed be missing. If the hard drive is actually OK, then use the installation DVD (you may have to set the BIOS to use the DVD drive as your primary boot device) or the Windows Repair CD. In Windows 10, Windows 8/8.1, and Windows 7, go to System Recovery Options and choose Startup Repair.

4. A. If the system is unresponsive, then a soft reset will not work. A hard reset is the next choice. With Apple's iPhone, iPad, and iPod Touch, forcing a restart on the device is done by pressing and holding the Sleep/Wake and Home buttons for at least 10 seconds until you see the Apple logo.

5. B. When an application crashes, you want to isolate the cause of the crash—it could be a compatibility issue, hardware, or a host of other problems—and solve it. One step to take early on is to look for updates/patches/fixes to the application released by the vendor.

6. B. This is a classic symptom of browser redirection. The perpetrator has one goal, which is to direct you to websites that he wants you to visit, regardless of what you actually want to see. Removing the redirector might be as simple as uninstalling an application (by dragging it to the Trash and emptying the Trash), or it might require full-scale virus (malware) mitigation.

7. D. If the service refuses to start, even manually, it is possibly corrupt. (It is also possible that you have malware, but we'll focus on it being corrupt first.) The system file checker (SFC) utility can fix the key system files needed to run this Windows service. If that doesn't fix it, then follow the steps needed to mitigate malware, or reinstall Windows.

8. A. Unfortunately, the only solution to a locked phone (or system lockout) is to perform a reset to factory specifications. That means that all the data on the phone is gone, unless it was synced with iTunes or iCloud (or the appropriate Android equivalent).

9. D. iPads and iPhones are not large enough to have external DVI or other video ports. If you want to project to an external monitor, you need an adapter or an app that will allow you to broadcast to the monitor over Wi-Fi or Bluetooth.

10. B. Lack of Bluetooth connectivity is often caused when a device is not turned on and/ or has an improper setting for discoverability. Make sure the device is turned on and discoverable (checking the manufacturer's documentation if necessary).

11. D. The best practices for malware removal is a seven-step process. Identify malware symptoms, quarantine the infected system, disable system restore (in Windows), remediate infected systems (including update anti-malware software and scan and remove the malware), schedule scans and run updates, enable system restore and create a restore point (in Windows), and educate the end user.

12. C. Spam is defined as any unwanted, unsolicited email, and not only can the sheer volume of it be irritating, it can often open the door to larger problems. While spam is not truly a virus or a hoax, it is one of the most annoying things with which an administrator must contend. Installing or enabling a spam filter on the email server is the best solution.

13. A. A Wi-Fi analyzer can be used on your network to see signal strength, channels used, and various other network metrics. Any company with a wireless network should have one for troubleshooting purposes.

14. C. The first rule with BSOD errors is to reboot. If the problem goes away, it could have just been a one-time problem. But since you just installed the sound card, it's most likely the sound card driver that caused the issue. Reboot into Safe Mode and uninstall the driver. After you reboot again, look on the manufacturer's site for an updated driver.

15. B, C. There are a number of reasons intermittent wireless connections can occur, but the two most common are lack of a good signal and interference. Increasing the number of repeaters, or being closer to them, can address the lack of a good signal. Interference can be addressed by reducing the number of devices competing for the same channel or by moving away from walls or obstacles.

16. A. Because problems tend to happen no matter how careful you may be, it is important to back up devices and be able to restore from those backups after an incident. Google Sync is available for backups and synchronization of data between Android-based devices and PCs.

17. A. The best practices for malware removal is a seven-step process. Identify malware symptoms, quarantine the infected system, disable system restore (in Windows), remediate infected systems (including update anti-malware software and scan and remove the malware), schedule scans and run updates, enable system restore and create a restore point (in Windows), and educate the end user.

18. B, C. Neither a soft reset nor a hard reset will delete all data on the phone or reset the password. A hard reset will work if the touch screen is unresponsive, and a soft reset will keep the data of running applications. Hard resets should be performed only if the system is locked up or unresponsive.

19. D. During the Windows 10/8/7 boot process, the master boot record (MBR) determines the file system and loads `winload.exe`, which starts the official Windows boot process. In Windows 108/7, `winload.exe` replaces `NTLDR` from the Windows XP days.

20. B, C. The Windows Preinstallation Environment (PE) is a minimal operating system, designed to prepare a computer for installation or to boot into for launching troubleshooting tools such as the Windows Recovery Environment (RE). It is not intended to be an operating system on a computer but rather a stepping-stone to get an OS installed or repaired.

21. D. The `SFC /SCANNOW` command checks all system files and repairs any problems found. `SFC /OFFBOOTDIR` allows you to set the location of an offline boot directory that can then be used for offline repair. `SFC /VERIFYFILE` specifies a file to be scanned but not repaired if errors are found. `SFC /SCANFIX` is not a valid option.

22. A. Log files are created to record significant events. Those events can range from security incidents to system problems to just normal user activity. Windows includes Event Viewer for the purpose of looking at log files and identifying problems.

23. C. Creators of malware have a number of methods by which they can wreak havoc on a system. One of the simplest ways is to delete or rename key system files. Then, the operating system will not work. Just as harmful as deleting or renaming a file is to change the permissions associated with it so that the user can no longer access it or perform those operations.

24. B. An invalid certificate usually means that the certificate that you have (or the one the website has) has expired. It could mean that the site is fine. But it could also mean someone has set up a Trojan that imitates the site you are seeking. If it's a site you are not familiar with, the best bet is to avoid it altogether.

25. C. If when you boot Windows won't load completely (it hangs or is otherwise corrupted), you can often solve the problem by booting into Safe Mode. To access Safe Mode, you must press F8 when the operating system menu is displayed during the boot process. You'll then see a menu of Safe Mode choices.

26. C. Antivirus databases should be updated frequently (about once a week, although more often is better) to keep your antivirus program up-to-date with all the possible virus definitions. Most antivirus programs will automatically update themselves (if configured properly), just as Windows Update will update Windows, provided the computer has a live Internet connection. It's a good idea to let them automatically update.

27. B. Mail decryption depends upon certificates, and problems can occur when those certificates expire or you have a configuration problem (which can accompany upgrades). To address the problem, try reimporting S/MIME certificates or deleting/importing them from the source.

28. A, C. High resource utilization can be a telltale sign that a device is running more than you think it should be—perhaps the drives are being searched or the camera is recording your every move. Or, it could be that the user has too many apps open and the device is struggling with available resources.

29. A. In Windows 10/8/7, WINRESUME checks the system for installed devices and device configurations and initializes the devices it finds. It passes the information to WINLOAD, which collects this information and passes it to the kernel after this file is loaded. WINRESUME.EXE replaces NTDETECT.COM from the Windows XP days. WINRESUME is what Windows uses when it wakes from hibernation.

30. B, C. Generally speaking, there is no need to close running apps on mobile devices, unless there is a problem. A common misperception among iPhone users is that all apps in the "background" (when they double-tap the Home button) are still running, when in fact they are not. That is a list of recently used apps, and their preview windows are still visible, but they are not actually using system resources as if they were open. Swiping up on them to "close" them is the same motion you would need to do if an app was locked up and you needed to do a force quit.

31. A. One of the more clever ways of spreading a virus is to disguise it so that it looks like an antivirus program. When it alerts the user to a fictitious problem, the user then begins interacting with and allowing the rogue program to do all sorts of damage. One of the trickier things for troublemakers to do is to make the program look as if it came from a trusted source—such as Microsoft—and mimic the Windows Action Center interface enough to fool an unsuspecting user.

32. B. If Windows 7 (or Windows 10/8) does not load properly, it could be a problem with the BOOTMGR file. That file starts the loading of the Windows OS. It replaces the NTLDR file, which was used by Windows XP and earlier Windows versions. Numerous dynamic link library (DLL) files are required to boot, but usually the lack of corruption of one of them produces a noncritical error.

33. A. If you want to recover your computer and bring it back to the point where it was when it was new (minus any files that you added since purchasing the machine), you can use the recovery CD set or DVD. In Windows, you can create a system repair disc from the Backup And Restore interface (beneath the Control Panel options for System And Security). The system repair disc can be used to boot the computer, and it will contain the system recovery tools.

34. B. A restore point is a copy, or snapshot, of your system configuration at a given point in time. It's like a backup of your configuration but not your data. Snapshots are created within Windows from the System Restore program. Restore points are created in one of three ways. One, Windows creates them automatically by default. Two, you can manually create them yourself. Three, a restore point is created before the installation of some programs (that way, if the install fails, you can "roll back" the system to a preinstallation configuration).

35. B. If the hard drive gets to be under 10 percent free space, its performance can slow down dramatically. The Disk Cleanup utility will show how much disk space is being taken up by temporary files, log files, the Recycle Bin, and other items that can easily be deleted. This could free up some disk space. You will possibly need to delete some files as well.

36. A. Windows comes with many tools to help protect and repair system files and configuration, such as Last Known Good, the Emergency Repair Disk, SFC, and others. But nonsystem files are not covered. The only way to protect user-generated content is to back it up!

37. C. Mobile devices will overheat on occasion. Sometimes it happens after it's been charging, but it can also happen because of excessive ambient temperatures or too much use over an extended period of time. When the device does overheat, it's best to power it off. And, you can often help it cool down more quickly by removing any protective case that may be there—and putting it back on later.

38. C. The email could be real, but most likely it's a hoax. Worse yet, it could be malware itself, and by clicking the link you will activate it on your computer. Always check a reputable source, such as www.us-cert.gov, www.cert.org, or an anti-malware vendor (Symantec, McAfee, and so on) for information on the latest threats. At a minimum, delete the email and don't click the link!

39. B. If a touch screen device is not responsive, the first step is to reboot the device. (If the screen is bad enough, he may need to replace the device, but that will not help in the short term.) A force stop just closes an app. Resetting the phone to the factory default settings will erase the data on the phone, which will not help in this situation.

40. D. Weak signals are a common culprit, behind dropped signals. Before you engage in communication, signal strength on the device should be evaluated. If the signal is low (for example, no bars), then change location (step outside, drive out of the tunnel, exit the elevator, and so forth) and try for a better signal. A low battery can affect signal strength, so keep the battery charged as much as possible.

41. B. A soft reset will not work because the buttons do not respond, and neither does the touch screen, so you can't swipe to turn it off. You need to do a hard reset; press and hold the Sleep/Wake and Home buttons on an iPhone for at least 10 seconds until you see the Apple logo. If the restart does not work, try plugging in the device and letting it charge (an hour or more is recommended) and try restarting again.

42. B. When an app is unresponsive, you can do a force stop to close it. With iOS, press the Home button twice quickly, and small previews of your recently used apps will appear. Swipe left to find the app that you want to close and then swipe up on the app's preview to close it using a force stop. On the iPhone X, it's only necessary to swipe up from the left corner to the middle of the screen.

43. A. The Windows Event Viewer utility provides information about what's been going on with the whole system to help you troubleshoot problems. Event Viewer shows warnings, error messages, and records of things that have happened successfully. It's found in all current versions of Windows. The three most commonly referenced logs are Security (which includes information about logins), System, and Application.

44. B. The best practice for malware removal is a seven-step process. Identify malware symptoms, quarantine the infected system, disable system restore (in Windows), remediate infected systems (including update anti-malware software and scan and remove the malware), schedule scans and run updates, enable system restore and create a restore point (in Windows), and educate the end user.

45. C. If an app does not load, the first thing to try is rebooting. If that does not work, attempt to remove and reload the app. Be sure to check the vendor's site for any similar problems (and solutions) encountered by others.

46. B. There are many other forms of malware in addition to viruses. While a true antivirus program will scan for viruses, anti-malware programs are a superset of virus scanners and will look for more than just traditional viruses. They can scan for spyware, ransomware, adware, and other malicious programs as well.

47. B. In the Unix/Linux world, a kernel panic is when the OS crashes, much like a blue screen of death in Windows. This occurs when the operating system detects an error from which it cannot safely recover—rather than one app crashing, the whole system does. First, reboot. If it comes back, solutions usually include updating hardware, firmware, software, and the OS itself. You can also check drives and RAM for errors that might be causing the crash and correct any problems that you uncover.

48. B. A computer slowdown could happen because of many things, such as hardware failure, an excessively full hard drive, not enough virtual memory, or malware. Rogue antivirus, hijacked email, and invalid certificates will cause problems but not computer slowdowns.

49. A, C. iPads and iPhones are not large enough to have external DVI or other video ports. If you want to project to an external monitor, you need an adapter, Apple TV, or an app that will allow you to broadcast to the monitor over Wi-Fi or Bluetooth.

50. C, D. It's most likely the driver that's causing the problem. One of the quickest (and best) ways to proceed is to boot to Safe Mode, which loads a standard VGA driver. Then you can uninstall the new video card driver. The other way is to boot to the Last Known Good configuration. Last Known Good will roll back the system to the state it was in when the last person logged in. So, if that was before the faulty driver was installed, it might solve the problem.

51. C. The MSCONFIG utility helps troubleshoot startup problems by allowing you to selectively disable individual items that are normally executed at startup. There is no menu command for this utility; you must run it with the Run command (on the Start menu). Choose Start ➤ Run, and type **MSCONFIG**. It works in most versions of Windows, although the interface window is slightly different among versions.

52. A. Creators of malware have a number of methods by which they can wreak havoc on a system. One of the simplest ways is to delete key system files. Then, the operating system will not work.

53. D. The Linux terminal is where commands are typed into. (It's the equivalent of a Windows command prompt.) Then, the commands are processed by the shell. The most common shell in Linux systems is bash, which stands for Bourne Again Shell.

54. B. Hijacked email is when an attacker sends out an email from your address to your contacts or as spam to others. One of the easiest ways to spread malware is to capture the email contacts of a user and send it as an attachment to all of those in their circle. The recipient is more likely to open the attachment because it seemingly comes from a trusted source.

55. C, D. The best practice for malware removal is a seven-step process. Identify malware symptoms, quarantine the infected system, disable system restore (in Windows), remediate infected systems (including update anti-malware software and scan and remove the malware), schedule scans and run updates, enable system restore and create a restore point (in Windows), and educate the end user.

56. C. The BIOS or UEFI will contain the boot order, which is what you need to change. You can set the system to boot to a hard drive, optical drive, network card, or other options.

57. D. Pop-ups are annoying but not necessarily an indication that your computer is infected with anything. Adware pop-ups usually spam your desktop with multiple (if not dozens of) windows at the same time. Spyware generally doesn't announce its presence, and viruses generally do more damage than a simple pop-up ad does.

58. A. Hijacked email is when an attacker sends out an email from your address to your contacts or as spam to others. One of the easiest ways to spread malware is to capture the email contacts of a user and send it as an attachment to all of those in their circle. The recipient is more likely to open the attachment because it seemingly comes from a trusted source.

59. D. In the Unix/Linux world, a kernel panic is when the OS crashes, much like a blue screen of death in Windows. This occurs when the operating system detects an error from which it cannot safely recover—rather than one app crashing, the whole system does. The first step in troubleshooting a kernel panic is to reboot and see whether the error persists.

60. C. Don't click the button! This is some sort of hoax. When you click the button, something bad will happen—something like malware being installed on your computer. Attackers are very creative about making their pop-ups look like legitimate security alerts. Clicking the X to close the window may work, but clicking anything related to this box is an unpleasant prospect.

61. A. Numerous dynamic link library (DLL) files are required to boot, but usually the lack of corruption of one of them produces a noncritical error. Within the Windows toolkit, the best utility to use to tackle this problem is the System File Checker (SFC).

62. A. If a touch screen device is not responsive, the first step is to reboot the device. In the case of an iPhone, a soft reset won't likely work (because the touch screen is not responsive), so try a hard reset. Press and hold down the Home and Sleep/Wake buttons for about 10 seconds, and then the Apple logo will appear. The phone will shut off. Then use the Sleep/Wake button to power it back on.

63. C. First, make sure that the service is configured to start properly. You can do this in the Services MMC app. An easy way to open Services is to click Start and type services in the search box. Then find Security Center and see what it's set to. It should be set to a Startup type of Automatic (Delayed Start).

64. C. If the Bluetooth devices have not been used together previously, they need to be paired to work. Pairing is usually a simple process where one device locates the other, a PIN is entered for security, and connectivity is tested. Then the two will work together. Otherwise, lack of Bluetooth connectivity is often caused when a device is not turned on and/or has an improper setting for discoverability.

65. B. Defragmenting a disk involves analyzing the disk and then consolidating fragmented files and folders so that they occupy a contiguous space, thus increasing performance during file retrieval. In Windows, there are a few different ways that you can get to the Disk Defragmenter, but the command prompt version is DEFRAG. The need for defragmenting the drive is only necessary on a drive with platters (HDDs), not solid-state drives (SSDs).

66. D. Windows 10/8/7 use Boot Configuration Data (BCD), which holds information about which OSs are installed on the computer. If BCD isn't able to find the OS bootstrap files (BOOTMGR in this case), then Windows won't load. BCD, which is edited with BCDEDIT.EXE, replaces the BOOT.INI file, which was used in Windows XP and other older versions of Windows.

67. C. The best practice for malware removal is a seven-step process. Identify malware symptoms, quarantine the infected system, disable system restore (in Windows), remediate infected systems (including update anti-malware software and scan and remove the malware), schedule scans and run updates, enable system restore and create a restore point (in Windows), and educate the end user.

68. B. While apps, usage, and so on can contribute to a power drain, one of the biggest offenders is the search for a cellular signal.

69. A, C. The NTLDR loader file is a key component of the Windows XP boot process, and the system will not boot without it. The file can be retrieved from the Recovery Console, from SFC, or from bootable media (recovery DVD, repair disk, and so on).

70. B. iPhones are susceptible to malware, just like any other computer device. Some malware can be configured to perform unauthorized location tracking. To help prevent this, always patch and update iOS as soon as updates are available and install anti-malware software. She can also disable Location Services in Settings⊁ Privacy⊁ Location Services.

71. A, C. Tips for increasing battery life include keeping OS updates applied (they may include energy-saving patches), avoiding ambient temperatures that are too high or too low, letting the screen automatically dim, and turning off location-based services. You should also disconnect peripherals and quit applications not in use (Bluetooth, for example, uses power when enabled, even if you are not using it to connect to anything).

72. C. Viruses do exist for Android; some industry estimates say that 90 percent of mobile-based viruses are targeted at Android OSs. Install an antivirus app and make sure it's kept up-to-date, just as you would on a PC.

73. A. Windows 7 has a Performance Information And Tools applet in the Control Panel. Once in there, click Advanced Tools to see a list of different tools that can help you monitor system performance. A lot of these tools are also located elsewhere, such as Event Viewer, Task Manager, Performance Monitor, DEFRAG, and others.

74. B. Check the settings on the device to see whether it is possible to brighten the screen. You can also change how quickly the phone dims with inactivity, as perhaps it's automatically dimming too quickly.

75. B. A restore point is a copy, or snapshot, of your system configuration at a given point in time. It's like a backup of your configuration but not your data. Snapshots are created within Windows from the System Restore program. If Windows will not load, Safe Mode can be used to run `rstrui.exe`, which will open a version of System Restore so you can use a snapshot.

76. C. When you need to get to a safe state—such as when you are disposing of a device or assigning it to a new user—you can reset it to the factory default settings. To do this, tap Settings and then General. Scroll down until you see the Reset option and choose it. Tap Erase All Content And Settings. At this point, the iPhone or iPad will ask you to confirm the reset, and when you tap OK, it will start the process.

77. A, D. Slow performance is often related to RAM. Look for any apps that are running and can be closed, or perform a soft reset to try to free up memory. Resetting to the factory default will delete all data on the device. You can't upgrade the RAM in an iPad.

78. A. Different versions of Windows use different files to identify what operating systems are installed and where their boot files can be found. With Windows XP and earlier versions (something you need to know only because `NTLDR` is an objective), the text file `Boot.ini` is used to identify the operating systems installed, their locations, and the boot options to use. Windows 10, Windows 8, and Windows 7 use the Windows Boot Configuration Data (BCD) file instead.

79. C. Light can quickly drain a battery on a mobile device, and thus most of them include the ability to dim the display both manually and automatically after a period of inactivity. While you normally want these actions, if the settings are incorrect, the screen can be too dim to work with. Check the settings on the device to see whether it possible to brighten the screen and/or keep it from automatically dimming within a short period of time.

80. B. One option for an inaccurate touch screen is to clean the screen, but that doesn't often solve the problem. A better solution is to calibrate the screen. Each mobile OS handles it differently, so check the manufacturer's website for help.

81. C. In Windows 10/8/7, `WINLOAD.EXE` is responsible for switching the system from real mode (which lacks multitasking, memory protection, and those things that make Windows so great) to protected mode (which offers memory protection, multitasking, and so on) and enables paging. In Windows 10/8/7, `WINLOAD.EXE` replaces `NTLDR` from the Windows XP days.

82. B. The easiest thing to try is to change the monitor orientation. This can be done through Control Panel, but an easy way to get to the setting is to right-click the Windows Desktop, choose Screen Resolution, and then change the orientation.

83. D. At times, a system will become corrupted to the point where it will only boot into Safe Mode and not allow a normal boot. While a hardware issue can cause this, it can often be associated with a damaged/missing driver. To address the problem, boot into the Recovery Console and scan for problems. You can also choose to boot to the Last Known Good configuration or resort to the recovery DVD.

84. A. Apps that are not used should be removed from a device to free up resources, namely, memory. To be fair, when users run out of storage space on their mobile devices, it's usually more because of videos, music, or pictures than apps. But apps do take up space and should be deleted if they are not being used.

85. A. When autoconnect is enabled on mobile devices, it is possible for them to seek out open Wi-Fi networks and try to connect to them automatically. This setting should be disabled for all devices because an untrusted connection is a possible place for a DNS or man-in-the-middle attack to occur.

86. B. It's true that enabling Bluetooth will cause more of a drain on the battery, but that's not the biggest risk here. When anonymous devices are allowed to connect to Bluetooth-enabled devices, this is known as unintended Bluetooth pairing, and it represents a security threat. Mobile security policies should be created and enforced to prevent this from occurring.

87. A. When a Mac cursor turns into a pinwheel and stays there, the system will not respond. Opening Apple Diagnostics won't work. You need to force a reboot of the system. There is no need to boot into Safe Mode yet; see whether the problem goes away first.

88. C, D. Because problems tend to happen no matter how careful you may be, it is important to back up devices and be able to restore from those backups after an incident. In the Apple world, there is iTunes and iCloud. iTunes is installed on a desktop or laptop PC, and iCloud is cloud-based storage, as its name implies. Be sure that your computer meets the necessary hardware and software requirements to install iTunes or other mobile synchronization software.

89. A, D. Not shutting down properly can result in lost data from open applications or corrupted operating system files. Neither option is good. Train all users on how to shut down properly.

90. A. If your computer is set to an incorrect time and date (we're talking years off, not just a few minutes), then it can cause invalid certificate errors for the websites you want to visit. It's never recommended to lower your security settings for the Internet zones.

91. D. While spam is not truly a virus or a hoax, it is one of the most annoying things with which an administrator must contend. Spam is defined as any unwanted, unsolicited email, and not only can the sheer volume of it be irritating, it can often open the door to larger problems. Administrators can help stop spam with spam filters on email servers. In addition, users can help themselves by not giving out their email addresses to websites that ask for them. Some companies will sell their lists of email addresses to other firms for "marketing" purposes, and then you start to get piles of spam.

92. B, D. Slow data speeds can be caused by too much interference or by a weak signal. If there is too much interference, try changing the channel on Wi-Fi routers to less-used channels; performance should increase. Solve weak signals by installing more access points or by moving closer to an existing access point.

93. B. The best practice for malware removal is a seven-step process. Identify malware symptoms, quarantine the infected system, disable system restore (in Windows), remediate infected systems (including update anti-malware software and scan and remove the malware), schedule scans and run updates, enable system restore and create a restore point (in Windows), and educate the end user.

94. A. Fixing this issue is just like fixing a missing operating system or missing system files. Using the installation DVD (you may have to set the BIOS to use the DVD drive as your primary boot device) or the Windows Repair CD, go to System Recovery Options and choose Startup Repair.

95. A. There are a number of reasons intermittent wireless connections can occur, but the two most common are lack of a good signal and interference. Increasing the number of repeaters, or being closer to them, can address the lack of a good signal.

96. A. Security holes in mobile device operating systems can leave back doors into which users can get unauthorized account or root access. The majority of these holes are closed by patches and upgrades as soon as they are discovered, so be sure to keep operating systems current.

97. D. Configurations and settings need to be personalized to the user using the device. Except for apps, choosing Settings on the device usually does this, followed by finding the areas that you want to modify and then making the desired changes and saving them.

98. C. Malware can change more settings than you might be aware of on a computer. For example, adware might be obvious because of the pop-ups and browser redirects, but it can also change the client-side IP settings that point to a DNS or proxy server. Check the IP configuration on the client and be sure it's set properly.

99. A, B. When authorized users access devices through unintended connections or unauthorized users access absconded devices (such as with root access), they can access the data on the device. Every firm should have a policy for protecting data (encryption) and dealing with leaks when they occur.

100. C. Going over the limit on your phone's data plan is generally not a major risk, other than to your finances. Data overage charges can be high, depending on your provider and service plan.

101. D. If an app does not load, try rebooting (forcing the device to restart, if necessary). If that does not work, attempt to remove and reload the app. Be sure to check the vendor's site for any similar problems (and solutions) encountered by others.

102. A, D. When an application crashes, you want to isolate the cause of the crash—it could be a compatibility issue, hardware, or a host of other problems—and solve it. One step to take early on is to look for updates/patches/fixes to the application released by the vendor. You can also try to repair the installation through Control Panel. If needed, you can remove and reinstall the software.

103. C. Occasionally, a rogue system will begin automatically shutting down and/ or restarting while in use. While it could be indicative of a hardware problem (malfunctioning motherboard, for example), it can also indicate a setting misconfiguration or driver problem. The most likely setting problem is with sleep settings, such as hibernation mode. If that's not it, then it could be a driver. To begin ruling out possibilities, boot the system into Safe Mode and see whether the problem continues. If the problem does not occur while in Safe Mode, then boot normally and begin testing what occurs as you eliminate drivers/devices one by one (sound, video, and so forth) until you find the culprit.

104. C. Occasionally, a device can be unknowingly put into silent mode, and this will keep sound from coming to the speakers, headphones, or other connected devices. When troubleshooting, always check to see that silent mode is not enabled (or the volume has been turned completely down) and restart the device if necessary.

105. A. REGSVR32.EXE, known as the REGSVR32 tool, allows you to register and unregister modules and controls for troubleshooting purposes. It is often associated with Internet Explorer, but it can be used with any control or module. The command-line syntax is REGSVR32 *DLLNAME.*

106. B. Malware can change more settings than you might be aware of on a computer. For example, adware might be obvious because of the pop-ups and browser redirects, but malware can also change the client-side IP settings that point to a DNS or proxy server. Check the IP configuration on the client and be sure it's set properly.

107. C. In Linux, there are two common boot loaders used. LILO (LInux LOader) is the older one but has been replaced by GRUB (GRand Unified Bootloader) in most instances. The most likely cause of a GRUB/LILO error is a missing or corrupt master boot record (MBR). The method to fix it depends on the version of Linux you are running, but generally speaking, you need to boot to the Linux installation CD/DVD, go into Linux rescue mode, and re-create the MBR.

108. C. A soft reset is the gentlest of the resets. In fact, it will retain data for running applications. Many iPhone users will know the soft reset as the way they turn their phone off and on normally. Press and hold the Sleep/Wake button until the red slider appears and then drag the slider to turn the device off. To turn the phone back on, press and hold the Sleep/Wake button again until you see the Apple logo.

109. D. If you have just updated a driver and the device isn't functioning, rolling back the driver installation can sometimes solve the problem. To roll back a driver, right-click the device name in Device Manager and choose Properties. On the Drivers tab, click the Roll Back Driver button. The Last Known Good configuration will not work because she logged in again. It will therefore be configured with the new (presumably bad) driver.

110.   D. He won't be able to open his anti-malware software because the computer is locked. Paying the fine is not a good option because this is a ransomware attack. Deleting and reinstalling Windows will work, but it's overkill. Simply boot into Safe Mode and use system restore to roll back the system. It's not guaranteed to work, but it's the best choice here. He could also boot to a recovery disk from his anti-malware provider (if he has one) and try a remediation.

111.   A. Sometimes a driver or application will give you compatibility errors in Windows. Microsoft has provided a Program Compatibility Assistant to help you troubleshoot errors and also fix them. To use Compatibility Assistant, right-click the program and choose Troubleshoot Compatibility.

112.   C, D. Unintended Bluetooth connections, whether it means to receive unsolicited messages (called Bluejacking) or have information stolen as a result of a connection (called Bluesnarfing) is a real risk to mobile users. Unintended Wi-Fi connections also pose a significant risk if mobile users are not aware how to mitigate it.

113.   C. One of the more clever ways of spreading a virus is to disguise it so that it looks like an antivirus program. When it alerts the user to a fictitious problem, the user then begins interacting with the program and allowing the rogue program to do all sorts of damage. One of the trickier things for troublemakers to do is to make the program look as if it came from a trusted source—such as Microsoft—and mimic the Windows Action Center interface enough to fool an unsuspecting user.

114.   A. All else being equal, airplane mode will actually conserve a bit of battery life because all the wireless signals are disabled. Apps, usage, and searching for a cellular signal will all drain the battery.

115.   D. If when you boot Windows it won't load completely (it hangs or is otherwise corrupted), you can often solve the problem by booting into Safe Mode. To access Safe Mode, you must press F8 when the operating system menu is displayed during the boot process. You'll then see a menu of Safe Mode choices, one of which is Last Known Good configuration.

116.   B. The BOOTREC /FIXBOOT command will rebuild the boot sector to one that is compatible with Windows 7 (or Windows 10/8.1/8). BOOTREC /FIXMBR will fix the Master Boot Record, and BOOTREC /REBUILDBCD will rebuild the BCD file.

117.   B. Many mobile security software suites have multiple security features. For example, Avast Mobile Security & Antivirus has multiple antivirus and anti-malware capabilities built in. One of the features is an app scanner, which will scan all apps for issues or potential malware.

118.   B, C. Browser redirection happens any time you try to visit a site and your browser instead sends you to an alternate site. One of two things is causing this. First, and most likely, you have some sort of malware that is redirecting your browser. Removing it can be as simple as uninstalling a program by using Programs in Control Panel, or it might require virus (malware) mitigation. The second possibility is that the DNS server you use (likely your ISP's) has been poisoned. If this happened, your ISP would be attempting to fix it as soon as possible.

119. A. A computer slowdown could happen because of many things, such as hardware failure, an excessively full hard drive, not enough virtual memory, or malware. Run a scan from anti-malware software to see whether there are any issues. Event Viewer, MSCONFIG, and REGSRV32 are useful troubleshooting tools but not typically used for system slowdowns.

120. C. Apple Configurator simplifies mass configuration and deployment on iPhone, iPad, and iPod Touch devices. It is intended for use by schools, businesses, and institutions that need to deploy specific configurations to multiple devices.

121. C. The Windows configuration database is known as the Registry. It consists of five "hives," which essentially hold information about all of the hardware, software, configurations, and users associated with the given machine. REGEDIT is the command that opens the Registry Editor and will allow you to make changes to it, but be careful! Changes made here are immediate and a mistake can be disastrous. Be sure to back up the Registry before making any changes.

122. A. If an OS update fails, it could be a configuration issue or simply a one-time glitch in the process. Wait until Windows Update reverts the changes and then reboot and try the update again. If that does not work, you can unplug removable media from your computer and try again, or you can try the Windows Update Troubleshooter.

123. A. A restore point is a copy, or snapshot, of your system configuration at a given point in time. It's like a backup of your configuration but not your data. Snapshots are created within Windows from the System Restore program. If Windows will not load, Safe Mode can be used to run rstrui.exe, which will open a version of System Restore so you can use a snapshot.

124. B. OneDrive is Microsoft's cloud implementation for end users. It will allow the user to sync her phone and back it up to the cloud. She can also access the data from other devices.

125. A. The best practice for malware removal is a seven-step process. Identify malware symptoms, quarantine the infected system, disable system restore (in Windows), remediate infected systems (including update anti-malware software and scan and remove the malware), schedule scans and run updates, enable system restore and create a restore point (in Windows), and educate the end user.

126. D. Whatever message was appearing in the pop-up window is likely in the mobile application log.

127. C. The system and application logs should contain valuable information about the cause of the crash. Logs detailing events regarding the system and the applications and their security can be found in the Event Viewer.

128. A. Given the description, it might be best to roll back the printer driver to a known good version. Updating the boot order and network settings have no impact on the printer working. Killing any printer-related tasks may not have any impact.

129. B, C. Updating the network settings manually or rebooting should apply the new network information. Disabling the firewall or booting to safe mode will not help the issue.

130. D. In Windows 10, you can enter Safe Mode by hitting Restart while holding the Shift button. Windows 10 will restart into Safe Mode. From there, you can install a clean copy of Windows through the Refresh Windows tool. This tool is found under Settings in the Update And Security category. Within Update And Security, choose Recovery, then More Recovery Options to refresh the Windows installation but opting to keep personal files.

131. A. Given the description, it might be best to roll back the update. Until the business application and update can be proven compatible, the update cannot be installed as is. Killing the task is not acceptable as it may be a necessary task, such as `explorer.exe`.

132. B. The solution to rebuild Windows profiles will fix the issue. Roaming profiles, especially with Windows 10, tend to experience problems, which can be most reliably fixed by rebuilding the Windows profile.

133. A. One common indicator is that the profile loads slowly while the system is booting.

134. B. The black screen of death signifies a complete operating system crash. It first appeared with Windows 3.x and still occurs in Windows 7 and 8 when the OS has trouble booting. The more common indication of an OS crash is the blue screen of death, which provides an error code, unlike the black screen of death.

Chapter 9: Operational Procedures

1. D. Power strips come in all shapes and sizes and are convenient for plugging multiple devices into one wall outlet. Most of them even have an on/off switch so that you can turn all the devices on or off at the same time. Don't make the mistake of thinking that power strips will protect you from electrical surges, though. If you get a strong power surge through one of these $10 devices, the strip and everything plugged into it can be fried.

2. A. The security considerations of each access method seem to be overlooked for this server. A server hosting confidential data, located in an open, shared environment is not best practice.

3. B. One component that people frequently overlook is the case itself. Cases are generally made of metal, and some computer cases have sharp edges inside, so be careful when handling them. You can, for example, cut yourself by jamming your fingers between the case and the frame when you try to force the case back on.

4. C. If the user has third-party software offering file sharing capability, then the file could be shared with others. Encryption and establishing a VPN are not necessary. There is no need for USB sharing without a USB port.

5. D. One way to keep dust and debris out of your computer is to use an enclosure, which is basically an extra case. But if dust and debris do get inside your case, the best way to remove it is to use compressed air instead of vacuuming. Compressed air can be more easily directed and doesn't easily produce ESD damage as a vacuum could. Simply blow the dust from inside the computer by using a stream of compressed air. However, make sure to do this outside so that you don't blow dust all over your work area or yourself.

6. A. Cables are a common cause of tripping. If at all possible, run cables through drop ceilings or through conduits to keep them out of the way. If you need to lay a cable through a trafficked area, use a cable floor guard to keep the cables in place and safe from crushing.

7. D. Third-party software that includes a screen sharing feature would allow the technician to demonstrate a task using the user's own local desktop.

8. B. Both RDP and HTTPS do provide confidentiality of network traffic, but SSH is the equivalent of Telnet.

9. B. When you buy an application, you aren't actually buying the application. Instead, you're buying the right to use the application in a limited way as prescribed by the licensing agreement that comes with it. Don't like the terms? Too bad. No negotiation is allowed. If you don't accept the end-user license agreement (EULA), your only recourse is to return the software for a refund.

10. B. After the device or data has been preserved, someone needs to keep track of it before it's handed over to the proper authorities. The specific next step depends on your documented chain of custody policy. Depending on the situation, materials may be held in a safe, locked location at the office, or they may need to be turned over to local authorities. Have a documented procedure in place to follow, given a situation. Always document the findings and who has custody of the illegal materials.

11. A, C. Telnet uses text only, no graphics. It runs leaner but less secure than Remote Desktop Protocol. Also, RDP runs only on Windows platforms, while Telnet runs on Linux/*NIX systems and others.

12. D. One of the golden rules of customer service is, don't vent about customers on social media. You never know who will read it, and regardless, it's unprofessional to air dirty laundry. Depending on the situation, it may be advisable to discuss it with your manager or simply document it and move on with your day.

13. C. If you buy commercial software, you will receive a product key, which you will need to enter during installation or the first time the application is opened. (Some products may let you use them on a trial basis but will then deactivate until you purchase the software and enter the key.) The product key might be emailed to you, or it could be located on the physical media if you got an installation CD-ROM or DVD.

14. C. IT professionals often deal with confidential, private, or restricted information. Other users trust that IT professionals will treat the sensitive material as such and not spread information. Ignore the paychecks and focus on doing the job professionally.

15. B. Avoid distraction and/or interruptions when talking with customers. You need to make them feel that their problem is important and that it has your full attention. Distractions can include personal calls, texting or social media, talking to co-workers, and other personal interruptions. Taking notes and asking appropriate questions is part of good customer service.

16. D. Self-grounding is not as effective as using proper anti-ESD gear, but it makes up for that with its simplicity. To self-ground, make sure the computer is turned off but plugged in. Then touch an exposed (but not hot or sharp!) metal part of the case. That will drain electrical charge from you. Better yet is if you can maintain constant contact with that metal part. That should keep you at the same bias as the case.

17. A. Remote Desktop Protocol (RDP) lets you establish a connection to a remote client, showing the remote system's desktop.

18. B. The lowest static voltage transfer that you can feel is around 3,000 volts; it doesn't electrocute you because there is extremely little current. A static transfer that you can see is at least 10,000 volts. However, a component can be damaged with less than 300 volts.

19. C. Be culturally sensitive. Some people may have a language barrier that makes it difficult to explain their problem. (Think about how much computer language you learned in your high school language courses!) Others may have different habits or practices in their workplace. Be respectful of their world. In some cases, using the appropriate professional titles is a sign of respect, and not using them is an insult.

20. A, D. To use the ESD strap, you attach one end to an earth ground (typically, the computer case) and wrap the other end around your wrist. This strap grounds your body and keeps it at a zero charge. Never wear an ESD strap if you're working inside a monitor or inside a power supply. If you wear one while working on the inside of these components, you increase the chance of getting a lethal shock.

21. D. When batteries are thrown away and deposited into landfills, the heavy metals inside them will find their way into the ground. From there, they can pollute water sources and eventually find their way into the supply of drinking water. The best way to dispose of old batteries is to recycle them.

22. C. If you have your policy in place, then your incident response plan should be relatively scripted. Your first priority as the first responder is to identify the improper activity or content. Then you should always get someone else to verify the material or action so that it doesn't turn into a situation of your word against someone else's. Immediately report the situation through proper channels.

23. C. When dealing with a customer, always display professionalism. That means avoiding slang, jargon, and acronyms; not interrupting; and clarifying what the customer wants.

24. A. Static shielding bags are important to have at your disposal when servicing electronic components because they protect the sensitive electronic devices from stray static charges. This is in contrast to the familiar pink, antistatic bags, which only prohibit static buildup found in other plastic bags but do not shield from ESD. By design, the static charges collect on the outside of these silver or pink bags rather than on the electronic components. Unlike antistatic mats, antistatic bags do not "drain" the charges away, and they should never be used in place of an antistatic mat. But while mats are designed to be stationary on a bench, bags are built for portability.

25. B. The str() function in Python is to return a string, a variable that can contain digits or characters.

26. A. After the device or data has been properly secured and preserved, document everything that could be relevant to the situation. Many companies have standard documentation that is used in incident response in order to be sure that the responder captures important information and does not forget to ask critical questions or look for vital clues.

27. C. Set and meet—or exceed—expectations and communicate timelines and status. Customers want to know what is going on. In addition, offering different repair or replacement options will usually make the customer feel better because you are giving them an option in choosing a solution.

28. B. When dealing with customers, it's important to maintain a positive attitude and project confidence. They are counting on you to resolve the problem.

29. B. The Payment Card Industry Data Security Standard (PCI DSS) applies to any organization that handles credit card data or processes or stores payment transactions from bank cards.

30. C. LCD monitors do not use capacitors like CRT monitors did. Instead, they require an inverter, which provides the high-voltage, high-frequency energy needed to power the backlight. The inverter is a small circuit board installed behind the LCD panel that takes DC power and converts (inverts) it for the backlight. Inverters store energy even when their power source is cut off, so they have the potential to discharge that energy if you mess with them.

31. C. The toner itself is a carcinogen, and the cartridges can contain heavy metals that are bad for the environment. PC recycling centers will take old toner cartridges and properly dispose of them. Most toner cartridge manufacturers will also take them back for recycling.

32. D. A desktop computer you are working on has a failed power supply. Although it is possible to open a power supply to work on it, doing so is not recommended. Power supplies contain several capacitors that can hold lethal charges long after they have been unplugged! It is extremely dangerous to open the case of a power supply. Besides, power supplies are pretty cheap. It would probably cost less to replace one than to try to fix it, and this approach would be much safer. Open a power supply only if you have been specifically trained how to repair them.

33. B. Creating a policy is the most important part of dealing with prohibited content or actions. Without a policy in place that specifically defines what is and what isn't allowed and what actions will be taken when a violation of the policy occurs, you don't really have a leg to stand on when a situation happens. What is in the policy depends on the company for which you work. A good policy will also contain the action steps to be

taken if prohibited content or activity is spotted. It may involve disciplinary action, termination of employment, or contacting law enforcement.

34. A. Having too little power, such as when a blackout (a complete loss of power) occurs, can wreak havoc on electrical circuits. Power blackouts are generally easy to detect. Power sags without a complete loss, called a brownout, are also very damaging to electrical components but oftentimes go unnoticed.

35. D. Use proper language and avoid using jargon, abbreviations, and acronyms. Every field has its own language, and outsiders feel lost when they start hearing it. Put yourself in the position of someone not in the field and explain what is going on by using words they understand. Start off with basic terms. If the customer is tech savvy, they will usually let you know, and then you can use more advanced terms as needed.

36. A, B. Open-source software is free: not only is the application free, but the source code (code used by programmers) is also shared to encourage others to contribute to the future development and improvement of the application. Open-source software can't be sold, although it can be bundled with commercial products that are sold. Contrast open source with commercial licenses, where you pay per user and can't modify the program except for as allowed by the developer.

37. D. Devices that actually attempt to keep power surges at bay are called surge protectors. They often look similar to a power strip, so it's easy to mistake them for each other, but protectors are more expensive, usually starting in the $25 range. They have a fuse inside them that is designed to blow if it receives too much current and not to transfer the current to the devices plugged into it. Surge protectors may also have plug-ins for RJ-11 (phone), RJ-45 (Ethernet), and BNC (coaxial cable) connectors.

38. D. Computer monitors (CRT monitors, not LCDs) are big and bulky, so what do you do when it's time to get rid of them? Most monitors contain several pounds of lead as well as other harmful elements such as arsenic, beryllium, cadmium, chromium, mercury, nickel, and zinc. Take them to an authorized recycling center and dispose of them according to the organization's toxic waste handling procedures.

39. A. Active listening means paying attention to your customers (eye contact is good) and taking notes. Allow them to complete their statements, and avoid interrupting them. People like to know that they are being heard, and as simple an act as it is, this can make all the difference in making them feel at ease with your work.

40. C. Compressed air won't likely blow the grime away. Electronic connectors of computer equipment should never touch water. Instead, use a swab moistened in distilled, denatured isopropyl alcohol (also known as electronics or contact cleaner and found in electronics stores) to clean contacts.

41. A. The best device for power protection is called an uninterruptible power supply (UPS). These devices can be as small as a brick or as large as an entire server rack. Inside the UPS is one or more batteries and fuses. Much like a surge suppressor, a UPS is designed to protect everything that's plugged into it from power surges. UPSs are also designed to protect against power sags and even power outages. Energy is stored in the batteries, and if the power fails, the batteries can power the computer for a period of time so that the administrator can then safely power it down.

42. C. Whenever working inside the case, always turn off the power. There is some debate as to if you should unplug the system. Leaving it plugged in grounds the equipment and can help prevent electrostatic discharge. Many technicians swear by this method. According to the A+ objectives, though, you should disconnect power before repairing a PC.

43. A, C. The muscles in the lower back aren't nearly as strong as those in the legs or other parts of the body. Whenever lifting, you want to reduce the strain on those lower-back muscles as much as possible. To do that, bend at the knees and lift with your legs. Also observe weight limitations and partner-lift if needed. Better yet, partner-lift and use a cart to move items. Also, keep objects close to your body and at waist level to minimize stress on your body.

44. C. To use the ESD strap, you attach one end to an earth ground (typically, the computer case) and wrap the other end around your wrist. This strap grounds your body and keeps it at a zero charge. This helps prevent you from accidentally frying components.

45. A, C. Shareware generally does not require licensing, and payment may be handled via the honor system. But shareware is generally not a good choice for a corporate environment where you depend on the software. A single user license is good for only one user. You could buy a lot of single user licenses, but that is generally more expensive than buying a concurrent or corporate license. Corporate and concurrent licenses are designed for large groups of users.

46. C. Most computers contain small amounts of hazardous substances, so they should be recycled by professionals who know how to deal with those dangers. Many municipalities, states, and countries have regulations in place specifying appropriate measures to enforce their proper disposal. Search the Internet for certified recycling programs near you.

47. C. The General Data Protection Regulation (GDPR) of 2016 protects the privacy of individuals living in the EU and European Economic Area, with conditions placed on maintaining their information on servers globally.

48. A. Set and meet—or exceed—expectations and communicate timelines and status. After resolving a customer's issue, follow up with them to ensure that they were satisfied with the services provided. The follow-up shows professionalism and may earn you future business.

49. A. Even though it's not recommended that you repair monitors without specific training, the A+ exam may test your knowledge of the safety practices to use if you ever you need to do so. If you have to open a monitor, you must first discharge the high-voltage charge on it by using a high-voltage probe. This probe has a very large needle, a gauge that indicates volts, and a wire with an alligator clip. Do not use an ESD strap when discharging the monitor; doing so can lead to a fatal electric shock.

50. A. In difficult situations, it can be challenging to keep a level head. It's important to do so and avoid arguing and becoming defensive. Many times, clients are frustrated because things are not working as they should. Sometimes they will take their frustration out on you. Keep a level head and work to resolve the problem.

51.   A. If you have your policy in place, then your incident response plan should be relatively scripted. Your first priority as the first responder is to identify the improper activity or content. Then you should always get someone else to verify the material or action so that it doesn't turn into a situation of your word against someone else's. Immediately report the situation through proper channels.

52.   D. When humidity gets to be very low, around 20 percent or lower, the risk of electrostatic discharge (ESD) increases. Remember that computer components can be damaged with as little as 300 volts, whereas humans can't feel a shock until it gets to 3,000 volts.

53.   D. If you have your policy in place, then your incident response plan should be relatively scripted. After identifying illegal content, you need to preserve the device. The data or device should immediately be removed from the possession of the offending party and preserved. This will ensure that the data doesn't mysteriously disappear before the proper parties are notified.

54.   D. Personally identifiable information (PII) is anything that can be used to identify an individual person on its own or in context with other information. This includes someone's name, address, other contact information; the names of family members; and other details that people would consider private. PII should always be kept confidential and secure. Be sure that this information is properly secured and can be accessed only by authorized personnel.

55.   B, D. Freeware is an easy choice, because it's free. Open-source software is often also free, and you can modify the code free of charge as well (if you have the skills to do so). Some shareware is free, but it depends on the program. Single-user and corporate licenses generally cost money.

56.   B, C. It is possible to damage a device by simply laying it on a benchtop. For this reason, you should have an ESD mat in addition to an ESD strap. This mat drains excess charge away from any item coming in contact with it. ESD mats are also sold as mouse/keyboard pads to prevent ESD charges from interfering with the operation of the computer. Many ESD wrist straps can be connected to the mat, thus causing the technician and any equipment in contact with the mat to be at the same electrical potential and eliminating ESD.

57.   A. When compressed air is used, particles of dirt and debris can become airborne, and they can be inhaled or get into your eyes. Always wear proper safety gear, such as safety goggles and an air mask.

58.   B. A person's medical records and health information is classified as protected health information (PHI) and must be protected according to regulatory requirements such as HIPAA.

59.   A. While it's possible that the disposal information and risks may be on the container somewhere, you will always find it on the product's Safety Data Sheet (SDS). SDSs include information such as physical product data (boiling point, melting point, flash point, and so forth), potential health risks, storage and disposal recommendations, and spill/leak procedures. With this information, technicians and emergency personnel know how to handle the product as well as respond in the event of an emergency.

60. B, C. Computers generally tolerate temperature and humidity levels about the same as humans do, except electronic devices do like it a bit colder. The general rule of thumb is room temperature or cooler, average humidity, and good ventilation.

61. D. The first option should be a few, quick blasts of compressed air, to immediately blow out the crumbs and debris. If that first option does not work, then the demineralized water should clean anything spilled on a keyboard. Bear in mind that when you use demineralized water, it will then take a few days in order to dry out the keyboard.

62. C. Four major classes of fire extinguishers are available, one for each type of flammable substance: A for wood and paper fires, B for flammable liquids, C for electrical fires, and D (metal powder or NaCl [salt]) for flammable metals such as phosphorus and sodium. The most popular type of fire extinguisher today is the multipurpose, or ABC-rated, extinguisher. It contains a dry chemical powder that smothers the fire and cools it at the same time. For electrical fires (which may be related to a shorted-out wire in a power supply), make sure the fire extinguisher will work for class C fires.

63. D. Be on time. If you're going to be late, be sure to contact your customer. Not doing so indicates that you think her problem isn't important.

64. D. Providing good customer service involves proper communication and professionalism. Dismissing customer problems is not good. Neither is asking accusatory questions. Clarify the scope of the problem and ask clarifying questions to ensure that you understand what isn't working properly.

65. C. Cables are a common cause of tripping. If at all possible, run cables through drop ceilings or through conduits to keep them out of the way. If you need to lay a cable through a trafficked area, use a cable floor guard to keep the cables in place and safe from crushing. In a pinch, and without a floor cable guard, you can use tape, such as duct tape, to secure your cables to the floor. This is recommended only as a temporary fix for two reasons. First, it's not much less of a trip hazard than just having the cables run across the floor. Second, duct tape doesn't protect the cables from being crushed if people step on them or heavy objects are moved over them.

66. A, D. Both tablets and cell phones have batteries. Those, plus the circuitry contain toxic chemicals such as beryllium, arsenic, and lead as well as rare-earth metals that could be recycled. None of what is inside most electronic devices belongs in a landfill. The organization should have procedures on toxic waste handling. The other two options arguably belong elsewhere as well but are not considered toxic.

67. C. One unique challenge when cleaning printers is spilled toner. Getting it wet will make an inky mess. It sticks to everything and should not be blown into the air and inhaled— it's a carcinogen. Use an electronics vacuum that is designed specifically to pick up toner. A normal vacuum's filter isn't fine enough to catch all of the particles, so the toner may be circulated into the air. Normal electronics vacuums may melt the toner instead of picking it up.

68. B. Electricity can hurt people, but it can also pose safety issues for computer components. One of the biggest concerns for components is electrostatic discharge (ESD). For the most part, ESD won't do serious damage to a person other than provide a little shock. But little amounts of ESD can cause serious damage to computer components, and that damage can manifest itself by causing computers to hang or reboot or fail to boot at all.

69. A. PowerShell uses the `.ps1` filename extension. Perl uses `.pl`.

70. B. The environment variables, typically set in the first lines of a script, will specify the script's path, filename, and file location.

71. A. Visual Basic scripts are run on Windows platforms, so the Linux/*nix based editors Emacs and vi would not be used to view a VB script.

72. A. A `.sh` file (Shell script) would use the `echo` command. The options with the `print` command are for Python version 2.7 and 3, respectively. There is no `pscreen` command.

73. D. Batch scripting, which uses the filename extension `.bat`, is typically a series of DOS command-line commands. Such a script file would run on DOS, OS/2, and on the Windows systems' command line. The other filename extensions—`.js`, `.sh`, and `.py`— are JavaScript, shell, and Python, respectively. They each would require special additional software to be able to interpret the script.

74. A. JavaScript uses the `.js` filename extension.

75. D. Each scripting or programming language might use a different character to declare a comment. The first three options—semicolon, exclamation point, and two slashes—are for assembly, Fortran, and Java or C++, respectively.

76. B. The basic loop can provide a technique to issue a command (or multiple commands) repeatedly.

77. D. The variable in scripting and programming is a value that you can change, populate, and use during the script or program's execution.

78. C. Conventionally, for any scripting or programming language, an integer is only able to be a digit. It can be as long as you want, but it can only be digits.

79. D. Network topology diagrams will illustrate how the network connects and routes in and around the environment. Diagraming the network's hardware and paths show a topology of perimeters and boundaries.

80. A. Asset tagging hardware such as desktops and laptops can help an administrator quickly know the details of a particular asset. Inventory management is more easily accomplished with asset tagging.

81. C. Password policy would state the minimum requirements for passwords, including but not limited to length, complexity, history, and lockout conditions.

82. D. Barcodes printed on physical tags that are then affixed to hardware to be managed are an inexpensive option to RFID asset tags.

83. B. Writing knowledge base articles to share with others, namely for those with similar tasks or duties in your environment, can be very helpful. Compared to the time and money spent on repeated discovery for a solution, writing knowledge base articles is a small investment. A change board is a list of expected or recent changes to the environment.

84. C. Every documented change should include the reason or purpose of the change. The reason can explain the justification to those unfamiliar with the situation before the change. The scope of the change documents what is affected by the change. The approval, arguably the most important part, documents the management's support of the change. Documenting what applications are not affected by the change is an unnecessary step.

85. D. The backout plan documents the actions to take in the event the change is rejected for some reason. The plan for change documents detailed actions to take to implement the change. A risk analysis is performed to assess, and likely accept, any additional exposure caused by the change. But end-user acceptance documents that the change is welcomed and agreed upon by end users.

86. B. Implementing file level disaster prevention and recovery best practices will help quicken recovery from a similar incident in the future. If, for example, a virus spread across multiple desktops, then perhaps image level recovery procedures would be useful.

87. A. Until testing is done, backups cannot be considered reliable.

88. D. Applications, specifically critical applications, would most likely be backed up and recovered in the event of a disaster.

89. C. Depending on the disaster, the question of cloud storage vs. local storage backups can significantly affect the success of recovery. For example, for a server hardware failure or a recent malware incident, local storage provides adequate security of backups. However, catastrophic collapse of the building would mean local storage is not accessible.

90. A. Account recovery, such as a forgotten username ID or password, often proceeds with a text or phone call to a documented phone number. Other examples include security questions, such as your first pet or mother's maiden name.

91. B. Jewelry is very often conductive, posing a risk of bridging electrical contacts. Shorting the connection between points might lead to permanent damage to components, let alone potentially causing injury to yourself. Common sense says to remove any jewelry before handling exposed electronics.

Chapter 10: Practice Exam 1 (220-1001)

1. A. L1 cache is generally the smallest and fastest cache. Therefore, it's reasonable to expect that the computer will have less L1 cache than L2.

2. A. TCP printing's RAW protocol uses TCP port 9100 by default. The alternative, LPR, uses source ports 721–731 and the destination port 515.

3. D. If the device does not produce sound, first make sure that it's not set to silent operation. Most mobile devices will have a switch on the side that sets them to silent or vibrate mode, which will mute the device from making noises. Also check settings for volume as well as possible redirection of sound, such as an active Bluetooth pairing. If the speakers have failed on a mobile device, it's time for a new device.

4. B, D. SSDs have many advantages over HDDs, including producing less heat and being less susceptible to damage from shock or overheating. However, they are more expensive per byte and have less capacity.

5. A. The monitor has a resolution of 16:9. You can determine this by dividing the first number in the resolution by 16 and multiplying the result by 9. It should equal the second number. (Or, you can just multiply the second number by 1.778, and it should equal the first number. For 16:10, you would multiply the second number by 1.6, and it should equal the first.) 16:9 is the aspect ratio for high-definition television.

6. A, D. A groove or scratch in the EP drum can cause the problem of vertical black lines running down all or part of the page. Because a scratch is lower than the surface, it doesn't receive as much (if any) of a charge as the other areas. The result is that toner sticks to it as though it were discharged. The groove may go around the circumference of the drum, so the line may go all the way down the page. Another possible cause of vertical black lines is a dirty charging corona wire. A dirty charging corona wire prevents a sufficient charge from being placed on the EP drum. Because the charge on the EP drum is almost zero, toner sticks to the areas that correspond to the dirty areas on the charging corona.

7. B. To avoid communications problems, you need to set the wireless access points to have nonoverlapping channels. In 802.11g, the three nonoverlapping channels are 1, 6, and 11.

8. A. ATX power supplies provide the following voltages for the computer: +3.3 VDC, +5 VDC, –5 VDC (on older systems), +12 VDC, and –12 VDC. The 12 V connectors have either four or eight pins.

9. A. Memory problems can cause system lockups, unexpected shutdowns or reboots, or errors such as the blue screen of death (BSOD) in Windows or the rotating pinwheel in MacOS. CPUs problems can also cause intermittent rebooting.

10. D. Rule #1 of troubleshooting is to always check your connections first. The most common issue that prevents network connectivity on a wired network is a bad or unplugged patch cable.

11. A. You can immediately rule out client-side hardware issues because the user can connect to some resources. You just need to figure out why he can't connect to others. This is most likely caused by one of two things: a configuration issue or a connectivity device (such as a router) problem. Since it's only affecting him, it's probably a configuration issue. But since he hasn't received an IP address conflict message, it's most likely a subnet mask configuration problem.

12. B, D. A 32-bit OS can run on either a 32-bit or 64-bit processor, although you will not be able to fully utilize the 64-bit processor's capabilities with a 32-bit OS. A 64-bit OS will run only on a 64-bit processor.

13. C. The vast majority of consumer Bluetooth mobile devices are Class 2 devices, which have a maximum communication distance of 10 meters.

14. B. The Northbridge is responsible for managing high-speed peripheral communications. The Southbridge manages slower onboard peripherals.

15. D. Monitors have their own internal power supply, and they can overheat. Overheating was more common with CRT displays than LCDs, but it still happens. Make sure the air vents on the back of the monitor are dust and debris free. In this case, removing the monitor from the cabinet might help. If the problem persists, it's best to replace the monitor.

16. A, B. This user needs a virtualization workstation. To ensure that the operating systems have the most resources possible, optimize the processors (the more cores, the better) and memory.

17. A. The MicroATX form factor is designed to work in standard ATX cases as well as its own smaller cases.

18. C, D. PCI expansion buses operate at 33 MHz or 66 MHz (version 2.1) over a 32-bit (4-byte) channel, resulting in data rates of 133 MBps and 266 MBps, respectively, with 133 MBps being the most common, server architectures excluded.

19. C. ExpressCard 2.0 running in PCIe 2.0 has a maximum speed of 5.0. GExpressCard 1.x cards running in PCIe 1.0 x1 mode have a maximum speed of 2.5 Gbps. ExpressCard 1.x cards running in USB 2.0 mode have a maximum speed of 480 Mbps.

20. B, C. Simple Mail Transfer Protocol (SMTP), Post Office Protocol 3 (POP3), and Internet Message Access Protocol (IMAP) are all email protocols. SMTP is for sending email. POP3 and IMAP are for downloading email.

21. C. The DC power supply (DCPS) converts house current into three voltages: +5 VDC and −5 VDC for the logic circuitry and +24 VDC for the paper-transport motors.

22. A. Splitters generally have two effects on a network cable: They degrade the signal and limit the distance the signal will travel. Use them judiciously.

23. A. A wireless locator or a Wi-Fi analyzer can be either a handheld hardware device or specialized software that is installed on a laptop, and its purpose is to detect and analyze Wi-Fi signals.

24. A. Because of the much smaller space available for keys, some laptop keys are consolidated into special multifunction keys. These keys are accessed through the standard keys by using a special function (Fn) key. Video adjustments come in two varieties: changing the video output and dimming or brightening the screen. In this case, there is a sun icon and a minus symbol. Some laptops will use a smaller sun or a sun and down arrow to signify dimmer while using a larger sun or a sun with an up arrow to signify brighter.

25. C. A fairly common issue with the BIOS is it fails to retain your computer's settings, such as time and date and hard drive configuration. The BIOS uses a small battery (much like a watch battery) on the motherboard to help it retain settings when the system power is off. If this battery fails, the BIOS won't retain its settings. Simply replace the battery to solve the problem.

26. B. The four-pin power connector is called a Molex connector. It's used to provide power to hard drives and optical drives.

27. B, C. The correct printer driver needs to be installed for the printer and operating system. For example, if you have an HP LaserJet Pro and a Windows 10 computer, then you need to install an HP LaserJet Pro driver made for Windows 10. If this is not done, you will get garbage out of the printer. The other cause of several pages of garbage being printed is a bad formatter board. This circuit board takes the information the printer receives from the computer and turns it into commands for the various components in the printer. Usually, problems with the formatter board produce wavy lines of print or random patterns of dots on the page.

28. D. If you have a swollen battery, turn the device off immediately and make sure that it's not plugged into a charger. It may be possible to remove the battery, but swollen batteries are more prone to explosions than normal ones because the casing is already compromised. The best course of action is to purchase a new device. Take the battery or device to a proper recycling center to dispose of it. Never just throw it in the trash because it can explode and harm sanitation workers as well as cause significant damage to the environment.

29. B. When your system refuses to boot into anything other than VGA mode, it indicates one of two problems. Either the video card is set to a resolution that it can't handle or the video card driver isn't loading properly. When in VGA mode, reset the video resolution to something you know the card can handle and reboot. If that doesn't solve it, reinstall the driver. If it still doesn't work, replace the video card.

30. A, C. The beeps are a BIOS beep code produced because there is an error in the POST routine. The manufacturer's website will likely tell you what the beep code means, and you can also troubleshoot using a USB POST card. Laptops do not have PCIe slots, and there is no specific tool called a BOOT tester.

31. B. Gaming PCs should have multicore processors, high-end video cards, high-definition sound cards, and high-end cooling systems.

32. A, B. DIMM DDR2 and DDR3 have 240 pins, while DDR4 has 288 pins. DDR4 SODIMM has 260 pins.

33. C. A personal area network (PAN) is a small-scale network designed around one person within a limited boundary area. The term generally refers to networks that use Bluetooth technology.

34. C. The x8 card won't completely fill the x16 slot, but it will work at x8 speeds if up-plugging is supported by the motherboard. Otherwise, the specification requires up-plugged devices to operate at only the x1 rate.

35. C. Wi-Fi Protected Access 2 (WPA2) is a huge improvement over WEP and WPA. It uses Counter Mode CBC-MAC Protocol (CCMP), which is a protocol based on the Advanced Encryption Standard (AES) security algorithm. CCMP-AES was created to address the shortcomings of TKIP, so consequently it's much stronger than TKIP.

36. C. The correct order for a T568A patch (straight through) cable is white/green, green, white/orange, blue, white/blue, orange, white/brown, brown.

37. B. The `ipconfig` command is used in Windows to check a computer's IP configuration information. `ifconfig` is used in Unix, Linux, and MacOS.

38. A. The connectors shown are ST connectors for fiber-optic cable. They connect with a BNC-type locking mechanism.

39. C. A DB15 connector is most often used for VGA, or analog video, connections. Therefore, a monitor is the best choice.

40. D. In the exposing step, the image is written to the photosensitive imaging drum. Wherever the laser beam touches, the photosensitive drum's charge is severely reduced from −600 VDC to a slight negative charge (around −100 VDC). As the drum rotates, a pattern of exposed areas is formed, representing the image to be printed.

41. A. Mobile devices often make use of small form factor memory cards, such as Secure Digital (SD), miniSD, or microSD cards. Higher-capacity versions of these cards are SDHC, SDXC, miniSDHC, microSDHC, and microSDXC. The standard versions can hold up to 4 GB in storage, HC up to 32 GB, and XC up to 2 TB.

42. C. For DDR2, multiply the bus speed by 8 to identify the type of memory needed. In this case, 667×8 equals 5336. The PC industry rounds this off to 5300.

43. B. A laser printer's DC power supply provides three different DC voltages to printer components. Using the multimeter, you should find the following voltages: pin 1 +5 v, pin 5 −5 v, pin 9 +24 v.

44. D. To use secure printing, go into the printer preferences (or a similar place) and indicate that it's a secure print job. The document will not print until you physically go to the printer and enter the PIN.

45. C. Because of the much smaller space available for keys, some laptop keys are consolidated into special multifunction keys. These keys are accessed through the standard keys by using a special function (Fn) key. Nearly every laptop has a video connector on the back or the side to plug in an external monitor or a projector. You will need to use the video toggle key to get this external port to work.

46. A. Private IP addresses are not routable on the Internet. The private IP address range for class C networks is 192.168.0.0/16.

47. D. Nearly every hard drive is built with Self-Monitoring, Analysis, and Reporting Technology (S.M.A.R.T.) software installed on it, which monitors hard drive reliability and theoretically can warn you in the event of an imminent failure.

48. D. If a key on the laptop keyboard is stuck, you need to determine whether the contact is having problems or whether the key itself is stuck. If the key is not physically stuck but the laptop thinks it is, rebooting generally solves the problem.

49. C. Network Address Translation (NAT) is a service that translates private IP addresses on your internal network to a public IP address on the Internet. He may also choose to configure DHCP to make IP address configuration easier, but DHCP does not translate addresses like NAT does.

50. D. RAID-10 is a mirrored striped set. As long as one drive in each mirrored pair is functional (just as in RAID-1), you shouldn't lose any data. Simply replace the failed disk and rebuild the array.

51. B. RAID-0 is called disk striping. Data can be written to or read from multiple devices at the same time, increasing data access speed. However, if one drive fails, all data is lost. (Back up early and often!) RAID-1 is a mirror set, which does not increase data access but provides fault tolerance. RAID-5 is disk striping with parity, which provides both speed and fault tolerance but requires three hard disks.

52. D. VGA devices are analog and therefore cannot be driven passively by digital HDMI ports directly. An HDMI-to-VGA adapter must be active in nature, either powered externally or through the HDMI interface itself.

53. B. During the charging step, the charging corona uses a high voltage to apply a strong, uniform negative charge (around –600 VDC) to the surface of the imaging drum.

54. C. Mini PCIe cards running in PCIe 1.0 x1 mode have a maximum speed of 2.5 Gbps. Mini PCIe cards running in USB 2.0 mode have a maximum speed of 480 Mbps, and those running in USB 3.0 or PCIe 2.0 x1 mode have a maximum speed of 5.0 Gbps.

55. B. Resistive touch screens respond to pressure, and they are highly accurate in detecting the position of the touch. These types of touch screens require the use of a stylus or other hard object, such as a fingernail.

56. C. SATA 1 has throughput of 1.5 Gbps, SATA 2 is rated at 3 Gbps, and SATA 3 is rated at 6 Gbps. SATA speeds can be confusing because the naming does not line up well with the data rates.

57. A. Fluorescent lighting, and LCD backlights in particular, require fairly high-voltage, high-frequency energy. The component that provides the right kind of energy is the inverter. The inverter is a small circuit board installed behind the LCD panel that takes DC current and inverts it to AC for the backlight.

58. C. If you have scorch marks on a component, say a video card or a motherboard, it could be that the specific component went bad. It could also be a sign of a problem with the power supply. If you replace the component and a similar problem occurs, definitely replace the power supply as well as the damaged component.

59. A. The connector on the left is a USB micro connector.

60. D. CAT7 UTP can handle 10 Gbps transmissions over 100 meters. CAT6 will transmit at 10 Gbps, but only for 55 meters, while CAT6A can handle the same transmission speed up to 100 meters. CAT5 has a maximum speed of 100 Mbps, and CAT5e has a maximum of 1 Gbps.

61. D. You can use the Windows chkdsk utility to create and display status reports for the hard disk. chkdsk can also correct file system problems (such as cross-linked files) and scan for and attempt to repair disk errors.

62.   B. The POST routine verifies the BIOS integrity as well as the presence of multiple hardware devices, including RAM, boot devices, and system buses. It does not verify the integrity of the hard drive (such as looking for bad sectors).

63.   D. A crimper is a handy tool for helping you put connectors on the end of a cable. Most crimpers will be a combination tool that strips and snips wires as well as crimps the connector onto the end.

64.   C, D. Dynamic Host Configuration Protocol (DHCP) dynamically assigns IP addresses and other IP configuration information to network clients. It's not considered a critical service requiring guaranteed data delivery, so it uses the connectionless UDP as its host-to-host layer protocol. It uses UDP 67 and UDP 68.

65.   A, C. Most e-readers use a technology called electrophoretic ink, or E Ink, which is a proprietary type of electronic paper. It's available in color but is often used in grayscales or black and white. E Ink allows for less energy use than other LCD displays, giving longer battery life, and it's much easier to read in bright conditions. E-readers generally have less memory than tablets do.

66.   C. The most common cause of an IP address conflict is if someone configures a computer with a static IP address that's part of the DHCP server's range. The DHCP server, not knowing that the address has been statically assigned somewhere, doles out the address and now there's a conflict. Rebooting the computer won't help, and neither will be releasing the address and getting a new lease from the DHCP server—it's just going to hand out the same address again because it doesn't know that there's a problem.

67.   D. If you're using RAID-5 (disk striping with parity), a single drive failure usually means that your data will be fine, provided you replace the failed drive. If you lose multiple drives at the same time, you will need to restore from backup.

68.   A. The net share command is used to share folders on a network. (And net use will allow users to connect to them.) The proper syntax is net share *<share_name>=*
<drive_letter>:<path>.

69.   C. MicroSD cards are 15mm × 11mm. xD Picture Cards are 25mm × 20mm, and miniSD cards are 21.5mm × 20mm. There is no current standard for an 11mm × 8mm memory card. For comparison, standard SD cards measure 32mm × 24mm.

70.   B. The first thing to try is to remove the battery and then see whether it will power up using AC power. This usually works. Longer term, you may want to replace the battery.

71.   D. The DHCP server can provide all required and optional TCP/IP configuration information to clients. This includes an IP address, subnet mask, default gateway, and DNS server address.

72.   A. If print jobs are processed very slowly or if you are continually seeing "low memory" error messages, it might be a good time to upgrade the memory in the printer.

73.   D. 802.11g operates at 2.4 GHz, whereas 802.11ac operates at 5 GHz. Therefore, her network adapter may not see the 802.11ac network. Many 802.11ac routers are dual-band, which means they do support 2.4 GHz devices for backward compatibility. But the standards themselves operate on different frequencies.

74. C. The charging corona or wire applies a strong positive charge (+600 VDC) to the paper. This allows the paper to attract the negatively charged toner from the imaging drum.

75. D. The audio settings can often be adjusted using the special function keys. To lower the volume, look for icons with a speaker. The differentiator between lowering or raising the volume can vary. In this example, the speaker is coupled with a plus and minus sign. The speaker mute button has a speaker with a line through it, and the microphone mute shows a microphone with the same.

76. B. A RAID-10 array is a mirror of a striped set. You need two drives to create the striped set, and the other two will mirror the first two. Therefore, you have only 2 TB worth of storage in this configuration.

77. C. The easiest way is to install an external NIC. Windows should detect the new card and disable the old one. If it doesn't, you can disable it manually in Device Manager.

78. D. Trying another monitor quickly narrowed down this problem. It's not the monitor, so it's the video card. Video connectors are not field replaceable, so just replace the entire video card.

79. A. The order of steps is as follows: processing, charging, exposing, developing, transferring, fusing, and cleaning.

80. A. There are three types of addresses in IPv6: unicast, anycast, and multicast. A unicast address identifies a single node on the network. An anycast address refers to one that has been assigned to multiple nodes. A multicast address is one used by multiple hosts. IPv6 does not use broadcasts.

81. C. At the Internet layer of TCP/IP, Address Resolution Protocol (ARP) resolves logical IP addresses to physical MAC addresses built into network cards. Reverse ARP (RARP) resolves MAC addresses to IP addresses.

82. B. The memory module shown is a MicroDIMM. You can tell the difference between a MicroDIMM and SODIMMs because a MicroDIMM does not have a notch on the connector side. MicroDIMMs are also more square than SODIMMs.

83. D. The FF00::/8 range in IPv6 is for multicasts. Remember that IPv6 does not use broadcasts. The closest IPv6 gets is the use of multicast addresses.

84. D. GPS systems were designed to require multiple satellites. Receivers use a process called triangulation, which they use to calculate the distance between themselves and the satellites (based on the time it takes to receive a signal) to determine their location. They require input from four satellites to provide location and elevation or from three to provide location.

85. D. Infrared is a short-distance, line-of-sight wireless communication method. If line of sight is broken, the communication will end.

86. A. When configuring a router, you should take five steps. Change the router's SSID, change the administrator username and password, select strong encryption such as AES or WPA2, choose a high-quality security passphrase, and connect the clients using the passphrase.

87. D. Hubs can be either active or passive. Passive hubs connect all ports electrically but do not have their own power source. Active hubs use electronics to amplify and clean up the signal before it is broadcast to the other ports.

88. B. There are four major versions of PCIe currently specified: 1.x, 2.x, 3.0, and 4.0. For the four versions, a single omnidirectional lane (such as in x1) operates at a data rate of 250 MBps, 500 MBps, approximately 1 GBps, and roughly 2 GBps, respectively. A bidirectional slot doubles the data rate. An x16 slot will operate 16 times as fast as x1.

89. D. The two most popular methods of manufacturing LCD panels are twisted nematic (TN) and in-plane switching (IPS). Of the two, IPS is regarded as having the best color representation in all angles, while TN is faster and less expensive. Fluorescent and LED are types of backlighting.

90. C. Of the three optical disc technologies, Blu-ray provides the most capacity over DVD and CD-ROM. Blu-ray double-sided, dual-layer (DS, DL) provides 100 GB of storage space, whereas single-sided, single-layer (SS, SL) provides 25 GB.

Chapter 11: Practice Exam 2 (220-1002)

1. A, B. When working with customers, you need to avoid personal interruptions such as phone calls or texts. Exceptions can be made if it's an emergency situation, but in those cases notify the client that you might get a call or text and explain that you will deal with it only if it's the emergency. Otherwise, ignore the personal interruption until you are not working with a client.

2. A. You can change the priority of a process in Task Manager's Details tab for Windows 8 or 10. (For Windows Vista and Windows 7, it's the Processes tab.) Under the Details tab, you right-click the process name and choose Set Priority. The six priorities, from lowest to highest, are low, below normal, normal, above normal, high, and real-time. Only an administrator can set a process to run at real-time priority. Task Manager changes the priority only for that instance of the running application. The next time the process is started, priorities revert to that of the base (typically normal).

3. B, C. The New Technology File System (NTFS) is available with all current versions of Windows. NTFS is an advanced file system that includes such features as individual file security, compression, and RAID support as well as support for extremely large file and partition sizes and disk transaction monitoring.

4. D. The easiest way to upgrade to Windows 10 from within Windows 8 Pro is to run the Microsoft utility called Windows Update Assistant.

5. D. A virtual private network (VPN) is a private network connection that occurs through a public network. A private network provides security over an otherwise unsecure environment. VPNs can be used to connect LANs together across the Internet or other public networks. With a VPN, the remote end appears to be connected to the network as if it were connected locally.

6. B. Self-grounding is not as effective as using proper anti-ESD gear, but it makes up for that with its simplicity. To self-ground, make sure the computer is turned off. Then touch an exposed metal part of the case. That will drain an electrical charge from you. Better yet is if you can maintain constant contact with that metal part.

7. B. 802.11n is a wireless networking standard. Therefore, choose wireless as the network connection type.

8. C. Unfortunately, the only solution to a locked phone (or system lockout) is to perform a reset to factory specifications. That means that all of the data on the phone is gone. There is no back door. In 2016, there was a publicized case of law enforcement wanting to do this in California, and there was even some discussion of the case going to the US Supreme Court. But Apple was steadfast that there is no back door, and they do not believe it's appropriate to create one, which would also create a potential security hole.

9. B. The sudo ("substitute user do" or "superuser do") command is used to run a command with a different privilege level than the current user logged in. Typically this means running a command with superuser or root permissions.

10. A. In Linux, there are two common boot loaders used. LILO (LInux LOader) is the older one, but it has been replaced by GRUB (GRand Unified Bootloader) in most instances. The most likely cause of a GRUB/LILO error is a missing or corrupt master boot record (MBR). The method to fix it depends on the version of Linux you are running, but generally speaking, you need to boot to the Linux installation CD/DVD, go into Linux rescue mode, and re-create the MBR.

11. C. Biometric devices use physical characteristics to identify the user. Biometric systems include fingerprint/palm/hand scanners, retinal scanners, and soon, possibly, DNA scanners. To gain access to resources, you must pass a physical screening process.

12. B. Many companies rely upon digital rights management (DRM) to protect digital assets such as online photos or videos. DRM is not as established as licensing agreements are, but you should still respect the property of the owners of digital content.

13. B. Tailgating refers to being so close to someone when they enter a building that you are able to come in right behind them without needing to use a key, a card, or any other security device. Using mantraps, which are devices such as small rooms that limit access to one or a few individuals, is a great way to stop tailgating.

14. A. The MSINFO32 tool displays a thorough list of settings on the machine. You cannot change any values from here, but you can search, export, and save reports. When run from a command prompt, the /computer option allows you to specify a remote computer on which to run the utility, and the /report option saves the report as a .txt file. Another option is, while in the GUI, you may click on View, then Remote Computer to collect information related to the chosen PC.

15. C. The two primary methods of installing Windows 10 (and most versions of Windows) are a clean install and an upgrade. With a clean install, no traces of any previous operating system are kept. With an upgrade, the focus is on keeping user-related data from the operating system that was installed previously on the machine. The user-related data may be user accounts, data, apps, or almost anything else. When the upgrade is done without removing the existing operating system (the norm), this is known as an in-place upgrade. A custom installation implies a clean installation.

16. B. Even if you disable the SSID broadcast, potential attackers still have many simple tools available to see your wireless network traffic and get the SSID anyway. It is a weak form of security that will keep out only the most casual intruders. Enabling MAC filtering can help you allow access only to certain hosts, but MAC addresses can be spoofed. WPA2 is still the best commonly available form of encryption for wireless routers. WEP has not been acceptable for years, and WPA is usually available alongside of WPA2. Changing the default username and password is always recommended.

17. D. Slow data speeds can be caused by too much interference, a weak signal, or an oversaturated wireless access point. If there is too much interference, try changing the channel on Wi-Fi routers to less-used channels and performance should increase. Solve weak signals by installing more access points or by moving closer to an existing access point. More access points can also help the oversaturation problem. If it was just one user, a low battery could cause problems, but that seems unlikely if the problem is widespread.

18. B, C. To ensure your personal safety, always remember some important techniques before moving equipment. The first thing to check for always is to see whether it's unplugged. There's nothing worse (and potentially more dangerous) than getting yanked because you're still tethered. Remove any loose jewelry, and secure long hair or neckties. Lift with your legs, not your back (bend at the knees when picking something up, not at the waist).

19. C. To combine both hard drives into one volume, you need to create a spanned, striped, or mirrored volume. A mirrored volume, like a RAID-1 array, will make one of the disks redundant, so in this case it would not give the user 1 TB of storage. A striped volume is like RAID-0 and will give you a slight performance boost.

20. A. Referenced by CompTIA as "Bit-Locker," Microsoft calls it BitLocker, and it allows you to use drive encryption to protect files, including those needed for startup and logon. BitLocker can be turned on only by administrators.

21. B. Using near-field communication (NFC), a user will simply move their device within range (about 4 inches, or 10 centimeters) of the merchant's receiver and the payment will be processed. In most cases, a PIN is required. This method is of course used when the customer and merchant are in the same physical location. Charges are usually linked to a bank account, credit card, or online payment service.

22. D. Privacy filters are either film or glass add-ons that are placed over a monitor or laptop screen to prevent the data on the screen from being readable when viewed from the sides. Only the user sitting directly in front of the screen is able to read the data.

23. C. The best way to remove data from the device is to perform a remote wipe. Ideally you have backed up or synced the device before then or you will lose data. Full device encryption is a good security practice, but that should have been completed prior to the phone being stolen.

24. D. When you create a partition in Windows 8 or newer, it will ask if you want to create a master boot record (MBR) or GUID Partition Table (GPT) one. GPT is newer and has far more features. One of those features is that you can create an unlimited number of logical partitions on it. Only the operating system will limit you; Windows will only allow 128 partitions on one drive.

25. A. An overwrite, also frequently called a drive wipe, replaces all data on a hard drive with 0s. This effectively makes it so that people can't recover old data from the drive and makes the drive safe to recycle.

26. D. If this is a first-time error, just reboot and see whether it goes away. Windows is pretty stable, but sometimes (although rarely) a blue screen of death does result and you need to reboot. If it doesn't happen again, it's very likely not a problem. If it continues to happen, boot into Safe Mode.

27. A. One of the best ways to avoid overheating is to avoid ambient temperatures that are too hot or too cold: Avoid having the device in direct sunlight for extended time periods, in a hot car on a summer day, or on top of a heat source. When the device does overheat, you can often help it cool down quicker by removing any protective case that may be there—and putting it back on later.

28. D. Netboot is the process of booting the OS from the network, such as from a thin client. This can be done with Windows 8 using Microsoft Desktop Virtualization. This is a useful option for environments where hardware is kept to a minimum. After DHCP is used to obtain network configuration parameters from a server, the thin client can locate a PXE boot server to send it the files that it needs to boot.

29. C. The `taskkill` command is used to terminate processes, just as you can do in Task Manager in Windows. To kill a process by its name, use the `/IM` switch. If you know the process ID, use the `/PID` switch. The `/S` switch is used to specify a remote system, and the `/FI` switch applies a filter to a set of tasks. The `/T` switch terminates child processes, and `/F` terminates the process forcefully.

30. B. During the Windows 10 boot process, `WINLOAD.EXE` processes a file that resides in the root directory specifying what OSs are installed on the computer and where they reside on the disk. During this step of the boot process, you may be presented with a list of the installed OSs (depending on how your startup options are configured and whether you have multiple OSs installed). In Windows 10/8.1/8/7, `WINLOAD.EXE` replaces `NTLDR` from the Windows XP days.

31. C. The best device for power protection is an uninterruptible power supply (UPS). These devices can be as small as a brick or as large as an entire server rack. Inside the UPS is one or more batteries and fuses. Much like a surge suppressor, a UPS is designed to protect everything that's plugged into it from power surges. UPSs are also designed to protect against power sags and even power outages. Intelligent UPSs can even alert the administrator by email. Energy is stored in the batteries, and if the power fails, the batteries can power the computer for a period of time so that the administrator can then safely power it down.

32.   A. DHCP servers are configured with a scope, which contains the information that the server can provide to clients. DHCP servers need at least one scope, but they can also have more than one. The scope contains the address pool for DHCP clients as well as other pertinent information for configuration.

33.   A, B. There are three tools that quickly show you CPU and memory usage in Windows. They are Resource Monitor, Performance Monitor, and Task Manager. Performance Monitor can also be accessed through Computer Management.

34.   A, B. Only Windows 10 Home and Professional will do an in-place upgrade to Windows 10 Education.

35.   A. If the printer is on your local computer and you want others to use it, you need to share the printer. You do this by right-clicking the printer, choosing Printer Properties, and then going to the Sharing tab. Check the box that reads Share This Printer. The share name will appear. You map a network printer if you are the one connecting to a remote printer.

36.   B. A brute-force attack is an attempt to guess passwords until a successful guess occurs. Because of the nature of this attack, it usually occurs over a long period of time. To make passwords more difficult to guess, they should be much longer than two or three characters (Microsoft recommends eight as the minimum) and be complex, and you should have password lockout policies.

37.   A. Pop-ups are annoying but not necessarily an indication that your computer is infected with anything. Antivirus and anti-malware programs don't generally deal with pop-ups unless those pop-ups are associated with malware, and most pop-ups aren't—they are just coded into the website. A firewall won't help here either.

38.   B. Going over the limit on data plans can be symptomatic of a hacked account. Closely monitor account usage.

39.   A, B, D. Windows 10 Professional, Enterprise, and Education have BitLocker included. Windows 10 Home does not have BitLocker, but drive encryption is possible.

40.   A. Acceptable use policies (AUPs) describe how the employees in an organization can use company systems and resources, both software and hardware. This policy should also outline the consequences for misuse. In addition, the policy (also known as a use policy) should address the installation of personal software on company computers and the use of personal hardware such as USB devices. The AUP may be part of an employee handbook but is not required to be.

41.   B. This is a form of ransomware, which can be programmed to take control over a user's webcam. It's just another layer of complexity to scare users. Deleting and reinstalling Windows will work, but it's not necessary. The system will be locked, so you can't open the anti-malware software. You can, however, boot to a bootable CD or DVD from the anti-malware software provider and start a remediation that way.

42. D. While it's possible that the disposal information and risks may be on the container somewhere, you will always find it on the product's Material Safety Data Sheet (MSDS). It should be stated that, while CompTIA still refers to these sheets as MSDS as an exam objective, the proper name has been changed to SDS. SDSs include information such as physical product data (boiling point, melting point, flash point, and so forth), potential health risks, storage and disposal recommendations, and spill/leak procedures. With this information, technicians and emergency personnel know how to handle the product as well as respond in the event of an emergency.

43. A, C. When authorized users access devices through unintended connections or unauthorized users access absconded devices, they can access the data on the device. Disable auto-connect to avoid unintended connections, and encrypt data on devices to help protect the data on them in the event they are stolen.

44. D. An intrusion detection system (IDS) is a passive device. It watches network traffic, and it can detect anomalies that might represent an attack. For example, if an attacker were to try to flood a network with traffic on a specific port, the IDS would sense that the additional traffic on that port was unusual. Then the IDS would log the anomaly and send an alert to an administrator. Note that it does nothing to prevent the attack; it simply logs relevant information pertaining to the attack and sends an alert.

45. A. The dir command shows a directory listing. The /p switch displays only one page at a time. Think of it as the pause switch.

46. C. A Type 1 hypervisor sits directly on the hardware, and because of this, it's sometimes referred to as a bare-metal hypervisor. In this instance, the hypervisor is basically the operating system for the physical machine. This setup is most commonly used for server-side virtualization, because the hypervisor itself typically has very low hardware requirements to support its own functions. Type 1 is generally considered to have better performance than Type 2, simply because there is no host OS involved and the system is dedicated to supporting virtualization. The hypervisor is also called a virtual machine manager (VMM).

47. B. Software running on infected computers called zombies is often known as a botnet. Bots, by themselves, are but a form of software that runs automatically and autonomously and are not harmful. *Botnet*, however, has come to be the word used to describe malicious software running on a zombie and under the control of a bot-herder. Denial of service attacks—both DoS and DDoS—can be launched by botnets, as can many forms of adware, spyware, and spam (via spambots).

48. C. Inheritance is the default behavior throughout the permission structure, unless a specific setting is created to override it. For example, a user who has Read and Write permissions in one folder will have that in all the subfolders unless a change has been made specifically to one of the subfolders. Modify access does not give users permissions to change permissions for others. Only Full Control allows that.

49. A. Monitor settings such as resolution, orientation, and location of secondary monitors are changed through Screen Resolution.

50. C. If an app does not load, try rebooting (forcing the device to restart, if necessary). If that does not work, attempt to remove and reinstall the app. Be sure to check the vendor's site for any similar problems (and solutions) encountered by others.

51. D. If you have your policy in place, then your incident response plan should be relatively scripted. Your first priority as the first responder is to identify the improper activity or content. Then you should always get someone else to verify the material or action so that it doesn't turn into a situation of your word against someone else's. Immediately report the situation through proper channels.

52. B. Device Manager has been present in every version of Windows since Windows 95. It allows you to manage all of your hardware devices, including updating drivers and disabling the device. It is found within the Computer Management console.

53. D. Microsoft Windows User State Migration Tool (USMT) version 10.0 allows you to migrate user file settings related to the applications, Desktop configuration, and accounts. It is intended to be used by administrators, and it requires a client computer connected to a Windows Server–based domain controller. USMT allows transfers to be scripted for several systems, while a Microsoft partner tool, PCmover Express, can be used when migrating user data for only a few machines. WET is no longer available for Windows 10.

54. D. In MacOS, there is a bar of icons that runs along the bottom (or side, if so configured) of your screen. That set of icons is known as the Dock, and it provides easy access to key apps that come with the Mac (such as Safari, Mail, Videos, and Music) or others that you choose to add there.

55. C. With ransomware, software—often delivered through a Trojan horse—takes control of a system and demands that a third party be paid. The "control" can be accomplished by encrypting the hard drive, by changing user password information, or via any of a number of other creative ways. Users are usually assured that by paying the extortion amount (the ransom), they will be given the code needed to revert their systems to normal operations. Even among malware, ransomware is particularly nasty.

56. D. The purpose of the system file checker (SFC) utility is to keep the operating system alive and well. SFC.EXE automatically verifies system files after a reboot to see whether they were changed to unprotected copies. If an unprotected file is found, a stored copy of the system file overwrites it.

57. B. A common cause for a lack of wireless connectivity is for a device to be in airplane mode. Since the user has a cellular signal, the phone definitely isn't in this mode. The other wireless signal types (Wi-Fi, Bluetooth) can be individually disabled, so check them as well.

58. A, C. Do not attempt to repair a CRT monitor without specific training. Even if the monitor has not been used for some time, capacitors can still hold a lethal charge. Also, be careful with the tubes in a CRT monitor. They are vacuum sealed, and if the glass breaks, it can be sent flying in any direction.

59. B. The best practices for malware removal is a seven-step process. Identify malware symptoms, quarantine the infected system, disable system restore (in Windows), remediate infected systems (including update anti-malware software and scan and remove the malware), schedule scans and run updates, enable system restore and create a restore point (in Windows), and educate the end user.

60. B, C. BitLocker and EFS can both be used for encrypting files on an NTFS volume. Encrypting File System (EFS) is available in most editions of Windows, and all users can use EFS. BitLocker is available on Windows 10 Pro (but not on Home). Only administrators can turn on BitLocker. As an additional distinction, EFS can encrypt just one file, if so desired, while BitLocker encrypts the whole volume and whatever is stored on it.

61. D. The recommended way to assign permissions on Microsoft systems is to grant them to groups. Then, users can be assigned to groups depending on their access needs. This is far less work than managing permissions on a user-by-user basis.

62. D. From a networking standpoint, each of the virtual desktops will typically need full network access. Virtualization is possible provided the hardware and the Windows 10 edition support it (Pro, Enterprise, and Education). The VM will create a virtual NIC and manage the resources of that NIC appropriately. The virtual NIC doesn't have to be connected to the physical NIC. Administrators will often configure a virtual switch within the hypervisor to manage the traffic to and from the virtual NICs and logically attach the virtual switch to the physical NIC.

63. A. The copy command makes a copy of a file in a second location. It cannot be used to copy directories. To copy a directory, you need to use the xcopy command.

64. C. If there is sufficient space on a machine and the hardware will support it, you can have more than one operating system and choose which one to run when you boot. If you create a multiboot environment, always install each OS on its own partition; that way, the key OS files remain separated and don't conflict with each other.

65. C, D. bootrec /rebuildbcd will rebuild the Boot Configuration Data (BCD) file, and bceedit allows you to edit the file. The bootrec /fixboot command will rebuild the boot sector to one that is compatible with Windows 10 (or Windows 7/8/8.1). bootrec / fixmbr will fix the Master Boot Record.

66. A. Troubleshooting theory for the A+ exam consists of six steps: identify the problem; establish a theory of probable cause; test the theory to determine cause; establish a plan of action to resolve the problem and implement the solution; verify full system functionality and, if applicable, implement preventive measures; and document findings, actions, and outcomes.

67. D. Don't click the buttons! This is some sort of hoax. When you click either button, something bad will happen—something like malware being installed on your computer. Attackers are very creative about making their pop-ups look like legitimate security alerts. Shut your computer down, and after you reboot, run a virus scan.

68. A. Keychain is a password management system from Apple. It allows you to store passwords for websites, mail servers, Wi-Fi, and so forth. There is an iCloud variant (iCloud Keychain) that keeps such information as Safari usernames/passwords and credit card information.

69. D. The System Configuration tool allows you to force the operating system to boot into Safe Mode, using the Boot tab. System configuration (MSCONFIG.EXE) has five tabs: General, Boot, Services, Startup, and Tools.

70. D. The one big advantage of share permissions is that they can be used if the NTFS file system is not in place. Of course, share permissions are in effect only when the user connects to the resource via the network. NTFS permissions are able to protect you at the file level. Share permissions can be applied to the directory level only. NTFS permissions can affect users logged on locally or across the network to the system where the NTFS permissions are applied.

71. A. Antivirus databases should be updated frequently to keep your antivirus program up-to-date with all the possible virus definitions. Most antivirus programs will automatically update themselves (if configured properly) just as Windows Update will update Windows, provided the computer has a live Internet connection. The best bet is to let them automatically update. Otherwise, at least once a week is good.

72. A. Personally identifiable information (PII) is anything that can be used to identify an individual person on its own or in context with other information. This includes someone's name, address, and other contact information; the names of family members; and other details that people would consider private. A first name is considered to be generally common enough that it is not PII. A full name, if not common, would be PII.

73. C. When a problem pops up with the Windows 8 operating system, you can boot into the Windows Recovery Environment (Windows RE) and repair it by choosing to refresh, reset, or restore it. Refreshing it keeps personal files and settings along with the default apps and those that you installed from the Windows Store. Resetting reinstalls Windows and deletes all but the default apps (meaning that you lose your personal files and settings). Restoring allows you to just undo recent system changes.

74. D. When you move a file or folder on the same NTFS volume, it will keep its original permissions. If you copy it or move it to a different volume, it will inherit permissions from its new parent directory.

75. A. No unintended or unauthorized event is a good thing for mobile users. The one that leaves a user most susceptible to a man-in-the-middle attack is an unintended Wi-Fi connection. This is because the device at the other end that the user is connecting to could be intercepting data or storing it for a possible attack later.

76. A. The way to protect against this is to implement a BIOS/UEFI password. If a user can get into the BIOS, then he can change the boot sequence, boot to an unauthorized device, and then do some damage to the system. A strong Windows password will help protect Windows but does not protect the computer in general. Autorun is a feature of Windows and does not affect the boot process.

77. D. In hibernate mode, the computer saves all the contents of memory to the hard drive, preserves all data and applications exactly where they are, and allows the computer to power off completely. When the system comes out of hibernation, it returns to its previous state.

78. C. A restore point is a copy, or snapshot, of your system configuration at a given point in time. It's like a backup of your configuration but not your data. Snapshots are created within Windows from the System Restore program. If Windows will not load, Safe Mode can be used to run `rstrui.exe`, which will open a version of System Restore so you can use a snapshot.

79. C. When accessing the NTFS-based resource over the network, both NTFS and share permissions are applied. If there is a difference between the two of them, the most restrictive permissions are used. Therefore, the user has Read & Execute access.

80. C. A snapshot is an exact copy of a logical volume that has been frozen at a specific point in time. When creating the snapshot, you don't need to worry about users changing files or taking the volume offline.

81. C. To run the SFC, you must be logged in as an administrator or have administrative privileges. If you attempt to run SFC from a standard command prompt, you will be told that you must be an administrator running a console session in order to continue. Rather than opening a standard command prompt, choose Start ➢ All Programs ➢ Accessories; then right-click Command Prompt and choose Run As Administrator. The UAC will prompt you to continue, and then you can run SFC without a problem.

82. C. The Windows Event Viewer utility provides information about what's been going on with the whole system to help you troubleshoot problems. Event Viewer shows warnings, error messages, and records of things that have happened successfully. It's found in all current versions of Windows. The three most commonly referenced logs are Security (which includes information about logins), System, and Application.

83. A. The user needs at least Read & Execute access to be able to run programs, and Write will allow him to make changes to files. Neither will allow him to delete files. Modify and Full Control will allow everything he needs as well, but Modify allows him to delete files (or the folder), and Full Control also gives him the ability to take ownership and assign permissions to others.

84. D. A community cloud is created when multiple organizations with common interests combine to create a cloud. In a sense, it's like a public cloud with better security. The clients know who the other clients are and, in theory, can trust them more than they could trust random people on the Internet. The economies of scale and flexibility won't be as great as with a public cloud, but that's the trade-off for better security.

85. A. Windows 7 incorporates Windows Firewall, which can be used to stop incoming and outgoing network traffic. Traffic is allowed or denied by specific rules that are part of an access control list (ACL). By default, Windows Firewall blocks incoming traffic. By creating exceptions, you can configure what incoming traffic you want to allow through.

86. B. Set and meet—or exceed—expectations and communicate timelines and status. Customers want to know what is going on. In addition, offering different repair or replacement options will usually make the customer feel better, as you are giving them an option in choosing a solution.

87. C. When formatting a hard drive, you can usually choose between a quick format or a full format. With a quick format, a new file table is created on the hard disk, but files are not fully overwritten or erased from the disk. Someone with data recovery software could easily access the data. A full format removes old files, creates a new file allocation table, and scans the hard drive for bad sectors.

88. B. When synchronizing an iPhone with a desktop, both the iOS and the desktop authenticate each other. This two-way authentication is called mutual authentication, and it lets multiple services on the iOS device communicate with the appropriate services on the desktop.

89. C, D. Social engineering is a process in which an attacker attempts to acquire information about your network and system by social means, such as talking to people in the organization. When this is done via email or instant messaging, it's called phishing. Phishing attempts that appear to come from a trusted source are called spear phishing. Another form of social engineering is known as shoulder surfing, and it involves nothing more than watching someone when they enter their sensitive data.

90. A, C. If an OS update fails, it could be a configuration issue or simply a one-time glitch in the process. Wait until Windows Update reverts the changes; then reboot and try the update again. If that does not work, you can unplug removable media from your computer and try again, or you can try the Windows Update Troubleshooter.

Index

OUs (organizational units), 248, 440
overheating
    avoiding, 335, 475
    laptops, 23, 356
    mobile devices, 130, 262, 392, 445
    troubleshooting, 130, 392
    wireless routers, 150, 401
overwriting drive, 243, 334, 438, 475

P

PaaS (Platform as a Service), 111, 385
packet filters, firewalls, 236, 434
page-description language (PDL), 84, 375
paging files, virtual memory, 176, 180,
    407, 409
pairing, Bluetooth to device, 20, 355
PANs (personal area networks)
    Bluetooth devices using, 40, 361
    overview of, 316, 467
paper jams, troubleshooting printers,
    124, 389
parallel ATA drives. *see* PATA (parallel
    ATA) drives
parallel bus, compared with serial, 86, 376
parity errors, within memory, 66, 369
partitions
    active, 185, 412
    creating, 334, 475
    diskpart utility, 141, 397
    extending, 184, 411
    factory recovery partition, 210, 425
    logical, 190, 414
    managing, 182, 410
    primary and extended, 189, 414
    recovery, 183, 410
    splitting, 211, 425
    swap (Linux), 174, 407
passive cooling systems, 93, 379
passwords
    Administrator accounts and, 241, 437
    attacks, 229, 430
    BIOS/UEFI, 224, 345, 427, 480
    brute-force attacks, 336, 476
    changing in Linux, 206, 423
    Keychain managing, 209, 343, 427, 479
    policies, 242, 303, 438, 463
    renaming default accounts, 226, 429
    resetting, 247, 440
    strong, 244, 439
    syncing between devices, 205, 422
PATA (parallel ATA) drives
    master and slave drives, 127, 390
    Northbridge management of, 84, 375
patches
    applying, 224, 427
    managing, 214, 426
    managing in Linux, 208, 423
    managing updates and, 175, 407
    web browsers, 234, 433
PCI DSS (Payment Card Industry Data
    Security Standard), 293, 458

PCI expansion bus
    overview of, 313, 466
    power requirements, 76, 372
    speeds, 70, 370
PCIe
    connectors, 76, 372
    data rates, 69, 87, 370, 377
    Express Card 2.0, 313, 466
    internal video adapters, 96, 380
    lanes and, 72, 371
    Mini PCIe, 320, 469
    mixing cards with expansion slots,
        93, 379
    slots, 91, 378
    up-plugging, 68, 73, 371
    versions, 327, 472
PCI-X
    adapters compatibility with PCI-X
        slots, 97, 380
    maximum throughput of PCI-X
        adapters, 77, 373
PCs (personal computers). *see* computers
PDF files, 92, 378
PDL (page-description language), 84, 375
PE (Preinstallation Environment), Windows
    OSs, 259, 443
performance
    hardware, 174, 407
    RAM and, 270, 449
Performance Information and Tools,
    Control Panel, 269, 448
Performance Monitor, 194, 416
peripherals
    device examples, 97, 380
    Northbridge and Southbridge, 312,
        465
Perl, comparing with PowerShell, 301, 463
permissions. *see also* NTFS permissions
    accessing networked printers, 130, 392
    ACLs (access control lists), 227, 429
    assigning, 226, 341, 428, 479
    changing file permissions (Linux),
        204, 421
    comparing, 231, 233, 432
    effective, 235, 434
    Full Control, 237, 435
    inheritance, 230, 431
    installation process failure and, 212,
        426
    most restrictive apply, 231, 431
    Read & Execute, 346, 481
    superuser or root permissions, 331, 473
    volumes and, 243, 438
personal area networks. *see* PANs (personal
    area networks)
personal computers (PCs). *see* computers
personally identifiable information (PII),
    298, 344, 461, 480
PGA (pin grid array), CPU socket, 94, 379
phablet device, 14, 352
PHI (protected health information),
    299, 461

phishing attacks, 239–240, 348, 436–437,
    482
photosensitive imaging drum, laser printers,
    317, 468
physical barriers, access control, 242, 438
pickup rollers, printers, 88, 377
pico-ITX motherboard, 64, 368
piconet, wireless Bluetooth, 14, 352
PII (personally identifiable information),
    298, 344, 461, 480
pin grid array (PGA), CPU socket, 94, 379
ping command
    sending ICMP packets, 198, 418
    uses, 141, 397
piracy, of software, 171, 405
pixels
    dead, 137, 396
    resolution and, 179, 409
Pixie (PXE) boot, 194, 416
plasma display
    for fast-motion programs, 82, 375
    technology in, 69, 370
Platform as a Service (PaaS), 111, 385
plenum cable, 45, 102, 363, 382
PoE (Power over Ethernet)
    distance from ethernet device, 50, 366
    installing a wireless hub, 45, 364
policies
    BYOD, 235, 433
    creating, 294, 458–459
    incident response, 298, 339, 461, 478
    password, 242, 303, 438, 463
polymorphic viruses, 232, 432
POP3 (Post Office Protocol 3)
    email protocols, 313, 466
    sending email, 38, 361
    storage email, 26, 358
pop-ups
    dealing with, 337, 476
    overview of, 266, 447
port replicator
    compared with a docking station,
        15, 353
    using, 25, 357
port triggering, 42, 362
ports
    accessing RDP, 39, 361
    disabling unneeded, 243, 438
    expansion ports, 10, 351
POST (power-on self test)
    BIOS and, 127, 146, 322, 391, 400,
        470
    boot routine, 77, 373
POST card, 123, 388
Post Office Protocol 3. *see* POP3 (Post
    Office Protocol 3)
power
    backouts, 295, 459
    DC to AC inverters, 321, 469
    disconnecting before working inside
        computer case, 296, 460
    surge protectors, 295, 459

Comprehensive Online Learning Environment

Register to gain one year of FREE access to the online interactive learning environment and test bank to help you study for your CompTIA A+ certification exams—included with your purchase of this book!

The online test bank includes the following:

- **Practice Test Questions** to reinforce what you've learned
- **Bonus Practice Exam** to test your knowledge of the material

Go to http://www.wiley.com/go/sybextestprep to register and gain access to this comprehensive study tool package.

Register and Access the Online Test Bank

To register your book and get access to the online test bank, follow these steps:

1. Go to bit.ly/SybexTest.
2. Select your book from the list.
3. Complete the required registration information, including answering the security verification to prove book ownership. You will be emailed a PIN code.
4. Follow the directions in the email or go to https://www.wiley.com/go/sybextestprep.
5. Enter the PIN code you received and click the "Activate PIN" button.
6. On the Create an Account or Login page, enter your username and password, and click Login. A "Thank you for activating your PIN!" message will appear. If you don't have an account already, create a new account.
7. Click the "Go to My Account" button to add your new book to the My Products page.

SYBEX
A Wiley Brand